Early human development

Early human development

EDITED BY

S. J. HUTT
PROFESSOR OF PSYCHOLOGY, UNIVERSITY OF KEELE

AND

CORINNE HUTT
SENIOR RESEARCH FELLOW, DEPARTMENT OF PSYCHOLOGY, UNIVERSITY OF KEELE

OXFORD UNIVERSITY PRESS

1973

Oxford University Press, Ely House, London W. 1

GLASGOW NEW YORK TORONTO MELBOURNE WELLINGTON
CAPE TOWN IBADAN NAIROBI DAR ES SALAAM LUSAKA ADDIS ABABA
DELHI BOMBAY CALCUTTA MADRAS KARACHI LAHORE DACCA
KUALA LUMPUR SINGAPORE HONG KONG TOKYO

PRINTED AND BOUND IN GREAT BRITAIN
BY RICHARD CLAY (THE CHAUCER PRESS) LTD
BUNGAY, SUFFOLK

Preface

THE range of journals and specialized texts containing material relevant to the study of early human behaviour is ever widening. The subject matter demands—perhaps more than in any other area of psychology—that traditional boundaries between disciplines are crossed, and that findings from genetics, endocrinology, neurophysiology and so on, be explored. We can no longer count on key papers appearing in just a few 'mainstream' journals. This inevitably places a strain upon library resources, especially in a small academic institution. The present collection is a small corrective to this problem. It grew out of the needs of our own students for a set of readings; while concentrating upon certain issues in developmental psychology, it adopts an essentially biological viewpoint. We are grateful to our former colleagues in the Human Development Research Unit, University of Oxford, and in the Department of Psychology, University of Reading, for their comments, and to our students in the Universities of Oxford and Reading whose suggestions greatly aided the selection of these readings.

S.J.H.
C.H.

University of Keele
February 1973

Acknowledgements

GRATEFUL acknowledgement is made to the authors, editors, and publishers of the following works and journals for permission to use material from their publications:

Behavioral Science; *British Journal of Medical Psychology*; *British Journal of Psychiatry*; *Child Development*; *Child Development II* (Appleton-Century-Crofts, New York); *Eugenics Quarterly*; Foss (Ed.), *Determinants of Infant Behaviour* (Methuen, London); Jones (Ed.), *Nebraska Symposium on Motivation* (University of Nebraska, Lincoln); *Journal of Child Psychology and Psychiatry*; *Journal of Experimental Child Psychology*; Lipsitt and Reese (Eds.), *Advances in Child Development and Behaviour* (Academic Press, New York); *Merrill-Palmer Quarterly*; Michael (Ed.), *Endocrinology and Human Behaviour* (O.U.P., London); *Nature*; *Psychological Monographs*; *Psychonomic Science*; *Quarterly Review of Biology*; *Science*; Tanner and Inhelder (Eds.), *Discussions on Child Development* (Tavistock, London); World Health Organization, *Maternal Care and Mental Health*.

Contents

List of Plates

Introduction

THIS collection is concerned with structure–function relationships between brain and behaviour in early development: how the environmental input is dealt with by the existing machinery, how this input modifies the structures, and how these factors produce the behaviour that results.

The early development of the brain and its relationship to behaviour are important from at least four points of view:

(1) It provides a 'natural experiment' in physiological psychology. Most of our information about the relationship between brain function and behaviour is derived from studies of animals, involving lesions or stimulation with micro-electrodes. Comparable studies in man have generally been restricted to studies of adults or patients with tumours, epileptogenic lesions, or damage caused by accidents. Thus, the study of the relationship between brain structure, physiological activity, and observed behaviour at various stages in ontogeny provides a unique natural experiment in the intact organism.

(2) One of the oldest controversies of psychology is the nature–nurture question, and its resolution in the area of perception has long been a matter of debate. The prelude to Bower's article [1] inquires: 'Does an infant see things in the same general way adults do, or must he learn to do so?' Fantz's belief [2, 3, 4] that some aspects of form perception are innate has generated a wealth of experimentation in the last decade. But not one of these reports has dealt with the question of what attributes of stimuli *can* be perceived with the infants' immature apparatus.

(3) The idea that the child is father of the man is as old as civilization itself and the systematic investigation of the later effects of infantile experiences has been given especial impetus by psychoanalytic theories. The fact that the adult manifestations of personality are closely tied to brain function leads inevitably to a quest for the antecedents of personality in the relationship of brain and behaviour in early infancy.

(4) The notion that such interrelationships may indeed have predictive value clearly leads to a practical question of whether later abnormalities of behaviour may be anticipated by studying the human infant and whether this in turn, may lead to some adequate prophylactic measures. It seems reasonable to assume that the earlier such abnormalities can be detected the better the chances of protecting the child from the consequences.

We hope that the organization of these readings in the present form may illuminate the structure–function relationships to which Bronson (Chap. 8) originally drew attention, and a consideration of which has been our own concern in the last few years.

References

1. BOWER, T. G. R. (1966). Visual perception in infancy. *Sci. Amer.* **215**, 2–10.

2. FANTZ, R. L. (1965). Ontogeny of perception. *In* (Schrier, A. M., Harlow, H. F., and Stolinitz, H. (Eds.)) *Behaviour of non-human primates.* Vol. II. Academic Press, New York.

3. —— (1965). Visual perception from birth as shown by pattern selectivity. *Ann. N. Y. Acad. Sci.* **118**, 793–814.

4. —— (1967). Visual perception and experience in early infancy: a look at the hidden side of behaviour development. *In* (Stevenson, Hess, and Rheingold (Eds.)) *Early behaviour: comparative and developmental approaches.* Wiley, New York.

Genetic determinants of behaviour

THERE is a common but fallacious assumption that to acknowledge genetic control is to embrace a determinism. The paradoxical situation often occurs in which the genetic control of physical characters will be accepted, but a similar control of psychological or behavioural characters repudiated. One misconception results from a semantic confusion, from the substitution of unequal for different: it is that the demonstration of individual differences proves that people are not equal. As Dobzhansky [3] emphasizes:

What biology has shown is that people are genetically diverse; every human being is a genetically unique, and unrepeatable individual. It cannot be reiterated too often that equality and inequality are sociological, similarity and diversity are biological, phenomena. A society can grant equality of opportunity to its members, or it can withhhold such equality; genetic diversity is biologically given, and could not be stamped out even if this were desirable (p. 130).

Dobzhansky equally firmly disposes of yet another misconception—that biological evolution stopped when cultural evolution began. Cultural evolution he claims, rather than supplanting biological evolution, has been superimposed upon it, since culture itself is a biological phenomenon.

Indeed, one wonders with Gottesman [10] that 'in this day and age, enlightened students of man's behaviour should entertain doubts, if not outright disbelief, about the appreciable genetic contribution to variation in certain human traits'. In Gottesman's view, much of the difficulty in accepting genetic control is attributable to the inappropriateness of the question asked, viz., how much of trait x is caused by heredity and how much by environment? Neither agent alone can produce the trait—'each genotype has its own more-or-less natural habitat'. The very fact of our ability to plan for the future, to remember much of our past experience and thus profit from it, to ratiocinate, to invent, and to create—abilities singularly human—is a result of our well-developed and differentiated neocortex. This property, which distinguishes us from our phylogenetic kin, is guaranteed its universality and perpetuity by being genetically coded and hence resident within the human gene pool. Thoday [16] has been quite unambiguous about the role of genes and environment: 'Every character is both genetic and environmental in origin . . . Genotype determines the potentialities of an organism. Environment determines which or how much of these potentialities shall be realized during development (p. 95).'

The question with which we, as behavioural scientists, should be concerning ourselves, as Gottesman [10] suggests, should be more searching. How much of the variance of scores on a particular trait under certain environmental conditions can be attributed to genetic factors? How modifiable is the phenotypic expression of such a trait? How do genetic and environmental influences interact? The subtlety of this interaction is illustrated by the classic finding of Skodak and Skeels [15]. These authors determined the IQs of children who had been adopted at varying periods after their birth, and followed them up into adolescence. Initially there was more resemblance between the IQs of the children and those of their adoptive mothers than those of their biological mothers. With increasing age, however, the children's IQs diverged from those of their adoptive mothers and came increasingly to resemble the IQs of their biological mothers. Other characteristics, such as weight, are also liable to show varying degrees of heritability during the course of development [17].

Theoretically, the *operon* model of gene action [11], which assumes the existence of two functionally different genes—regulator and structural genes—has provided a satisfactory basis for the explanation of such developmental phenomena. When a trait or characteristic is normally distributed in a population (e.g. height, intelligence) it must be polygenically determined, since single gene determination would result in a discontinuous distribution. In humans most traits and characteristics are polygenic in origin. When several genes have a small but constant effect in determining a trait it is likely that not all the genes become operative simultaneously. In fact, the research on chromosome puffing [1] supports the hypothesis that genes switch on or off, and do so at different developmental stages. Thus the Skodak and Skeels findings could be accounted for in terms of different sets of genes determining the several constituent abilities comprising IQ, all these genes being manifest only at or after puberty.

The case for regarding intelligence as being constituted of several, and perhaps independent, abilities has been strongly made by Vandenberg [23], whose evidence suggests that IQ consists of at least six independent abilities, each reflecting genetic factors to a different degree in the following order of decreasing magnitude: spatial visualization, word fluency, vocabulary, number ability, and some forms of reasoning; memory apparently shows no effect of hereditary influence. The work of Vandenberg [18–23], and of Gottesman ([7–9] and Chap. 3) has done much to further our knowledge of the inheritance of intelligence and personality, and Freedman ([4, 5], and Chap. 1) has made an important contribution in departing from conventional psychometric procedures to demonstrate that social behaviours like smiling and fear of strangers are under some measure of genetic control. Gottesman (Chap. 3) provides a stimulating discussion of the biological adaptiveness of such social responses and of the advantage that accrues from having these under genetic control. More recently Freedman has found that consanguinous similarities in certain behavioural responses are manifested during the first or second day of life; he also observed differences in infantile reflex patterns between Caucasian, African, and Navaho infants in their first 32 hours of life [6].

As McClearn [12] points out, an important concept in quantitative genetics is *heritability*. In very general terms this may be seen as the proportion of phenotypic variance attributable to genetic sources. Twin studies have usually formed the basis for the estimation of this factor, and Nichols

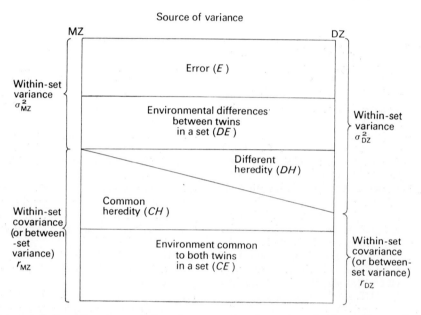

FIG. 0.1. Schematic representation of sources of variance in twin data. (From Nichols [14].)

[14] has provided a useful schematic representation of the sources of variance in such data (Fig. 0.1). This representation however makes certain assumptions that are not always valid—in particular, the assumptions that the effect of the environment is the same for fraternal and identical twins and that there is no assortative mating of the parents. Mittler's [13] discussion of the procedures employed in deriving estimates of heritability is most instructive. Erlenmeyer-Kimling and Jarvik (Chap. 2) have performed a most valuable service in collating the results of 52 twin studies to show the inheritance of IQ with different degrees of consanguinity.

Scarr's contribution (Chap. 4) is significant in that it helps resolve a controversy of long standing: empiricists have objected to the genetic interpretation of the findings of twin studies on the grounds that mono-zygotic twins are likely to share a more similar environment than are dizygotic twins. Scarr's analysis of twin data in which zygosity was some-times mistaken by the parent, showed quite unambiguously that mono-zygotic twins were rated more alike in their demeanour, even though the parent had considered them to be dizygotic.

As a general rule, we can expect that the more homogeneous the environment the more the observed differences will reflect differences in genotypes, and the more homogeneous the genotypes the more the observed differences will be a function of environmental factors [2].

References

1. BEERMAN, W. (1963). Cytological aspects of information transfer in cellular differentiation. *Am. Zool.* **3**, 23–32.

2. DOBZHANSKY, T. (1965). *Heredity and the nature of man.* Allen and Unwin, London.

3. —— (1968). Genetics and the social sciences. *In* (Glass, D. C. (Ed.)) *Genetics.* Rockefeller University Press, New York.

4. FREEDMAN, D. G. (1965). An ethological study of human behaviour. *In* (Vandenberg, S. G. (Ed.)) *Methods and goals in human behaviour genetics.* Academic Press, New York.

5. —— (1965). Hereditary control of early social behaviour. *In* (Foss, B. (Ed.)) *Determinants of infant behaviour.* Vol. III. Methuen, London.

6. —— (1971). Genetic variations on the hominid theme: individual, sex, and ethnic differences. *1st Symp. of the Int. Soc. for the Study of Behavioural Development, Nijmegen.*

7. GOTTESMAN, I. I. (1963). Heritability of personality: a demonstration. *Psychol., Monogr.* **77** (9), whole No. 572.

8. —— (1963). Genetic aspects of intelligent behaviour. *In* (Ellis, N. R. (Ed.)) *Handbook of mental deficiency: psychological theory and research.* Mc-Graw-Hill, New York.

9. —— (1965). Personality and natural selection. *In* (Vandenberg, S. G. (Ed.)) *Methods and goals in human behaviour genetics.* Academic Press, New York.

10. —— (1968). Beyond the fringe—personality and psychopathology. *In* (Glass, D. C. (Ed.)) *Genetics.* Rockefeller University Press, New York.

11. JACOB, F. and MONOD, J. (1961). On the regulation of gene activity. *Cold Spring Harbor Symp. Quart. Biol.* **26**, 193–209.

12. McCLEARN, G. E. (1970). Genetic influences on behaviour and development. *In* (Mussen, P. H. (Ed.)) *Carmichael's manual of child psychology.* Wiley, New York.

13. MITTLER, P. (1971). *The study of twins.* Penguin Books, Harmondsworth.

14. NICHOLS, R. C. (1965). The national merit twin study. *In* (Vandenberg, S. G. (Ed.)) *Methods and goals in human behaviour genetics.* Academic Press, New York.

15. SKODAK, M. and SKEELS, H. M. (1949). A final follow-up study of one hundred adopted children. *J. genet. Psychol.* **75**, 85–125.

16. THODAY, J. M. (1965). Geneticism and environmentalism. *In* (Meade, J. E. and Parkes, A. S. (Eds.)) *Biological aspects of social problems.* Oliver and Boyd, London.

17. THOMPSON, W. R. (1968). Genetics and social behaviour. *In* (Glass, D. C. (Ed.)) *Genetics.* Rockefeller University Press, New York.

18. VANDENBERG, S. G. (1962). The hereditary ability study: hereditary components in a psychological test battery. *Am. J. human Genet.* **14**, 220–37.

19. —— (1965). Multivariate analysis of twin differences. *In* (Vandenberg, S. G. (Ed.)) *Methods and goals in human behaviour genetics.* Academic Press, New York.

20. —— (1966). Contributions of twin research to psychology. *Psychol. Bull.* **66**, 327–52.

21. —— (1966). Hereditary factors in psychological variables in man, with special emphasis on cognition. *In* (Spuhler, J. N. (Ed.)) *Behavioural consequences of genetic differences in man.* Viking Fund, Chicago.

22. —— (1967). Hereditary factors in normal personality traits (as measured by inventories). *In* (Wortis, J. (Ed.)) *Recent advances in biological psychiatry.* Vol. IX. Plenum Press, New York.

23. —— (1968). The nature and nurture of intelligence. *In* (Glass, D. C. (Ed.)) *Genetics.* Rockefeller University Press, New York.

I

Inheritance of behaviour in infants

D. G. FREEDMAN AND BARBARA KELLER†

THE majority of longitudinal studies of infants and children have indicated that there is consistency in personality within individuals over the years [1, 2], but the role that heredity has played in this can only be surmised. We have applied the twin method to a longitudinal study in order to investigate the role of heredity.

Twenty pairs of twins of the same sex were examined on a monthly basis in their own homes in their first year. Zygosity was determined at the end of the study on the basis of non-concordance or concordance on 13 bloodgroup factors. We found an N_1 of 11 fraternal pairs and an N_2 of 9 identical pairs. All families entered the study voluntarily, apparently because of an interest in gauging the development of their twins. None was paid. Most were middle class and represented a variety of racial and cultural backgrounds. The tests included the mental and motor scales and the infant behaviour profile developed by Nancy Bayley of the National Institute of Mental Health. Our report is based on the scores of these instruments.‡

The present approach has several advantages: (1) According to Piaget [3], deferred imitation of other children, that is, imitation independent of immediate perception, starts after the first year. Such imitation was not observed in our group. Our observations also bear out Ahrens' findings [4] that infants have little interest in one another before the 10th month, after which interest gradually increases. Thus, mutual imitation and 'contagion' within pairs can be ruled out as factors in our results. (2) Differential treatment of identical and fraternal twins by parents can also be effectively ruled out as a contaminating factor. Neither examiners nor parents were certain of zygosity, since determinations were made only at the end of the study. Parents who ventured an

† From 'Inheritance of behaviour in infants'. *Science* **140**, 196–8 (1963). Copyright © 1963 by the American Association for the Advancement of Science. Reprinted by permission of the authors and the Association.

‡ These instruments are in current use in the nationwide 'Collaborative Study' sponsored by the National Institute of Neurological Diseases and Blindness. Standard scores on the Mental and Motor Scales are based on norms given by Nancy Bayley (The California First Year Mental Scale and The California Infant Scale of Motor Development, University of California Syllabi Nos. 243 and 249 (1933 and 1936)). The Infant Behaviour Profile consists of 21 items covering 12 categories of behaviour: social orientation (two items), object orientation, goal directedness, attention span, cooperativeness, activity (four items), sensory reactivity, tension, fearfulness, general emotional tone, endurance, and sensory mode (six items). Each item is rated along a scale from deficient to over-endowed with five steps specifically spelled out; a nine-point scale was obtained by adding half-steps. An unpublished study of tester–observer reliability resulted in 70 per cent full agreement on these items (median), with an interquartile range of only 6 per cent.

opinion tended to believe their twins were fraternal; hence parents of fraternals were correct, and parents of identicals were incorrect in six out of the nine pairs. Obstetricians were of little help in determining zygosity, for they were incorrect 9 out of 19 times. (Our observations and careful discussions with parents indicated that, as a

suggests that the results are readily reproducible (Figs. 1.1, 1.2, and 1.3).

Fig. 1.1 [shows the distribution of intra-pair differences on the combined mental and motor scales, and it is clear that identical pairs and fraternal pairs form two distinct but overlapping populations. ($p < 0.01$; all p values are based on one-tailed tables

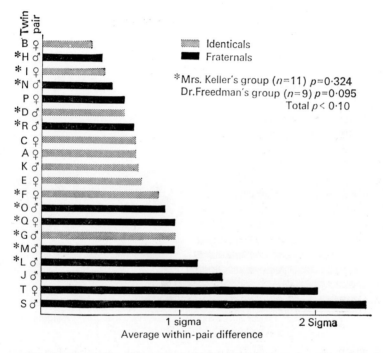

FIG. 1.1. The Bayley mental and motor scales averaged to form a single distribution.†
Average within-pair differences in the first year, based on 8- to 12-monthly administrations.

rule, differential behaviour of infants drew different rather than the same responses from parents. In no case did a parent 'create' differences where none previously existed.) (3) Two investigators worked independently, each seeing approximately half the twin pairs. Their data formed similar distributions on all measures used and

† See footnote on p. 8.

of the Mann-Whitney non-parametric test [5, 6].) The mental scale ($p < 0.10$) and the motor scale ($p < 0.005$) follow a similar order when plotted individually. Fig. 1.2 illustrates the distribution of intra-pair differences on the infant behaviour profile, where once again fraternal pairs exhibit greater differences ($p < 0.001$).

The extent of within-pair consistency over the first year is indicated by the following: on the mental scales, in identical twins within-pair changes in superiority occurred in 37 per cent of the tests administered; fraternal twins switched positions on 23 per cent of consecutive tests. Likewise, on the 21-item infant behaviour profile [2]. Fraternal pairs averaged 4·36 items on which no more than one switchover in relative position occurred over the first year, and on which there was an average within-pair difference of two or more points, that is, items in which

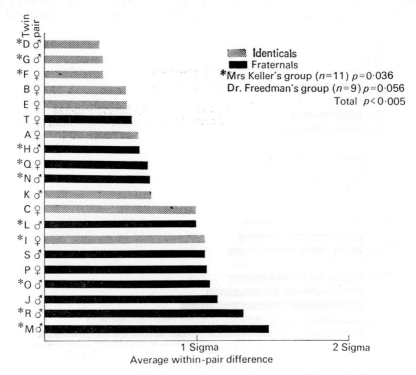

FIG. 1.2. The Bayley infant behaviour profile, a rating scale consisting of 21 items covering 12 categories of behaviour.† Average within-pair differences in the first year, based on 8- to 12-monthly administrations.

motor scales, identical pairs switched positions on 35 per cent of the tests compared to 15 per cent in fraternal pairs. Ranking indicated that fraternal pairs exhibited significantly fewer changes *vis-à-vis* each other on both the mental scales ($p = 0.05$) and the motor scales ($p = 0.005$).

Similar results were obtained on the
† See footnote on p. 8.

intra-pair differences were decidedly persistent and large; identical twins averaged 1·12. Ranking on this basis again differentiated identical from fraternal twins ($p < 0.025$). Items rated on the basis of motor activity most often met the above criteria, although other categories of behaviour proved equally discriminating in particular pairs.

Judgement of behaviour from films is perhaps the best-controlled aspect of this study. Monthly motion pictures were taken in which each twin of a pair was filmed separately in the same situations. At the end of the study the films of one twin were shown to a group of four professionals who had

twins were distinctly larger ($p < 0.005$) (Fig. 1.3). The rank-order correlation between the distributions in Figs. 1.2 and 1.3 is 0.44 ($p < 0.03$).

The distribution of within-pair differences on the infant behaviour profile (Fig. 1.2) reflects our experiences in recording data after visits to

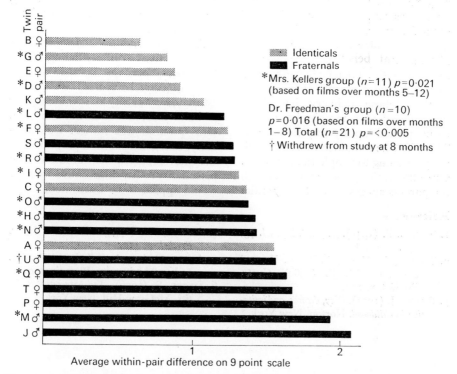

FIG. 1.3. Within-pair differences on the Bayley infant behaviour profile, based on 8 consecutive months of filmed behaviour (either months 1 to 8, or 5 to 12).

worked with infants, and the films of the other were shown to a second comparable group. In this way we avoided a possible 'halo' effect. The judges rated each child on the infant behaviour profile, and the scores were averaged for each infant. The difference within each pair was ascertained, the differences ranked, and again intra-pair differences among fraternal

the homes of identical pairs A, B, C, and D. In each of these pairs the personalities merged into a single picture after a few hours, and unless our impressions of differences were recorded immediately, it became impossible to do so later. This merger could not be ascribed to similar appearance, for there was no difficulty in recording other identical looking pairs who exhibited some clear-cut behavioural differences.

Consistent behavioural differences within some identical pairs deserves special attention. In pair E, following normal births, only the second-born was startled by noises in the first two months, cried at the jack-in-the-box at 3 months, and became extremely fearful of strangers during the last half of the first year. In pair K, the second-born twin, after a traumatic breech birth, slept much of the time over the first $1\frac{1}{2}$ months. Then he began smiling to people more readily than did his brother whose delivery had been normal, and at 5 months he wanted to be picked up by any newcomer. Thereafter he remained more immediately outgoing to people than his twin. Our observations and interviews with the parents suggested that differential treatment played no role in producing these differences, and obstetrical and pediatric records yielded no clues. The following categories were examined, and none could be reasonably associated with such differences: birth order, traumatic delivery, large differences in birth weight, Apgar ratings (an assessment of viability at birth), and monochorionic versus dichorionic embryogenesis.

Although motor behaviour was most effective in differentiating within twin-pairs, perhaps because it was most objectively scored, we cannot estimate heritability for specific aspects of behaviour, nor was this our aim. Our question was rather: Does heredity, in a general sense, play a role in the development of abilities and personality? An affirmative answer would appear to be warranted.

References

1. NEILON, P. (1948). *J. genet. Psychol.* **73**, 175.
2. THOMAS, A., CHESS, S., BIRCH, H., and HERTIZIG, M. E. (1960). *Compr. Psychiat.* **1**, 103.
3. PIAGET, J. (1951). *Play, dreams, and imitation in childhood*. Norton, New York.
4. AHRENS, R. (1954). *Z. exptl. Angew, Psychol.* **2**, 412.
5. AUBLE, D. (1953). *Bull. Inst. Educ. Res.* Indiana University, Bloomington.
6. SIEGEL, S. (1956). *Non-parametric statistics*. McGraw-Hill, New York.

2 Genetics and intelligence

L. ERLENMEYER-KIMLING AND LISSY F. JARVIK[†]

No MOTHETIC psychological theories have been distinguished by the tendency to disregard the individual variability which is characteristic of all behaviour. A parallel between genetic individuality and psychologic individuality has rarely been drawn because the usual assumption has been [1] that the organisms intervening between stimulus and response are equivalent 'black boxes', which react in uniform ways to given stimuli.

While behaviour theory and its analytic methods as yet make few provisions for modern genetic concepts, the literature contains more information than is generally realized about the relationship between genotypic similarity and similarity of performance on mental tests. In a search for order among the published data on intellectual ability, we have recently summarized the work of the past half century.[‡] By using the most commonly reported statistical measure, namely,

the correlation coefficient,[ʳ] it has been possible to assemble comparative figures from the majority of the investigations.

Certain studies giving correlations had to be excluded from this compilation for one of the following reasons: (1) type of test used (for example, achievement tests, scholastic performance, or subjective rating of intelligence); (2) type of subject used (for example, mental defectives); (3) inadequate information about zygosity diagnosis in twin studies;[§] (4) reports on too few special twin pairs.

The 52 studies[‡] remaining after these exclusions yield over 30 000 correlational pairings[¶] for the genetic relationship categories shown in Fig. 2.1. The data, in aggregate, provide a broad basis for the comparison of genotypic and phenotypic correlations. Considering only *ranges* of the observed measures, a marked trend is seen towards an increasing degree of intellectual resemblance in direct pro-

† From 'Genetics and intelligence: a review'. *Science* **142**, 1477–9 (1963). Copyright © 1963 by the American Association for the Advancement of Science. Reprinted by permission of the authors and the Association.

‡ This material was included in a report presented at the XVII International Congress of Psychology, Washington, D.C. (1963), (Erlenmeyer-Kimling, L., Jarvik, L. F., and Kallmann, F. J.). Detailed information about the data presented here is available upon request.

§ This survey does include reports on opposite-sex (hence dizygotic) twin pairs from these studies.

¶ Correlation pairings refer to the number of individual pairs used in deriving the correlation coefficients. Some investigators constructed a large number of pairings on the basis of a relatively small number of individuals. Altogether, we have been able to identify the following minimum numbers: twins, 3134 pairs (1082 monozygotic and 2052 dizygotic); sibs apart, 125 pairs plus 131 individuals; sibs together, 8288 pairs plus 7225 individuals; parent–child, 371 pairs plus 6812 individuals; fosterparent–child, 537 individuals; unrelated apart, 15 086 pairings; unrelated together, 195 pairings plus 287 individuals.

portion to an increasing degree of genetic relationship, regardless of environmental communality.

Furthermore, for most relationship categories, the *median* of the empirical correlations closely approaches the theoretical value predicted on the basis of genetic relationship alone. The average genetic correlation between parent and child, as well as that able difference between the groups. Since only two studies dealt with siblings reared *apart*, it is possible to state only that the reported correlations for that group fall within the range of values obtained for siblings reared together and exceed those for unrelated children living *together*.

For unrelated persons in a large random-mating population, the theoretical

Category		0·00 0·10 0·20 0·30 0·40 0·50 0·60 0·70 0·80 0·90	Groups included
Unrelated persons	Reared apart		4
	Reared together		5
Fosterparent-child			3
Parent-child			12
Siblings	Reared apart		2
	Reared together		35
Two-egg	Opposite sex		9
	Like sex		11
One-egg	Reared apart		4
	Reared together		14

FIG. 2.1. Correlation coefficients for 'intelligence' test scores from 52 studies. Some studies reported data for more than one relationship category; some included more than one sample per category, giving a total of 99 groups. Over two-thirds of the correlation coefficients were derived from IQs, the remainder from special tests (for example, primary mental abilities). Mid-parent–child correlation was used when available, otherwise mother–child correlation. Correlation coefficients obtained in each study are indicated by dark circles; medians are shown by vertical lines intersecting the horizontal lines which represent the ranges.

between siblings (including dizygotic twins) is 0·50. The median correlations actually observed on tests of intellectual functioning are: 0·50 for parent–child, 0·49 for siblings reared together, and 0·53 for dizygotic twins, both the opposite-sex and like-sex pairs. Although twins are presumably exposed to more similar environmental conditions than are siblings spaced apart in age, the correlations for mental ability do not indicate a sizeable difference between the groups.
genetic correlation is usually considered to be zero; for smaller populations, or those that deviate substantially from panmixia, however, the genetic correlation between presumably unrelated individuals in fact may be considerably higher. The observed median for unrelated persons reared apart is −0·01. Medians for unrelated individuals reared together (children reared in the same orphanage or foster home from an early age) and for the

fosterparent–child group are 0·23 and 0·20, respectively. The relative contributions made by environmental similarity and sample selection to these deviations from zero are still to be analysed.

At the other end of the relationship scale, where monozygotic twins theoretically have 100 per cent genetic correlation, medians of the observed correlations in intellectual functioning are 0·87 for the twins brought up together, and 0·75 for those brought up apart.† The correlations obtained for monozygotic twins reared together are generally in line with the intra-individual reliabilities of the tests. The median for the separated twins is somewhat lower, but clearly exceeds those for all other relationship groups.

In further reference to twin studies, our survey ‡ shows that mean intra-pair differences on tests of mental abilities for dizygotic twins generally are between 1½ to 2 times as great as those between monozygotic twins reared together. Such a relationship appears to hold also for the upper age groups, as suggested by a longitudinal study of senescent twins [2].

Taken individually, many of the 52 studies reviewed here are subject to various types of criticism (for example, methodological). Nevertheless, the overall orderliness of the results is particularly impressive if one considers that the investigators had different backgrounds and contrasting views regarding the importance of heredity. Not all of them used the same measures of intelligence (see caption, Fig. 2.1),

and they derived their data from samples which were unequal in size, age structure, ethnic composition, and socio-economic stratification; the data were collected in eight countries on four continents during a time span covering more than two generations of individuals. Against this pronounced heterogeneity, which should have clouded the picture, and is reflected by the wide range of correlations, a clearly definitive consistency emerges from the data.

The composite data are compatible with the polygenic hypothesis which is generally favoured in accounting for inherited differences in mental ability. Sex-linkage is not supported by these data (for example, under a hypothesis of sex-linkage the correlations for like-sex dizygotic twins should be higher than those for opposite-sex twins), although the possible effects of sex-linked genes are not precluded for some specific factors of ability.

We do not imply that environment is without effect upon intellectual functioning; the intellectual level is *not* unalterably fixed by the genetic constitution. Rather, its expression in the phenotype results from the patterns laid down by the genotype under given environmental conditions. Two illustrations of the 'norm of reaction' concept in relation to intellectual variability are seen in early total deafness and in phenylketonuria. Early deafness makes its stamp upon intellectual development, in that it lowers IQ by an estimated 20 score points [3]. Phenylketonuria is ordinarily associ-

† Correlation data are now available on 107 separated pairs of monozygotic twins from four series: NEWMAN, H. H., FREEMAN, F. N., and HOLZINGER, K. J. (1937), *Twins: A Study of Heredity and Environment*, University of Chicago Press, Chicago; CONWAY, J. (1958), *Brit. J. stat. Psychol.* **11**, 171; JUEL-NIELSEN, N.

and MOGENSEN, A. (1962) cited by Strömgren, E., in *Expanding goals of genetics in psychiatry*, Kallmann, F. J. (Ed.), Grune and Stratton, New York, p. 231; SHIELDS, J. (1962), *Monozygotic twins brought up apart and brought up together*, Oxford Univ. Press, London.

ated with an even greater degree of intellectual impairment. However, early alteration of the nutritional environment of the affected child changes the phenotypic expression of this genetic defect [4]. Individual differences in behavioural *potential* reflect genotypic differences; individual differences in behavioural *performance* result from the non-uniform recording of environmental stimuli by intrinsically non-uniform organisms.

References

1. HIRSCH, J. (1963). *Science* **142**, 1436.
2. JARVIK, L. F. and FALEK, A. (1963) *J. Gerontol.* **18**, 173.
3. SALZBERGER, R. M. and JARVIK, L. F. (1963). *In* (Rainer, J. D., *et al.* (Eds.)) *Family and mental health problems in a deaf population.* N.Y. State Psychiatric Institute, New York.
4. HOMER, F. A., STREAMER, C. W., ALEJANDRINO, L. L., REED, L. H., and IBBOTT, F. (1962). *New Engl. J. Med.* **266**, 79.

3 | Genetics and personality

IRVING I. GOTTESMAN†

Introduction

A renewed interest in the twin method in developmental psychology is a healthy sign that we are confronting our ignorance about the sources of variation in cognitive ability and personality traits. Despite a sometimes well-founded pessimism about the effectiveness of earlier efforts to contribute to an understanding of the roles of heredity and environment in human behaviour generally, greater sophistication about the complexities of genetics and personality measurement has resulted in significant advances in human behaviour genetics which are not generally appreciated [28]. Recent reviews of interest to developmental psychologists may be found in Gottesman [9], McClearn [19], and Vandenberg [29]. The present paper is a preliminary report in a broader research programme into the origins of individual differences in both normal and abnormal personality characteristics [8, 10, 11, 12].

One of the concerns of behaviour geneticists is the possible evolutionary significance of a trait. Simpson [26] has helped foster this concern by noting that the modern theory of evolution reinstated behaviour as one of the essential determinants of evolution. Mayr [18] succinctly summed up the

† From 'Genetic variance in adaptive personality traits'. *J. child Psychol. Psychiat.* **7**, 199–208 (1966). Reprinted by permission of Maxwell Microforms International Marketing Corp.

role of behaviour in evolution: 'The point that is important for us is that new habits and behaviour always start in a concrete local population. If the new behaviour adds to fitness, it will be favoured by selection and so will all genes that contribute to its efficiency' (p. 605). Fitness may be simply defined, for our purposes, as the number of offspring surviving to an age when they might reproduce. Needless to say, the gene to behaviour pathway involves a very complex chain of events [6, 21].

There are no genes for behaviour. The genes exert their influence on behaviour through their effects at a more molecular level of organization. Enzymes, hormones, and neurons mediate the path between the genes and those psycho-social aspects of behaviour termed personality. Even the latter complications have been compounded by discoveries in molecular genetics involving the concepts of regulator and operator genes (e.g. the work of Jacob and Monod [17]) that influence the sequential activation of well-established structural gene potential throughout the life of an organism. Henceforth, formulations in behavioural genetics will have to reckon with the fact that genetic variation in individual differences may arise from alterations in structural genes, either qualitative or quantitative, or by activation or inhibition of regulator genes, also qualitative or quantitative.

For our present purposes, it will be

sufficient to conceptualize the contribution of heredity to personality trait variation in terms of heredity's determining a reaction range [9]. Within this framework a genotype determines an indefinite but circumscribed assortment of phenotypes, each of which corresponds to one of the possible environments to which the genotype may be exposed. The theory of natural selection would lead us to expect that traits with adaptive significance evolved and endured because of such adaptive value. The processes underlying organic evolution should lead to appreciable genetic variation in those personality traits with patent adaptive value. However, a number of genetically conditioned traits may be anticipated whose adaptive value is no longer apparent in current environments; a case in point is the presence in Negro Americans of a type of haemoglobin with adaptive value in the malaria-infested regions of their African forebears [4].

Method

Of the few available methods for investigating the genetic aspects of human behaviour, the twin method is the most fruitful and economic. The underlying principle of the twin method is simple and sound: since identical (MZ) twins have identical genotypes, any observed dissimilarity within pairs must be due to environmental factors. The latter may be intra-uterine, peri-natal, or post-natal. Fraternal (DZ) same-sex twins, while on the average differing in 50 per cent of their genes, provide a measure of environmental control not otherwise possible by virtue of sharing such factors as birth rank, mother's age and experience, schooling, and nutrition. When both kinds of twins are studied

simultaneously from the same population a rough but useful estimate of the importance of genetic factors in the variance of a trait in that population may be obtained. The principle may be schematically illustrated with the following equations, once the within-pair variances (v_{MZ} and v_{DZ}) have been calculated:

$$v_{DZ} = v_{env} + v_{her}, \qquad (3.1)$$
$$v_{MZ} = v_{env}, \qquad (3.2)$$
$$v_{DZ} - v_{MZ} = v_{her}, \qquad (3.3)$$

where the subscripts 'env' and 'her' denote 'environmental' and 'hereditary', respectively. The assumptions necessary for the complete validity of the method are that the average intra-pair differences in trait-relevant environmental factors are substantially the same for both MZ and DZ twins, and that variance associated with the interaction of hereditary and environmental factors is small or equivalent in both (3.1) and (3.2). Criticisms of the method may be found in the references already cited.

Twin study statistics

Twin investigators in the behavioural sciences have elected different ways of expressing their findings. Allen [2] has found fault with any single way of statistically summarizing the data. When a trait is qualitative or can be arbitrarily but usefully dichotomized the simplest way of expressing results is in terms of the percentage of MZ and then DZ pairs that are concordant for the presence of the trait. Most responses in the purview of personality research do not lend themselves to a qualitative analysis. Since the inference that a trait has an appreciable component of its variance associated with genetic factors depends on the demonstration of greater similarity within MZ pairs than DZ pairs, other approaches are required for handling continuously distributed traits. One approach is to show that the (intra-class) correlation coefficient for MZ pairs is significantly higher than that for the DZ pairs. This method is straightforward and tells whether genetic factors are even worth enter-taining; it fails to tell us the strength of the genetic factors, however. The latter is sometimes hazardously inferred from a statistic known as heritability H. The heritability of a trait in the twin method is defined as the proportion of within-family trait variance associated with genetic factors. The values thus obtained are sample-specific until proved otherwise, and also suffer from not taking into account between-family genotypic variance. Twin method H values underestimate the role of genetic factors in the total population [5]. H is easily calculated from the within-pair variances:

$$H = \frac{v_{DZ} - v_{MZ}}{v_{DZ}}. \qquad (3.4)$$

The last statistic to be mentioned is the F or variance ratio formed by v_{DZ}/v_{MZ}. The statistical significance is easily found from tables and by itself permits us to infer the strength of genetic factors in eliminating MZ within-pair variation. The same F ratio is used to test the significance of H so that both F and H may be conveniently pre-sented together. The degrees of free-dom involved for F are equal to the number of DZ and MZ pairs, respectively.

Subjects

The sample will be referred to as the Harvard twins to distinguish it from a Minnesota twin sample of the same age which was given some of the same test [8]. Ss were same-sex, complete pairs of twins in grades 9–12, volun-teering from some 20 cooperating school systems in the Greater Boston area, other than Boston itself, with an enrolment of 33 617 and from some 15 other school systems in the same area that refused official cooperation, with an enrolment of 34 154. Cooperating schools provided a complete list of all twin pairs, numbering 180 pairs of same-sex twins. The latter number was almost exactly the number expected, based on a figure of 0·55 per cent of the 15-year-old population being in-tact pairs of same-sex twins [1]. Twins in the non-cooperating systems were contacted by advertisements in neigh-bourhood newspapers and through 'mothers of twins' clubs. The names of 59 additional pairs came from the latter sources, only 31 per cent of the potential number of pairs in that population. Only 11 pairs in the total list of 239 pairs came from the huge Catholic parochial school system (33 489 in the age range sampled).

Of the 180 pairs from the cooperat-ing systems, 132 (73 per cent) actually volunteered and completed the person-ality tests and procedures to be described. Of the 59 additional pairs, 46 (78 per cent) completed the requirements. Of the total of 178 pairs of tested volunteers, 94 were female and 84 male. In terms of social class as inferred from fathers' occupation (Minnesota scale for paternal occupa-tions), 22 per cent were professional (Class I), 25 per cent semi-professional and managerial (Class II), 38 per cent skilled trades and clerical (Class III), and 15 per cent semi-skilled or engaged in occupations requiring little training (Classes V–VII). In terms of religion, 48 per cent were Catholic, 19 per cent Jewish, 15 per cent Conservative

Protestants, and 18 per cent Liberal Protestants or non-denominational. It would appear that Catholics were well represented, despite the non-cooperating parochial system, because suburban Catholics sent their children to public schools.

Thirty-one pairs of twins were dropped from the sample of 178, leaving a final sample of 147 pairs of same-sex twins. The 31 pairs were eliminated because one or both members had invalidated their personality tests, either intentionally or through poor reading comprehension. Invalidity was determined by a raw score of 10 or higher on the Lie scale of the Minnesota multiphase personality inventory (MMPI) or a raw score of 22 or higher on the F scale of the MMPI. The final sample of 147 pairs was composed of 79 pairs of MZ twins, 34 male and 45 female, and 68 pairs of DZ twins, 32 male and 36 female. For reasons of economy, 40 of the original 178 pairs who were clearly MZ or DZ were excused from blood typing; zygosity of the remaining 138 pairs was determined by the extensive blood grouping procedure suggested by Smith and Penrose [8].

Procedures

All twins were administered the California psychological inventory (CPI) [14], MMPI [3], a brief vocabulary test of intelligence (Shipley-Hartford, cf. [27]), and a biographical data sheet. Parents were asked to volunteer and took the same tests and, in addition, filled in the adjective check list [13] for themselves and each of their two twins; 177 parents were tested. Siblings of the twins who were the same sex and between the ages of 14 and 25 were asked to participate and 58 came

forward. Only certain of the twins' CPI results will be discussed in this paper (cf. [10]).

No report has yet been made of twin similarities on the 18 scales of the CPI, nor has anyone suggested that some of the variance on the scales may reflect genetic variability in a population.

Results

The within-pair MZ and DZ variances for each of the 18 CPI scales are given for the total group, females and males in Tables 3.1, 3.2, and 3.3 together with the heritability (H) of each scale and its F ratio.

For the total sample of MZ twins (Table 3.1) all 18 of the CPI scale intra-class vs were significant at less than the 0·01 level. The vs ranged from 0·29 to 0·60.

Only half the DZ vs were significant at the 0·01 level with five more at the 0·05 level. The calculations of H values for the total sample of twins showed that seven traits had approximately one third or more of the within-family variance significantly associated with genetic factors: sociability, dominance, self-acceptance, social presence, socialization, good impression, and psychological mindedness. A further five traits had H values greater than 25 per cent. Interpretation of the results is facilitated by looking at the meaningful clusters or factors in the CPI. Table 3.4 presents the major results of the analysis from a behavioural genetics viewpoint.

The first 4 of the 7 traits named above completely define 1 of the 2 factors derived from the CPI by Nichols and Schnell [22] which they named Person Orientation. The factor scale correlated −0·66 with the social–introversion scale of the MMPI. Thus

TABLE 3.1. *Genetic Components of Variance for the CPI (Total Twin Sample)*

Scale	V of DZ $N = 68$	V of MZ $N = 79$	H	F‡
Dominance	80·706	41·342	0·49	1·95†
Capacity for status	71·816	53·532	0·25	1·34
Sociability	90·838	46·082	0·49	1·97†
Social presence	79·603	51·405	0·35	1·55*
Self-acceptance	99·787	53·848	0·46	1·85†
Sense of well-being	101·80	91·437	0·13	1·11
Responsibility	67·206	49·960	0·26	1·35
Socialization	88·904	60·184	0·32	1·48*
Self-control	71·559	51·994	0·27	1·38
Tolerance	86·456	62·924	0·27	1·37
Good impression	70·824	44·158	0·38	1·60*
Communality	79·772	64·677	0·19	1·23
Achievement via conformance	66·625	76·297	0·00	0·87
Achievement via independence	83·059	63·291	0·24	1·31
Intellectual efficiency	72·559	59·405	0·18	1·22
Psychological mindedness	82·912	56·639	0·32	1·46
Flexibility	70·309	60·044	0·15	1·17
Femininity	60·868	44·576	0·27	1·36

‡ $F_{0.05} = 1·47$ indicated by *, $F_{0.01} = 1·72$ indicated by †.

TABLE 3.2. *Genetic Components of Variance for the CPI (Female Twins)*

Scale	V of DZ $N = 36$	V of MZ $N = 45$	H	F‡
Dominance	56·389	32·978	0·42	1·71*
Capacity for status	88·528	58·278	0·34	1·52
Sociability	93·917	40·844	0·56	2·30†
Social presence	65·194	48·411	0·26	1·35
Self-acceptance	81·569	47·467	0·42	1·72*
Sense of well-being	83·125	67·756	0·18	1·23
Responsibility	61·722	31·056	0·50	1·99*
Socialization	68·194	44·706	0·34	1·53
Self-control	91·514	48·333	0·47	1·89*
Tolerance	93·194	63·622	0·32	1·46
Good impression	74·736	44·678	0·40	1·67
Communality	65·319	57·567	0·12	1·13
Achievement via conformance	79·458	61·789	0·22	1·29
Achievement via independence	101·15	54·344	0·46	1·86*
Intellectual efficiency	77·264	42·067	0·46	1·84*
Psychological mindedness	80·625	61·756	0·23	1·31
Flexibility	77·625	56·011	0·28	1·39
Femininity	57·694	49·200	0·15	1·17

‡ $F_{0.05} = 1·68$ indicated by *, $F_{0.01} = 2·09$ indicated by †.

TABLE 3.3. *Genetic Components of Variance for the CPI (Male Twins)*

Scale	V of DZ $N = 32$	V of MZ $N = 34$	H	F ‡
Dominance	108·06	52·412	0·51	2·06*
Capacity for status	53·016	47·250	0·11	1·22
Sociability	87·375	53·015	0·39	1·65
Social presence	95·812	55·368	0·42	1·73
Self-acceptance	120·28	62·294	0·48	1·93*
Sense of well-being	122·81	122·78	0·00	1·00
Responsibility	73·375	74·353	0·00	0·99
Socialization	12·20	80·676	0·28	1·39
Self-control	49·109	56·838	0·00	0·86
Tolerance	78·875	62·000	0·21	1·27
Good impression	66·422	43·471	0·35	1·53
Communality	96·031	74·088	0·23	1·30
Achievement via conformance	52·187	95·500	0·00	0·55
Achievement via independence	62·703	75·132	0·00	0·83
Intellectual efficiency	67·266	82·353	0·00	0·82
Psychological mindedness	85·484	49·868	0·42	1·71
Flexibility	62·078	65·382	0·00	0·95
Femininity	64·437	38·456	0·40	1·68

TABLE 3.4. *Heritability of CPI Extraversion–Introversion Scales*

Factor	CPI scale	H	F
Person	Sociability	0·49	1·97†
Orientation	Self-acceptance	0·46	1·85†
or	Social presence	0·35	1·55*
Extraversion–introversion	Dominance	0·49	1·95†

TABLE 3.5. *Heritability of CPI Dependability–Undependability Scales*

Cluster	CPI scale	H	F
Value	Responsibility	0·26	1·35
Orientation	Socialization	0·32	1·48*
or	Self-control	0·27	1·38
Dependability–Undependability	Tolerance	0·27	1·37
	Good impression	0·38	1·60*
	Communality	0·19	1·23

‡ $F_{0.05} = 1·79$ indicated by *, $F_{0.01} = 2·28$ indicated by †.

the factor can also be conceptualized as a dimension of extraversion–introversion with variation equally determined by genetic and non-genetic substrates.

Table 3.5 gives *H* results for the scales in the other major factor of the CPI. Gough [14] considered it to be a dimension of dependability–undependability and Nichols and

Schnell [22] have termed the factor 'value orientation'. It is difficult to relate the latter concept to ideas of adaptation and evolution but not the former. The dimension has a low but appreciable genetic component.

Sex differences in heritability of personality traits have been broached in an earlier paper [8]. Both sex role

0·60 in females and 0·84 in males. Corresponding values for the Harvard sample [10] were 0·33, 0·35, and 0·29. The combined probability for the two studies using the MMPI makes the genetic component of variance in the social–introversion dimension highly significant, $p < 0.005$. The high heritability found for the person-orienta-

TABLE 3.6. *Sex Differences in CPI Scale Heritabilities*

Scale	H Female ($N = 81$ pairs)	H Male ($N = 66$ pairs)
Responsibility	0·50	0·00
Self-control	0·47	0·00
Achievement via independence	0·46	0·00
Intellectual efficiency	0·46	0·00
Sociability	0·56	0·39
Dominance	0·42	0·51

typing and sexual selection in the Darwinian sense were suggested as relevant to an evaluation of such differences. The area is a fascinating one in need of a great deal of thought. Table 3.6 shows the largest differences found with the CPI for the present sample.

Discussion

Scarr [23] has made the point that both longitudinal studies in child development (e.g. [16]) and twin studies find a consistent, perhaps constitutional component in a dimension of personality like extraversion–introversion that emerges despite differences in age, sex, social class, and, within limits, culture. She reported an H value of 0·83 for the Fels child behaviour scale of social apprehension in a large sample of 52 pairs of primary school girl twins. The author reported [8] an H of 0·71 for the social introversion scale of the MMPI in a sample of 68 pairs of adolescent twins,

tion or extraversion–introversion factor of the CPI for the present study adds to evidence for the latter statement.

An interpretation of the above findings that appeals to the author involves a linkage with the idea that individual differences in the strength of social attachments in infancy observed by Schaffer and Emerson [24, 25] have a large genetic component and that such a trait has obvious evolutionary significance and adaptive value.

The infant–mother affectional system has also been singled out for importance in non-human primates. Harlow, Harlow, and Hansen [15], from their observations of Rhesus monkeys, posited the infant–mother (different from mother–infant) system as one of five affectional systems. It is interesting to conjecture that the child and adolescent derivatives of social attachment observed in infants are what we term sociability or are reflected in the dimension of extraversion–introversion. Might the adult derivatives of social attachment be related to the mother–infant and father–infant affectional systems? Meehl [20] suggested that interpersonal aversiveness characterized the schizophrenic and the schizotype. Schizophrenics were observed to be less fit than normals, i.e. to have fewer children, males more so than females [7]. The framework provided by evolutionary biology may be a useful one for synthesizing the observations listed above.

Any speculation about the mode of transmission for the genetic substrate of personality variation must limit itself to a polygenic theory as opposed to classical Mendelian models. As such, the relative absence of some of the genes in the polygenic system that may underlie the dimension of extraversion–introversion could lead to pathological degrees of non-attachment. Perhaps some infants characterized as autistic, and some children and adults labelled as schizophrenic, have an inherited defect in the strength of their 'attachment systems' as a necessary but not usually sufficient condition for their abnormal behaviour.

Conclusions

The scientific era of human behavioural genetics is relatively young. The attempts to study the evolution of behaviour and to elucidate possible selective forces that made some behaviours more adaptive than others are fraught with disconcerting vagueness but compensatory satisfactions. With few exceptions most comprehensive efforts in human behavioural genetics have focused on mental illness and mental deficiency. Such efforts should continue. The present paper attempted to provide some data and speculations that might be useful in bringing adaptive or non-pathological personality traits into the light cast by the modern theory of evolution.

References

1. ALLEN, G. (1955). Comments on the analysis of twin samples. *Acta Genet. med. Gemell.* **4**, 143–59.
2. —— (1965). Twin research: problems and prospects. *In* (Steinberg, A. G., and Bearn, A. G. (Eds.)) *Progress in medical genetics.* Grune and Stratton, New York, pp. 242–69.
3. DAHLSTROM, W. G. and WELSH, G. S. (Eds.) (1960). *An MMPI handbook.* University of Minn. Press, Minneapolis.
4. DOBZHANSKY, T. (1962). *Mankind evolving.* Yale Press, New Haven.
5. FALCONER, D. S. (1960). *An introduction to quantitative genetics.* Ronald, New York.
6. FULLER, J. and THOMPSON, W. (1960). *Behaviour genetics.* Wiley, New York.
7. GOLDFARB, C. and ERLENMEYER-KIMLING, L. (1962). Mating and fertility trends in schizophrenia. *In* (Kallmann, F. J. (Ed.)) *Expanding goals of genetics in psychiatry.* Grune and Stratton, New York, pp. 42–51.
8. GOTTESMAN, I. I. (1963). Heritability of personality: a demonstration. *Psychol. Monogr.* **77**, No. 9, whole No. 572.
9. —— (1963). Genetic aspects of intelligent behaviour. *In* (Ellis, N. (Ed.)) *Handbook of mental deficiency: psychological theory and research.* McGraw-Hill, New York, pp. 253–96.
10. —— (1965). Personality and natural selection. *In* (Vandenberg, S. G. (Ed.)) *Methods and goals in human behaviour genetics.* Academic Press, New York.
11. —— and SHIELDS, J. (1966). Schizophrenia in twins: 16 years' consecutive admissions to a psychiatric clinic. *Br. J. Psychiat.* **112**, 809–18.

12. —— and —— (1966). Contributions of twin studies to perspectives on schizophrenia. *In* (Maher, B. A. (Ed.)) *Progress in experimental personality research*. Vol. 3. Academic Press, New York, p. 1–84.

13. GOUGH, H. G. (1960). The adjective check list as a personality assessment research technique. *Psychol. Rep.* **6**, 107–22.

14. —— (1965). Conceptual analysis of psychological test scores and other diagnostic variables. *J. abnorm. Psychol.* **70**, 294–302.

15. HARLOW, H. F., HARLOW, MARGARET K., and HANSEN, E. W. (1963). The maternal affectional system of Rhesus monkeys. *In* (Rheingold, Harriet L. (Ed.)) *Maternal behaviour in mammals*. Wiley, New York, pp. 254–81.

16. HONZIK, MARJORIE P. (1964). Personality consistency and change: some comments on papers by Bayler, Macfarlane, Moss and Kagan, and Murphy. *Vita hum.* **7**, 139–42.

17. JACOB, F. and MONOD, J. (1961). On the regulation of gene activity. *Cold Spring Harbor Symp. on Quant. Biol.* **26**, 193–209.

18. MAYR, E. (1963). *Animal species and evolution*. Harvard University Press, Cambridge.

19. McCLEARN, G. E. (1964). Genetics and behaviour development. *In* Hoffman, M. L. and Lois W. (Eds.)) *Review of child development research*. Vol. 1. Russell Sage, New York, pp. 433–80.

20. MEEHL, P. E. (1962). Schizotaxia, schizotypy, schizophrenia. *Am. Psychol.* **17**, 827–38.

21. MEISSNER, W. W. (1965). Functional and adaptive aspects of cellular regulatory mechanisms. *Psychol. Bull.* **64**, 206–16.

22. NICHOLS, R. C. and SCHNELL, R. R. (1963). Factor scales for the California psychological inventory. *J. consult. Psychol.* **27**, 228–35.

23. SCARR, SANDRA (1965). The inheritance of sociability. *Am. Psychol.* **20**, 524 (Abstract).

24. SCHAFFER, H. R. and EMERSON, PEGGY E. (1964). The development of social attachments in infancy. *Monogr. Soc. Res. Child Dev.* **29**, Ser. 94.

25. —— and —— (1964). Patterns of response to physical contact in early human development. *J. Child Psychol. Psychiat.* **5**, 1–13.

26. SIMPSON, G. G. (1958). The study of evolution: methods and present status of theory. *In* (Roe, Anne and Simpson, G. G. (Eds.)) *Behaviour and evolution*. Yale Press, New Haven, pp. 7–26.

27. SINES, L. K. (1958). Intelligence test correlates of Shipley-Hartford performance. *J. clin. Psychol.* **14**, 399–403.

28. VANDENBERG, S. G. (Ed.) (1965). *Methods and goals in human behaviour genetics*. Academic Press, New York.

29. —— (1966). Contributions of twin research to child development. *Psychol. Bull.* **66**, 327–52.

4 Environmental bias in twin studies

SANDRA SCARR†

THE twin study method attempts to estimate genetic contributions to variation in human behaviour by comparing intra-pair differences of monozygotic (MZ) and same-sex dizygotic (DZ) pairs. The resulting estimates of heritability and comparisons of intraclass correlations are based upon a perhaps questionable assumption: that the environments of DZ co-twins are no more dissimilar than the environments of MZ co-twins. Since excess MZ correlations are interpreted as being genetic in origin, additional DZ differences created by greater environmental variance would lower their intra-class correlations and hence bias the results in favour of high genetic estimates.

Environmental biases of both ante- and post-natal origins must be considered. Price [6] and Allen [1] suggested that some variance in co-twins may be accounted for by differences in ante-natal nourishment, especially in monochorial MZ twins. If this ante-natal environmental bias exists, it reduces rather than raises genetic estimates by introducing environmental differences between genetically identical twins. Differences in birth weight of co-twins are also thought to influence later similarities in development; in this study, how-

† From *Eugenics Quart.*, **15**, 34–40 (1968). Reprinted by permission of the University of Chicago Press.

ever, there were no differences between MZ and DZ groups in the similarity of co-twins' birth weights.

Vandenberg [11] examined the issue of equal environmental (postnatal) variances for MZ and DZ twins with emphasis on the dependent variables. He concluded that unequal environmental variances for the two kinds of twins would have little effect on anthropometric and physiological measures. For psychomotor and cognitive traits, and for personality measures, unequal variances could be more significant. Vandenberg defended the assumption of equal environmental variances for MZ and DZ groups by pointing to the multivariate analysis of twin differences, which has shown little evidence of a general within-family environmental factor which would lead one of the twins to score higher on most tests. A devoted environmentalist might reject Vandenberg's argument based on multivariate analysis; he might counter that number ability could be encouraged in one twin in one family while verbal reasoning was favoured in one of another pair. There might be no general pattern of abilities affected, yet all genetic estimates would be contaminated by differences in parental treatment.

Leaving cognitive abilities aside, it seems likely that behavioural and personality measures would be biased by *increased* environmental variances in DZ pairs and by *decreased* environmental variances between MZ co-twins. Several investigators have already shown that MZ co-twins are indeed more similar than DZ co-twins in the treatment they receive from their parents as well as in the development of mutually interdependent roles [4], choice of friends, sports attendance, and some food preferences [10]. Additional data to be presented in this paper support their contention that the home environments of MZ co-twins are in general more similar than those of DZ co-twins, but questions the assumption that this is necessarily *prima facie* evidence for environmental bias in twin studies.

Behavioural Similarities of co-twins

Smith [10] interviewed 164 pairs of adolescent twins about work, school, sports, leisure, sleep, dress, study habits, and food and beverage preferences. He found that, in general, MZ co-twins were more similar than DZ co-twins, with the results more positive for females than for males. Two of the eight MZ correlations were significantly greater than DZ correlations. MZ co-twins were more likely to have the same friends and the same patterns of attendance at sports events. Habits of work, school, sports participation, sleep, and study did not significantly differentiate between MZ and DZ pairs. For household chores and food and beverage preferences, MZ females tended to be more similar than DZ females, but the effect was not as strong for males. Adolescent MZ co-twins were more likely to consider themselves similar in habits and activities, and the MZ females were more likely to dress alike. For males,

there were no differences in dressing alike for MZ and DZ pairs. Smith concluded that these results cast doubt upon the validity of the assumption of equal environmental variances for MZ and DZ twins.

In a study of 61 pairs of twin girls in grade school in the Boston area, MZ co-twins were also found to be somewhat more similar than DZ pairs in their behaviours and in the parental treatment they received [7, 8]. Unlike Smith's [10] sample, there were no differences in the socio-economic status or educational level of the parents of MZ and DZ twins. The modal parents of both kinds of twins were high-school graduates in lower white collar occupations—policemen, firemen, salesmen, office workers, and so forth. The twin groups showed no differences in IQ (total group mean, 100·4) or age (total group mean, 95 months).

Both the MZ and the DZ co-twins were likely to prefer the same kinds of activities, but the MZ co-twins were more similar in the number of activities they engaged in. This finding was interpreted as variation in activity motivation, for which genetic contributions were found, not only in ratings but behavioural measures as well [7]. The behavioural similarities and differences of MZ and DZ co-twins doubtless result from both genetic and environmental factors: but are MZ co-twins more similar mainly because of environmental pressures for similarity, as Smith [10] implies? Or are the greater similarities of MZ co-twins principally a reflection of greater genetic similarity, resulting in phenotypic similarity, behavioural and otherwise? From these data it is impossible to separate the sources of behavioural variation.

Parental Behaviour

Many of the arguments presented by critics of the twin study method have focused on the differences in parental treatment of identical and fraternal twins. Since MZ twins are supposed to be alike, parents may emphasize their similarities; and since DZ twins are not supposed to be alike, parents may concentrate on differentiating them. The measurement of parental behaviour towards their children is a hazardous but worthy goal [9]. The differences of treatment received within the family by MZ and DZ co-twins are difficult to measure from an 'objective' point of view; and in the brief time we spent in the homes of our sample, objective measures were impossible to obtain. It was possible, however, to obtain a subjective evaluation of parental behaviour by interviewing the mothers and by having them rate the attitudes and expectations they held for their twins.

The mothers were interviewed about their twins' present and past behaviour. They were asked, 'How similar or different do you feel Twin A and Twin B are?' Their answers were coded on a scale from 1 (very different) to 5 (very similar). The Vineland social maturity scale [2] was completed during the interviews to measure the amount of responsibility and independence the mothers believed each twin could accept. The mothers were also asked to recall the twins' early development and behaviour 'problems', from which scales of co-twin similarity were constructed. The anamnestic data on the twins' early years are not necessarily accurate, but rather reflect the mothers' selective recall of similarities and differences in their twins. The results of the mothers' interviews are given in Table 4.1.

TABLE 4.1. *Percentage of MZ and DZ Pairs Rated as Similar for Several Characteristics*

Mothers' ratings of co-twins	MZ ($N = 23$)	DZ ($N = 29$)
Similar now	78	17
Similar social maturity expected	91	62
Dressed alike	74	48
Similar early behaviour problems	83	59
Similar early development	78	59

The twins were all extensively blood-grouped and their zygosity established at or beyond 0·95 probability. The investigator did not know the results of the zygosity diagnosis until all of the measures had been completed and scored.

The data are shown as percentages of pairs reported to be similar for each measure in order to make the scores comparable. The original calculations were either comparisons of intraclass correlations or chi-square tests of the MZ and DZ distributions, all of which showed significant differences at or beyond the 0·05 level of probability, one-tailed, except early development.

It is abundantly clear that the mothers of MZ twins believe them to be more similar than the mothers of DZ pairs believe their twins to be, both at the present time and in the past. Of the 52 pairs for whom complete data and blood-grouping were available, the MZ pairs were more likely to be considered generally similar at the time of the study, and their mothers were more likely to expect the same levels of social responsibility and independence from them. MZ co-twins were also more likely to be dressed alike by their mothers or to choose to dress alike.

The mothers of DZ twins recalled more differences between their children at an early age. If one DZ twin had a behaviour 'problem', involving eating, sleeping, thumb sucking, toilet training, or something else, the co-twin might or might not have had a similar 'problem'. But if one MZ twin was said to have had a problem, her sister was very likely to have 'shown' the same behaviour. The early development of most MZ co-twins was recalled by their mothers as somewhat more similar than the early development of DZ co-twins. In general, the mothers of MZ twins believed that their children had been similar and continued to be similar, while the mothers of DZ twins noticed more differences between their children.

The mothers were also asked to complete the 'adjective check list' [3] separately for each twin. This instrument contains 300 adjectives which comprise 26 personality scales. The *need* (n) scales are empirically derived clusters of adjectives based on Murray's [5] personality theory of the interaction between organismic *needs* and environmental *presses*. Personality is conceived as a pattern of needs, some more prepotent than others, which characterize individuals. Of the 20 scales which describe the twins, the MZ co-twins were rated as significantly similar on 11 scales, and the DZ pairs on 5, as shown in Table 4.2. Three of the scales have significantly higher MZ than DZ intra-class correlations: n affiliation, n change, and counselling readiness, a measure that Gough [3] calls 'available anxiety'.

The mothers of MZ twins again perceived their twins as relatively more similar than the mothers of DZ twins perceived their children, significantly so on measures of sociability

(n affiliation), flexibility (n change), and anxiety. The results from the mothers' interviews, and Vineland social maturity scale, and the adjective check list indicated that DZ co-twins were perceived and treated more differently by their mothers than MZ twins.

The assumption of equal environmental variances

Even if most investigators now agree that MZ co-twins experience generally more similar environments than DZ co-twins, does this imply that we have to abandon the twin study method? Not yet. The real problem with the assumption of equal environmental variances for MZ and DZ co-twins is that when parents are correct about their twins' zygosity two important factors are confounded: (1) the greater genetic differences of DZ co-twins, with accompanying physical, intellectual and behavioural differences; and (2) the greater differences of parental treatment of DZ pairs, which might create additional intra-pair dissimilarities.

If parents are simply reacting to the existing differences between their DZ twins' behaviour, then no bias is introduced into twin studies. But, if parents effectively train differences, then these environmentally determined differences would bias the comparisons of intra-class correlations in favour of genetic hypotheses by reducing the possible similarities of DZ co-twins. By the same token, the parents of MZ twins who know their twins are identical may react to existing similarities or seek to train greater similarities than would otherwise exist. When parents are correct about their twins' zygosity, it is impossible to distinguish between parental behaviour that is a reaction to the phenotypic behaviour of their twins and parental treatment that seeks to train greater differences or similarities.

A method for estimating environmental bias

Not all parents of twins are correct about their twins' zygosity, however, and these parents offer a critical test of environmental bias in twin studies.

are wrong about their twins' zygosity. Smith [10] reported the following percentages of misclassification by parents, using blood-grouping as the criterion diagnosis:

MZ males: 15 per cent (6 pairs)
MZ females: 12 per cent (6 pairs)
DZ males: 20·6 per cent (7 pairs)
DZ females: 35 per cent (14 pairs)

Results of the Boston female-twin

TABLE 4.2. *Intra-class Correlations of Mothers' Ratings for MZ and DZ Pairs on the Adjective Check List*

	Intra-class coefficients			
	MZ		DZ	
Scales	($N = 23$)	p	($N = 29$)	p
Self-confidence	0·24	—	0·12	—
Sel-controlf	0·51	$< 0·01$	0·31	—
Lability	0·53	$< 0·01$	0·40	0·05
Personal adjustment	0·57	$< 0·01$	0·40	0·05
n Achievement	0·17	—	−0·05	—
n Dominance	−0·04	—	−0·16	—
n Endurance	0·10	—	0·11	—
n Order	0·29	—	0·05	—
n Intraception	0·42	$< 0·05$	0·34	—
n Nurturance	0·55	$< 0·01$	0·50	$< 0·01$
n Affiliation	0·83	$< 0·001$	0·56	$< 0·01$
n Heterosexuality	0·57	$< 0·01$	0·54	$< 0·01$
n Exhibition	0·39	0·05	0·09	—
n Autonomy	0·40	0·05	0·11	—
n Aggression	0·35	—	−0·08	—
n Change	0·70	$< 0·001$	−0·12	—
n Succorance	−0·16	—	−0·02	—
n Abasement	0·00	—	0·00	—
n Deference	0·19	—	0·02	—
Counselling readiness (available anxiety)	0·56	$< 0·01$	0·03	—

By examining the cases of parents who are *wrong* about their twins' zygosity, it is possible to separate parental reactions to similarities and differences based on *genetic relatedness* from parental behaviours which arise from their *belief* that their twins should or should not be similar.

When parents are asked, 'Are your twins identical or fraternal?' a surprising number either do not know or

sample are similar: 17·4 per cent of the MZ pairs were believed by their mothers to be DZ; and 31·2 per cent of the DZ pairs were believed to be MZ. The total number of incorrect diagnoses is small, because twin samples are generally small, but the 11 error cases, for whom complete data are available, provide a critical test for environmental variance as a bias in twin studies.

A comparison of the behaviours and ratings of parents who were wrong about their twins' zygosity with those who were correct will yield results in one of the two following directions:

(1) MZ pairs, misclassified as DZ, will be treated like correctly diagnosed MZ pairs; and DZ pairs, thought to be MZ, will be raised like correctly identified DZ pairs. From these results, we would conclude that the degree of *genetic relatedness* of the twins is a more important determinant of similar or different parental treatment than the parents' *belief* that their children should or should not be similar.

An approximate method of estimating the amount of environmental bias is the *direction* of results as predicted by the alternate hypotheses. With a large twin sample, it would be possible to calculate the degree to which results for correctly identified pairs deviate from those of misclassified pairs, and to correct for environmental variance in genetic estimates. Unfortunately, these data are too limited to permit such a refinement.

Results and discussion

To test these hypotheses, the same measures of similarity and differences reported for the whole sample were

TABLE 4.3. *Percentage of Correctly and Incorrectly Classified Pairs Rated as Similar for Several Characteristics*

Mothers' ratings of co-twins	Correctly classified		Misclassified	
	MZ $(N = 19)$	DZ (N = 22)	MZ $(N = 4)$	DZ $(N = 7)$
Similar now	79	9	75	43
Similar social maturity expected	95	67	75	43
Dressed alike	74	45	75	57
Similar early behaviour problems	79	59	100	57
Similar early development	79	54	50	71

(2) MZ pairs, misclassified as DZ, will be treated like correctly diagnosed DZ pairs; and vice versa for DZ pairs misclassified as MZ. From these results we would conclude that the parents' *beliefs* about zygosity determine the similarities and differences in their behaviour towards their twins. If parental beliefs are important determinants of environmental similarity for co-twins, then differences are probably accentuated between presumed and real DZ co-twins and minimized for presumed and real MZ co-twins, thereby introducing environmental bias into genetic estimates from twin studies.

calculated separately for the misclassified and correctly classified pairs. The results for four misjudged MZ pairs and seven misclassified DZ pairs are given with the results for the correctly classified pairs in Table 4.3.

The data generally confirm the first hypothesis: that genetic relatedness of the twins determines the similarity of parental treatment. Although the numbers are too small to yield statistical significance, the trends are clear. The mothers of MZ twins, whom they wrongly believe to be DZ, treat them more like correctly identified MZ twins. And the mothers of DZ twins, whom they believe to be MZ, treat them more like correctly classified DZ pairs. Despite the mothers' erroneous beliefs, the twins are recognized as having similarities and differences appropriate to their degree of genetic relatedness.

In the interview, the mothers of MZ twins, wrongly believed to be DZ, tended to say that they are similar at the present time. The misclassified DZ pairs were said to be less similar despite their mothers' beliefs that they were identical twins. The social maturity scores more clearly reflect this trend; a larger percentage of the MZ pairs believed to be DZ were treated similarly by the mothers than the DZ pairs believed to be MZ. The mothers expected independence and allotted responsibility similarly or differently according to their twins' actual zygosity. Actual DZ co-twins probably receive more differentiated parental treatment because they *are* different, not because the mothers believe they should be.

Dressing alike was more frequent among MZ females regardless of the mothers' diagnosis of zygosity. The proportions of MZ and DZ co-twins dressed the same was approximately the same in correctly and incorrectly diagnosed groups. Dressing alike does not seem to be a function of simply looking alike, since the DZ twins who were mistaken for MZ did not dress alike as frequently as the MZ's who were mistaken for DZ.

Results from the mothers' recall of early 'problems' indicated again that MZ twins are more similar than DZ twins, even when the mothers had misclassified them. However, the mothers' recall of their twins' early development reversed the direction of previously reported findings. The mothers of DZ pairs, believed to be MZ, reported greater developmental similarity for their children than did the mothers of MZ twins believed to be DZ. Perhaps developmental similarities and differences were an important basis for the parental misdiagnosis of zygosity when the twins were very young. The recall of early development was the only measure which reversed the direction of the findings.

The adjective check list scales corroborated previous results. Differences between misclassified DZ pairs were greater than those between misclassified MZ co-twins for the three scales which showed significantly greater DZ differences for the whole sample. The Vineland social maturity scores continued this trend with DZ differences greater than MZ differences, regardless of the correctness of parental diagnosis (Table 4.4). These results support the first hypothesis, that the degree of genetic relatedness is a more important determinant of parental treatment than parents' beliefs that their twins should or should not be similar. But this is not to say that no bias exists.

Venturing farther out on the slim branch of small numbers, we might also note that DZ twins misclassified as MZ are treated more similarly than correctly classified DZ twins. Data from the Vineland social maturity scale and the adjective check list suggest that beliefs about zygosity also have an effect on MZ pairs, whose reported differences are greater when they are misclassified as DZ. There is evidence for some bias towards minimizing differences between MZ pairs (and those DZ pairs believed to be MZ) and emphasizing differences between DZ pairs (and those MZ pairs believed to be DZ).

The comparisons of parental behav-

TABLE 4.4. *Mean Co-twin Difference on Significant Adjective Check List and Vineland Scales for Correctly and Incorrectly Classified Groups*

	Correctly classified		Misclassified	
	MZ ($N = 19$)	DZ ($N = 22$)	MZ ($N = 4$)	DZ ($N = 7$)
Adjective check list scales				
n Affiliation	4·1	8·5	5·7	6·6
n Change	5·6	15·8	7·3	9·7
Counselling readiness (anxiety)	4·7	12·0	4·0	5·9
Vineland social maturity	0·4	1·1	1·3	1·8

iour for correctly and incorrectly classified pairs suggests, however, that environmental determinants of similarities and differences between MZ and DZ co-twins are not as potent as the critics charge. Differences in the parental treatment that twins receive are much more a function of the degree of the twins' genetic relatedness than of parental beliefs about 'identicalness' and 'fraternalness'.

Although the small number of twins involved in this study limits the significance of the results, the method of estimating environmental bias in twin studies may be useful to investigators with larger samples. Hopefully, some of the questions about the influence of differential parental treatment of MZ and DZ twins can be answered by a study of a larger sample of mis-diagnosed twins.

References

1. ALLEN, G. (1965). Twin research: Problems and prospects. *In* (Steinberg and Bearn (Eds.)) *Prog. Med. Genet.* Grune and Stratton, New York.
2. DOLL, E. A. (1947). *Vineland social maturity scale manual.* Educational Test Bureau, Minneapolis.
3. GOUGH, H. G. (1960). The adjective check list as a personality assessment research technique. *Psychol. Rep.* **6**, 107–22.
4. JONES, H. E. (1955). Perceived differences among twins. *Eugen. Quart.* **5**, 98–102.
5. MURRAY, H. A. (1938). *Explorations in personality.* Oxford University Press, New York.
6. PRICE, B. (1950). Primary biases in twin studies: a review of pre-natal and natal differences producing factors in monozygotic pairs. *Am. J. Hum. Genet.* **2**, 293–352.
7. SCARR, SANDRA (1966). Genetic factors in activity motivation. *Child Dev.* **37**, 663–73.
8. —— (1966). The origins of individual differences in adjective check list scores. *J. consult. Psychol.* **30**, 354–7.
9. SHAEFER, E. S. and BELL, R. Q. (1958). Development of the parental attitude research instrument. *Child Dev.* **29**, 339–61.
10. SMITH, R. T. (1965). A comparison of socioenvironmental factors in monozygotic and dizygotic twins, testing an assumption. *In* (Vandenberg, S. G. (Ed.)) *Methods and goals in human behaviour genetics.* Academic Press, New York.
11. VANDENBERG, S. G. (1966). Contributions of twin research to psychology. *Psychol. Bull.* **66**, 327–52.

Hormonal determinants of behaviour

II

THE controversy raging over the past decade concerning the matter of psychosexual differentiation might be regarded as one of the more fruitful debates in clinical psychology. It resulted in greater attention being paid to experimental endocrinological work, in informative and critical reviews of the animal and human literature, and in attempts to understand the mechanisms whereby steroid hormones, and in particular the sex hormones, exerted their pervasive influence.

On the basis of their analyses of several cases of sexual anomalies and hermaphrodites, Money and the Hampsons ([16–18]) put forward their theory of *psychosexual-neutrality at birth*. They found that, despite genetic, gonadal, or hormonal sex, the individual successfully adopted the sex role to which he was assigned and in which he was reared. The conclusions drawn by these authors was that the human organism was completely flexible as far as psychosexual identity was concerned, and, provided it was done early and before many sex-appropriate behaviours were learned, sexual reassignment was quite feasible too. This view was of course in accord with the empiricist outlook prevailing in North America, and it was a considerable while before an examination was made of the evidence upon which Money and the Hampsons relied. Milton Diamond (Chap. 5) was the first to question both the generality and the unequivocality of the Money and Hampson conclusions. He submitted clinical evidence of hermaphroditism and an impressive body of data from developmental, endocrinological, anthropological and comparative sources in rebuttal of the psychosexual-neutrality view and in support of a contrary hypothesis of *psychosexual-differentiation at birth*. More recently Zuger [22] has also questioned the psychosexual-neutrality view on conceptual and logical grounds.

The publication in 1966 of an entire volume on sex differences [15] seemed to bring the topic very much into the forefront of developmental psychology, although good reviews of this subject had already been available [20, 21]. With this book, however, came the first attempt to relate the experimental endocrinological work on animals to mechanisms underlying human behaviour [5]. The significance of this work results from its demonstration of the following: (1) the mechanisms of sexual differentiation in all mammals are essentially similar; (2) there is no neuter sex in mammals the natural propensity being to differentiate as a female even in the absence of any gonads [9–11]; (3) the gonadal hormones have a dual action—an organizing action in early life and an activating action in adult life [6]; (4) it is not simply the reproductive system that is organized in a male or female manner but the brain as well ([8, 13, 7]); (5) there is a species-specific critical period in foetal or early post-natal life during which this organization takes place; and (6) that the most potent organizing agent is the testicular hormone ([19, 1–3]).

The importance of early androgenic influences on both reproductive structures and behaviour in the human is illustrated by the careful analysis of genetic females exposed to androgens *in utero* made by Money and Ehrhardt (Chap. 6). The finding that the synthetic drug Progestin, when administered to ensure implantation of the embryo in women prone to mis-carry, virilized foetal genetic females was disconcerting, and rightly led to its discontinuation. It led too to an investigation of the effects of the normal female hormone progesterone upon the developing foetus (Chap. 7). Dalton's finding that progesterone accelerated development and maturation and enhanced IQ is significant, but cannot readily be explained. It is congruent however with the Money and Ehrhardt finding that the IQ of androgenized females were on average higher than those of normal females. Recent evidence also suggests that hormones other than the sex hormones have a facilitative action upon brain functions ([12, 14]) and elucidation of these effects promises to be a fruitful area of psychoendro-crinology.

References

1. Goy, R. W. (1966). Role of androgens in the establishment and regulation of behavioural sex differences in mammals. *J. Anim. Science* **25**, Suppl. 21–35.

2. —— (1968). Organizing effects of androgen on the behaviour of Rhesus monkeys. *In* (Michael, R. P. (Ed.)) *Endocrinology and human behaviour.* Oxford University Press, London.

3. —— BRIDSON, W. D., and YOUNG, W. C. (1964). Period of maximal susceptibility of the pre-natal female guinea pig to masculinizing actions of testosterone proprionate. *J. comp. Physiol. Psychol.* **57**, 166–74.

4. ——, MITCHELL, J. C., and YOUNG, W. C. (1962). Effect of testosterone proprionate on O_2 consumption of female and female pseudoherma-phroditic guinea pigs. *Am. Zool.* **2**, 525.

5. HAMBURG, D. A. and LUNDE, D. T. (1966). Sex hormones in the development of sex differences in human behaviour. *In* (Maccoby, E. (Ed.)) *The development of sex differences.* Tavistock, London.

6. HARRIS, G. W. (1964). Sex hormones, brain development, and brain function. *Endocrinology* **75**, 627–48.

7. —— (1970). Hormonal differentiation of the developing central nervous system with respect to patterns of endocrine function. *Phil. Trans. R. Soc. (Lond.)* B 259, 165–77.

8. —— and LEVINE, S. (1965). Sexual differentiation of the brain and its experimental control. *J. Physiol.* **181**, 379–400.

9. JOST, A. (1953). Problems of foetal endocrinology: the gonadal and hypophyseal hormones. *Rec. Progr. horm. Res.* **8**, 379–418.

10. —— (1958). Embryonic sexual differentiation: morphology, physiology, abnormalities. *In* (Jones, H. W. and Scott, W. W. (Eds.)) *Hermaphroditism, genital anomalies, and related endocrine disorders.* Williams & Wilkins, Baltimore.

11. —— (1960). Hormonal influences in the sex development of bird and mammalian embryos. *In Sex differentiation and development.* Mem. Soc. Endocrin. No. 7, Cambridge University Press, London.

12. KASTIN, A. J., MILLER, L. H., GONZALEZ-BARCENA, D., HAWLEY, W. D., DYSTER-AAS, K., SCHALLY, A. V., DE PARRA, L. V., and VELASCO, M. (1971). Psycho-physiologic correlates of MSH activity in man. *Physiol. Behav.* **7**, 893–6.

13. LEVINE, S. (1966). Sex differences in the brain. *Scient. Amer.* **214**, 84–90.

14. —— (1971). Stress and Behaviour. *Scient. Amer.* **224**, 26–31.

15. MACCOBY, E. E. (Ed.) (1966). *The development of sex differences.* Tavistock, London.

16. MONEY, J., HAMPSON, J. G., and HAMPSON, J. L. (1955). Hermaphroditism: Recommendations concerning assignment of sex, change of sex, and psychologic management. *Bull. Johns Hopkins Hosp.* **97**, 284–300.

17. —— —— and —— (1955). An examination of some basic sexual concepts: The evidence of human hermaphroditism. *Bull. Johns Hopkins Hosp.* **97**, 301–19.

18. —— —— and —— (1956). Sexual incongruities and psychopathology: the evidence of human hermaphroditism. *Bull. Johns Hopkins Hosp.* **98**, 43–57.

19. PHOENIX, C. H., GOY, R. W., GERALL, A. A., and YOUNG, W. C. (1959). Organizing action of pre-natally administered testosterone proprionate on the tissues mediating mating behaviour in the female guinea pig. *Endocrinology* **65**, 369–82.

20. TERMAN, L. M. and TYLER, L. E. (1954). Psychological sex differences. *In* (Carmichael, L. (Ed.)) *Manual of child psychology*, 2nd ed. Wiley, New York.

21. TYLER, L. (1965). *The psychology of human differences*, 3rd ed. Appleton-Century-Crofts, New York.

22. ZUGER, B. (1970). Gender role determination: a critical review of the evidence from hermaphroditism. *Psychosom. Med.* **32**, 449–67.

5 Psychosexual neutrality or psychosexual differentiation at birth

MILTON DIAMOND†

Introduction

A review of the many areas pertinent to the field of sexual behaviour over the last decade reveals the development and elaboration of various psychosexual medical aspects. This in itself is not surprising in view of the greater all-round interest in the psychological field coupled with the increased publicity given to studies bearing on sexual behaviour. What is surprising, however, is a certain direction this development has taken and the relative ease with which one view has been accepted.

Starting in 1955, articles written by John Money and Joan and John Hampson, either in collaboration or separately, began to appear with regularity. Within two years these investigators had produced a book and almost a dozen papers (see the chapter references). The content of their articles details clinical examinations, descriptions, interviews, and therapy of various individuals with sexual abnormalities. Particular attention was given to those patients classified as sexually precocious or as hermaphroditic.

The term 'hermaphroditic' is broadly

† From 'A critical evaluation of the ontogeny of human sexual behaviour'. *Quart. Rev. Biol.* **40**, 147–75 (1965). Reprinted by permission of the author, of the University of Hawaii, School of Medicine, and the editor of the journal.

used here to indicate sexual deviance from the normal condition in any two or more of the following ways: (a) external genital morphology; (b) internal accessory reproductive structures; (c) hormonal sex and secondary sexual characteristics; (d) gonadal sex; and (e) chromosomal sex.

This work must be considered of value in giving new insight into various clinical areas previously almost taboo, and in shedding light on some particularly intriguing questions of human sexuality. The articles went further, however, into theorization about the ontogeny of human sexual behaviour and its modifiability, and included a reappraisal of classical notions of sex roles. Probably on the strength of the clinical aspects, this revised theory seems to have gained favour and gone without serious challenge.

Essentially the theory advocated by Money and the Hampsons holds that gender role—all those things that a person says or does to disclose himself or herself as having the status of boy or man, girl or woman, respectively, and sexual orientation as a male or female—is independent of chromosomal sex, gonadal sex, genital morphology, hormonal balance, or other commonly used indicators of sex [68, 72]. In their own words:

...in place of a theory of instinctive masculinity or femininity which is innate, the evidence of hermaphroditism lends support to a conception that psychologically, sexuality is undifferentiated at birth and that it becomes differentiated as masculine or feminine in the course of the various experiences of growing up [130].

Now it becomes necessary to allow that erotic outlook and orientation is an autonomous psychologic phenomenon independent of genes and hormones, and moreover, a permanent and ineradicable one as well [124].

It is more reasonable to suppose simply that, like hermaphrodites, all the human race follow the same pattern, namely, of psychosexual undifferentiation at birth [125].

Thus, in the place of the theory of an innate, constitutional psychologic bisexuality ... we must substitute a concept of psychologic sexual neutrality in humans at birth [68].

In brief, their theory may be called a psychosexual 'neutrality-at-birth' theory, as opposed to a 'sexuality-at-birth' theory. Although other investigators have supported and projected evidence and theory of a similar nature, the present focus is placed on the works originating from the authors just cited, since they, starting almost with a formal challenge to the classical concept of human sexuality [130] are perhaps at present most closely associated with this approach and most prolific and influential in this area of thought, particularly in regard to clinical considerations.

It is my present intention to review the evidence relative to this theory, and to suggest in contradistinction that the very same data may not be inconsistent with more classical notions of inherent sexuality at birth. This inherent sexuality, like other biological characters, need not necessarily manifest itself at birth as it might be first revealed at puberty or during adulthood. Nevertheless, inherent sexuality may, from birth, provide a built-in 'bias' with which the individual interacts with his environment.

Generally the concept of psychosexual neutrality at birth may be considered to draw support from the following three broad areas: (1) clinical cases; (2) the imprinting phenomenon; and (3) learning theory. The clinical material will be considered first, as it has figured most prominently in the formation and presentation of this theory. Wherever possible, counterevidence will be drawn primarily from human data.

Clinical evidence in support of the existence of sexual neutrality at birth

The basic arguments in favour of a psychosexual-neutrality at birth theory are derived from clinical investigations by Money, Hampson, and Hampson with patients manifesting various sexual anomalies. Each patient was rated in regard to the usual criteria of sex assignment, namely, gonadal sex, hormonal sex, chromosomal sex, and internal and external genitalia. In addition, these patients were rated as to the assigned sex in which they were reared and their gender role. Each of the first five categories was separately compared with the last two, and the last two were compared with each other.

Gonadal sex

Among 20 patients in whom a contradiction was found between the gonadal sex and the sex of rearing, 17 disclosed themselves in a gender role concordant with their rearing. The gonadal structure was an unreliable prognosticator of such an individual's gender role [130].

Hormonal sex

Of 27 patients whose hormonal functioning and secondary sexual body morphology contradicted their sex of rearing, 4 became ambivalent with respect to gender role as male or female, but 23 of them established gender roles consistent with their sex of rearing despite the embarrassment and worry occasioned by such contradictions [130].

Chromosomal sex

Without a single exception among 20 patients, it was found that the gender role and sexual orientation were in accordance with the socially assigned sex and rearing rather than in accord with the chromosomal sex [72].

Internal and external genitalia

In 22 of 25 individuals, the gender role agreed with the assigned sex and rearing and was not in accord with the predominant male or female internal accessory structures [72]. And in cases where the sex of rearing was contradictory to the sex of the external genitalia, 23 of 25 individuals had been able to come to terms with their anomalous appearance and to establish a gender role consistent with their assigned sex and rearing [72].

Assigned sex and gender role

Despite the extent of the various sexual anomalies and incongruities involved, only 8 of 131 comparisons (6 per cent) did not show concordance of assigned sex and gender role. It seems that the best indication of psychosexual orientation (gender role) for hermaphroditic individuals is the sex of initial parental assignment. This would be a better index than chromosomal sex, gonadal sex, or any other of the five standard criteria of sex dimorphism [72].

Conclusions and comments

The conclusions drawn from evidence such as that cited above are perhaps stated most succinctly by Money, Hampson, and Hampson [130] as follows:

In the light of hermaphroditic evidence, it is no longer possible to attribute psychologic maleness or femaleness to chromosomal, gonadal or hormonal origins, nor to morphological sex differences of either the internal accessory reproductive organs or the external genitalia. . . . From the sum total of hermaphroditic evidence the conclusion that emerges is that sexual behaviour and orientation as male or female does not have an innate, instinctive basis. In place of a theory of instinctive masculinity or femininity which is innate, the evidence of hermaphroditism lends support to a conception that psychologically, sexuality is undifferentiated at birth and that it becomes differentiated as masculine or feminine in the course of the various experiences of growing up.

During these experiences of growing up the normal human is assumed (from hermaphroditic (pathological) data) to be imprinted as well as taught a sexual role. The first $2\frac{1}{2}$ or 3 years of life are supposedly the critical period for human imprinting, and cases are cited where alteration of sex after this age is traumatic [129, 131, 132, 72, 124]. This age is correlated by Money with the development of verbalization. He believes that the critical period for the imprinting of gender role and orientation corresponds with a critical period for the establishment of a native language. Another critical period for limited modification of gender imprints is postulated to occur at puberty [124]. To further the idea that a psychosexual imprint is fixed and irreversible, 5 cases of genetic females born with fused labia and enlarged clitorides are cited. Two of these were reared as boys and three as girls, and yet all seemed to be psychologically content in their present sex [72].

The extent and depth of the imprint and subsequent learning is supposedly such that alteration after 4 years of age is fraught with psychological danger and is usually unsuccessful [67, 71]. 'With only 1 exception the 6 patients reassigned later than the first birthday were rated as inadequately adjusted' [72].

Given the evidence presented, what may we conclude? It has been shown that hermaphroditic individuals in our society find it possible to assume sexual roles opposite to their genetic sex, morphological sex, etc., and they can assume this role so well that they can function socially as 'normal' members of society, engage in erotic activities, and receive pleasure in their reared roles. To best assume this role it is most advantageous in our society for them to start early in life, preferably before the first birthday. Beyond these conclusions, however, much has been extrapolated. Maybe it has been strongly demonstrated that humans, particularly hermaphroditic ones, are flexible when it comes to the assumption of an incongruous sex role. Yet to assume that a sex role normally is exclusively or even mainly a very elaborate, culturally fostered deception and imprinting phenomenon, and that it is not also reinforced by taboos and potent defence mechanisms superimposed on a biological prepotency or pre-natal organization and potentiation seems unjustified and, from the present data, unsubstantiated.

Considerations regarding inherent sexuality at birth

Any theory has to contend with various types of data. Whereas the theory of psychosexual-neutrality at birth is primarily derived from observations of clinical deviations from the normal, there is not only clinical but anthropological, and multidisciplinary experimental evidence for the existence of psychosexual-sexuality at birth.

Before further consideration of such data, the following two points are to be regarded as fundamental:

(1) It should be readily obvious that man and his behavioural parameters follow the natural scheme of evolution, although it is often difficult to apply animal data to man. In the face of abundant evidence that nonhuman species are behaviourally as well as morphologically fixed in a particular sex at birth, a 'neutrality-at-birth' theory would indirectly infer that man's sexual behaviour patterns are different from those of all other vertebrates by not being instinctively mediated.

.   .   .   .   .

I will hold that man in regard to his sexual behaviour patterns is, like all other vertebrates, subject to prenatally organized mediation. The manner or extent of this mediation is not yet clear but is believed to involve the foetal organization and potentiation of certain neural tissues which are, within genetic limits, post-natally modifiable but not to the extent of complete reversal or negation. This effect on the nervous system is believed primarily to be a function of the genetically induced endocrine environment of the presexually differentiated individual. For man as well as most other vertebrates this is a pre-natal occurrence. Ontogenetic experiences are superimposed on this potentiated nervous system and serve to give emphasis and further direction to predisposed tendencies. Man is probably more flexible in regard to this organization than any other species, but that would not justify our saying he is free of it.

(2) It is significant that no criteria or definition of human male or female behaviour has found universal acceptability. Humans, as well as many other species of animal, *normally* exhibit elements of sexual behaviour usually attributed to members of the opposite sex. The capability and frequency of such behaviour is neither rare nor bizarre. I will defend the point, that although humans *can adjust* to an erroneously imposed gender role, (a) it does not mean that pre-natal factors are not normally influential, and (b) they do so with difficulty if not pre-natally and biologically predisposed.

. . . . .

Thus, both normal human beings or hermaphrodites who exhibit various so-called anomalous sexual behaviour still are performing within the biological continuum predictable by evolution. Evolving from a highly stereotyped pattern among primitive organisms, humans are capable of displaying highly flexible sexual behaviour patterns. An evolutionary trend starting with inflexible stereotyped sexual behaviour and progressing to flexibility in behaviour is consistent with modern genetic and evolutionary concepts [171]. The very considerable extent of this flexibility, particularly in hermaphrodites, may account for the many cases of maintained gender role which are incompatible with morpho-logical criteria of sex. This same flexibility may account for the erroneous theory of psychosexual neutrality for normal individuals.

Evidence in support of sexuality at birth

The evidence presented in support of the concept of psychosexual-neutrality at birth primarily involves hermaphroditic individuals who have successfully adapted themselves to an assigned gender role inconsistent with one or more morphological criteria of sex. Once reared in a mal-assigned sex past the age of four, these individuals are supposedly unable to negotiate a change in their gender role without severe emotional trauma [72]. The neutrality theory is supported by no normative data. A theory that psychosexuality exists at birth, on the other hand, can use the same evidence and demonstrate (1) that humans, hermaphrodites in particular, are flexible enough to maintain an atypical gender role, either by choice or accident, even when contradictory to their normal external genitalia; (2) that a gender role, if mal-assigned may be reassigned after the age of four without undue trauma; and (3) irrespective of the foregoing conclusions, that normal as well as hermaphroditic individuals are predisposed towards a particular gender role at birth.

Studies of normal children

Although the literature is scanty in this regard, various studies of neonatal, preverbal, and pre-school children indicate that there are differences which may be considered indicative of sexual differences existing from birth and which are psychosexually predisposing to adult male or female roles.

Terman [172], in an extensive review of normal psychological sex differences in children, wrote: 'Sex differences have been found for almost every physical variable, including body build, gross and fine anatomy, physiological functioning, and biochemical composition. Indeed, every cell in a human body bears the stamp of its sex.' He then proposed that some of these differences, such as height, weight, body build, strength, endurance, motor ability, and rate of maturation, might be expected to reflect themselves behaviourally. In this regard he lists the following. (a) *Body size*. The mean weight of boys at birth exceeds that of girls by approximately 5 per cent, and their body length is greater by 1 or 2 per cent. This superiority continues until about the age of 11. (b) *Vital capacity*. As one of the determiners of the sustained energy output which is possible for an individual, vital capacity may considerably influence sex differences in play interests, and other activities. Boys show a 7 per cent superiority in vital capacity by age 6 and rapidly increase their lead to about a 35 per cent superiority at age 20. (c) *Muscular strength*. Tests of strength in grip, back, and legs show boys to be superior at all ages tested. At age 7 boys show about 10 per cent superiority and this increases to a 50 to 60 per cent advantage at age 18. (d) *Rate of maturation*. It is widely recognized that girls generally exhibit more rapid physical development than boys. In skeletal development girls are superior to boys at birth and increase this superiority at a fairly steady rate until growth is complete. 'Girls of all races precede boys on the average by twelve to twenty months in pubertal development, and their adolescent growth

changes are correspondingly accelerated.'

These obvious examples of constitutional differences are reflected in the individual choice of the more muscular forms of behaviour of male children, such as running, climbing, and wrestling, compared with the more conservative and sedentary activities of female children, such as hopping and skipping. This was extensively reported by Lehman and Witty [101], as early as 1927, in a classical study involving some 19 000 children. Walker [178], studying the somato-types and behaviour of pre-school children 2 to 4 years old, has presented much data to indicate that there is a good correlation between sex-related behaviour traits and body build as rated by endomorphy, mesomorphy, and ectomorphy. He concludes that 'in this group of pre-school children, important associations do exist between individuals' physiques and particular behaviour characteristics'. Further, these associations show considerable similarity to those described by Sheldon for college-aged men, though the strength of association is not as strong as he reports. It is suggested that the relations are multiple determined, arising from primary body conditions (e.g. strength, energy, sensory thresholds). ' . . . In particular, variations in physical energy, in bodily effectiveness for assertive or dominating behaviour, and in bodily sensitivity appear as important mediating links between physique structure and general behaviour.'

In areas such as conation and cognition we also note early manifest sex differences. This is especially significant, since these categories are believed to reflect traits less influenced by culture. There is considerable evidence that from early childhood boys show more aggression and anger than girls. Goodenough [51] reported this to be manifest as early as 7 months of age. In regard to personality Walters, Pearce, and Dahms [180] have demonstrated that 2- to 5-year-old girls are significantly more friendly, sympathetic, and helpful to others ('affectionate') than are boys of the same age; while boys tend to display more actual or threatened hostility to others ('aggressive'). Walker [178] found similar results for children of the same age range and in fact remarks that the difference is as great at 2 years of age as later.

Boys and girls are seen to show different perceptual responses to Rorschach forms [2]. They have shown, for example, that throughout the first ten years of life boys give more responses than do girls in every category. Girls respond differently to colour than do boys, and they respond more often to the perceived form alone. The type of response also seems sex-dependent. At $3\frac{1}{2}$ years of age boys give more responses than do girls and verbalize more. Boys see more movement in the figures, and boys make more mention of urogenital structures. At 7 years of age sex differences in perceptual responses are the most marked. Girls' responses tend to be neater and more concise. Boys' records are longer and more involved, their comments and explanations complicated and rambling. Girls give more global responses, boys more details and tiny details. Boys give more aggressive responses.

Ames and Learned [1] showed significant sex differences in developmental trends in block building and block construction. Like the Rorschach test, this block-building and construction test supposedly reveals inherent differences and forms of behaviour not significantly influenced by culture. Ames and Learned used 350 children equally divided between the sexes at ages 2 through 6 years. Conspicuous sex differences occurred at all ages tested. For example, at 2 years 'boys build in a more complex and detailed manner than do girls'. Boys show more responses and show more compact designs. At 4 years, 'The structures of girls fall more than those of boys. Twice as many boys as girls make one large compact structure, and many more boys than girls make scenes.' At 6 years: 'Nearly twice as many boys as girls build symmetrically. Many more boys than girls build one large compact structure. Girls show more interest in size and colour. More girls than boys purposely destroy their products.'

Many more normative studies of similar character could be presented. In effect, the conclusions and implications of their findings are summarized by the pediatrician Benjamin Spock. Spock [168], in an article entitled 'Are we minimizing differences between the sexes?' lists sex differences noticeable from birth in areas of interest, aptitude, and personality, and concludes: 'In terms of basic temperament and drive there are fairly consistent differences between the sexes, though they may be accentuated or obscured by upbringing.' He then prescribes that for greater security in adult roles it is better to capitalize on these differences rather than to minimize them.

.   .   .   .   .

Predisposition of gender orientation

Genetic considerations

Primary in any discussion of predisposition towards or away from a particular pattern of sexual behaviour would be consideration of the possible genetics involved. That animals are subject to inherited tendencies in relation to their sex roles cannot be disputed. Young [180] has reviewed many of the nonclinical studies and presents evidence not only showing innate manifestations of sexual behaviour patterns but describing how different animal strains can react differently to the environment. Many recent studies corroborate these findings [54, 84, 109–112]. In regard to man, however, our knowledge is a little more obscure. Kinsey, Pomeroy and Martin [93] state this theme thus: 'The most important biologic factors affecting the nature and frequency of sexual response in the human animal are the hereditary forces which account for the differences between male and female. Within either of these sexes, heredity must also account for some of the variation in sensory structures and in the mechanisms which are concerned with emotional response.' However, no other area in the study of human sexuality seems beset with as many difficulties as a study of inherited sexuality. Not only would a proper investigation involve a broad longitudinal survey over many years but it would have to cover succeeding generations. Nevertheless some data are available.

Kallmann's work [87, 88] and that of Schlegel [154] are probably the most conclusive. Kallmann studied 40 monozygotic and 45 dizygotic twin pairs in which one of the co-twins was a known overt homosexual. He found 100 per cent of the monozygotic twins concordant for homosexuality; whereas the dizygotic co-twins were essentially similar to the general male population. Strikingly, the monozy-

gotic twins were even comparable in the mode and extent of their deviance and type of displayed behaviour, and although they had developed their gender roles independently when separated from each other. Kallmann considers this evidence, and I would agree, to throw 'considerable doubt upon the validity of purely psychodynamic theories of predominantly or exclusively homosexual behaviour patterns in adulthood and correspondingly strengthens the hypothesis of a genically determined disarrangement in the balance between male and female maturational (hormonal) tendencies' [87].

Schlegel [154] reviewed reports on 113 twin couples and found 95 per cent concordant homosexuality in the monozygotic twins and only 5 per cent concordance among the dizygotic twins. His evidence is in excellent agreement with Kallmann's data.

. . . . .

In a most recent work Kallmann [89] reviews much of the more recent genetic data and still maintains that genetics are crucially involved in psychosexual development, the mechanism, however, still to be determined.

Hampson and Hampson [72] and J. L. Hampson [71] have considered Kallmann's work, but regard his evidence as being outweighed by two types of studies. The first of these is exemplified by the work of Pare [139], who, using the Barr technique for sex chromatin analysis, investigated male homosexuals for presence of the female chromatin body in the cell nucleus. Pare found no difference between the sex chromatin of the homosexuals and control males. This is a weak counter argument to the genetic one, since a negative finding of this sort is not necessarily evidence against the importance of genetic differences. With present techniques, chromosomal studies can do little more than indicate the presence of an extra sex chromosome or deficiency of an entire sex chromosome, or a gross translocation. They cannot reveal a single deviant gene or even several. The second type of study is more weighty, and consists of psychiatric and psychological reports which claim psychosexual disorders to be the result of social learning. These are exemplified by the reports of a multitude of workers who describe family situations and experiences which supposedly provide a basis for homosexuality. Green and Money [60, 61] also attribute sexual deviation to certain kinds of experiences. In discussing the possible aetiology of effeminacy in 5 pre-pubertal boys they cursorily review and dismiss the possible influence of a genetic involvement and prefer instead to consider only improper imprint experiences at an early age, despite the fact that common imprint experiences could not be proved.

.   .   .   .   .

Undoubtedly we are dealing with an interaction of genetics and experience; the relative contribution of each, however, may vary with the particular behaviour pattern and individual concerned. Effeminacy and other sexual deviations are not altogether rare in our society. Without contending that inheritance is the whole cause, we may well consider it influential and predisposing. A quotation from Mead is again applicable: 'It seems safe to assume that any behaviour which can be institutionalized in a culture and regarded as a recurrent possible human choice has some hereditary base' [114]. This hereditary base is what, especially

for other animals, is usually termed an innate and instinctual framework within which the individual develops, meets, and contends with his environment.

Most individuals, falling within the range of normal sexual behaviour for our society, may be considered as following a path of genetic least resistance—that of their 'innate instincts'. In analysing human behaviour, trying to separate genetics and experience may be like trying to separate hydrogen and oxygen in their importance with respect to the properties of water. Those misassigned individuals who go against the predisposition inherent in their genetic make-up overcome it only to the extent their genetic flexibility will allow.

.   .   .   .   .

In the development of any behaviour pattern we must consider not only the stimuli serving to mould the pattern but the nature of the receptive medium which is to be moulded. Many humans, siblings in particular, can be subjected to extremely diverse experiences and still develop similar personalities; conversely, humans may be subjected to like experiences and develop quite differently. The individual's constitutional capacity to respond to these environmental stimuli exerts its influence, too. It is the genetic heritage of an individual which predisposes him to react in a particular manner so that the learning of a gender role can occur. Even if one thinks in terms of imprinting and innate releasing mechanisms (IRM) [137, 118], these concepts must be recognized as implying that the individual possesses a genetic heritage. The IRM does not appear *de novo* but is species-specific and, as its name says, innate.

Hormonal organization of sexual behaviour
To support the theory of psychosexual neutrality at birth we have been presented with no instance of a normal individual appearing as an unequivocal male and being reared successfully as a female, or vice versa. Wherever the aetiology of the hermaphroditism was determined the particular patients had been subjected, during their pre-natal or neo-natal existence, to a genetic or hormonal imbalance, or both [72]. This imbalance may provide the requisite basis for what seems to be psychosexual neutrality.

It has long been recognized that various hormones are potent regulators of human behaviour. Earlier cultures had a knowledge of the effects of castration, and much recent evidence is available to confirm the role that androgens serve in sexual drive and activity in men.

Occasional studies to the contrary, the bulk of evidence indicates that testicular androgens activate libido, and that castration or other androgen loss due to some pathological condition reduces libido. Reviews [102, 170, 11, 12, 93] and more recent case studies [22] can readily document this conclusion. Females too are influenced by their endocrines. The early work of Foss [44], Shorr, Papanicolaou, and Stimmel [164], Loeser [104], Geist [46], Salmon and Geist [148], Kupperman and Studdiford [98], and the recent work from the Sloan-Kettering Institute is probably quite definitive in this respect [181, 182, 157, 165, 183]. These studies show the significant role androgens usually play in contrast to the 'female' hormones, the oestrogens and progesterone, in maintaining and stimulating erotic inclination, sexual desire, and behaviour in females. In males the origin of the androgen is primarily from the testes, in the female from the adrenal and the ovary itself.

The androgenic influences are acknowledged by Money [120]. However, he sees them as supporting the neutrality theory essentially on the following line of reasoning. Sexual desire and erotic functioning of both men and women are dependent upon a similar group of substances—androgens. Since men react to androgens with male sexual behaviour and females react to androgens with female sexual behaviour, the hormones are non-directional, only activational, and the direction comes from another source. 'The direction or content of erotic inclination in the human species is not controlled by the sex hormones. Hormonally speaking, the sex drive is neither male nor female but undifferentiated—an urge for the warmth and sensation of close body contact and genital proximity' [120]. The direction taken by the drive is assumed to be learned or imprinted purely from the sex of rearing. Hampson and Hampson [72] have stated that among patients whose sex hormones and secondary sexual body development contradicted the sex of rearing *only* 16 per cent were unable to adjust unambivalently to the assigned sexual role. Thus they reason that sex hormones do not act as causal agents in the establishment of an individual's gender role and psychosexual orientation.

Perloff [140, 141], Kinsey and his associates [93, 94], and others also suggest that in the adult human individual endocrines are not the *sole* instigator or *sole* director (or both) of sexual behaviour. Indeed, this position is not under contention. But to say that something is not the cause or sole director of a particular effect does not mean that it has little or no influence. Admittedly, hormones are probably not the single causal agent that induces gender role orientation, but their influence is undeniable and strong. Money [124] has said, 'The sex hormones, it appears, have no direct effect on the direction or content of erotic inclination in the human species. These are assumed to be experientially determined.' But the importance of the hormones in this regard was implicitly admitted, since hormonal therapy was recommended for correction of psychosexual and physical doubt [72].

.   .   .   .   .

These hormones, however, can affect behaviour only to an extent that is inherent and previously organized within the soma. Boss [21], in considering the activating properties of hormones in regard to a somatic base of sexual behaviour, stressed that genetic factors are strongly involved, not only in determining the specific pattern of the taxonomic unit, but also of the sex. She considered this to be demonstrated by the widely if not generally valid rule that the same amounts of hormone do not produce identical reactions in the two sexes of a given species. Young [189] has expressed a similar idea as follows: 'We feel that the responses that the members of different sexes give to hormonal stimulation are predetermined; in this sense a specific rather than a nonspecific relationship exists.' Harris [78] most recently presented the idea in this manner: 'This (sex-specific differential behaviour response to hormones) reflects, in all probability, some anatomical or biochemical difference in the central nervous system of the two sexes.'

A most critical point to be elaborated here is that although endocrines may be primarily activational in the adult, in the foetus or neonate they must be considered directional. Phoenix, Goy, Gerall, and Young [143] have clearly demonstrated that female guinea pigs are behaviourally as well as somatically masculinized by an androgen, testosterone propionate, pre-natally injected into the mother. Post-natal behaviour, more than the genitalia, was shown to be liable to alteration by the androgen, as even somatically unaffected females were behaviourally masculinized. Genetic females, if potentiated by androgens, manifested a suppression of the capacity to display lordosis following oestrogen and progesterone treatment, and male-like mounting behaviour was displayed by many of these animals even when lordosis could not be elicited [143]. Similar studies with the Rhesus monkey afforded comparable results, that is, pre-natally administered androgens will alter the normal female behaviour patterns and genital structures to those of the male [191]. These data may be taken as evidence of the organizing ability of pre-natally acting androgens on the neural tissues mediating sexual behaviour. Human females, *in utero*, also have been shown to be structurally modified by androgens [187, 64, 65, 34]. Although it has yet to be adequately demonstrated that these embryonic individuals were behaviourally affected, the possibility is within reason and not without zoological precedent. A possible mechanism for genes and hormones to interact and provide direction has recently been suggested. In contrast to the well-known evidences that genes can control hormonal activities, Karlson [90] proposes and cites experimental evidence to show that steroid hormones are capable of altering and controlling gene activity. If such an alteration were to occur in cells within the (behaviour mediating) nervous system we might expect an influence on subsequent behaviour, certainly if the change were to occur during a critical pre-natal period.

Just as the presence of androgen has been demonstrated to be crucial, the pre-natal absence of androgens is also crucial for the organization of mammalian tissues.

. . . . .

Jost [86] and Burns [27], in excellent reviews, have cited the experimental evidence indicating that sexual differentiation of the normal male and female is dependent upon the presence of testicular substances. If testicular substances are present the differentiation is masculine; if absent, the differentiation is feminine. Males castrated prior to sexual differentiation develop structurally as females; in them there is an absence of external male genitalia and maintenance of derivatives of the Müllerian duct, e.g. the fallopian tubes, uterus, etc. Comparable human evidence is available from different types of hermaphroditic individuals; those with gonadal (testicular) aplasia [63, 66, 85, 185, 138, 4] and testicular feminization [134, 63, 85, 106, 6, 91, 135, 138, 4] in particular. These genetic males are phenotypically female. Hampson, Hampson, and Money [33] have claimed that since these individuals who possess a male chromatin pattern, can assume a gender role as normal females it means that the gender role is assumed independently of the genetic sex. It must be recognized that these genetic anomalies deprive the developing foetus of proper gonadal substances

which in the human species, as demonstrably in other animals, may potentiate and organize the nervous system for masculine behaviour. The deprivation of typical hormones or the presence of heterotypical ones may simultaneously potentiate and organize the nervous system for female behaviour.

Most significant are the findings which bridge the hormonal induction phenomenon discussed above and the resulting demonstrable sex-specific differences in the nervous system, in the hypothalamus in particular. Harris and Jacobsohn [79, 80], Martinez and Bittner [107], Harris [78], and Gorski and Wagner [53] have shown that early in development the hypothalamus is differentiated into a male or female type. Their studies emphasize this in regard to the hypothalamo-hypophyseal axis in particular. Pituitaries transplanted beneath the hypothalamus from males or females into hypophysectomized castrated males will not cycle, whereas hypophysectomized females bearing either male or female pituitary grafts show complete and normal estrus cycles.

Later Barraclough [7], Barraclough and Gorski [8, 9], Harris and Levine [81], Whalen and Nadler [184] demonstrated how this sexual differentiation of the hypothalamus may be achieved relatively simply with a single injection of steroid in a neonatal animal whose nervous system is still undifferentiated sexually. These experiments reflect on the organization of neural tissues implied in the work of Phoenix, Goy, Gerall, and Young [143] and most probably occur in nature by means of the induction of gonadal substances.

The implications are clear. The well-known and documented instances of hormonal regulation of sexual behaviour below the human level are seen to be brought under neural mediation. With a broader outlook we see that genetic forces induce gonadal development, and gonadal development is normally followed by the elaboration of foetal or neonate gonadal substances responsible for the sexual differentiation of the nervous system. The neuro-endocrine relations of the hypothalamus are the most obvious entities affected but it may be surmised that other, purely neural, aspects are also differentiated or potentiated at this time.

Since most sexual anomalies are under genic control [63, 85, 138, 4, 17, 26], it may be inferred that it is via such indirect and subtle means, as through hormonal action, that genes may be expected to influence organization of the nervous system and to mould sexual behaviour. Thus rearing and assignment based on phenotype are not all that is involved in analysing the aetiology of sexual behaviour in hermaphrodites. Those individuals with a male chromatin pattern who successfully assume a female gender role do so with the absence of crucial (hormonal) potentiating factors that may, in a normal male, establish a male constitution and a predisposition for the assumption of a male gender role.

In the only behavioural studies of their kind to date, Grady and Phoenix [56] and Feder and Whalen [41], working with William C. Young, have completed studies which show that male sexual behaviour is influenced by the loss of the neonatal gonad. They castrated male rats prior to sexual differentiation and observed that when reaching the normal age of maturity these rats fail to show masculine behaviour and can readily be induced to show female behaviour.

Phoenix, Goy, Gerall, and Young [143] aptly summarize these sorts of data:

For the neural tissues mediating behaviour, corresponding relationships (to the development of the genital tracts) seem to exist. The embryonic and foetal periods are periods of organization or 'differentiation' in the direction of masculinization or feminization. Adulthood, when gonadal hormones are being secreted, is a period of activation; neural tissues are the target organs and mating behaviour is brought to expression. Like the genital tracts, the neural tissues mediating mating behaviour respond to androgens or to estrogens depending on the sex of the individual, but again the specificity is not complete (Antliff and Young, 1956; Young, 1961).

.   .   .   .

Therefore, when we consider prenatal as well as post-natal existence, hormones may be regarded as directional as well as activational; and at birth the individual may be considered to have been neurally predisposed by genetic and hormonal means towards one sex. Since this predisposition is demonstrated so vividly in animals, including anthropoids, we may logically assume that it persists in the human after birth, although manifestations of it may be suppressed or modified. In a recent review article Young, Goy, and Phoenix [191] expressed such confidence about this point that in relation to the theory of Hampson and Money they stated: 'In view of what we have learned an endocrinological basis which is consistent with the concept of psychologic bisexuality exists for the interpretation of most if not all of the cases they report.'

The nervous system

In discussing behaviour, we find it inevitable to consider in some detail its medium—the nervous system. The point at issue here is whether the nervous system is just a neutral responsive system intermediate between stimulus and response, or is a system with a built-in diasthetic bias. This consideration is crucial, since it is on the nervous system that potentiation and organization must exert their influence and it is on the nervous system that learning (to be discussed below) exerts its effect.

Previously, genetic and hormonal factors were seen to be capable of organizing the nervous system to direct future sexual behaviour. More direct, immediate, and independent influences of the nervous system may be understood from clinical studies and from experiments investigating behaviour by means of ablation, lesion placement direct stimulation, direct application of hormones, electrical self-stimulation, or electrical recording. These various methods reveal different functional levels of activity and the sites of so-called 'sex-centres'—loci for the integration of the component activities of a particular sex behaviour pattern. Significantly, these studies often reveal inherent differences of the nervous system dependent upon gender. Were a 'neutral' nervous system to exist, identical effects would be expected from individuals of both sexes.

The majority of direct studies do not set out primarily to investigate response differences between the sexes. These differences are in fact taken for granted, and sex-specific response patterns such as lordosis and oestrus behaviour are used as dependent variables. The functional role of a specific locus or structure is thus usually analysed only in relation to the anticipated patterns applicable to the sex of the animal investigated. But although male–female comparisons are not usually made, direct studies are of value in illustrating that loci within the nervous system possess inherent properties related to sexual disposition, behaviour, and manifestations of gender role.

The most significant differentiation of the hypothalamus has been mentioned above in discussing the role of the endocrines in sexual differentiation. The hypothalamus has for quite some time been implicated both indirectly and directly in influencing sexual behaviour patterns. Its indirect functioning via the hypophysis has been discussed by Harris [75–78], Green [57], Greer [62], Sawyer [150, 151], Szentágothai, Flerkó, Mess, and Halász [169], Nalbandov [136], Everett [40], and others. The significance of this functional pattern was discussed in an earlier section (p. 49).

.   .   .   .   .

Many reviews (Beach [14]; Goldstein [49]; Sawyer [150, 151]) detail the relative dependence of the male and independence of the female on the cortical mass in relation to the competent expression of sexual behaviour. Complete removal of the cortex will not prevent mating responses in the female rat, cat, rabbit, or guinea pig, whereas destruction or removal of 75 per cent of the male cortex completely abolishes the male mating pattern. In female rats which spontaneously exhibit male-like mounting, decortication stops this behaviour whereas the usual female behaviour components are unimpaired [10]. While it may be argued that most of the data are from non-humans, Ford and Beach [43] have suggested that the human male and female are also differentially dependent upon cortical mass relative to their expression of sexuality. These, then, are indices of sexually differentiated nervous tissues.

The classical work of Klüver and Bucy [76] in 1939 and by Klüver [95] afterwards showed that sexually mature male macaques respond to bilateral removal of the temporal lobe by hypersexual activity: heterosexual, homosexual, and autosexual in direction. The female does not show this. Significantly, however, Klüver [95] remarked, '. . . an intensification of sexual responses may occur even in a pseudohermaphrodite or in a female from which the uterus and both ovaries have been removed prior to extirpating the temporal lobes.' Later in his review Klüver added, 'There is no doubt that age, sex, species, and many other factors influence the picture of behaviour alterations produced by a bilateral temporal lobectomy.' Schreiner and Kling [158–160] and Green, Clemente, and De Groot [58] have similarly demonstrated that lesions in the piriform cortex of the male cat induced hypersexual changes, whereas hypersexuality was not usually observed in female cats with similar lesions. Analogous functioning of the human cerebrum may be inferred from clinical reports of the Klüver–Bucy syndrome [149, 173] and other disorders of the temporal lobe [38, 39]. Interestingly, these reports show sexual deviation manifested only in men.

Lansdell has reported a sex difference in verbal ability [99] and in design preference [100], which reacts differentially to temporal lobe surgery. After surgery to the dominant lobe, women maintain their previous 'artistic judgement' while men lose theirs. 'The effects of the operations suggest that some physiological mechanisms underlying artistic judgement and verbal ability may overlap in the female brain, but are in opposite hemispheres in the male' [100].

On a more subtle level, perceptual differences between males and females can be considered. In children, the work mentioned earlier with Rorschach tests [2] and block building [1] is suggestive of the presence within the nervous system of perceptual and cognitive processes which are early manifested sex differences. On a purely neurophysiological basis Lipsitt and Levy [103] have shown that as early as the first three days of life females show a lower threshold to electric shock stimulation than do males.

Adult women usually have greater olfactory acuity than men [156] and this has been seen to vary with hormone levels [155]. Kinsey *et al.* [94] reported that males, more often than females, are erotically oriented to visual cues. Females may be more susceptible to tactile stimuli. Sexual distinctions such as these cannot help but influence various aspects of an individual's life, including the way he or she views and reacts to the world, and hence gender role.

It may be argued, as Money [125] does, that differences such as perceptual responses are *results* of learning rather than inherent in the nervous system and *causal*. However, Money presents no model to explain how or why perceptual thresholds to stimuli which are obscure and novel, such as those used by Lansdell may be differentially altered and learned, particularly where the patient is unaware of a desirable direction for the change. Because of the nature of the tests and the early ages at which they were administered, it would also be difficult to explain how the Rorschach and block-building tests were biased by learning.

It may be concluded that the nervous systems of males and females are differentially reactive to the environment. And there is good reason to believe that these differences, so definite in humans as well as in other animals, are present and influential at birth and afterwards.

Imprinting

Hampson and Hampson [72] contend that:

The premise that behaviour is based primarily on instincts is gradually disappearing from scientific writing and the traditional concept of instinct is undergoing revision and modification. In its place has emerged the view that early experience importantly structures subsequent behaviour. This is not to say, lest misunderstanding arise, that the animal organism—human or subhuman—is merely a blank slate to be written upon by the capricious finger of life experiences. Quite the contrary, for there are now many studies in the literature dealing with genetic constitution and the inheritance of basic capacities affecting later learning, temperament, and personality.

This theme is developed so that the constitutional factors are considered insignificant when compared with ontogenetic factors. Difficulty in incongruous sex orientation or modification of sex is thought of in ontogenetic terms of crucial timing and imprinting.

. . . . .

Since no experimental studies on the imprinting of human sexuality *per se* are available, animal experiments may provide further insight into such a possibility. Young [189], in reviewing isolation experiments with the guinea pig, stated, 'The data as a whole indicate that the emergence of sexual behaviour patterns in the male guinea pig is not restricted to an early critical period comparable with that described in the literature dealing with imprinting' (Lorenz [105]). Rats, too, have been shown to be relatively free from the need of sexual imprinting [15], and so have mice [92]. Since lower mammalian species are free of an imprinting requirement for competent sexual behaviour, it seems that it would be difficult to defend the proposition that humans, a behaviourally more flexible species, are subject to such an imprinting stereotype.

Admittedly, although many species and individual variations exist [162], 'critical periods' do exist for mammals in regard to reproductive phenomena. But while reproduction may be affected, assumption of a sexual role may not be. A normal Rhesus monkey raised in isolation may not react sexually sufficiently to mate, but a male still follows male behaviour patterns (albeit deviantly); and a female, female patterns. Harlow [74] has mentioned that many types of sexually dimorphic behaviour patterns such as play, aggression, and receptivity, which are as much a part of the proper gender role as coitus, arise spontaneously in isolated male and female monkeys. He said, 'It is unreasonable to account for these sex differences as learned, culturally ordered patterns of behaviour because there is no opportunity for acquiring a cultural heritage, let alone a sexually differentiated one, from an inanimate cloth surrogate' [74]. This conclusion is in contradistinction to the response of the female Rhesus which, as mentioned earlier, when potentiated by pre-natal androgen injections, behaves not as a deviant female but as a male. There seems to be little doubt that normal

humans would manifest sexually dimorphic behaviour patterns even if
raised in isolation.

It is interesting here to consider the
following point. If imprinting were
involved to any great extent and the
gender role independent of a more
significant sexual instinct, then a
neutrality theory would have to contend with the fact that for the first
three years of life babies are almost
exclusively with their mothers (or
some other female), and yet male
children are usually *not* imprinted as
females. This fact must be considered
in the light of the observations that
imprinting, as we see it in birds, occurs
within the brief space of a few hours
and irrespective of sex. Nothing really
comparable to imprinting has been
demonstrated to occur in human
sexuality.

Learning and reinforcement

. . . . .

Much of the psychosexual 'neutrality
at birth' theory depends upon the
great part that learning plays in the
instillation of masculine and feminine
gender roles [72, 118, 124]. Sears,
Maccoby, and Levin [163], Rabban
[144], and others are cited by Hampson and Hampson as indicating that
culture and learning shape subsequent
behaviour. Ehrmann [37] has recently
provided an excellent review of various studies investigating the social
determinants of human sexual behaviour. These studies indeed indicate that
gender personality is influenced by
society and thus, in part, is learned.
But Ehrmann wisely started his review
by emphasizing that in looking for the
social determinants of sexual behaviour one must take into account biological considerations and not simply
learning processes. Benjamin [18] in a

very recent study of trans-sexual
individuals could find no evidence that
childhood conditioning is involved in
the aetiology of the trans-sexualism in
47 out of 87 patients. Of the remaining
40 patients conditioning was of 'doubtful' influence in 24 individuals and
definitely influential in only 16 cases.

As a function of learning, assumption of a gender role presumably
should follow the characteristics of a
normal learning curve. But, when
viewed properly, modifiability of sex
behaviour by learning must be seen
also as a disproof of the imprinting
theory, for the same modifications of
behaviour cannot be caused both by
learning and by imprinting in the same
species. The basic incompatibilities
are that learning requires reinforcement while imprinting does not, and
that imprinting is fixed and irreversible while learning is not. But even to
grant that assumption of a gender role
by an individual in our society may be
moulded by learning in no way proves
that it is the sole or dominant deter-
miner of the gender role. Money,
Hampson, and Hampson would have
us believe so.

. . . . .

It is not obvious, when we examine
the best possible evidence, how the
criteria of learning can be logically
applied to the hermaphroditic evidence. Yet to do just that is the core
of their philosophy, which asserts that
if gender roles are modified by learning or are established by imprinting,
then sexual behaviour patterns are
not pre-natally mediated. Here is a
subtle *non sequitur*. All evinced learning, be it operant or classical, is by
definition a modification of behaviour
[177]. The evidence presented in this
paper indicates that the learning of a
gender role is a culturally fostered

ontogenetic phenomenon of development superimposed on a prenatally determined pattern and mechanism of sexual behaviour. As Tinbergen [175] has stated, 'There is a close relationship between innate equipment and learning processes, in that learning is often predetermined by the innate constitution. Many animals inherit predispositions to learn special things, and these dispositions to learn therefore belong to the innate equipment.' This predisposition may be considered also in terms of differential endocrine sensitivity. The nervous systems of males and females subjected to genetic and hormonal factors may present an altered learning capability that sets limits to or extends the range of sexual behaviour possible to the individual. Hutchinson [83] has pro-posed that the individual's genetic endowment operates to mould behaviour by affecting 'the rates and extent of development of the neuropsychological mechanisms underlying the identification process and other aspects of object relationships in infancy'. An extensive search of the literature reveals no case where a male or female without some sort of biological abnormality, e.g. chromosomal, hormonal, or gonadal, accepted an imposed gender role opposite to that of his or her phenotype. If such an individual is available he has not been referred to by proponents of a 'neutrality at birth' theory. It may be assumed that such an individual will be hard to find, since this anomalous behaviour would be outside normal limits.

See note at end of references.

References

1. AMES, L. B. and LEARNED, J. (1954). Developmental trends in child kalcidoblock responses. *J. genet. Psychol.* **84**, 237–70.

2. —— —— MÉTRAUX, R. W., and WALKER, R. N. (1952). *Child Rorschach Responses: Developmental trends from two to ten years.* Hoeber-Harper, New York.

3. ARMSTRONG, C. N. (1955). Diversities of sex. *Brit. Med. J.* **1**, 1173–77.

4. —— (1964). Intersexuality in man. *In* (Armstrong, C. N. and Marshall, A. J. (Eds.)) *Intersexuality in vertebrates including man.* Academic Press, London, pp. 349–93.

5. BALL, J. (1937). Sex activity of castrated male rats increased by estrin administration. *J. comp. Psychol.* **24**, 135–44.

6. BARNO, A. (1962). Testicular feminization syndrome in male pseudohermaphrodites. *Am. J. obstet. Gynecol.* **84**, 710–18.

7. BARRACLOUGH, C. A. (1961). Production of anovulatory, sterile rats by single injections of testosterone propionate. *Endocrinology* **68**, 62–7.

8. —— and GORSKI, R. A. (1961). Evidence that the hypothalamus is responsible for androgen-induced sterility in the female rat. *Endocrinology* **68**, 68–79.

9. —— and —— (1962). Studies on mating behaviour in the androgen-sterilized female rat in relation to the hypothalamic regulation of sexual behaviour. *J. Endocrinol.* **25**, 175–82.

10. BEACH, F. A. (1943). Effects of injury to the cerebral cortex upon the display of masculine and feminine mating behaviour by female rats. *J. comp. Psychol.* **36**, 169–99.

11. —— (1948). Sexual behavior in animals and men. *Harvey Lect. Ser.* **43**, 254–80.

12. —— (1948). *Hormones and behavior.* Hoeber-Harper, New York.

13. —— (1949). A cross-species survey of mammalian sexual behavior. *In* (Hoch, P. H. and Zubin, J. (Eds.))

Psychosexual development in health and disease. Grune and Stratton, New York, pp. 52–78.

14. —— (1951). Instinctive behavior: Reproductive activities. *In* (Stevens, S. S. (Ed.)) *Handbook of experimental psychology.* John Wiley and Sons, New York, pp. 387–606.

15. —— (1958). Normal sexual behavior in male rats isolated at fourteen days of age. *J. comp. Physiol. Psychol.* **51**, 37–8.

16. —— and JAYNES, J. (1954). Effects of early experience upon the behavior of animals. *Psychol. Bull.* **51**, 239–63.

17. BEATTY, R. A. (1964). Chromosome deviations and sex in vertebrates. *In* (Armstrong, C. N. and Marshall, A. J. (Eds.)) *Intersexuality in vertebrates including man.* Academic Press, London, pp. 17–143.

18. BENJAMIN, H. (1964). Nature and management of transsexualism. *West. J. Surg. Obstet., Gynecol.* **72**, 105–11.

19. BERG, I., NIXON, H. H., and MAC-MAHON, R. (1963). Change of assigned sex at puberty. *Lancet* **2**, 1216–17.

20. BETTINGER, H. F. (1950). Genetic and hormonal aspects of intersexuality. *In* (King, E. S. J. (Ed.)) *Studies in pathology.* University Press, Melbourne, pp. 113–32.

21. BOSS, W. R. (1943). Hormonal determination of adult characters and sex behavior in herring gulls (*Larus argentatus*). *J. exp. Zool.* **94**, 181–209.

22. BREMER, J. (1959). *Asexualization, A follow-up study of 244 cases.* Macmillan, New York.

23. BROOKHART, J. M. and DEY, E. L. (1941). Reduction of sexual behavior in male guinea pigs by hypothalamic lesions. *Am. J. Physiol.* **133**, 551–4.

24. BROWN, J. B. and FRYER, M. P. (1957). Hypospadias—Complete construction of penis, with establishment of proper sex status. *Postgrad. Med.* **22**, 489–91.

25. —— and —— (1964). Plastic surgical correction of hypospadias with mistaken sex identity and transvestism resulting in normal marriage and parenthood. *Surg. gynecol. Obstet.* **118**, 45–6.

26. BRUNNER-LORAND, J. (1964). Intersexuality in mammals. *In* (Armstrong, C. N. and Marshall, A. J. (Eds.)) *Intersexuality in vertebrates including man.* Academic Press, London, pp. 311–47.

27. BURNS, R. K. (1961). Role of hormones in the differentiation of sex. *In* (Young, W. C. (Ed.)) *Sex and internal secretions*, 3rd ed. Williams and Wilkins, Baltimore, pp. 76–158.

28. CHALL, L. P. (1963). An attempt at descriptive integration. *In* (Winokur, G. (Ed.)) *Determinants of human sexual behavior.* Charles C. Thomas, Springfield, pp. 167–86.

29. CLEGG, M. T., SANTOLUCITO, J. A., SMITH, J. D., and GANONG, W. F. (1958). The effect of hypothalamic lesions on sexual behaviour and estrous cycles in the ewe. *Endocrinology* **62**, 790–7.

30. CORNER, G. W. (1942). *The hormones in human reproduction.* Princeton University Press, Princeton.

31. DEESE, J. E. (1958). *The psychology of learning*, 2nd ed. McGraw-Hill, New York.

32. DENGROVE, E. (1961). Sex differences. *In* (Ellis, A. and Abarbanel, A. (Eds.)) *The encyclopedia of sexual behavior.* Hawthorn Books, New York, pp. 931–8.

33. DEWHURST, C. J. and GORDON, R. R. (1963). Change of sex. *Lancet* **21**, 1213–16.

34. DIAMOND, M. and YOUNG, W. C. (1963). Differential responsiveness of pregnant and non-pregnant guinea pigs to the masculinizing action of testosterone propionate. *Endocrinology* **72**, 429–38.

35. DICKS, G. H. and CHILDERS, A. T. (1934). The social transformation of a boy who had lived his first fourteen years as a girl: A case history. *Am. J. Orthopsychiat.* **41**, 508–17.

36. DOBZHANSKY, T. (1962). *Mankind evolving: The evolution of the human species.* Yale University Press, New Haven.

37. EHRMANN, W. (1963). Social determinants of human sexual behavior. *In* (Winokur, G. (Ed.)) *Determinants of human sexual behavior.* Charles C. Thomas, Springfield, pp. 142–63.

38. EPSTEIN, A. W. (1960). Fetishism: A study of its psychopathology with particular reference to a proposed disorder in brain mechanisms as an etiological factor. *J. nerv. ment. Dis.* **130**, 107–19.

39. —— (1961). Relationship of fetishism and transvestism to brain and particularly to temporal lobe dysfunction. *J. nerv. ment. Dis.* **133**, 247–53.

40. EVERETT, J. W. (1964). Central neural control of reproductive functions of the adenohypophysis. *Physiol. Rev.* **44**, 373–431.

41. FEDER, H. H. and WHALEN, R. E. (1965). Feminine behavior in neonatally castrated and estrogen treated male rats. *Science* **147**, 306–7.

42. FLETCHER, R. (1957). *Instinct in man: In the light of recent work in comparative psychology.* Int. Univ. Press, New York.

43. FORD, C. S. and BEACH, F. A. (1951). *Patterns of sexual behavior.* Harper Bros., New York.

44. FOSS, G. L. (1937). Effect of testosterone propionate on a postpuberal eunuch. *Lancet* **2**, 1307–9.

45. GEDDA, L. (1963). Aspetti genetici dell'osmosessuality. *Acta Genet. Med. Gemellol.* **12**, 213–27.

46. GEIST, S. H. (1941). Androgen therapy in the human female. *J. clin. Endocrinol.* **1**, 154–61.

47. GHABRIAL, F. and GIRGIS, S. M. (1962). Reorientation of sex. Report of two cases. *Int. J. Fertility* **7**, 249–58.

48. GILDEA, E. F. and ROBINS, L. N. (1963). Suggestions for research in sexual behavior. *In* (Winokur, G. (Ed.)) *Determinants of human sexual behavior.* Charles C. Thomas, Springfield, pp. 193–4.

49. GOLDSTEIN, A. C. (1957). The experimental control of sex behavior in animals. *In* (Hoagland, H. (Ed.)) *Hormones, brain function, and behavior.* Academic Press, New York, pp. 99–123.

50. GOODALE, H. D. (1918). Feminized male birds. *Genetics* **3**, 276–99.

51. GOODENOUGH, F. L. (1931). Anger in young children. *Inst. Child Welfare Monogr. Ser., No. 9.* Univ. Minn. Press, Minneapolis.

52. GORSKI, R. A. and BARRACLOUGH, C. A. (1963). Effects of low dosages of androgen on the differentiation of hypothalamic regulatory control of ovulation in the rat. *Endocrinology* **73**, 210–16.

53. GORSKI, R. A. and WAGNER, J. W. (1965). Gonadal activity and sexual differentiation of the hypothalamus. *Endocrinology* **76**, 226–39.

54. GOY, R. W. and JAKWAY, J. (1959). The inheritance of patterns of sexual behavior in female guinea pigs. *Anim. Behav.* **7**, 142–9.

55. —— and PHOENIX, C. H. (1963). Hypothalamic regulation of female sexual behavior; establishment of behavioural oestrus in spayed guinea pigs following hypothalamic lesions. *J. reprod. Fertil.* **5**, 23–40.

56. GRADY, K. L. and PHOENIX, C. H. (1963). Hormonal determinants of of mating behavior; the display of feminine behavior by adult male rats castrated neonatally. *Am. Zool.* **3**, 482–3.

57. GREEN, J. D. (1956). Neural pathways to the hypophysis. *In* (Fields, W. S., Guillemin, R., and Carton,

C. A. (Eds.)) *Hypothalamic hypophysial interrelationships*. Charles C. Thomas, Springfield, pp. 3–16.

58. CLEMENTE, C. D. and DEGROOT, J. (1957). Rhinencephalic lesions and behavior in cats: An analysis of the Klüver–Bucy syndrome with particular reference to normal and abnormal sexual behavior. *J. comp. Neurol.* **108**, 505–45.

59. —— and MONEY, J. (1960). Incongruous gender role: Nongenital manifestations in prepubertal boys. *J. nerv. ment. Dis.* **130**, 160–8.

60. —— and —— (1961). Effeminacy in prepubertal boys. Summary of eleven cases and recommendations for case management. *Pediatrics* **27**, 286–91.

61. —— and —— (1961). 'Tomboys' and 'Sissies'. *Sexology* **28**, 2–5.

62. GREER, M. A. (1957). Studies on the influence of the central nervous system on anterior pituitary function. *Recent Prog. horm. Res.* **13**, 67–104.

63. GRUMBACH, M. M. and BARR, M. L. (1958). Cytologic tests of chromosomal sex in relation to sexual anomalies in man. *Recent Prog. horm. Res.* **14**, 255–334.

64. —— and DUCHARME, J. R. (1960). The effects of androgens on fetal sexual development: Androgen-induced female pseudohermaphrodism. *Fertility sterility* **11**, 157–80.

65. —— —— and MOLOSHOK, R. E. (1959). On the fetal masculinizing action of certain oval progestins. *J. clin. Endocrinol. Metab.* **19**, 1369–80.

66. —— VAN WYK, J. J. and WILKINS, L. (1955). Chromosomal sex in gonadal dysgenesis (ovarian agenesis): Relationship to male pseudohermaphrodism and theories of human sex differentiation. *J. clin. Endocrinol. Metab.* **15**, 1161–93.

67. HAMPSON, J. G. (1955). Hermaphroditic genital appearance, rearing and eroticism in hyperadrenocorti-

cism. *Bull. Johns Hopkins Hosp.* **96**, 265–73.

68. —— (1964). The case management of somatic sexual disorders in children: psychologic considerations. *In* (Lloyd, C. W. (Ed.)) *Human reproduction and sexual behavior*. Lea and Febiger, Philadelphia, pp. 250–64.

69. —— and MONEY, J. (1955). Idiopathic sexual precocity in the female: Report of three cases. *Psychosomat. Med.* **17**, 16–35.

70. —— —— and HAMPSON, J. L. (1956). Hermaphrodism: Recommendations concerning case management. *J. clin. Endocrinol. Metab.* **16**, 547–56.

71. HAMPSON, J. L. (1964). Deviant sexual behavior; homosexuality; transvestism. *In* (Lloyd, C. W. (Ed.)) *Human reproduction and sexual behavior*. Lea and Febiger, Philadelphia, pp. 498–510.

72. —— and HAMPSON, J. G. (1961). The ontogenesis of sexual behavior in man. *In* (Young, W. C. (Ed.)) *Sex and internal secretions*, 3rd ed., Williams and Wilkins, Baltimore, pp. 1401–32.

73. —— —— and MONEY, J. (1955). The syndrome of gonadal agenesis (ovarian agenesis) and male chromosomal pattern in girls and women: Psychologic studies. *Bull. Johns Hopkins Hosp.* **97**, 207–26.

74. HARLOW, H. (1961). Sexual behavior in the rhesus monkey. *Minutes of conference on sex and behavior*. (Beach, F. A. (moderator)). University of California, Berkeley.

75. HARRIS, G. W. (1955). *Neural control of the pituitary gland*. Arnold and Co., London.

76. —— (1956). Hypothalamic control of the anterior lobe of the hypophysis. *In* (Fields, W. S., Guillemin, R., and Carton, C. A. (Eds.)) *Hypothalamic-Hypophysial interrelationships*. Charles C. Thomas, Springfield, pp. 31–45.

77. —— (1960). Central control of pituitary secretion. *In* (Field, J., Magoun, H. W., and Hall, V. E. (Eds.)) *Handbook of physiology*; Section 1, Neurophysiology. Vol. II. Waverly Press, Baltimore, pp. 1007–33.

78. —— (1964). Sex hormones, brain development and brain function. *Endocrinology* **75**, 627–48.

79. —— and JACOBSOHN, D. (1950). Proliferative capacity of the hypophysial portal vessels. *Nature* **165**, 854.

80. —— and —— (1951). Functional grafts of the anterior pituitary gland. *Proc. R. Soc.* B, **139**, 263–76.

81. —— and LEVINE, S. (1962). Sexual differentiation of the brain and its experimental control. *J. Physiol.* **163**, 42P–43P.

82. HULL, C. L. (1952). *A behavior system: An introduction to behavior theory concerning the individual organism.* Yale University Press, New Haven.

83. HUTCHINSON, G. E. (1959). A speculative consideration of certain possible forms of sexual selection in man. *Am. Natur.* **93**, 81–91.

84. JAKWAY, J. (1959). Inheritance of patterns of mating behavior in the male guinea pig. *Anim. Behav.* **7**, 150–62.

85. JONES, H. W. and SCOTT, W. W. (1958). *Hermaphroditism, genital anomalies and related endocrine disorders.* Williams and Wilkins Co., Baltimore.

86. JOST, A. (1958). Embryonic sexual differentiation (Morphology, Physiology, Abnormalities). *In* (Jones, Jr., H. W. and Scott, W. W. (Eds.)) *Hermaphroditism, genital anomalies and related endocrine disorders.* Williams and Wilkins Co., Baltimore, pp. 15–45.

87. KALLMANN, F. J. (1952). Twin and sibship study of overt male homosexuality. *Am. J. human Genet.* **4**, 136–46.

88. —— (1952). Comparative twin study on the genetic aspects of male homosexuality. *J. nerv. ment. Dis.* **115**, 283–98.

89. —— (1963). Genetic aspects of sex determination and sexual maturation potentials in man. *In* (Winokur, G. (Ed.)) *Determinants of human sexual behavior.* Charles C. Thomas, Springfield, pp. 5–18.

90. KARLSON, P. (1963). New concepts on the mode of action of hormones. *Perspect. biol. Med.* **6**, 203–14.

91. KENDALL, B. and LOEWENBERG, L. S. (1962). Testicular feminization: Report of 2 cases occurring in siblings. *Obstet. Gynecol.* **20**, 551–4.

92. KING, J. A. (1957). Relationships between early social experience and adult aggressive behavior in inbred mice. *J. genet. Psychol.* **90**, 151–66.

93. KINSEY, A. C., POMEROY, W. B., and MARTIN, C. E. (1948). *Sexual behavior in the human male.* W. B. Saunders Co., Philadelphia.

94. —— —— MARTIN, C. E., and GEBHARD, P. H. (1953). *Sexual behavior in the human female.* W. B. Saunders Co., Philadelphia.

95. KLÜVER, H. (1952). Brain mechanisms and behavior with special reference to the rhinencephalon. *Lancet* **72**, 567–74.

96. —— and BUCY, P. C. (1939). Preliminary analysis of functions of the temporal lobes in monkeys. *A.M.A. neurol. Psychiat.* **42**, 979–1000.

97. KRAFT, I. A. and BEDFORD, Z. C. (1963). Psychologic preparation of a five-year-old pseudohermaphrodite for surgical sexual change. *Pediat. clin. N. Amer.* **10**, 257–64.

98. KUPPERMAN, H. S. and STUDDIFORD, W. E. (1953). Endocrine therapy in gynecologic disorders. *Postgrad. Med.* **14**, 410–24.

99. LANSDELL, H. (1961). The effect of neurosurgery on a test of proverbs. *Am. Psychol.* **16**, 448.

100. —— (1962). A sex difference in effect of temporal lobe neurosurgery on design preference. *Nature* **194**, 852–4.

101. LEHMAN, H. C. and WITTY, P. A. (1927). *The psychology of play activities.* Barnes, New York.

102. LIPSCHÜTZ, A. (1924). *The internal secretions of the sex glands: The problem of the 'puberty gland'.* Williams and Wilkins, Baltimore.

103. LIPSITT, L. P. and LEVY, N. (1959). Electrotactual threshold in the neonate. *Child Dev.* **30**, 547–54.

104. LOESER, A. A. (1940). Subcutaneous implantation of female and male hormone in tablet form in women. *Brit. Med. J.* **1**, 479–82.

105. LORENZ, K. (1937). The companion in the bird's world. *Auk* **54**, 245–73.

106. MARSHALL, H. K. and HARDER, H. I. (1958). Testicular feminizing syndrome in male pseudohermaphrodites; report of 2 cases in identical twins. *Obstet. Gynecol.* **12**, 284–93.

107. MARTINEZ, C. and BITTNER, J. J. (1956). A non-hypophyseal sex difference in estrous behavior of mice bearing pituitary grafts. *Proc. Soc. Exp. biol. Med.* **91**, 506–9.

108. MASTERS, W. H. and JOHNSON, V. E. (1963). The clitoris: An anatomic baseline for behavioral investigation. *In* (Winokur, G. (Ed.)) *Determinants of human sexual behavior.* Charles C. Thomas, Springfield, pp. 44–57.

109. MCGILL, T. E. (1962). Reduction in 'Headmounts' in the sexual behavior of the mouse as a function of experience. *Psychol. Rep.* **10**, 284.

110. —— (1962). Sexual behavior in three inbred strains of mice. *Behaviour* **19**, 341–50.

111. —— and BLIGHT, W. C. (1963). The sexual behavior of hybrid male mice compared with the sexual behavior of males of the inbred parent strains. *Anim. Behav.* **11**, 480–3.

112. —— and —— (1963). Effects of genotype on the recovery of sex drive in the male mouse. *J. comp. Physiol. Psychol.* **56**, 887–8.

113. MEAD, M. (1928). *Coming of age in Samoa.* William Morrow, New York.

114. —— (1961). Cultural determinants of sexual behavior. *In* (Young, W. C. (Ed.)) *Sex and internal secretions*, 3rd ed., Williams and Wilkins, Baltimore, pp. 1433–79.

115. MELICOW, M. M. and USON, A. C. (1964). A periodic table of sexual anomalies. *J. Urol.* **91**, 402–25.

116. MONEY, J. (1955). Hermaphroditism, gender and precocity in hyperadrenocorticism: Psychologic findings. *Bull. Johns Hopkins, Hosp.* **96**, 253–64.

117. —— (1957). *The psychologic study of man.* Charles C. Thomas, Springfield.

118. —— (1960. Components of eroticism in man: Cognitional rehearsals. *In* (Wortis, J. (Ed.)) *Recent advances in biological psychiatry.* Grune and Stratton, New York, pp. 210–25.

119. —— (1960). Phantom orgasm in the dreams of paraplegic men and women. *Arch. genet. Psychiat.* **3**, 373–82.

120. —— (1961). Components of eroticism in man: The hormones in relation to sexual morphology and sexual desire. *J. nerv. ment. Dis.* **132**, 239–48.

121. —— (1961). Components of eroticism in man: II. The orgasm and genital somesthesia. *J. nerv. ment. Dis.* **132**, 289–97.

122. —— (1961). Hermaphroditism. *In* (Ellis, A. and Abarabanel, A. (Eds.)) *Encyclopedia of sexual behavior.* Hawthorn Books, New York, pp. 472–84.

123. —— (1961). Too early puberty. *Sexology* **28**, 2–8.

124. —— (1961). Sex hormones and other variables in human eroticism. *In* (Young, W. C. (Ed.)) *Sex and internal secretions*, 3rd ed. Williams and Wilkins, Baltimore, pp. 1138–400.

125. —— (1963). Cytogenetic and psychosexual incongruities with a note on space-form blindness. *Am. J. Psychiat.* **119**, 820–7.

126. —— (1963). Factors in the genesis of homosexuality. *In* (Winokur, G. (Ed.)) *Determinants of human sexual behavior.* Charles C. Thomas, Springfield, pp. 19–43.

127. —— (1963). Psychosexual development in man. *In* (Deutch, Albert (Ed.)) *Encyclopedia of mental health.* Franklin Watts, New York, pp. 1678–709.

128. —— and HAMPSON, J. G. (1955). Idiopathic sexual precocity in the male. *Psychosomat. Med.* **17**, 1–15.

129. —— —— and HAMPSON, J. L. (1955). Hermaphroditism: Recommendations concerning assignment of sex, change of sex, and psychologic management. *Bull. Johns Hopkins Hosp.* **97**, 284–300.

130. —— —— and —— (1955). An examination of some basic sexual concepts: The evidence of human hermaphroditism. *Bull. Johns Hopkins Hosp.* **97**, 301–19.

131. —— —— and —— (1956). Sexual incongruities and psychopathology: The evidence of human hermaphroditism. *Bull. Johns Hopkins Hosp.* **98**, 43–57.

132. —— —— and —— (1957). Imprinting and the establishment of gender role. *A.M.A. Arch. neurol. Psychiat.* **77**, 333–6.

133. —— and HIRSCH, S. R. (1963). Chromosome anomalies, mental deficiency and schizophrenia. *Arch. Genet. Psychiat.* **8**, 242–51.

134. MORRIS, J. M. (1953). The syndrome of testicular feminization in male pseudohermaphrodites. *Am. J. Obstet. Gynecol.* **65**, 1192–211.

135. —— and MAHESH, V. B. (1963). Further observations on the syndrome 'testicular feminization': *Am. J. Obstet. Gynecol.* **87**, 731–48.

136. NALBANDOV, A. V. (Ed.). (1963). *Advances in neuroendocrinology.* University of Illinois Press, Urbana.

137. NORRIS, A. S. and KEETEL, W. C. (1962). Change of sex during adolescence: A case study. *Am. J. Obstet. Gynecol.* **84**, 719–21.

138. OVERZIER, C. (Ed.). (1963). *Intersexuality.* Academic Press, New York.

139. PARE, C. M. B. (1956). Homosexuality and chromosomal sex. *J. Psychosomat. Res.* **1**, 247–51.

140. PERLOFF, W. H. (1949). Role of the hormones in human sexuality. *Psychosomat. Med.* **11**, 133–7.

141. —— (1963). The role of hormones in homosexuality. *J. Albert Einstein Med. Cen.* **11**, 165–78.

142. PHOENIX, C. H. (1961). Hypothalamic regulation of sexual behavior in male guinea pigs. *J. comp. physiol. Psychol.* **54**, 72–7.

143. —— Goy, R. W., GERALL, A. A., and YOUNG, W. C. (1959). Organizing action of prenatally administered testosterone propionate on the tissues mediating mating behavior in the female guinea pig. *Endocrinology* **65**, 369–82.

144. RABBAN, M. (1950). Sex-role identification in young children in two diverse social groups. *Genet. Psychol. Monogr.* **42**, 81–158.

145. RADO, S. (1940). A critical examination of the concept of bisexuality. *Psychosomat. Med.* **2**, 459–67.

146. ROBISON, B. L. and SAWYER, C. H. (1957). Loci of sex behavioral and gonadatrophic centers in the female cat hypothalamus. *Physiologist* **1**, 72 (Abstr.).

147. ROTH, M. and BALL, J. R. B. (1964). Psychiatric aspects of intersexuality. *In* (Armstrong, C. N. and Marshall, A. J. (Eds.)) *Intersexuality in vertebrates including man.* Academic Press, London, pp. 395–443.

148. SALMON, U. J. and GEIST, S. H. (1943). Effect of androgens upon libido in women. *J. clin. Endocrinol.* **3**, 235–8.

149. SAWA, M., UEKI, Y., ARITA, M., and HARADA, T. (1954). Preliminary report on the amygdaloidectomy on the psychotic patients, with interpretation of oral-emotional manifestation in schizophrenics. *Folia psychiat. neurol., Japan* **7**, 309–29.

150. SAWYER, C. H. (1960). Reproductive behavior. *In* (Field, J., Magoun, H. W., and Hall, V. E. (Eds.)) *Handbook of physiology;* Section 1, Neurophysiology, Vol. II. Waverly Press, Baltimore, pp. 1225–40.

151. —— (1962). Gonadal hormone feedback and sexual behavior. Proceedings of the I.U.P.S. XXII International Congress, Leiden, *Excerpta Med. Int. Congr. Ser. No. 47*, pp. 642–9.

152. —— and ROBISON, B. (1956). Separate hypothalamic areas controlling pituitary gonadotropic function and mating behavior in female cats and rabbits. *J. clin. Endocrinol. Metab.* **16**, 914–15 (Abstr.).

153. SCHILLER, C. H. (Ed.). (1957). *Instinctive behavior: The development of a modern concept.* Int. Univ. Press, New York.

154. SCHLEGEL, W. S. (1962). Die Konstitutionsbiologischen Grundlagender Homosexualitat. *Z. Menschl. Vererb. Konstitutionslehre* **36**, 341–64.

155. SCHNEIDER, R. A., COSTILOE, J. P., HOWARD, R. P., and WOLF, S. (1958). Olfactory perception thresholds in hypogonadal women; changes accompanying administration of androgen and estrogen. *J. clin. Endocrinol.* **18**, 379–90.

156. —— and WOLF, S. (1955). Olfactory perception thresholds for citral utilizing a new type olfactorium. *J. app. Physiol.* **8**, 337–42.

157. SCHON, M. and SUTHERLAND, A. M. (1960). The role of hormones in human behavior. III. Changes in female sexuality after hypophysectomy. *J. clin. Endocrinol. Metab.* **20**, 833–41.

158. SCHREINER, L. and KLING, A. (1953). Behavioral changes following rhinencephalic injury in cat. *J. Neurophysiol.* **16**, 643–59.

159. —— and —— (1954). Effects of castration on hypersexual behavior induced by rhinencephalic injury in cat. *A.M.A. Arch. neurol. Psychiat.* **72**, 180–6.

160. —— and —— (1956). Rhinencephalon and behavior. *Am. J. Physiol.* **184**, 486–90.

161. SCHULTZ, J. H. (1963). Intersexuality and transvestism. *In* (Overzier, C. (Ed.)) *Intersexuality.* Academic Press, New York, pp. 514–33.

162. SCOTT, J. P. (1962). Critical periods in behavioral development. *Science* **138**, 949–58.

163. SEARS, R. R., MACCOBY, E. E., and LEVIN, H. (1957). *Patterns of child rearing.* Row Peterson, Evanston.

164. SHORR, E., PAPANICOLAOU, G. N., and STIMMEL, B. F. (1938). Neutralization of ovarian follicular hormone in women by simultaneous administration of male sex hormone. *Proc. Soc. exp. biol. Med.* **38**, 759–62.

165. SOPCHAK, A. L. and SUTHERLAND, A. M. (1960). Psychological impact of cancer and its treatment. VII. Exogenous sex hormones and their relation to life-long adaptations in women with metastatic cancer of the breast. *Cancer* **13**, 528–31.

166. SOULAIRAC, A. (1959). Les lésions gonadiques et les troubles du compartment sexual. *Prob. Act. d'Endocrinol.* **3**, 1–6.

167. —— and SOULAIRAC, M. L. (1956). Effets de lésions hypothalamiques sur le comportement sexuel et le tractus génital du rat male. *Ann. Endocrinol. (Paris)* **17**, 731–45.

168. SPOCK, B. (1964). Are we minimizing differences between the sexes? *Redbook* **122**, 20–30.

169. SZENTÁGOTHAI, J., FLERKÓ, B., MESS, B., and HALÁSZ, B. (1962). *Hypothalamic control of the anterior pituitary.*

An experimental-morphological study. Akadémia: Kiadó, Budapest.

170. TAUBER, E. S. (1940). Effects of castration upon the sexuality of the adult male. *Psychosomat. Med.* **2**, 74–87.

171. TAX, S., and CALLENDER, C. (Eds.) (1960). *Issues in evolution. Evolution after Darwin.* Vol. III. University of Chicago Press, Chicago.

172. TERMAN, L. M. (1946). Psychological sex differences. *In* (Carmichael, L. (Ed.)) *Manual of child psychology.* John Wiley and Sons, New York, pp. 954–1000.

173. TERZIAN, H. and DALLE ORE, G. (1955). Syndrome of Klüver and Bucy: Reproduced in man by bilateral removal of the temporal lobes. *Neurology* **5**, 373–80.

174. THORNDIKE, E. L. (1913). *The psychology of learning (Educational psychology II).* Teachers College, New York.

175. TINBERGEN, N. (1951). *The study of instinct.* Oxford University Press, London.

176. VERPLANCK, W. S. (1955). Since learned behavior is innate, and vice versa, what now? *Psychol. Rev.* **62**, 139–44.

177. —— (1957). A glossary of some terms used in the objective science of behavior. *Psychol. Rev* **64**, Supplement.

178. WALKER, R. N. (1962). Body build and behavior in young children. *Monogr. Soc. Res. Child Dev.* **27**, 1–94.

179. WALLIN, P. and CLARK, A. L. (1963). A study of orgasm as a condition of women's enjoyment of coitus in the middle years of marriage. *Human Biol.* **35**, 131–9.

180. WALTERS, J., PEARCE, D., and DAHMS, L. (1957). Affectional and aggressive behavior of preschool children. *Child Dev.* **28**, 15–26.

181. WAXENBERG, S. E. (1963). Some biological correlatives of sexual behavior. *In* (Winokur, G. (Ed.))

Determinants of human sexual behavior. Charles C. Thomas, Springfield, pp. 52–75.

182. —— DRELLICH, M. G., and SUTHERLAND, A. M. (1959). The role of hormones in human behavior. I. Changes in female sexuality after adrenalectomy. *J. clin. Endocrinol. Metab.* **19**, 193–202.

183. —— FINKBEINER, J. A., DRELLICH, M. G., SUTHERLAND, A. M. (1960). The role of hormones in human behavior. II. Changes in sexual behavior in relation to vaginal smears of breast-cancer patients after oophorectomy and adrenalectomy. *Psychosomat. Med.* **22**, 435–42.

184. WHALEN, R. E. and NADLER, R. D. (1963). Suppression of the development of female mating behavior by estrogen administered in infancy. *Science* **141**, 273–4.

185. WILKINS, L. H. (1960). Abnormalities of sex differentiation. Classification, diagnosis, selection of gender of rearing and treatment. *Pediatrics* **26**, 846–57.

186. —— (1964). Embryonic sex differentiation, controlling factors and abnormalities, diagnosis and treatment. *Clin. proc. Child. Hosp.* **20**, 1–8.

187. —— JONES, H. W., HOLMAN, G. H., and STEMPFEL, R. S. JR., (1958). Masculinization of the female fetus associated with administration of oral and intramuscular progestins during gestation: non-adrenal female pseudohermaphrodism. *J. clin. endocrinol. Metab.* **18**, 559–85.

188. YOUNG, W. C. (1957). Genetic and psychological determinants of sexual behavior patterns. *In* (Hoagland, H. (Ed.)) *Hormones, Brain function and behavior.* Academic Press, New York, pp. 75–98.

189. —— (1961). The hormones and mating behavior. *In* (Young, W. C. (Ed.)) *Sex and internal secretions,* 3rd

ed. Williams and Wilkins, Baltimore, pp. 1173–239.

190. —— DEMPSEY, E. W., MEYERS, H. L.,
and HAGQUIST, C. W. (1938). The
ovarian condition and sexual behavior in the female guinea pig.
Am. J. Anat. **63**, 457–87.

191. —— GOY, R. W., and PHOENIX, C. H.
(1964). Hormones and sexual behavior. *Science* **143**, 212–18.

NOTE: The author of the article adds:

Following the publication of this article, Dr. John Money has altered his thinking regarding the ontogeny of human sexual development and recently himself has provided data which supports the idea that human sexuality is subject to biological and ontogenetic influences. Further case work pertinent to this article would be found in 'Genetic and endocrine interactions and human psycho-sexuality' in M. Diamond (Ed.) (1968), *Perspectives in reproduction and sexual behavior*, Indiana Univ. Press, Bloomington.

6 Pre-natal hormonal exposure

JOHN MONEY AND ANKE A. EHRHARDT†

Experimental animal background

It has been apparent, since the justly famed experiments of Jost [7] in the fifties, that androgen or an analogous substance, plays a special role in embryonic sexual differentiation. The principle of differentiation somewhat simplified appears to be: add androgen and obtain a male. Logical symmetry would seem to dictate that, from a neutral state, the addition of androgen produces a male and of oestrogen, a female. Not so! Nature's actual plan may be stated as: add nothing and obtain a female. In other words, the differentiation of the male is one step further in complexity than the differentiation of the female. This point is well worth holding in mind with respect to psychosexual differentiation, and with respect to the differentiation of the central nervous system that mediates psychosexual function.

The principle of androgen as a masculinizing additive appears to hold, also, in the sexual differentiation of the hypothalamus, according to the evidence of the new experimental work reported elsewhere in this symposium by some of its leading proponents (see reviews by Money [10]

† From 'Prenatal hormonal exposure: possible effects on behaviour in man'. In *Endocrinology and human behaviour*, (Michael, R. P. (Ed.)), Oxford University Press, London, pp. 32–48 (1968). Reprinted by permission of the publishers.

and Gorski [6]). In particular, the presence of androgenic steroids at a critical period of embryonic development will, in at least some of the lower species, have a permanent influence on neurohormonal releasing centres in the region of the median eminence, so that they will, henceforth, be incapable of stimulating pituitary gonadotrophic functioning in the periodic, female fashion to produce oestrous cycles. Instead, these centres will function acyclically in the male fashion.

Additionally, there is some evidence to suggest that when the centres of the median eminence that regulate the pituitary's release of gonadotrophins are being androgenized, corresponding centres in the preoptic area are androgenized also. They will subsequently be responsible for the suppression of behavioural patterns typical of the female role in reproduction—which need not, however, be entirely abolished—and the expression of the typically masculine patterns. Recent experiments suggest that hypothalamic sexual differentiation may be a matter not only of centres governing sexual activation, but also of centres governing the appropriate inhibition or 'turning off' of sexual behaviour. Inhibitory centres have been identified in proximity to the mammillary bodies.

Some work has already been accomplished on the influence of pre-natal androgens on sex-related behavioural differentiation in the primate, notably at the Oregon Regional Primate Research Centre. By injecting androgens into the pregnant Rhesus mother, it was possible to obtain female offspring with ovaries, uterus, and tubes internally, but with total external masculinization, namely a penis and empty scrotum. Such an animal, during childhood, is observed to exhibit rough-and-tumble play and assertive dominance with a frequency approaching that of the normal control male more closely than the normal control female. In the sexual play of childhood, the experimental animal also exhibits more behaviour typical of the normal male than of the female. At adolescence, hormonal puberty is that of the female, with normal menstrual cycles. Post-pubertal sexual behaviour has not yet been reported upon. The full story will not be known until enough masculinized monkeys have been produced to permit an experimental design with four categories, namely, those regulated at puberty with exogenous male hormone versus those not; and those surgically feminized at birth, versus those not.

The obverse of these masculinizing experiments is now possible as the result of the recent discovery of the androgen-antagonistic property of the drug cyproterone [13, 14]. This drug, administered to the pregnant female at a critical period of gestation causes the male offspring to be born with normal-appearing female external genitalia. The internal genitalia are male. In rats, it has been reported that the experimentally-produced simulant females are responded to as females by stud males and react as such, if they have been post-natally castrated and brought into oestrus by hormonal substitution treatment.

In the human organism, developmental pliability during the post-natal phase of psychosexual differentiation is probably much greater than in the lower, especially the oestrous, species, and more dependent on social interaction.

As everyone knows, it is ethically not possible to manipulate the pre-natal hormonal environment of a human foetus for experimental purposes. One must turn instead to the ready-made experiments of nature and learn what one can from them. There are, among others, three clinical syndromes to which we have recently directed our attention in this particular connection. They are the syndromes of progestin-induced hermaphroditism, the congenital adreno-genital syndrome (or female hyperadrenocortical hermaphroditism), and Turner's syndrome.

The rationale for choosing progestin-induced and hyperadrenocortical hermaphroditism, is that both these conditions illustrate the principle that masculinization represents something added. In each case the female foetus is exposed respectively to an excess of exogenous and endogenous androgen, the timing being such that, though the internal sexual organs are unaffected, the external genitalia are masculinized. The degree of masculinization varies from a mildly enlarged clitoris to a normal-appearing penis and empty scrotum. The progestin-induced condition, now generally avoidable, occurs as an untoward side-effect of an effort to preserve a pregnancy in a woman who otherwise repeatedly miscarries. Post-natally, the child needs, if the deformity is severe, only surgical correction as early as possible, and no hormonal treatments. The hyper-adrenocortical condition occurs as a recessive genetic trait. It requires life-time hormonal control with cortisone and early surgical feminization of the external genitalia, with a resultant good prognosis.

The rationale for choosing Turner's syndrome is that it represents the principle that feminine differentiation ensues in the absence of an added masculine factor. Girls with this syndrome have no gonads and, there-fore, no foetal gonadal hormones to influence foetal differentiation. The basic aetiologic defect is genetic, typi-cally a missing sex chromosome—

childhood and teenage. Table 6.1 gives the numbers in each group, along with various other identifying characteristics.

Categories of sex differences

The categories for analysis of sex differences in behaviour and psycho-sexual differentiation, as well as the techniques for assessing them, are still largely a matter of empirical trial and error. Our efforts at categorization have made us attentive to the following:

(1) *Energy expenditure level, particularly as represented by the organized movements of an athletic type of play.* This kind of

TABLE 6.1. *Size and Age Composition of three Diagnostic Groups*

Diagnostic group	No. of patients	Age range in years	Mean age in years
Progestin-induced hermaphroditism†	10 (all white)	$3\frac{9}{12}-14\frac{3}{12}$	$7\frac{10}{12}$
Hyperadrenocortical hermaphroditism	12 (11 white, 1 Negro)	$6\frac{8}{12}-16\frac{6}{12}$	$10\frac{2}{12}$
Turner's syndrome	15 (12 white, 3 Negro)	$8\frac{6}{12}-16\frac{5}{12}$	$12\frac{7}{12}$

† See [5].

occasionally a mosaic—so that the chromosomal count is usually 44 + XO. The missing chromosome might have been an X or a Y.

For the present special study of possible pre-natal hormonal influences on behaviour, we selected sub-samples from our larger clinical population of each syndrome, with proper attention to the avoidance of intentional samp-ling bias. For the groups to be roughly corresponding in age, our clinic files dictated that we favour middle to late

activity has traditionally been recog-nized as a feature of tomboyishness in girls. It may or may not be associated with play or sports traditionally identi-fied as boyish. It probably corresponds to the rough-and-tumble play reported as a characteristic, in the Rhesus monkey, of juvenile males.

(2) *Play, toy, and sports preferences.* These preferences have long been popularly recognized as an index of either boy-ishness or girlishness in children. In games of playing house or mother and

father, the relationship of play to the development of psychosexual identity is transparently clear.

(3) *Clothing preference.* Children become sensitized to what may be considered the regalia of a boyish or girlish identity at the same early age as they do to toy preferences, irrespective of the fact that fashion permits considerable overlap for girls. The same applies to what may loosely be called cosmetic preference, including haircut.

(4) *Maternalism.* It is more or less universally understood that motherhood is rehearsed in the doll play of girls. Boys' play rehearsal of the father's parental role may include direct handling of infants, dependent on the home model. Individual childhood differences in the anticipation of

TABLE 6.2. *Six Indices of Psychosexual Identity in three Diagnostic Groups*

	Progestin-induced hermaphroditism $N = 10$		Adrenogenital hermaphroditism $N = 12$		Turner's syndrome $N = 15$	
	Number	Per cent	Number	Per cent	Number	Per cent
1. (a) Intense outdoor physical and athletic interests	10	100	11	92	0	0
(b) Moderate interest and ability in outdoor activities	0	0	0	0	6	40
2. (a) Known to self and to others as tomboy	9	90	9	75	? 1	7
(b) Psychosexual ambivalence but not a tomboy	0	0	1	8	0	0
3. (a) Interest in boys' toys only	6	60	3	25	0	0
(b) Boys' toys preferred and dolls only occasionally	3	30	7	58	0	0
(c) Dolls preferred and no boys' toys	1	10	2	17	13	87
(d) Dolls preferred and boys' toys only occasionally	0	0	0	0	2	13
4. (a) Priority of marriage versus career	0	0	0	0	4	27
(b) Priority of career versus marriage	2	20	5	42	1†	7
(c) Marriage and career	6	60	6	50	9	60
(d) No information	2	20	1	8	1	7
5. (a) Slacks, shirts, and shorts strongly preferred	8	80	9	75	0	0
(b) Pretty dresses, plus slacks, shorts, and shirts	2	20	2	17	6	40
(c) Pretty dresses and no slacks, shirts, or shorts	0	0	1	8	9	60
6. Own sex depicted first in draw-a-person test	7	70	7	58	15	100

† Wanted to be a nun.

parenthood show up clearly with advancing age, as when some girls seek every chance to care for a young baby, as well as expressing their longing for, and intense interest in attending to the needs of infants.

(5) *Career ambition.* When these ambitions are chiefly vocational or professional, they do not exclude motherhood, but mothering tendencies take second place in a growing girl's or adolescent's anticipation of adulthood.

(6) *Body image.* Normally the body image, which is inferred from verbal or graphic representations, agrees with body morphology and function. When a contradiction or ambiguity occurs with reference to sex, the altered body image is an indication of incomplete or erroneous psychosexual differentiation.

(7) *Perceptual erotic arousal.* After puberty, visual and narrative stimuli are more potent in inducing genitopelvic arousal—as contrasted with romantic and sentimental arousal—in males than females. Females are more dependent specifically on the sense of touch for genitopelvic arousal. This sex difference may be a function of androgen, and possibly of androgenic influences during foetal development.

In the light of the foregoing seven aspects of sex difference, we obtained, by means of interviews and projective tests, information from each girl in each of our three groups and from at least one parent each on the following topics: tomboyishness, play and toy preference, clothing preference, maternalism, career preference, and sex of first figure depicted by choice in the draw-a-person test. The respective frequency incidences obtained are given in Table 6.2. The table shows rather clearly that the two forms of hermaphroditism resemble one another and differ very markedly from Turner's syndrome.

Intellectual comparisons

We obtained also a Wechsler IQ on each girl (Table 6.3). Our surveys of IQ in larger groups in the case of the adrenogenital syndrome (Fig. 6.1) [12] and Turner's syndrome [9, 1] produced results in accord with these present ones.

The fact that the three means differ is almost certainly not accidental. In the case of Turner's syndrome, it is known that difficulty in space-form organization is one of the many characteristic traits of the syndrome (Fig. 6.2). It is probably related to the genetic defect that produces the syndrome. It is responsible for a sometimes large disparity between verbal and performance IQ and pulls down the level of the full IQ.

The above-average level of the mean IQ in the adrenogenital syndrome is not, to the best of our ability to evaluate, an artifact of sampling. It leaves open the possibility that the recessive genetic factor responsible for adrenocortical dysfunction in the syn-

TABLE 6.3. *IQ Data in three Diagnostic Groups*

		Progestin-induced hermaphroditism $N = 10$	Adrenogenital hermaphroditism $N = 12$	Turner's syndrome $N = 15$
IQ	Mean	125	112	101
	Range	105–137	91–131	65–125

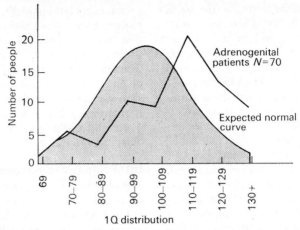

Fig. 6.1. IQ distribution in 70 cases of the adrenogenital syndrome.

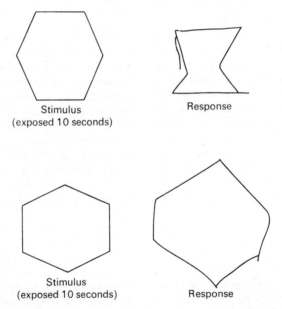

Fig. 6.2. Two figures from the Benton visual retention test reproduced by a girl aged 10 years with Turner's syndrome, showing space-form perceptual difficulty. (IQ 106.)

drome is associated with another genetic trait that favours IQ. Alternatively, the exposure of the central nervous system to a flood of foetal androgen may in some way be beneficial to IQ.

The latter possibility is lent some credence by the findings in the case of progestin-induced hermaphroditism. Six of the 10 girls had an IQ above 130, the expected number in random sampling being 2 per 100.

Even allowing for the fact that the lower social and educational classes were not represented in this sample, it is difficult (though permissible) to explain away so many high IQs as an artifact of sampling or of chance. They may equally be a side-effect of progestin on the foetus, and this possibility should be further investigated (see [2]).

Discussion

The data presented suggest that there may well be a foetal hormonal effect on subsequent psychosexual differentiation. If so, it is limited in scope and does not induce anything approaching a complete psychosexual reversal in a genetic female. Rather, it bestows a special quality on behavioural development as a female. Though the juvenile age of many of the girls in the present study does not permit a definitive statement regarding dating, romance, and erotic object choice, there was no evidence of lesbianism among the older ones. Moreover, one does not find a prevalence of homosexuality among a large number of older and long-untreated adrenogenital female hermaphrodites. Psychosexual differentiation in the human must, evidently, be understood as a composite or end result of various component factors, and not as a single or global entity.

It is interesting to speculate on nature's plan of psychosexual differentiation as compared with morphologic sexual differentiation. There are two plans of morphologic differentiation. The one applies to the gonads and internal organs and represents the principle of development versus vestigiation of one of parallel pairs, the vestige always being residually in evidence, even though only in minute degree. The other applies to the external organs, the principle being a single anlage with homologous outcomes; there is no residual of an alternative organ, but differentiation may be incomplete and ambiguous in some cases.

It is possible that the different components of psychosexual differentiation follow in some cases the one, and in some cases the other principle. The over-all effect, however, seems to be more compatible with the first rather than the second principle—at least, if one judges from such phenomena as bisexuality and episodic transvestism. In these conditions, it is apparent that two separate psychosexual systems are each intact. When one comes to the fore, the other recedes, and vice versa, unless, perhaps, a time arrives when one stays suppressed for ever.

There is less cause for surprise in this duality than may at first appear, for the development of psychosexual identity after birth (and do not underestimate the potency of post-natal events) is not unlike the development of language in an infant exposed to bilingualism. In order to know what constitutes English vocally and linguistically, the bilingual infant has to discriminate what constitutes non-English, that is the other language, from English. Thus, the two language systems differentiate as entities, independent of one another. Analogously in the psychosexual differentiation of a child, the system of that which constitutes masculinity is, and should, become, one entity, discriminate from the system that constitutes femininity. Ordinarily, the two systems are not activated alongside one another. The one has positive valence and the other negative. The negative system, appropriate to the other sex, functions as a reminder, so to speak, of what not to do and how not to behave in order to be all boy, or conversely all girl. Theoretically, the important point here is that the negative or other-sex system, exists as a neurocognitional entity, albeit subliminal, so that it may, under specified developmental or experimental circumstance, be evoked and made operational.

Finally, and with respect to IQ, the findings of difference between the three groups indicate that one may use special diagnostic groups to study the relationship of genetics and foetal hormones to the development of the brain and intelligence. Further, these findings open new avenues for the investigation of sex differences in cognitional function and intelligence.

References

1. ALEXANDER, D. and MONEY, J. (1966). Turner's syndrome and Gerstmann's syndrome: neuropsychologic comparisons. *Neuropsychologia* **4**, 265–73.

†2. DALTON, K. (1968). Ante-natal progesterone and intelligence. *Brit. J. Psychiat.* **114**, 1377–85.

†3. EHRHARDT, A. A., EPSTEIN, R., and MONEY, J. (1968). Foetal androgens and female gender identity in the early-treated adrenogenital syndrome. *Johns Hopkins Med. J.* **122**, 160–7.

†4. —— EVERS, K., and MONEY, J. (1968). Influence of androgen and some aspects of sexually dimorphic behaviour in women with the late-treated adrenogenital syndrome. *Johns Hopkins Med. J.* **123**, 115–22.

5. —— and MONEY, J. (1967). Progestin-induced hermaphroditism: IQ and psychosexual identity in a study of 10 girls. *J. sex Res.* **3**, 83–100.

6. GORSKI, R. A. (1966). Localization and sexual differentiation of the nervous structures which regulate ovulation. *J. reprod. Fertil. Suppl.* **1**, 67–88.

7. JOST, A. (1961). The role of the foetal hormones in prenatal development, *Harvey Lect.* **55**, 201–26.

†8. LEWIS, V. G., MONEY, J., and EPSTEIN, R. (1968). Concordance of verbal and nonverbal ability in the adrenogenital syndrome. *Johns Hopkins Med. J.* **122**, 192–5.

9. MONEY, J. (1964). Two cytogenetic syndromes: psychologic comparisons. I. Intelligence and specific-factor quotients. *J. psychiat. Res.* **2**, 223–31.

10. —— (1965). Influence of hormones on sexual behaviour. *A. Rev. Med.* **16**, 67–82.

†11. —— EHRHARDT, A. A., and MASICA, D. (1968). Foetal feminization induced by androgen insensitivity in the testicular feminizing syndrome. Effect on marriage and materialism. *Johns Hopkins Med. J.* **123**, 105–14.

12. —— and LEWIS, V. (1965). IQ, genetics and accelerated growth: adrenogenital syndrome. *Bull. Johns Hopkins Hosp.* **118**, 365–73.

13. NEUMANN, F. and ELGER, W. (1965). Proof of the activity of androgenic agents on the differentiation of the external genitalia, the mammary gland and the hypothalamic-pituitary systems in rats. Excerpta Medica International Congress Series No. 101, Androgens in normal and pathological conditions. *Proceedings of the 2nd Symposium on steroid hormones, Ghent, 1965.*

14. —— and —— (1966). Permanent changes in gonadal function and sexual behaviour as a result of early feminization of male rats by treatment with an antiandrogenic steroid. *Endokrinologie* **50**, 209–25.

† References added by the editors, and published since 1967.

7 Effects of pre-natal progesterone

KATHARINA DALTON†

Introduction

Toxaemia of pregnancy remains the 'disease of theories' both in respect of its causation and treatment. Among the many treatments suggested, although not generally accepted, is the administration of progesterone from the middle trimester for the relief of toxaemic symptoms [1, 2, 3]. An unexpected finding has been the clinical observation that children of progesterone-treated mothers appear to reach their milestones earlier and to make excellent progress at school.

Pilot study in educational ability

To determine whether children whose mothers had received ante-natal progesterone (progesterone children) had thereby acquired any educational advantage over normal children, a pilot study was undertaken. Thirty-two progesterone children, aged 6 to 13 years, were matched with an equal number of controls, whose mothers had attended the practice for antenatal care and were healthy throughout pregnancy. Controls were matched for age, social class, and parity. Head teachers were given an unannotated list of 64 children and asked to grade each child's intelligence as 'above average', 'average', and 'below aver-

† From 'Ante-natal progesterone and intelligence'. *Brit. J. Psychiat.* **114**, 1377–82 (1968). Reprinted by permission of the author and the Editor of the *British Journal of Psychiatry*.

age'. They assessed 55 per cent of progesterone children as being above average intelligence compared with 41 per cent of the control children, which confirmed the clinical observation of the intellectual advantage of progesterone children.

Design for follow-up of progesterone children

The successful pilot study was followed by a larger survey of progesterone children, with testing, (a) at the first birthday, when the milestones could most easily be determined, and (b) at the ages of 9 and 10 years, when school tests in preparation for the Eleven Plus examinations were being made. For this survey, the names of progesterone children and controls were obtained from hospital registers; of the 262 children participating only seven were known to the author (progesterone five, control two). Assessments of development and intellectual ability were made by doctors, health visitors, and head teachers, who were unaware of the category of the child. The progesterone had been administered to the mothers by intramuscular injections in dosages varying from 50 to 300 mg daily for the relief of toxaemic symptoms.

Method of follow-up at first birthday

The subjects were the children of mothers included in a previous study entitled, 'Controlled trials in the prophylactic use of progesterone in the treatment of pre-eclamptic toxaemia' [3]. The mothers had been allocated to the progesterone or control treatment group by random envelope method between the 16th and 28th week of pregnancy. At the child's first birthday, the clinic doctor completed a prepared questionnaire, or if the child did not attend a health visitor completed the questionnaire in the home. All mothers cooperated and questionnaires were completed within three weeks of the first birthday.

Only 29 of the 64 progesterone children and 31 of the 66 control children were traced, but Table 7.1

TABLE 7.1. *Characteristics of Groups in Follow-up at One Year*

	Progesterone	Control
Number of children	29	31
	per cent	per cent
Boys	45	45
Birth weight		
Under 6 lb	14	6
6–7 lb	55	55
8 lb and over	31	39
Immunization schedule		
completed	65	61

shows that the characteristics of the two groups of children were similar in sex distribution, birth weight, and immunization schedule. The traced children were a representative sample of the original 130 children in respect of sex and birth weight. The failure to trace the children appeared to be due to adoption, moving from the area without leaving an address, and residence at the local gipsy encampment.

Method of educational follow-up

Children studied were those whose mothers were included in the report

'Toxaemia of pregnancy treated with progesterone during the symptomatic stage' [2]. The 44 progesterone children were each matched to two controls:

1. The next born child in the labour ward register whose mother had a normal pregnancy and delivery (normal control);
2. The next child to be delivered from a mother who developed toxaemia (toxaemic control).

Toxaemia was defined as a blood pressure of 140/90 mm Hg or over together with either oedema or albuminaria after the 28th week and before the onset of labour, provided that prior to the 28th week the blood pressure had always been below 140/90 mm Hg and there had been no albuminaria.

All mothers were sent a letter asking permission for an education assessment from the child's head teacher. The head teacher was asked to complete a form stating whether the named child was 'above', 'average', or 'below' standard in verbal reasoning, English, arithmetic, craftwork (practical ability), and physical education (co-ordination of movement and muscular control).

Of the 132 children under review educational assessments were received from 76 teachers in respect of 79 children (progesterone 29, normal controls 21, toxaemic controls 29). A further 15 children (5 from each group) were traced, but no educational assessment was possible (left U.K. 7, not registered with N.H.S. doctor so recent address unknown 3, died 2, adopted 1, permission refused 1, and 1 child remained at the named school for only 3 weeks). Thirty-eight children (29 per cent) have remained untraced in spite of every effort by the General Register Office and the co-operation of the Ministry of Health. Two progesterone children had in-complete assessments, one was not graded for verbal reasoning and another for craftwork. One child (toxaemic control) is mentally re-tarded.

Table 7.2 shows the characteristics

TABLE 7.2. *Characteristics of the Groups in the Educational Follow-up*

	Progesterone	Control
Number of children	29 †	50
	per cent	per cent
Mother's age		
Under 25 years	29	50
26–35 years	42	40
36 and over	29	10
Parity		
1	29	58
2 and 3	68	38
4 and over	3	4
Previous abortions	32	2
Birth weight		
Less than 5 lb	7	2
5–7 lb	65	74
8 lb and over	28	12
Boys	62	58

† Including a set of twins.

of the group, the progesterone mothers tend to be older and of higher parity, and progesterone children tend to be heavier than controls. The greatest discrepancy is in the significantly higher proportion of previous abor-tions suffered by the progesterone mothers, in fact 9 of the 28 mothers had experienced 15 previous abor-tions.

Results of developmental and educational follow-up

The attainments of 60 children at their first birthday are shown in Fig. 7.1.

There is a similarity in the two groups in the time of eruption of the first tooth, total number of teeth, and in talking ability, but significantly more progesterone children were able to stand unaided and walk unaided than control children, and more progester-one children were breast-fed until 6 months.

Analysis of the educational grading of 79 children aged 9 to 10 years revealed that the progesterone children received significantly more 'above average' grades than either the normal or toxaemic controls (Fig. 7.2). The better grades obtained by progesterone children exceeded that of the controls by 10 per cent in all subjects, 14 per cent in academic subjects, 13 per cent verbal reasoning, 11 per cent English, 14 per cent arithmetic and 10 per cent craftwork, and it is only in physical education that the progesterone chil-dren are similar to controls. These results are significant as shown by the chi-square test with one degree of freedom on two-tailed tests in respect of all subjects, academic subjects and arithmetic.

To determine whether progesterone could account for the advantages observed at the first birthday follow-up and in the educational follow-up, the progesterone children were divided into a 'high dosage' group, whose mothers received 8 g or over during pregnancy (e.g. 100 mg from 24th week to delivery), and 'low dosage' group, whose mothers received less than 8 g progesterone. Fig. 7.3 shows a progressive decrease in attainments, from the 'high dosage' group through the 'low dosage' group to the controls whose attainments were lowest. This decrease was observed in respect of (a) breast feeding at 6 months, (b) stand-ing and (c) walking at the first birth-

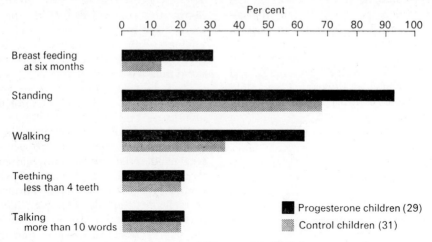

FIG. 7.1. Attainments of 60 children at first birthday examination.

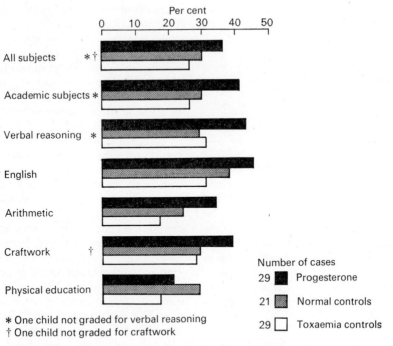

FIG. 7.2. Above average school grades of 79 children at 9–10 years.

day, and in the 'above average' grades of (d) all school subjects, (e) in academic subjects, (f) verbal reasoning, (g) English, and (h) arithmetic.

In the educational follow-up an analysis was made of the time in pregnancy when progesterone was first administered. A significant improvement in educational performance was demonstrated among children who received progesterone before the 16th week (Fig. 7.4). In respect of children studied at the first birthday a similar comparison was not possible as the mothers were not entered into the controlled trials until after the 16th week.

The questionnaire completed at the first birthday asked for information about genital development. No case of masculinization of the girls was noticed, but one boy in the progesterone group had small testes and in the control group two boys had undescended testes and three had neo-natal breast engorgement.

Discussion

Mammary development is dependent on endogenous progesterone. The exogenous progesterone administered to these mothers during pregnancy would be expected to further increase this development. This could account for more progesterone mothers breast-feeding at 6 months, and for the success at breast-feeding to be related to the dosage of progesterone administered.

Reifenstein [4] analysed 82 pregnancies treated with 17-α-hydroxy-progesterone caproate for habitual abortion and described the babies as 'tending to reach maturity more rapidly'. The progesterone children in this study are only ahead in standing and walking, but not in the other

milestones of teething and talking, suggesting a selective rather than general maturation. The educational follow-up suggests an intellectual advantage as opposed to increased physical ability.

No cases of masculinization occurred among the girls. Wilkins [5] reviewed 101 cases of masculinization but found only two girls who had received progesterone (as opposed to progestogens) whereas ten had received no hormone therapy at all.

Ehrhardt and Money [6] have described ten girls aged 3–14 years whose mothers had been treated with synthetic progestogens for the prevention of threatened abortion, in whom nine had evidence of hermaphroditism. They found a high IQ in six of them and a marked tendency to be tomboys. Gronroos *et al.* [7] and more recently Barker and Edwards [8] have shown that toxaemia in the mother is often associated with diminished intelligence in the child.

The first child's intelligence score may be expected to be the highest, with a progressive decline in subsequent children [8]. This educational survey included considerably less first children among the progesterone group (29 per cent) compared with control children (58 per cent), but nevertheless the intellectual advantage of the progesterone group was significant.

The progesterone mothers had a high incidence of previous abortions and it may be that the more intense maternal care given to a much-wanted child could account for the high incidence of breast-feeding and even the earlier development of activities (standing and walking) as opposed to teething and talking, but

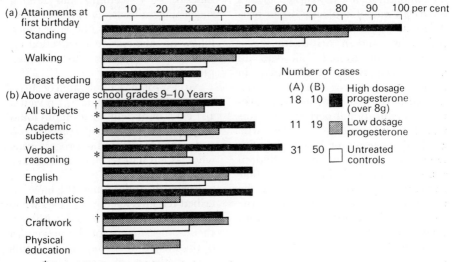

FIG. 7.3. Effect of high dosage progesterone on attainments.

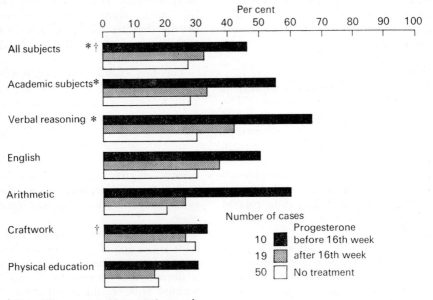

FIG. 7.4. Above average school grades and time of progesterone administration.

this would not account for better developmental and educational attainments being related to dosage or to the time of administration. The developmental attainments were further analysed for a relationship between breast and bottle feeding. The method of feeding could not account for the observed differences as 45 per cent of the 22 breast-fed children were walking compared with 46 per cent of the 37 bottle-fed; and again 86 per cent of breast-fed children were standing compared with 75 per cent of bottle fed.

It may be argued that this survey is incomplete. It is based on a clinician's observation of bright schoolchildren whose mothers had received progesterone during pregnancy. It is hoped that this paper will stimulate others to make a closer examination of the intelligence of further groups of progesterone children.

References

1. DALTON, K. (1954). Similarity of symptomatology of premenstrual syndrome and toxaemia of pregnancy and their response to progesterone. *Brit. med. J. ii*, 1071.
2. —— (1957). Toxaemia of pregnancy treated with progesterone during the symptomatic stage. *Brit. med. J. ii*, 378.
3. —— (1962). Controlled trials in the prophylactic value of progesterone in the treatment of pre-eclamptic toxaemia. *J. Obstet. Gynaec. Brit. Cwlth.* **69**, 465.
4. REIFENSTEIN, E. C. (1958). Clinical use of 17-α-hydroxy progesterone 17-n-caproate in habitual abortion. *Ann. New York Acad. Sci.* **71**, 762.
5. WILKINS, L. (1960). Masculinization of the female foetus due to the use of orally given progestogens. *J. Am. med. Ass.* **172**, 1028.
6. EHRHARDT, A. A. and MONEY, J. (1967). Progestogen-induced hermaphroditism: IQ and psychosexual identity in a study of ten girls. *J. Sex Res.* **3**, 1, 83.
7. GRONROOS, M., KIVIKOSKI, A., and RAURAMO, L. (1961). A comparative study of the obstetrical history of pupils in schools for backward children and elementary school pupils. *Acta obstet. gynaec. Scand.* **40**, 321.
8. BARKER, D. J. P. and EDWARDS, J. H. (1967). Obstetric complications and school performance. *Brit. med. J., ii*, 695.

Summary

A study has been made of 90 children whose mothers received ante-natal progesterone, compared with matched controls. More progesterone children were breast-fed at 6 months, more were standing and walking at one year, and at the age of 9–10 years the progesterone children received significantly better gradings than controls in academic subjects, verbal reasoning, English, arithmetic, craftwork, but showed only average gradings in physical education.

The developmental and intellectual advantages were all related to the dose of progesterone received by the mothers, those receiving over 8 g being related to earlier walking and standing and also better school gradings. The intellectual advantage was greatest in children whose mothers received progesterone before the 16th week of pregnancy.

III

Early brain mechanisms

USING nine indices of neural maturation, Conel ([3, 4]) † has shown that in comparison with the adult cerebral cortex, that of the human infant is grossly immature at birth, and remains thus for at least the first month of life. This has led some workers (see [1]) to describe the newborn infant as essentially 'pre-corticate'. The most mature cortical area at birth is the pre-motor cortex, in particular, the area which later controls movements of the upper trunk and limbs. The sensory receiving areas lag far behind and the frontal lobes show no visible development. From the age of 3 months, however, there is marked acceleration in the maturity of the sensory receiving areas, particularly of the visual cortex, which by 6 months begins to show many of the features of the adult brain ([5, 6]). Some development is also seen in the frontal area, particularly the mid-frontal gyrus, which is concerned with the control of eye movements.

Similarly, using myelination as their index, Yakovlev and Lecours [15] have shown that many of the structures of the subcortical forebrain only begin to mature after birth, often after the first month of life, even though in some areas (e.g. the optic tract and optic radiation) an adult complement of myelin is achieved by about the third month of life. In contrast, the brain stem and spinal cord are well developed at birth, which is to be expected, since most of the infant's life-preserving homeostatic mechanisms are regulated at this level.

We may thus loosely characterize the development of the central nervous system in the first year of life as the progressive maturation of structures at three different levels: brain stem, subcortical forebrain, and cortex. This somewhat over-simplified, but heuristically useful picture has been employed by Bronson (Chap. 8) to postulate three critical periods in early development, each defined by the particular level of neurological development attained by the infant at different ages. It seems reasonable to assume that the more a particular level of the brain approximates the degree of maturity seen in the adult, the more it is likely to sustain adult psychological functions. Conversely, the greater the immaturity of a particular

† Conel's six-volume neurohistology of the cerebral cortex presents a forbidding prospect to even the most dedicated neuroanatomist, and to the non-specialist it makes no concessions at all. Fortunately, a number of authors have attempted to write short, accessible paraphrases of Conel's work, one of the most recent being W. A. Marshall's excellent book: *The development of the brain.* Oliver and Boyd, Edinburgh (1970).

area, the less likely it is to be implicated in the mediation of a function with which it is associated in adulthood. Thus, the infant's capacity for selective attention, for learning, and for responsiveness to the effects of early stimulation will all be determined by the availability of particular neural networks at particular ages. Consideration of such structural changes will affect both our expectation as to the aspects of the environment to which the infant is responding and our interpretation of the mechanisms whereby he responds.

The relative dominance of brain-stem structures in the neo-natal period will have a number of implications. Firstly, the motor activity of the organism will be restricted to a number of circumscribed reflexive behaviours known to be integrated at a brain-stem level. Secondly, behaviour will be much more influenced by endogenous cyclic factors, or 'biological clocks' than at later ages.

Perhaps the most definitive evidence for the brain-stem organization of some behaviours is provided by studies of anencephalic babies. Monnier's (Chap. 9) short summary shows that the anencephalic's motor repertoire at birth is remarkably similar to that of normal babies. More recent studies of the sensory behaviour of such babies have added two further items of information: (1) that such babies manifest an optokinetic response [10]; (2) that they are capable of responding differentially to the *intensity* dimension of auditory stimuli [2]. These are important points to remember when considering the apparently sophisticated perceptual capacities of newborn infants (Part IV).

Many studies have shown that sensory or stimulus deprivation in early life has deleterious consequences upon development of the brain ([7, 8, 13]). How then does the human brain mature, normally adequately, during the time when the sense organs are immature and the baby spends at least 75 per cent of its time asleep? Roffwarg, Muzio, and Dement (Chap. 10) provide an answer in suggesting that the anatomical organization of the central nervous system is such that during rapid eye movement (REM) sleep much of the brain—particularly the occipital cortex and visual pathways—receive massive neural bombardment from the pontine reticular system. This suggestion goes far towards resolving yet another puzzle, namely the function of REM sleep in the human neonate, since REM sleep is associated with dreaming in adults. Roffwarg *et al.* suggest that in early life the function of REM sleep is to provide an endogenous source of neural excitation while the brain is 'off-line', so to speak. Since, with increasing age the provision of stimulation is fulfilled by experiences in the waking state, the proportion of REM sleep progressively decreases.

The clock-like behavioural rhythms of the human neonate were first systematically investigated by Wolff [14] who demonstrated that certain recurrent constellations of behavioural signs, which he termed *states*, followed each other in a consistent and predictable manner and appeared to be largely independent of external stimuli. Such states are almost certainly determined by slowly-changing metabolic processes. Wolff's work was restricted to behavioural observations but, subsequently, Prechtl [11] supplemented these with physiological parameters and made the definition of a 'state' more rigorous.

'State' is not a term with a well defined connotation, but is a concept used to describe a behaviour condition that: (1) is stable over a period of time; (2) occurs repeatedly in an individual infant; and (3) is encountered in similar forms in other individuals. Prechtl [11] differentiates five states:

State I: eyes closed, regular respiration, no movement, except sudden generalized startles;

State II: eyes closed, irregular respiration, small muscular twitches, no gross movements;

State III: eyes open, no gross movements;

State IV: eyes open, movements of head, limbs and trunk;

State V: crying.

This nomenclature is employed by Hutt *et al.* in their discussion of the state concept in Chapter 11.

One of the hazards of a failure to recognize the presence of biological clocks in the human neonate is that the data obtained in relation to a perfectly legitimate question about attention, perception, or memory, may be contaminated by changes in the state of the organism which are quite unrelated to the experimental variables being studied. The experimental paradigm upon which many psychologists operate assumes that there is a causal relationship between the stimulus presented and the response observed. Studies which have attempted to take state into account have shown that in the human newborn both the probability of response to a given stimulus and its magnitude are a function of the baby's state (Chap. 11). In fact, the observed behaviour may be obtained *despite* the presence of particular stimuli rather than *because* of them. For instance, when one observes that on repeated presentation of an auditory stimulus the baby passes from quiet wakefulness to REM sleep and eventually to non-REM sleep, it is tempting to suppose that it has 'habituated' to the stimulus. However, in studies of the effects of repetitive elicitation of monosynaptic and polysynaptic reflexes [12] and auditory stimulation [9], it was found that the mean duration of the various states in stimulated babies did not differ significantly from those observed in unstimulated babies [11]. Hutt, Lenard, and Prechtl stress the importance of taking account of state in all studies of so-called psychological processes in newborn infants, and challenge the interpretation of some psychological experiments in which state was not treated as an experimental variable.

References

1. BOUSFIELD, W. A. and ORBISON, W. D. (1952). Ontogenesis of emotional behavior. *Psychol. Rev.* **59**, 1–7.

2. BRACKBILL, Y. (1971). The role of the cortex in orienting: orienting reflex in an anencephalic human infant. *Dev. Psychol.* **5**, 195–201.

3. CONEL, J. L. (1939). *The post-natal development of the human cerebral cortex. I: Cortex of the newborn.* Harvard University Press, Cambridge, Mass.

4. —— (1941). *The post-natal development of the human cerebral cortex. II: Cortex of the one-month infant.* Harvard University Press, Cambridge, Mass.

5. —— (1947). *The post-natal development of the human cerebral cortex. III: Cortex of the three-month infant.* Harvard University Press, Cambridge, Mass.

6. —— (1951). *The post-natal development of the human cerebral cortex. IV: Cortex of the six-month infant.* Harvard University Press, Cambridge, Mass.

7. CRAGG, B. G. (1967). Changes in visual cortex on first exposure of rats to light. *Nature* **215**, 251–3.

8. HUBEL, D. H. and WIESEL, T. N. (1963). Receptive fields of cells in striate cortex of very young, visually inexperienced kittens. *J. Neurophysiol.* **26**, 994–1002.

9. HUTT, C., BERNUTH, H. VON, LENARD, H. G., HUTT, S. J., and PRECHTL, H. F. R. (1968). Habituation in relation to state in the human neonate. *Nature* **220**, No. 5167, 618–20.

10. JUNG, R. and HASSLER, R. (1960). The extra pyramidal system. *In* (Field, F. (Ed.)) *Handbook of physiology.* Vol. 2. Section 1, *Neurophysiology.* American Physiol. Soc., Washington D.C.

11. PRECHTL, H. F. R. (1968). Polygraphic studies of the full-term newborn infant, II. Computer analysis of recorded data. *In* (Bax, M. C. O. and MacKeith, R. C. (Eds.)) *Studies in Infancy. Clinics in developmental medicine No. 27.* Heinemann, London.

12. —— VLACH, V. LENARD, H. G., and KERR GRANT, D. (1967). Exteroceptive and tendon reflexes in various behavioural states in the newborn infant. *Biologia Neonat.* **11**, 159–75.

13. RIESEN, A. H. (1961). Stimulation as a requirement for growth and function in behavioural development. *In* (Fiske, D. W. and Maddi, S. R. (Eds.)) *Functions of varied experience.* Dorsey, Homewood, Ill.

14. WOLFF, P. H. (1959). States in newborn infants. *Psychosom. Med.* **21**, 110–18.

15. YAKOVLEV, P. I. and LECOURS, A.-R. (1967). The myelogenetic cycles of regional maturation of the brain. *In* (Minkowski, A. (Ed.)) *Regional development of the brain in early life.* Blackwell, Oxford.

8 Hierarchical organization of the central nervous system

GORDON BRONSON†

THE evolutionary history of man is reflected in the emergence of adaptive mechanisms of increasing complexity in the course of early development. This paper focuses on two of these ontogenetic sequences which seem of particular importance for understanding adult behaviour: 'critical-period' phenomena, and the development of learning capacities. Evidence is discussed defining three critical periods characterized by the relatively enduring consequences of the quality of stimulation experienced during these stages. Many data suggest that learning capacities of increasing complexity emerge with a chronology paralleling the development of these critical periods. An attempt is made to clarify and interrelate these two ontogenetic sequences by considering the behavioural data in light of evidence on the concurrent maturation of mediating neural systems.

The use of neurological evidence to clarify the meaning of behavioural data requires a conceptual model which focuses on aspects of nervous system functioning pertinent to the issues at hand. The first part of this paper presents such a neurological

† From 'The hierarchical organization of the central nervous system: implications for learning processes and critical periods in early development'. *Behavior. Sci.* **10**, No. 1, 7–25 (1965). Reprinted by permission of the author and the Editor of *Behavioral Science*. Copyright © 1965.

model. It emphasizes the hierarchical nature of central nervous system (CNS) organization in postulating a series of three 'levels' within the nervous system. More complex ('higher') levels are seen as a product of the evolution of successively more differentiating neural networks which in part supersede, and in part build upon, the less complex adaptive mechanisms mediated by the phylogenetically older levels. Ontogenetically, the emergence of new behavioural capacities is seen as a function of the sequential maturation of networks within the different levels.

The second part of the paper considers the different characteristics of learning phenomena mediated by networks at the three CNS levels. Differences in learning capacities are discussed in terms of varying degrees of perceptual and motor differentiation and, more significantly, in terms of the kinds of events which serve as adequate 'reinforcement' for learning mediated by neural systems of the different levels. This leads to the proposal of a rough developmental chronology of learning from classical conditioning, through instrumental learning, to latent learning phenomena, a sequence which parallels the maturation through early infancy of neural networks of increasing cognitive and motivational differentiation. The adult organism, it is assumed, may acquire

information under any of these paradigms, depending upon the circumstances of acquisition.

The final part of the paper attempts
to interpret evidence from studies of
critical-period phenomena in light of

which are of behavioural relevance.
In a few instances where neurological
evidence is lacking, inferences from
behavioural observations are tentatively introduced to complete the
model.

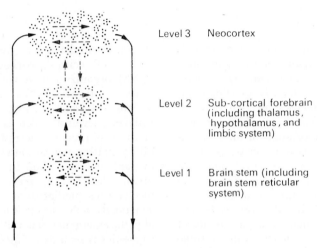

Level 3   Neocortex

Level 2   Sub-cortical forebrain
(including thalamus,
hypothalamus, and
limbic system)

Level 1   Brain stem (including
brain stem reticular
system)

Fig. 8.1. Basic characteristics of a hierarchical model of CNS functioning.

the postulated theory of the emergence
of learning capacities. Three major
critical periods in early development
are suggested, each defined by a
shifting saliency of different environmental events, and each related to the
emergence of more complex learning capacities. Neurologically, each
critical period is seen as beginning
with the maturation of neural systems
of a given CNS level and terminating
through several possible mechanisms,
including functional inhibition im-
imposed by subsequent maturation of
higher-level networks.

The neurological model, which
sections an integrated nervous system
into 'levels' is, of course, a heuristic
device. Some degree of neurological
accuracy is necessarily sacrificed in the
interest of presenting general patterns

Hierarchical model of CNS functioning

The conceptual model

Fig. 8.1 represents the basic characteristics of the model. A gross dichotomy
is made between neural tissue which
consists of networks of short axon
neurons with multiple interconnec-
tions (stippled areas of Fig. 8.1) and
the systems of long axon neurons which
interconnect these areas (broken lines).
These latter systems are found both
within levels (horizontal broken lines)
and between levels of the CNS
(vertical broken lines); they constitute
an innate programming system channelling the flow of excitation patterns
among the areas of short axon networks. Peripheral afferents and
efferents (solid lines) connect with the

CNS at the several levels so that increasingly refined sensory and motor discriminations can be made directly by the successively more differentiating networks. The networks for vertical integration between levels enable the more primitive systems to exercise an upward control for the general programming of patterns of cerebral activation, while higher levels projecting downward effect a more highly differentiated over-all functioning through tonic inhibition plus a more selective phasic excitation and inhibition of lower-level systems. (References documenting the general functional characteristics encompassed by the model are presented below, as each level is considered in detail.) Finally, note that the increasing diversity of stippled areas within successive levels of Fig. 1 represents the increasingly differentiated character of higher-level CNS networks.† This evolutionary refinement brings an increasing development of specialized functions among the short axon networks of the higher levels.

Input into all levels is both from peripheral afferents and from connections from other areas in the CNS; activity in levels 1 and 2 is also strongly affected by changes in the internal chemical environment. Information resulting from the interplay of these factors at level 1, projected upward to primary sensory and motor areas within the neocortex, affects the general (tonic) level of sensory alertness and motor responsiveness. Similarly, networks within level 2 integrate input from various sources

and project output to level 3, modulating the more varied (phasic) activation patterns in 'association' areas of the neocortex to effect a more focal alertness to particular stimulus patterns [60]. Since the networks within levels 1 and 2 include areas particularly responsive to internal biochemical changes, the more discriminative neocortical processes are partially affected by, and therefore adaptive to, the physiological condition of the organism.

Functions mediated by the various levels

Turning to a more specific consideration of structures incorporated within each of the three levels of Fig. 8.1, it is possible to specify further the functional capacities of the various levels. While the generalizations to follow at times require some qualification, the exceptions are not crucial to the main arguments of the paper.

Level 1 networks. The phylogenetic primacy of brain-stem networks of level 1 is reflected in the gross motor functions mediated at this level. The brain-stem reticular system and the various motor nuclei of this level constitute a system for co-ordinating gross body movement; for example, innate mechanisms for bilateral co-ordination of head, eyes, and trunk, producing orienting responses to tactile and vestibular, visual, and auditory stimuli, are mediated at this level (i.e. postural reflexes, the optokinetic reflex, and auditory orienting reflexes). Present also are more discrete stimulus-response systems such as the

---

† Since the neocortex is anatomically continuous, the model at this point reflects the functional rather than the gross structural properties of the neocortex. As excitation spreads minimally, and only from activated

cortex, and in normal functioning activation is discretely patterned by thalamocortical circuits, from a functional perspective the short axon networks of the neocortex are best represented by numerous rather discrete areas.

sucking reflex, rooting reflex, pupillary reflex, etc. [34]. Brain-stem response patterns are representative of the total behaviour repertoire of simple vertebrates; in man they either provide the background pattern for support of the more differentiated motor responses controlled from higher neural systems [34], or in the case of more discrete reflexes they may disappear shortly after birth under inhibition from neocortical networks [41].

Berlyne [5] has surveyed the extensive data refining an 'orientation reaction' mediated by networks of this level. It consists of a complex of responses including: orienting of receptor organs (e.g. turning of head, eyes, and ears); a general skeletal response (arrest of ongoing actions, increase of muscle tonus); autonomic system reactions preparatory for action; changes in receptor organs (e.g. pupil dilation); and an EEG arousal reaction. Its adaptive function in providing a poised alertness to external stimuli is clearly evident. The nature of the adequate sensory stimulus depends on the level of sensory development of the organism. Sharpless and Jasper [62], working with cats, have demonstrated that brain-stem preparations respond to changes in mode or intensity of stimuli but not to variations of pattern within modes, showing that direct sensory mediation at this level is possible, but that sensory discrimination is severely limited. Berlyne presents data from Russian investigators indicating that the acquired 'signal value' of a complex stimulus can influence its saliency in producing an orienting response in humans, a mechanism which must involve the downward control of level-1 processes by perceptual systems of the neocortical level. Congruent

with this are neurological studies showing that direct electrical stimulation of the sensory areas within the neocortex can produce orienting responses [70].

Berlyne further describes a 'defensive reaction' which apparently can also be mediated by the brain-stem level. It consists of a constellation of responses, largely overlapping with the orienting responses but including 'freezing', 'blinking', 'gasps', and some variations in the reaction pattern within the autonomic system. He notes very intense stimuli, and pain, as being capable of producing this defensive reaction. In addition, the many studies of the conditioning of complex stimuli, using some form of pain as the unconditioned stimulus, demonstrate that the defensive reaction, like the orienting reaction, can follow from neocortically mediated perceptual patterns, as well as from direct level 1 sensory input.

Turning to processes of vertical integration with higher levels of the CNS, the reticular network of level 1 appears as a neocortical activating system. Diffusely projecting afferents to the neocortex affect the general level of neocortical activation, a mechanism influencing over-all sensory and motor responsiveness. In addition to mediating diurnal variations in sensory alertness and motor activity, this level 1 mechanism appears capable of overriding the more focal activation of limited cortical areas controlled by the thalamic reticular system, which is a level-2 mechanism underlying focused-attention phenomena (see [39], and below). This capacity appears to be a protective device for superseding level-2 mechanisms for focused attention, thereby producing a condition of over-all alertness in situations of potential danger. This alerting response is a component of both the orientation and defensive reactions discussed above.

The reticular system is known to be responsive to the level of nutrients in the blood, to various sex hormones, and to adrenalin. Decreases in the first and increases in the latter two factors heighten reticular activity [18]. With regard to peripheral input, the reticular system receives direct afferents from all sensory modalities, but pain and proprioceptor inputs are known to be particularly salient [60], and it is known also to be richly endowed with afferents from sexual organs [25]. The limited capacity for within-mode discrimination of afferent patterns by level-1 networks has been noted above. Downward control of reticular activity is present from many areas of the neocortex, but most particularly from the superior temporal, cingulate, and hippocampal gyrii, areas involved in memory and emotion [60]. Such control can effect a more discriminative reticular functioning through the selective excitation and inhibition of reticular networks by neocortical centres, following the recognition of significant objects.

It seems probable, as Berlyne [5] has suggested, that continued level 1 activation of the higher CNS levels can produce two different orientations in the intact mammal, depending on the intensity of the reticular system excitation. Moderate excitation, initially producing the transient orientation reaction, leads to exploratory investigation until terminated by familiarity with the stimulus object (habituation). This approach orientation, occurring under moderate degrees of level-1 excitation, presumably allows for the subsequent narrowing of attention to specific sensory modes as level-2 attention mechanisms resume control of neocortical activation patterns following the waning of the initial generalized alerting response. More intense reticular activation would produce an initial defensive reaction, followed by innate or acquired fear reactions, and terminated either by escape from the arousing stimuli, or by habituation to a level inducing exploration rather than fear [5, 69]. Response sequences in infant monkeys presented with novel stimuli [27], illustrate this latter phenomenon very clearly: the initial fear reaction of clinging to the (surrogate) mother decreases with visual examination, and is gradually replaced by approach and close investigation. These extensions of brief level-1 orientation and defensive reactions into more enduring exploratory or fear orientations under the control of higher-level perceptual processes will be discussed further below. (With regard to complex human functioning, it may be noted that since the individual need not be aware of stimuli producing intense activation of reticular networks [e.g. chemical factors in the blood; in the 'subception' phenomenon of 'perceptual defense' studies, and perhaps also in cases of clinically observed chronically repressed disturbing ideation], it would seem probable that in some situations innocent objects may become the focus of escape or attack behaviour. In circumstances where the environment fails to provide any adequate sensory support for the subsequent focusing of the defensive reaction, continued intense reticular activation could lead to the generalized irritability or diffuse anxiety which characterizes certain neurotic syndromes.)

Level 2 networks. While the highly complex networks interconnecting subcortical areas within the mammalian forebrain (level 2, Fig. 8.1) are not well understood, a general description of the functions supported by networks at this level is possible. For purposes of analysis the networks of level 2 can be classified as providing: (1) more refined sensory discrimination and motor co-ordination; (2) specific motivational and/or emotional orientations supporting ongoing purposive behaviour sequences; and (3) mechanisms for the control of attention. It is the latter two aspects of level-2 systems which are of the greatest interest here. (In man the level-2 networks for motor co-ordination—the corpus striatum, pallidium, and parts of the thalamus and subthalamus—function as higher integrating mechanisms within the extrapyramidal system. With loss of sensory or motor areas of the neocortex, subcortical areas can provide gross motor control over limbs and facial expression, particularly in conditions of high motivation [19], and rough location of somatosensory stimulation [25]. Without level-3 mediation, auditory and visual experiences are entirely lost in man, although this is not true for all mammals [45].

The motivational networks within level 2, which act to initiate and support diverse purposive orientations to the environment, are responsive (1) to changes in the internal chemical environment and probably (2) to direct input from pain and sexual afferents, and (3) are influenced also by complex auditory and visual perceptions mediated by way of neo-cortical systems. Within the hypothalamus are excitatory and inhibitory nuclei, responsive to internal nutritive and saline concentrations, which on stimulation activate or inhibit eating and drinking, as well as areas whose stimulation or ablation increases or inhibits sexual or aggressive behaviour [65], and which presumably are responsive to particular hormones. Peripheral pain and sexual sensations are conducted via the spinothalamic tract which, in contrast to pathways for other tactile sensations, has extensive collaterals to the brain-stem and particularly to thalamic areas outside of the primary neocortical relay nuclei [25]. Complex auditory and visual patterns of acquired motivational significance must, in man, involve downward activation from gnostic areas of the neocortex [36, 52]. Morgan [46] reviews animal studies which support the common experience that motivational networks can be activated by diverse types of stimulation: internal biochemical changes, direct level-2 afferents, and projections from neocortical networks. The complex networks of the limbic system which interconnect areas responsive to the internal environment (i.e. the hypothalamus) and to direct pain and sexual afferents (parts of the thalamus) with pathways from the neocortex (probably via the paleocortex), would appear to be central in the integration of diverse types of motivationally significant stimuli. For reviews of the varied and extensive motivational effects of ablation or excitation of different areas of the limbic system, see [49] and [65]. In addition to motivational functions, the limbic system is central to the mediation of emotional behaviour. Fear or rage reactions are the most frequent emotions reported in animal studies; however, when verbal report is possible human subjects indicate pleasant as well as unpleasant mood changes following diverse limbic system lesions, giving support to the contention of Olds and Olds [50] that stimulation in numerous limbic loci are 'pleasurable' to animals. For a review of studies of emotional functions of the limbic system, see [9].

The attention-mediating function of level-2 systems in mammals involves the vertical feedback networks between nuclei of the thalamic reticular system and various areas of the neocortex. In contrast with the global alerting capacity of brain-stem activation of the neocortex, the more rapidly fluctuating and more focal alerting mechanisms of the thalamic reticular system allow for the focus of attention to specific sensory modes, and probably to particular input patterns within modes. These diffusely projecting thalamic nuclei activate primarily parietal, occipital, and temporal areas adjacent to the various primary sensory-reception areas. As these cortical areas serve gnostic functions, the control which the neocortex exerts over the thalamic reticular system enables the neocortex to control partially its own excitation level for the selective attention to significant aspects of the contemporary input. For a review of evidence on this, see [60]. Neurological data on the functional relations between these attention mechanisms and networks underlying motivational orientation is lacking. Behavioural evidence to be discussed below indicates, however, that in circumstances where a specific motivational system is not dominant attention is guided by perceptual novelty rather than towards 'needs-relevant' objects, and the more flexible cognitive and motor activities associated with exploratory behaviour will appear.

Level-3 networks. For present purposes only a limited discussion of the contributions of level-3 systems is necessary. The highly developed perceptual, cognitive, and motor capacities of the neocortex need no review, and the role of these perceptual and motor capacities in initiating and supporting exploratory or fear reactions has been noted in discussing level-1-networks. Welker [69] notes that exploratory behaviour is more prominent in species with fewer inborn responses to specific stimulus patterns, and also that the dominant sensory mode for exploratory investigation relates to the relative degree of development of various sensory areas of the neocortex in the different species; these facts illuminate the major role of neocortical systems in the instigation and orientation of exploratory behaviour. Studies by Krechevsky [37], showing a decrease in the variability in maze behaviour proportional to the amount of neocortical damage in rats, as well as the 'lethargic' behaviour found in totally decorticate cats [3] and monkeys [68], also demonstrate the importance of neocortical processes in supporting an exploratory orientation in mammals. Situations in which neocortically mediated perceptions maintain alertness through a tonic excitation of lower-level networks will be discussed further in later sections.

The hierarchical organization of adaptive mechanisms

One of the consequences of the evolutionary development of the nervous system is what appears as a repetition of the various adaptive mechanisms, with refinements, at successive levels of the CNS. The increasingly differentiating sensory and motor mechanisms found at successively newer levels of the CNS is a well-known example; others of equal importance seem less noted and therefore call for further discussion. The interest of this hierarchical organization lies both in the sequential appearance of successively more refined adaptive mechanisms in early human development, and in the later complex interactions among systems of different levels serving analogous functions but with different degrees of complexity.

The hierarchy of learning mechanisms, a major focus of this paper, is considered in detail in a later section. For the moment consider what may be loosely called a 'motivational' hierarchy. Dell [18] notes that increases in physiological needs which affect the internal environment (food, drink, sex, etc.) produce cyclical periods of heightened activity. These periodic increases in 'appetitive' behaviour have phenotypical characteristics of exploratory behaviour, but are distinguished in the terminology of this paper (1) by being primarily instigated by internal factors rather than by perceptual novelty; and (2) in being oriented towards, and terminated by, particular stimulus patterns associated with the appropriate consummatory activity. Also, the 'exploratory' components of appetitive behaviour will disappear as the animal learns more about the location of appropriate consummatory stimuli within its environment. Neural tissue sensitive to changes in the internal environment is found both in the reticular system of level 1 and in the hypothalamus within level 2. While both levels are sensitive to the same range of biochemical factors, present evidence indicates that the hypothalamus is more differentiated (1) in having discrete nuclei specifically responsive to particular biochemical changes, and (2) in producing behaviour sequences oriented towards various specific goals following the activation of localized hypothalamic areas. Stellar [65] reviews evidence showing that electrical or chemical stimulation of discrete hypothalamic areas selectively influences eating, drinking, or sexual activities; stimulation of the reticular system apparently affects only the general level of sensory alertness and motor activity [60]. It seems reasonable, therefore, to speak of a hierarchy of motivational systems: continued excitation of level-1 systems, in the absence of specific hypothalamic activity, produces flexible exploratory behaviour oriented towards perceptual novelty; the additional activation of level-2 motivational systems brings a channelling of behaviour towards specific goals. This is illustrated by Bruner, Matter, and Papanek [12], who find less 'trial-and-error' behaviour in the maze as hunger drive is increased in rats, as well as less incidental learning of non-essential cues. (See [69] for a review of other pertinent studies.) Some types of stimuli seem to activate motivational systems at both levels, i.e. internal biochemical changes can produce both the 'exploratory' components of appetitive behaviour (from level-1 activation) and the perceptual sensitivities to particular goal-related objects (associated with level-2 excitation). Other stimuli seem to activate primarily level-1 motivational systems, as when perceptual novelty brings the heightened alertness basic to exploratory behaviour. Perception of goal-relevant objects (e.g. food, sex partner) will activate level-2 motivational systems when internal biochemical factors are sufficiently close to 'threshold' values. (It is tempting to complete this motivational hierarchy by suggesting that in man neocortical networks have assumed motivational functions beyond the purely perceptual roles mentioned above. It seems likely that cognitive processes relatively independent of the immediate perceptual environment can maintain an alert purposive orientation through the continuous activation of levels-1 networks. The Gestalt studies of perseverance towards the completion of interrupted tasks and the desire for cognitive closure, as well as Allport's [1] early concept of 'functional autonomy', and Miller, Galanter, and Pribram's [43] recent emphasis on the major importance of acquired 'images' and 'plans' in guiding purposive behaviour, all call attention to the characteristically human capacity for maintaining, or returning to, a complex programme of flexible goal-oriented behaviour which is independent of immediate environmental stimulation, and remote from any recognized physiological need. Current theories of 'derived motives' (psychoanalysis) or 'secondary drives' (learning theories) perhaps place too exclusive an emphasis on phylogenetically older motivational systems which are activated by biochemical changes and maintained primarily by subcortical systems. In Freudian terms, ego 'energies' are not necessarily derived only from neutralized libido.)

One final pair of hierarchical systems needs brief discussion here: the development of the transient orientation and defensive reactions into the more enduring exploratory or fear orientations in circumstances where neocortically mediated perception maintains reticular system activity. Since reticular system activity is responsive only to changes in the mode or the intensity of the direct level-1 sensory input, and habituation is fairly rapid, the orientation reaction will be of relatively brief duration in any reasonably stable environment. With the addition of downward activation from perceptual systems of the neocortex, the pattern variability present in the normal environment becomes an adequate stimulus for maintaining a degree of level-1 reticular system activation sufficient for an alert interest in the environment. In conditions of moderate perceptual novelty, this interest outward is manifest in exploratory behaviour. The development of aversive response patterns, from the brief defensive reaction mediated directly at level 1 by intense stimulation or pain, to the more enduring fear orientation in response to complex stimulus patterns of extreme novelty, is more complicated. In the many species showing innate fearfulness in response to perceptual novelty, this reaction develops somewhat later than the capacity for complex pattern discrimination—a chronology often described as allowing time for the development of primary attachments (see section on critical periods, below). Fearfulness in response to novelty, therefore, either requires more extensive visual experience than does object recognition, or is dependent upon still further maturation within the CNS. Analysing Riesen's [56] data on the subsequent development of chimpanzees reared from birth to seven months in diffuse (unpatterned) light, it appears that in these animals the fear of strange objects appeared at about the same time as, or even before, clear evidence of visual recognition. This would indicate that maturational processes, which would normally occur subsequent to neocortically mediated object recognition, initiate the fear of strangeness. The maturation may be within any of the several areas within the limbic system known to be involved in fear behaviour [9, 24], but no direct data are available on maturational rates within these networks. If this is the case, the development in infancy from the brief defensive reaction to the more complex and enduring fear orientation is dependent on maturational processes within both level 2 and level 3.

The emergence of the more refined mechanisms within each of these adaptive hierarchies can be observed in early human development. Studies of the maturation of the human CNS [15, 16] indicate that for about the first month after birth neocortical systems are essentially nonfunctional. The behaviour repertoire during this first month is limited to functions noted above as capable of level-1 mediation [54]: adaptive motor patterns are reflexive and have been observed in anencephalitic infants in the same form as in normal neonates [34]; apart from specific reflexes, sensitivity to peripheral stimulation is limited to changes in intensity of input and to pain, with no clear evidence of pattern discrimination. (Data which give some indication of preferential fixation to different visual patterns during the first week of primate life [20] can be a product of intensity discrimination mediated at the retinal level [59]; visual following, a response to spatio-temporal intensity changes,

has been demonstrated in decorticate animals [63] as well as in anencephalitic infants [34] and can therefore be classified as a subcortically mediated reflex.)

In brief, the sensory and motor capabilities of the neonate reflect the differentiating capacities of level-1 systems. Analyses of the early development of 'emotional' capacities limit the neonate to a 'quiet-excitement' continuum [33], a behavioural range which can be mediated by changes in level-1 reticular activity. In the present terminology, this earliest 'emotional' range corresponds to the undifferentiated 'motivational' system of the brain stem organism. Furthermore, the range of stimuli influencing this infant motivational system (internal biochemical changes, sudden intense stimuli, and internal or external pain) is identical to the input sensitivities of level-1 networks. Since the non-specific nature of this primitive motivational state produces no behavioural cue as to the nature of the arousing stimuli [33], when not guided by additional information (i.e. hours since last feeding, etc.), the parent must adopt a trial-and-error approach to reducing the excitatory stimulus.

Conel's [17] histological studies show rapid neocortical maturation beginning in the second and third months. This period is marked by behavioural developments which require neocortical mediation, indicating that level-3 systems are maturing to functional levels. (For an analysis of the sequence of maturation among neocortical systems, see [11].) Perceptual and motor capacities now reflect neocortical mediation: the appearance of smiling in response to visual stimuli in the second month [2] is evidence of the achievement of pattern discrimination and recognition; in the motor area McGraw [41] documents the inhibition of reflexive responses as voluntary neocortical control brings greater flexibility to motor patterns. Various authors observing early 'emotional' development [33] give various terms to the emerging patterns, but all agree that the undifferentiated continuum of the newborn expands to a growing spectrum of emotional states beginning at about the second month. Assuming that emotional expression relates to the gratification or frustration of various motivational orientations, this expanding repertoire must reflect an increased motivational differentiation, as well as increased cognitive capabilities. While no neurological evidence on maturation rates within level 2 is available, studies referred to earlier show that level-2 networks are basic to the mediation of emotional and motivational processes. It seems reasonable that networks at this level, maturing along with neocortical systems, underlie this increasingly differentiated range of affective and motivational orientations.

The emergence of more refined adaptive mechanisms can also be seen in the transition from the transient orienting reaction of the newborn to the more enduring exploratory interest of the 3-month infant. As neocortical perceptual systems mature the complex of brief orienting responses present at birth [54] is extended to include reactions to neocortically mediated perceptions, producing a more enduring and more flexible exploratory interest in the environment. Piaget [53] and Bühler [13] mark the second month as the beginning of active visual interest in the environment, with the first overt

exploratory behaviour appearing around three months [53]. This development is reflected also in Kleitman and Engelmann's [35] studies of infants' sleep patterns. During the first month the infant is only briefly awake except when alerted by factors directly affecting level-1 systems (i.e. nutritional deficiencies, sudden intense stimulation, or pain). By around three months, there are appreciable periods of daytime wakefulness, with little change in the amount of night-time sleep. This daytime alertness is presumably maintained by the novelty of the perceptual environment. A similar development of increasingly complex aversive reactions can be seen in the early months of infant development. The initial defensive reaction to intense stimuli or pain is extended by neocortical mediation (and probably also by maturation of level-2 networks) to include more complex fear reactions to patterned stimuli. These developments bring the capacity for acquiring fears of specific objects in the environment, as well as an innate fear of perceptual strangeness. In all of these adaptive hierarchies—sensory-motor, motivational, attentive, and aversive—more refined mechanisms effect a more discriminating and more flexible functioning as higher-level systems add to the complexity of existing systems. Less emphasized in the above analysis are instances where phylogenetically newer systems supersede, rather than build upon and extend, the more primitive mechanisms. The inhibitory function of the neocortex in replacing the reflexive adaptations of the neonate with voluntary motor control is a well-documented example of this [41, 66].

Before proceeding to the consideration of learning phenomena, it will be helpful to review some general characteristics of the CNS functioning which emerge from the material presented so far. Three mechanisms are hypothesized to account for the increasingly complex behaviour patterns accompanying the development of the forebrain.

(1) Networks of higher levels are increasingly discriminative: capacities for sensory discrimination increase at successive levels; reactions to internal biochemical changes become more differentiated; and motor control is more complex at higher levels.

(2) Capacity for complex behaviour is also increased as downward control from newer systems extends and refines the responsiveness of lower-level networks through the selective excitation and inhibition of functional systems within the lower levels. Examples of this process of 'encephalization' are found in the neocortical activation of motivational networks at level-2 in response to learned visual and auditory patterns, and on the motor side, in the sequences of selective excitation and inhibition of reflexive motor systems within the brain-stem to give postural support for complex voluntary activity.

(3) Upward projection from integrative processes at lower levels modulates the activation levels of various neocortical systems, utilizing information from the integrative activities within lower levels for the general programming of complex level-3 capacities. Examples of this upward control are brain-stem modulation of over-all neocortical activation, affecting the general level of alertness in response to gross characteristics of the internal and external environment, and the more specific modulation of attention and

motivational orientations by subcortical forebrain networks capable of more limited activation of discrete systems within the neocortex.

The latter two processes of vertical integration will emerge as positive feedback networks in those instances where mutual facilitation occurs between two systems at different levels, i.e. systems activated by internal stimuli at level 2 will sensitize perceptual networks of the neocortex (level 3) towards relevant stimuli; such percepts will in turn further activate the level-2 motivational network.

(It is interesting to note that the integrative processes of successive levels of the CNS appear to contribute increasingly complex qualities of consciousness. Brain-stem activation mediates general alertness and probably also constitutes a basis for experiences of heightened tension and diffuse anxiety; motivational networks of level 2 appear to contribute more specific affective states which can be distinguished by quality as well as intensity; neocortical systems add awareness of pattern, giving ideational content to conscious experience. Since the model postulates multiple determinants for activation of various subcortical networks, the contemporary content of experience may or may not be the major determinant of the affective context in which it occurs.)

Hierarchy of learning processes

The conceptual model of the CNS presented above assumes that integrative processes occur within areas of multiply-interconnected short axon neurons (stippled areas of Fig. 8.1). These processes consist of interactions among various inhibitory and excitatory inputs coming from other parts of the nervous system, from peripheral afferents, and/or from changes in the internal chemical environment. The nature of input to which an area is responsive, and the qualities of innate structure within the area, in part determine the particular characteristics of the integrative processes occurring in the various areas. In addition, it seems a reasonable assumption that the integrative activities themselves produce internal structural changes which also affect the subsequent activation patterns within most, if not all, of these areas. Those changes in subsequent activation patterns which are relatively enduring underlie behavioural phenomena which would be included in a broad definition of learning.

A corollary to the hypothesis that the structural changes underlying learning can be found within integrative networks of all levels is the probability that differences in the complexity of the integrative processes of different levels are associated with behavioural evidence defining different kinds of learning. Within the broad conception of learning presented above are included habituation, classical conditioning, instrumental learning (including 'trial-and-error' learning and operant conditioning), and latent learning phenomena. Habituation, while it is recognized as ubiquitous through all levels of CNS and appears at times to be more than a transient effect [5, 29, 62], will be considered mainly in contrast to the remaining three learning processes. These latter classifications, developed as paradigms for the experimental study of learning processes, will be shown to fit well into the hierarchical conception of CNS functioning described earlier.

Two characteristics are proposed as distinguishing the quality of learning phenomena occurring through mediation by different levels of the nervous system. Most evident is the degree of sensory and motor differentiation involved: the increased capacities of the higher levels for perceptual differentiation and integration, and for complex motor control, allow for increasingly complex learning phenomena. (Differences in discriminative capacities when input is mediated by different levels of the CNS have been nicely demonstrated by Sharpless and Jasper [62] in a study of habituation in the cat: level-1 networks habituated to a given sound will respond only to changes in intensity; level-2 networks are capable of alerting the organism when the frequency is changed, and neocortical systems are required to respond to pattern variations. Morgan [45] reviews numerous studies demonstrating capacity for visual intensity discrimination, but loss of capacity for pattern recognition, following neocortical damage in mammals. These latter studies would account for Riesen's [57] finding that dark-reared cats can learn a visual intensity discrimination as rapidly as normals, while pattern discrimination is severely limited by the lack of previous visual experience.)

The second factor distinguishing learning phenomena mediated by networks of various levels is both more interesting and more difficult to specify clearly. It has to do with the nature of the neural excitation which is adequate for the inducement of the enduring structural changes underlying learning. The assumption that some form of central 'excitation' is necessary as a reinforcement in learning phenomena distinguishes the three traditional learning paradigms from habituation: repeated input that is not followed by such reinforcement produces only habituation to the afferent pattern.

(That some form of central excitation, rather than 'drive reduction', provides the major basis for reinforcement is increasingly evident. Morgan [46] reviews evidence distinguishing the excitatory effects of consummatory activity from the [often confounded] reduction of physiological needs as the effective reinforcement for learning. Work by Gastaut [22] on the changing EEG patterns during learning points to the 'reinforcing' role of excitatory activation from the reticular system in classical conditioning procedures. Recent studies analysing the reinforcing effects of direct electrical stimulation in various areas of the hypothalamus and limbic system [50] give strong evidence that it is excitation of level-2 networks which provides reinforcement for instrumental learning in birds and lower mammals; electrodes implanted within the brainstem or neocortical levels generally lack this reinforcing capacity. Berlyne [5], in his extensive review of the behavioural consequences of various central excitatory states, also concludes that excitatory processes are basic to reinforcement. However, he maintains a 'drive reduction' theory by inferring an 'arousal jag', i.e. a sudden decrease in excitation following CNS arousal, as the basis of reinforcement. For present purposes, whether it is the

subsequent rapid decrease of central excitation or the excitation itself which provides reinforcement is of no great consequence. From the neurological approach, Gerard [23], in his discussion of the probable mechanisms of structural change underlying learning, also concludes that it is increases in excitation level that effect the permanent encoding of input.) From an adaptive perspective, it seems reasonable that it is those sensory or motor events which prove significant to the organism, i.e. which lead to changes in excitation levels, which are remembered, while events not followed by such reinforcement will produce only habituation.

It is in the analysis of the various kinds of 'significant events' which are capable of providing such excitatory reinforcement that the second basis for a hierarchical ordering of learning capacities emerges.† The simplest of the traditional learning paradigms, demonstrated in newborn (i.e. 'precorticate') humans [54] and in decorticate mammals [54], is classical conditioning. A basic requirement for such learning is an unconditioned stimulus capable of exciting level-1 networks, thereby 'reinforcing' the conditioned stimulus. The unconditioned stimulus may be a stimulus innately associated with a reflexive network, or a sudden intense stimulus, or pain—all stimuli noted above as directly activating level-1 systems. In

---

† Note that in the following analysis, which relates different types of learning to excitatory reinforcement mediated by integrative networks of the different levels, the ultimate locus of structural change is not assumed to be always only within the level providing the excitatory reinforcement. The networks for the spread of excitation (vertical broken lines, Fig. 8.1) allow for transmission of excitatory reinforcement to other levels. The particular

types of learning associated with structural changes within the different levels cannot be fully specified: that habituation can occur at all levels seems well established [62]. Morgan [45] reviews evidence indicating that conditioned learning can occur within either neocortical or subcortical networks; the possible loci of structural changes underlying more complex types of learning remain unclear (see [45, 4, 51]).

the conditioning of intact adult mammals, a more complex stimulus of acquired significance may provide excitatory reinforcement by the downward activation of level-1 systems from neocortical networks. This latter instance, where classical conditioning procedures involve neocortical mediation, can apparently result in learning localized primarily within neocortical systems or mainly within lower-level networks, a complication which will be discussed further below. For the present, it is sufficient to establish that level-1 excitation is adequate for classical conditioning, and that certain types of reinforcement can be directly mediated at this level.

In instrumental learning procedures, the 'significance' of preceding events is established by reinforcement through 'reward', or by the absence of painful 'punishment'. Instrumental avoidance learning (learning of a response which prevents administration of 'punishment') may seem at first to present some difficulties for the present excitatory theory of reinforcement. There appear to be two possible explanations for the evident reinforcing capacities of a lack of (excitatory) punishment. It could be encompassed by Berlyne's 'arousal jag' discussed above: the first stage in avoidance learning, learning that a given stimulus signals impending pain, fits a classical conditioning model, with pain as the excitatory reinforcement; in a second stage, when the anticipated pain does not occur if a specified response is made, there would be a reinforcing decrease in excitation level. Solomon and Brush [64] present such an analysis, describing reinforcement in this second stage as 'anxiety reduction'.

As an alternate explanation, note that following the initial stage, which fits the more simple excitatory model, the second step, learning to make the correct avoidance response, could be encompassed within the model for latent learning.

As will be discussed below, the reinforcement in latent learning comes from perceptual novelty, which in this instance is an absence of the anticipated shock when the correct response is made. Since it is to be argued that latent learning phenomena, with 'novelty' as reinforcement, requires neocortical perceptual mediation in mammals, it is relevant that learning of instrumental avoidance problems of even moderate complexity seems impossible in decorticated mammals [26]. More simple avoidance problems, such as the conditioning of a decorticate cat to flex the to-be-shocked leg in response to a buzzer as conditioned stimulus [29], fit into the model of classical conditioning.

In other types of instrumental learning, the 'rewards' used as reinforcement are stimuli productive of consummatory activity (e.g. eating, copulation, etc.), and their salience is a rough function of the amount of activity produced and of the degree of physiological need [10]. The types of events which can be included in this concept of reinforcing 'consummatory activity' will, of course, vary greatly with species and age of organism, and must involve both innate and acquired stimulus sensitivities. The exclusive capacity of tissue within level 2 to effect the reinforcement of instrumental acts when stimulated by implanted electrodes was noted earlier [50]. No reference can be found to instrumental learning in the absence of level-2 networks, and damage to various areas of the neocortex does not preclude such learning when complex pattern discriminations are not required [45]. It seems probable, therefore, that in instrumental learning the reinforcing effects of consummatory activities are the result of excitation of level-2 networks.

There remain learning processes where the excitatory reinforcement is less evident, i.e. in latent learning phenomena, including sensory preconditioning and the sensori–sensory learning described by Hebb [28] as basic to early perceptual development in mammals. Learning in these situations, traditionally defined as occurring without reinforcement, is demonstrated in conditions of general alertness and in the absence of any consummatory activity (see review by Thistlethwaite [67]. This third type of learning seems to reflect the capacity of an alert neocortex to be adequately excited by variation in the immediate perceptual input. The earlier discussion described the role of perceptual novelty in instigating and maintaining exploratory behaviour, an orientation providing the basis for latent learning. Since the neocortex was shown to be basic to an exploratory orientation in mammals, and as there is no evidence for latent learning in mammals deprived of neocortical networks, it seems reasonable to assume that perceptual variation, mediated by level-3 systems, provides the adequate excitatory reinforcement for this third class of learning phenomena. (Butler's [14] evidence that monkeys will learn to open a window when 'rewarded' by a view of an adjoining room illustrates the reinforcing effect of perceptual novelty. Welker [69] reviews other evidence supporting this view of the role of perceptual novelty in latent learning.) In humans it seems reason-

able to extend the concept of perceptual novelty to encompass also conceptual novelty as an adequate reinforcement in those learning processes involving only cognitive activity.

Learning situations which allow for effective mediation of input by networks at more than one level introduce a further complexity. It has been long noted that in the classical conditioning of intact mammals the conditioned response may differ from the unconditioned response, both in being incomplete and in containing additional elements that indicate expectancy of the forthcoming unconditioned stimulus. This 'anticipatory' component of the conditioned response is a general characteristic of animals with a functional neocortex, and has been reported by Hernandez-Peon and Brust-Carmona [29] to be seen also in the decorticate cat. While the experimenter may be focused upon the reinforcing effects of the unconditioned stimulus upon the to-be-conditioned stimulus, the subject, human or otherwise, is also attending to, and learning from, other aspects of the experimental procedure. Maier and Schneirla [40] analyse this additional component as instrumental learning, and Razran [55] considers it to be 'discriminational and relational' learning. Both of these analyses point out that more complex learning processes, reinforced by consummatory activities (Maier and Schneirla), or perceptual novelty (Razran), may in many experimental procedures occur concurrently with classical conditioning. An analogous situation appears in examples of 'incidental learning' occurring in instrumental learning experiments. In such experiments, the subject is motivated towards, and reinforced by, one type of 'goal' but shows some evidence of the learning of incidental (i.e. goal-irrelevant) information in the process (see, for example, [12]). Instrumental learning and latent learning phenomena appear to occur concurrently in these latter experimental procedures. In brief, it appears that learning of different types, in response to aspects of the environment which are providing different types of reinforcement, may occur concurrently. This degree of complexity, probably ubiquitous in mammalian learning, would be expected from the hypothesis that mediational processes underlying learning can occur within integrative networks at various levels of the CNS.

The above analysis relates the three traditional types of learning to excitatory reinforcements mediated by different levels within the CNS. The variations in time factors observed in the different learning processes also suggest a hierarchical ordering. Classical conditioning, involving level-1 excitation for reinforcement, requires for effective learning that excitation from the unconditioned stimulus temporarily overlap the conditioned stimulus. Instrumental learning, involving level-2 excitatory reinforcement, allows for greater delay between the perceptual or motor events to be learned and the subsequent reinforcing activity. The perceptual organization or reorganization of the environment, reinforced by the excitatory effects of perceptual novelty mediated by level-3 systems, can under ideal circumstances be a relatively continuous process as neocortical mechanisms maintain the focus of attention to salient perceptual sequences for relatively long blocks of time.

As with the sensory-motor, motivational, attentional, and aversive hierarchies discussed earlier, the successively more refined learning phenomena also emerge during the postnatal maturation of the central nervous system. Learning in the human neonate seems limited to classical conditioning reinforced by excitatory activation mediated directly by level-1 networks [47]. During the next 2 or 3 months, maturation of networks of the higher levels brings evidence of instrumental and latent learning capacities. Ambrose [2] concludes that instrumental conditioning provides the basis for the development of social smiling during the second and third months, and Brackbill [8] has demonstrated differential changes in the strength of the smiling response in 4-month-old infants, depending on whether Brackbill responded to the smile by picking up, cuddling, and cooing at the infant, or by simply remaining a passive observer. Piaget [53] records the intentional repetition of arm movements in one of his children at about three months after the infant accidentally struck a rattle hung above his cot, which in the present terminology appears to be an early example of latent learning. The general perceptual organization of the sensory world, described by Hebb [28] as basic to later learning, probably also begins in the second and third months, when Piaget [53] and Bühler [13] note the beginnings of a general visual interest in the environment. Much of this early organization of the sensory environment must be independent of consummatory reinforcement and must, therefore, be classed as early instances of latent learning.

Critical-period phenomena

The data from critical-period studies can be described in terms of (1) the nature of the stimuli to which the organism is particularly sensitive during a critical period, (2) the nature of the behaviour patterns which are later affected, and (3) the developmental stage within which variations in the significant stimuli have their maximal effects on later behaviour. Using all of these characteristics as criteria for ordering the data from the numerous studies, three separate critical periods can be defined: (1) a critical period affecting the later 'emotionality' of the animal, with the sensitive period occurring directly after birth, and with the amount of general (unpatterned) stimulation as the significant variable; (2) a critical period affecting primary attachments, occurring at a somewhat later age and dependent on maturation of capacities for pattern discrimination; (3) a critical period when the 'richness' of the perceptual and behavioural environment influences later learning abilities, a phenomenon also dependent on the development of pattern discrimination, and probably upon the functioning of complex motor capacities as well, and whose upper age limit remains only vaguely defined.

Note that the defining variables (the significant stimuli, the behavioural effects, and the critical age-range) of each critical period correspond closely with the perceptual capacity, the behavioural influence, and the maturational chronology of one of the three levels of the conceptual model. This correspondence suggests that critical-period phenomena are products of the quality of activation patterns occurring in integrative networks of the different levels at the periods when the networks first become responsive to afferent excitation. Each critical period, therefore, begins as the networks involved mature to a level of functional significance. The upper limit may be set by at least two possible developmental factors.

First, the sensitivity of the neural network may decrease, ending the period when rapid structural changes, or more enduring excitatory reverberations, follow from afferent excitation. (This limiting development could be, in part, a product of the excitation itself, as well as of innate growth patterns. For reviews of the accelerating effect of stimulation on development, see [38] for behavioural data, and [57] for neurological evidence.) There is only rather indirect evidence in support of this first possible explanation: Roberts [58] finds that the inhibitory synaptic transmitter substance GABA, necessary for effective functioning of the innately inhibitory neurons within a neural network, is less present in the immature nervous system, which should make for more extensive and enduring activation patterns in the early stages of CNS development. (See also [56] for arguments favouring an early period of 'plasticity' of the CNS.)

The second type of developmental factor which might act to terminate some critical stages, is the maturation of neural systems which inhibit or prevent the activation of networks involved in the critical learning. This could be either a general inhibition, such as is found in the tonic effects of neocortical networks upon brain-stem activation, and which might be the terminating factor in the earliest critical stage, or a more specific interference, such as suggestions that the development of innate fear responses terminates imprinting [31]. The limited evidence available for distinguishing between these possible terminating mechanisms will be presented as each critical stage is considered in more detail.

The effects of unpatterned stimuli (disturbing the animal by shaking the cage, handling, tactile stimuli, electric shock, cooling, etc.; the specific characteristics of the adequate stimuli remain unclear) have so far been established in only a few species: rats, mice, and possibly dogs and cats [38]. The critical period for these effects appears limited to the earliest postnatal stage, before neocortical auditory and visual mechanisms mature. This should limit the phenomenon to those animals born with relatively immature nervous systems, a class including rats, mice, cats, dogs, and the larger primates. The stimuli so far found effective are those which were noted above as capable of directly affecting level-1 networks, a finding not surprising, since this critical period occurs at a developmental stage when higher-level perceptual capacities are, on behavioural evidence, essentially non-functional. Nearly all of these studies are on rats or mice, and the later behavioural effects of early stimulation have been clearly established only in these species. Behavioural measures include the rate of avoidance learning and measures of aggressiveness towards other mice, which Levine [38] interprets to be functions of the strength of a general fear reaction to noxious and/or novel situations in the first type of measure, and of variations in a tendency to 'freeze' in the second. Other behavioural measures show variations in autonomic activity in frightening situations, i.e. in open-field tests the amount of urination and defecation is affected by the degree of early stimulation. In the earlier analysis of the defensive reaction, it was noted that all of these kinds of behaviours are associated with an intense activation of level-1 networks. From the rather limited evidence available, it would, therefore, appear that the reactivity of these level-1 networks in later life is in part determined by the extent to which they are activated during very early development. This hypothesis includes this earliest critical-period phenomenon within the broad conception of learning defined above, but limits it to a developmental stage when level-1 networks are either possessed of greater sensitivity, or are characterized by a lack of inhibitory regulation from neocortical systems. With regard to the type of level-1 activation which is effective, the experimental data on rats and mice indicate that stimulation associated with normal sucking processes must be relatively insignificant, since the addition of a few minutes per day of diverse types of 'stressful' stimulation produces such marked effects. In the earlier discussion, it was noted that level-1 networks include both innate reflexive systems basic to neonatal survival, and the more diffuse systems responsive to diverse less specific stimuli. In view of the relative insignificance of the sucking process, it appears to be the latter more general type of activation, noted to be associated with the complex of defensive responses, which leads to the later behavioural effects.

One of the most striking aspects of critical-period phenomena is the delayed appearance of the behavioural effects of earlier experience. From the present perspective, this appears as a consequence of the hierarchical organization of adaptive mechanisms: later-maturing networks, mediating more complex behaviours, are affected by the degree of activation of level-1 systems. Early experience which affects the reactivity of these networks would, therefore, influence more complex behaviours at later stages. In brief, earlier experiences affecting the re-activity of level-1 networks determine the degree of emotionality of the organism, while later experiences, following maturation of higher-level systems, determine the objects of emotional significance.

The critical period determining primary affectional attachments in mammals appears with the development of neocortically mediated perceptual capacities and is dependent upon the visual and auditory discriminations of this level [61]. There is evidence, however, that the neo-cortex is not primarily involved in the mediation of reinforcement for this type of learning. While the parameters influencing the development of early attachments in mammals are only minimally explored, it appears that the animal becomes attached to that object towards which certain types of responses are directed during the sensitive period. The nature of these responses will vary with species—for example, clinging to soft objects seems basic to attachment formation in monkeys [27], a response which is outside the repertoire of puppy be-haviour, although puppies readily form attachments [61]. Chicks become attached to followed objects [30], while human infants show the be-ginnings of attachment at an age before following is possible. In his considera-tion of the possible responses providing the basis for forming attachments in humans, Bowlby [7] points out the innate species-common characteristics of the significant acts. This sug-gests that the formation of early attachments is a type of instrumen-tal learning: objects perceived while making consummatory responses are remembered and subsequently sought after when the appropriate motivation is aroused. While this analysis must be recognized as highly tentative, it sug-gests that neural networks within level 2 are primarily responsible for re-inforcement of experiences producing early attachment. (Such a conclusion also finds tangential support from the specific emotional quality associated with subsequent frustration of the acquired orientation, an affective response which is probably mediated by subcortical networks; note also that attachment formation is prominent in some species of birds, and that they are essentially subcorticate animals.)

It is interesting that evidence reviewed by Scott [61] and experi-ments by Moltz [44] indicate that experimental procedures which would have the effect of a general excitation of level-1 systems—food deprivation, electric shock, painful stimuli, etc.—are effective in producing more rapid attachment learning. This facilitory effect of level-1 excitation has been observed in instrumental learning at later ages also, where electric shock administered in association with the to-be-learned stimuli may increase the rate of learning [10]. These pheno-mena could be instances of level-1 excitation projecting upward to sup-plement reinforcement from level-2 excitation.

Mechanisms terminating this second critical period are far from clear. Many authors note the development of fearfulness in response to novelty as an orientation precluding the development of new affectional ties, but there is evidence indicating other mechanisms also may be involved (see reviews [31, 61]). It was suggested earlier that those neural mechanisms associated with fearful behaviour that are found within the limbic system may set a maturationally imposed upper limit, but lack of direct evidence on maturational sequences within subcortical forebrain networks prevents further analysis. As with the earlier critical period, the eventual consequences of experience within this stage depend on the influences of subsequent maturation and later learning. For example, the maturation of neural systems releasing sex hormones initiates sexual activities which are in part oriented by early attachments, and in the learning area, the complex vicissitudes of primary affectional bonds in response to later interpersonal experiences appears as a major theme in psychoanalytic theory.

The third type of critical-period phenomena involves the effect of opportunity for complex perceptual and motor experience at an early age upon various learning abilities in later life. Bingham and Griffiths [6], Forgays and Forgays [21], and Hymovitch [32] have shown that rats reared for various periods in cages filled with a diversity of objects inviting perceptual and motor exploration were better maze learners as adults. The latter study is particularly relevant since it included control conditions indicating that improved learning is not an expression of the development of specific motor abilities or of a particular motivational orientation, and that an 'enriched' environment provided to adult rats does not counter

the effects of early impoverishment. Evidence for similar effects in cats, dogs, and monkeys is available in studies which involve early sensory deprivation rather than enrichment. Melzack and Scott [42] reared puppies in isolation from weaning to eight months in conditions allowing only minimal perceptual and motor experience (and which incidentally also must have inhibited the development of the affectional bonds which normally would occur in this period). Even after two years experience in a normal environment, these animals showed severe deficits in the visual control of motor behaviour in avoiding painful stimuli. From the authors' description of the obtuse behaviour of these animals in learning to avoid painful stimuli, the deficiency seemed to be in the perceptual organization of the sensory environment, which contrasts with the hyperemotionality which interfered with avoidance learning in rats as a result of minimal stimulation in the earliest critical period. Riesen [57] reviews studies of cats reared in total darkness for nine months, or with only diffuse (unpatterned) illumination for five months, which when moved to normal environments failed in some cases to develop normal visual abilities. An apparently irreversible deficit in somesthetic perceptual ability in a chimpanzee reared with cardboard tubes on forearms and legs was shown by Nissen, Chow, and Semmes [48]. Many of the above studies were inspired by Hebb's [28] analysis of the role of early experience in the perceptual organization of sensory input. That the perceptual deficit following early sensory deprivation was to some degree irreversible often seems to be a secondary finding, and the studies vary in the degree to which this was carefully observed or conclusively demonstrated. There seems adequate evidence, however, to conclude that previous perceptual and motor experience is not only necessary for maximal performance in problems requiring perceptual discrimination and motor skills, but that such experience is more salient in its later effects if acquired when the neocortical systems mediating these capacities first mature. Evidence for setting any precise upper limit to this critical stage is lacking, but since it seems improbable that it is terminated by inhibitory effects due to the subsequent maturation of other functional systems, the waning of the period of maximum sensitivity is probably a very gradual process. (See [56] for evidence on 'loss of plasticity' with age.) The learning occurring at this stage fits the paradigm of latent learning, and this third critical period can be described as a

time of particularly rapid learning within this model. Note that in the sensory deprivation studies cited above the initial retardation often largely disappeared given an adequate environment subsequent to deprivation, and that in studies where deprivation was limited to a single sensory mode, the deficit that did remain was limited to that sensory capacity. This final critical period, therefore, seems to differ from the other two in that (1) the critical period is probably less sharply delineated, (2) effects of deprivation are probably relatively more reversible, and (3) the later effects appear in behavioural areas directly similar to those in which the critical experiences occur. All of these characteristics seem related to the absence of 'higher-level' systems to inhibit, or to build upon, the integrative networks involved in this third critical period.

References

1. ALLPORT, G. W. (1937). *Personality: a psychological interpretation*. Holt, New York.

2. AMBROSE, J. A. (1960). The development of the smiling response in early infancy. *In* (Foss, B. M. (Ed.)) *Determinants of infant behaviour*. Methuen & Co., Ltd., London.

3. BARD, P. and RIOCH, D. McK. (1937). A study of four cats deprived of neocortex and additional portions of the forebrain. *Johns Hopkins Hosp. Bull.* **60**, 73–147.

4. BENJAMIN, R. M. (1959). Absence of deficits in taste discrimination following cortical lesions as a function of the amount of preoperative practice. *J. comp. physiol. Psychol.* **52**, 255–8.

5. BERLYNE, D. E. (1960). *Conflict, arousal and curiosity*. McGraw-Hill, New York.

6. BINGHAM, W. E. and GRIFFITHS, W. J., JR. (1952). The effect of different environments during infancy on adult behavior in the rat. *J. comp. physiol. Psychol.* **45**, 307–12.

7. BOWLBY, J. (1958). The nature of the child's tie to his mother. *Int. J. Psychoanal.* **39**, 1–24.

8. BRACKBILL, YVONNE. (1958). Extinction of the smiling response in infants as a function of reinforcement schedule. *Child Dev.* **29**, 115–24.

9. BRADY, J. V. (1960). Emotional behavior. *In* (Field, J. (Ed.)) *Handbook of physiology. Sect. I: neurophysiology.* Vol. III. American Physiological Society, Washington D.C.

10. BROGDEN, W. J. (1951). Animal studies of learning. *In* (Stevens, S. S. (Ed.)) *Handbook of experimental psychology.* Wiley, New York.

11. BRONSON, G. A. (1963). A neurological perspective on ego development in infancy. *J. Am. Psychoanal. Ass.* **11**, 55–65.

12. BRUNER, J. S., MATTER, JEAN, and PAPANEK, MIRIAM. (1955). Breadth of learning as a function of drive level and mechanization. *Psychol. Rev.* **62**, 1–10.

13. BÜHLER, CHARLOTTE. (1930). *The first year of life*. Day, New York.

14. BUTLER, R. A. (1954). Incentive conditions which influence visual exploration. *J. exp. Psychol.* **48**, 19–23.

15. CONEL, J. LeR. (1939). *The postnatal development of the human cerebral cortex. I. Cortex of the newborn*. Harvard University Press, Cambridge, Mass.

16. —— (1941). *The postnatal development of the human cerebral cortex. II. Cortex of the one-month infant*. Harvard University Press, Cambridge, Mass.

17. —— (1947). *The postnatal development of the human cerebral cortex. III. Cortex of the three-month infant*. Harvard University Press, Cambridge, Mass.

18. DELL, P. C. (1958). Some basic mechanisms of the translation of bodily needs into behavior. *In* (Wolstenholme, G. E. W. and O'Connor, C. M. (Eds.)) *Symposium on the neurological basis of behavior*. Little, Boston.

19. DENNY-BROWN, D. (1960). Motor mechanisms—introduction: the general principles of motor integration. *In* (Field, J. (Ed.)) *Handbook of physiology. Sect. I: neurophysiology.* Vol. II. American Physiological Society, Washington D.C.

20. FANTZ, R. L. (1958). Pattern vision in young infants. *Psychol. Rec.* **8**, 43–7.

21. FORGAYS, D. G. and FORGAYS, JANET. (1952). The nature of the effect of free-environmental experience in the rat. *J. comp. physiol. Psychol.* **45**, 322–8.

22. GASTAUT, H. (1958). Conditioned reflexes and behavior. *In* (Wolstenholme, G. E. W. and O'Connor, C. M. (Eds.)) *Symposium on the neurological basis of behavior*. Little, Boston.

23. GERARD, R. W. (1960). Neurophysiology: an integration. *In* (Field, J. (Ed.)) *Handbook of physiology. Sect. I: neurophysiology.* Vol. III. American Physiological Society, Washington D.C.

24. GLOOR, P. (1960). The amygdala. *In* (Field, J. (Ed.)) *Handbook of physiology. Sect. I: neurophysiology.* Vol. II. American Physiological Society, Washington D.C.

25. GUYTON, A. C. (1961). *Textbook of medical physiology*. W. B. Saunders, Philadelphia.

26. HAMUY, T. P. (1961). The role of the cerebral cortex in the learning of an instrumental conditional response. *In* (Fessard, A., Gerard, R. W., and Konorski, J. (Eds.)) *Brain mechanisms and learning*. Charles C. Thomas, Springfield, Ill.

27. HARLOW, H. F. and ZIMMERMANN, R. R. (1959). Affectional responses in the infant monkey. *Science* **130**, 421–32.

28. HEBB, D. O. (1949). *The organization of behavior*. Wiley, New York.

29. HERNANDEZ-PEON, R. and BRUST-CARMONA, H. (1961). The functional role of subcortical structures in habituation and conditioning. *In* (Fessard, A., Gerard, R. W., and Konorski, J. (Eds.)) *Brain mechanisms and learning*. Charles C. Thomas, Springfield, Ill.

30. HESS, E. H. (1959). Imprinting. *Science* **130**, 133–41.

31. HINDE, R. A. (1962). Sensitive periods and the development of behavior. *In* (Barnett, S. A. (Ed.)) *Lessons from animal behavior for the clinician*. National Spastics Society Study Group and Heinemann Medical Books, Ltd., London.

32. HYMOVITCH, B. (1952). The effects of experimental variations on problem solving in the rat. *J. comp. Physiol.* **45**, 313–21.

33. JERSILD, A. T. (1946). Emotional development. *In* (Carmichael, L. (Ed.)) *Manual of child psychology*. Wiley, New York.

34. JUNG, R. and HASSLER, R. (1960). The extrapyramidal motor system. *In*

(Field, J. (Ed.)) *Handbook of physiology. Sect. I: neurophysiology.* Vol. II. American Physiological Society, Washington D.C.

35. KLEITMAN, N. and ENGELMANN, T. G. (1953). Sleep characteristics of infants. *J. appl. Physiol.* **6**, 266–82.

36. KLUVER, H. (1958). The temporal lobe syndrome. *In* (Wolstenholme, G. E. W. and O'Connor, C. M. (Eds.)) *Symposium on the neurological basis of behavior.* Little, Boston.

37. KRECHEVSKY, I. (1937). Brain mechanisms and variability: I. variability within a means-ends-readiness. *J. comp. Psychol.* **23**, 121–38.

38. LEVINE, S. (1962). The effects of infantile experience on adult behavior. *In* (Bachrach, A. J. (Ed.)) *Experimental foundations of clinical psychology.* Basic Books, New York.

39. LINDSLEY, D. B. (1960). Attention, consciousness, sleep, and wakefulness. *In* (Field, J. (Ed.)) *Handbook of physiology. Sect. I: neurophysiology.* Vol. III. American Physiological Society, Washington D.C.

40. MAIER, N. R. F. and SCHNEIRLA, T. C. (1942). Mechanisms in conditioning. *Psychol. Rev.* **49**, 117–34.

41. McGRAW, MYRTLE. (1943). *The neuromuscular maturation of the human infant.* Columbia University Press, New York.

42. MELZACK, R. and SCOTT, T. H. (1957). The effects of early experience on the response to pain. *J. comp. physiol. Psychol.* **50**, 155–61.

43. MILLER, G. A., GALANTER, E., and PRIBRAM, K. H. (1960). *Plans and the structure of behavior.* Holt, New York.

44. MOLTZ, H. (1960). Imprinting: empirical basis and theoretical significance. *Psychol. Bull.* **57**, 291–314.

45. MORGAN, C. T. (1951). The psychophysiology of learning. *In* (Stevens, S. S. (Ed.)) *Handbook of experimental psychology.* Wiley, New York.

46. —— (1957). Physiological mechanisms of motivation. *In* (Jones, M. R.

(Ed.)) *Nebraska symposium on motivation.* Univ. Nebraska Press, Lincoln.

47. MUNN, N. L. (1946). Learning in children. *In* (Carmichael, L. (Ed.)) *Manual of child psychology.* Wiley, New York.

48. NISSEN, H. W., CHOW, K. L., and SEMMES, JOSEPHINE. (1951). Effects of restricted opportunity for tactual, kinesthetic and manipulative experience on the behavior of a chimpanzee. *Am. J. Psychol.* **64**, 485–507.

49. OLDS, J. (1955). Physiological mechanisms of reward. *In* (Jones, M. R. W. (Ed.)) *Nebraska symposium on motivation.* Univ. Nebraska Press, Lincoln.

50. —— and OLDS, M. E. (1961). Interference and learning in paleocortical systems. *In* (Fessard, A., Gerard, R. W., and Konorski, J. (Eds.)) *Brain mechanisms and learning.* Charles C. Thomas, Springfield, Ill.

51. ORBACH, J. and FANTZ, R. L. (1958). Differential effects of temporal neocortical resections on overtrained and nonovertrained visual habits in monkeys. *J. comp. physiol. Psychol.* **51**, 126–9.

52. PENFIELD, W. (1958). The role of temporal cortex and experience. *In* (Wolstenholme, G. E. W. and O'Connor, C. M. (Eds.)) *Symposium on the neurological basis of behavior.* Little, Boston.

53. PIAGET, J. (1952). *The origins of intelligence in children* (1936). International Universities Press, New York.

54. PRATT, K. C. (1946). The neonate. *In* (Carmichael, L. (Ed.)) *Manual of child psychology.* Wiley, New York.

55. RAZRAN, G. (1955). Conditioning and perception. *Psychol. Rev.* **62**, 83–95.

56. RIESEN, A. H. (1958). Plasticity of behavior: psychological series. *In* (Harlow, H. F. and Woolsey, C. N. (Eds.)) *Biological and biochemical bases of behavior.* Univ. Wisconsin Press, Madison.

57. —— (1961). Stimulation as a requirement for growth and function in behavioral development. *In* (Fiske,

D. W. and Maddi, S. R. (Eds.)) *Functions of varied experience.* Dorsey, Homewood, Ill.

58. ROBERTS, E. (1960). Biochemical maturation of the central nervous system. *In* (Brazier, M. A. (Ed.)) *The central nervous system and behavior: transactions of the third conference.* Josiah Macy, Jr. Foundation, New York.

59. SACKETT, G. P. (1963). A neural mechanism underlying unlearned, critical period, and developmental aspects of visually controlled behavior. *Psychol. Rev.* **70**, 40–50.

60. SAMUELS, INA. (1959). Reticular mechanisms and behavior. *Psychol. Bull.* **56**, 1–25.

61. SCOTT, J. P. (1962). Critical periods in behavioral development. *Science* **138**, 949–58.

62. SHARPLESS, S. and JASPER, H. H. (1956). Habituation of the arousal reaction. *Brain* **79**, 655–80.

63. SMITH, K. U. and WARKENTIN, J. (1939). The central neural organization of optic functions related to minimum visual acuity. *J. genet. Psychol.* **55**, 177–95.

64. SOLOMON, R. L. and BRUSH, ELINOR. (1956). Experimentally derived conceptions of anxiety and aversion. *In* (Jones, M. R. (Ed.)) *Nebraska symposium on motivation.* Univ. Nebraska Press, Lincoln.

65. STELLAR, E. (1960). Drive and motivation. *In* (Field, J. (Ed.)) *Handbook of physiology. Sect. I: neurophysiology.* Vol. III. American Physiological Society, Washington D.C.

66. TERZUOLO, C. A. and ADEY, W. R. (1960). Sensorimotor cortical activities. *In* (Field, J. (Ed.)) *Handbook of physiology. Sect. I: neurophysiology.* Vol. II. American Physiological Society, Washington D.C.

67. THISTLETHWAITE, D. (1951). A critical review of latent learning and related experiments. *Psychol. Bull.* **48**, 97–129.

68. TRAVIS, A. M. and WOOLSEY, C. N. (1956). Motor performances of monkeys after bilateral partial and total cerebral decortications. *J. physic. Med.* **35**, 273–310.

69. WELKER, W. I. (1961). An analysis of exploratory and play behavior in animals. *In* (Fiske, D. W. and Maddi, S. R. (Eds.)) *Functions of varied experience.* Dorsey, Homewood, Ill.

70. WHITTERIDGE, D. (1960). Central control of eye movements. *In* (Field, J. (Ed.)) *Handbook of physiology. Sect. I: neurophysiology.* Vol. II. American Physiological Society, Washington D.C.

9 Response repertoire of the anencephalic infant

M. MONNIER†

WE have made a prolonged study of the scheme of integration of the motor functions by the central nervous system. Various methods can be used. The best way is to study the development of the motor paths in the embryo, foetus, and newborn, a method initiated by Monakov and Minkowski at Zürich and experimentally perfected by Windle at Chicago. Phylogeny and ontogeny supply us with concordant data which enable us to reconstitute the scheme of integration (Aufbauplan) of the motor functions provided that these data are analysed and interpreted according to functional criteria [2]. If we admit as a criterion of integration the synthesis of the elementary mechanisms in a function adapted to an aim, we can say that the scheme of integration advances by stages at well defined times. We have distinguished the following stages:

(1) Integration of motor functions in respiration and nutrition, functions of mime and vocal expression, protective functions with predominance of flexion mechanisms and functions of pre-

hension (end of foetal life, and birth);
(2) Functions of active orientation of head and eyes (2 to 3 months);
(3) Functions of lifting the head (2 to 3 months), the trunk (5 to 6 months), the legs, retaining position (7 to 10 months);
(4) Functions of progression, locomotion, and regulation of equilibrium (11 to 14 months);
(5) Articulate language (15 to 24 months);
(6) Technical manual dexterity characteristic of working man (adolescence).

Although it is always possible to study experimentally in the animal the correlations between the stages of development of motor functions and the stages of differentiation of anatomical functions, which give us information on the integrating function of the differentiated mechanisms, the same cannot be done with man. This is why the newborn anencephalics, with their rudimentary bulbo-spinal, ponto-bulbo-spinal or meso-ponto-bulbo-spinal brains afford us an exceptional opportunity of defining the correlation between a stage in the organization of motor functions and the corresponding stage in the morphological development of the nervous system. We shall describe the motor paths of ponto-bulbo-spinal anencephalics (rhombencephalic an-

† From behaviour of new-born anencephalics th various degrees of anencephaly'. *Discussions on child development* (Tanner, J. M. and Inhelder, B. (Eds.)), Vol. 1. Tavistock, London, pp. 62–7 (1956). Reprinted by permission of Tavistock Publications Ltd. and the World Health Organization.

encephaly), then those of a meso-rhombencephalic anencephalic and finally those of Gamper's anencephalic with a well developed mesencephalon. At the same time anatomical sections of the brain stem will be shown, illustrating the degree of development of the nervous integrating mechanisms.

Rhombencephalic anencephalus

We have been able to observe four anencephalics whose brain was limited

to noxious tactile stimulation or to acoustic or vestibular stimulation. Integration at this stage is characterized by poor localization of reflex responses, a tendency to irradiation, bilateralism, and even generalization of response (mass reflex). Stimulation of the sole of the foot, the malleolus, or the Achilles tendon produces, not a Babinski phenomenon confined to the big toe, but a triple retraction of the leg on the side stimulated, often also of the other side, and sometimes even

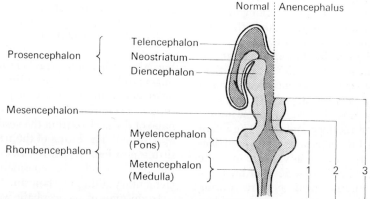

FIG. 9.1. Anencephalic newborns at various stages of anencephaly.

1. *Rhombencephalic Anencephalus*, Monnier and Willi, 1947.
2. *Meso-rhombencephalic Anencephalus*, Monnier and Willi, 1953.
3. *Mesencephalic Anencephalus*, Gamper, 1926.

to the pons, medulla oblongata, and cord. In such cases the vegetative functions are very poorly regulated. The blood supply to the peripheral area is insufficient and respiration is irregular. Ingestion of food is badly co-ordinated, especially sucking. The temperature is very labile (poikilo-thermy) and the infant can hardly survive more than one or two days. There was no spontaneous activity and no periodicity of states of wakefulness and sleep. Motor activity consists mainly of defence behaviour by flexion with intense protective reflexes

a reaction of the upper limbs accompanied by clonic trembling of hands and arms. Reflexes of flexion posture and prehension reactions are highly developed. Rudimentary balancing reactions are observed with extension of the arms and flexion of the head, as in Moro's reflex. Although conditions for development of mental activity do not perhaps exist it can at least be said that mechanisms for protection against noxious stimuli and prehension to counteract the dangerous effect of weight are accompanied by expression phenomena capable of interpreting certain rudimentary affective states. The mechanisms responsible for these primordial integrations are the reticular formations of the medulla oblongata and the pons (Tegmentum pontis), with the posterior cords and the cranial nerves V to XII [3].

Meso-rhombencephalic anencephalic

I had the opportunity of observing with H. Willi an anencephalic whose brain was limited to the caudal area of the mesencephalon (isthmus) together with the pons, medulla oblongata, and cord. It was possible to keep the newborn alive for fifty-seven days. It showed good circulation, irregular and sometimes periodic respiration, poikilothermy, and mediocre regulation of blood sugar. Spontaneous activity was limited to a few movements of the face and lips. The infant lay on one side with arms and legs flexed. It had the advantage over the type previously described of having a more physiological posture during sleep. The hands were prone and legs supine. It slept most of the time and showed little movement—only lazily or by fits and starts—when stimulated. The head sometimes moved slowly from one side to the other.

The somatic-motor integrated functions consisted mainly of defensive flexion reflexes released by exteroceptive tactile, thermic, or chemical stimuli, more or less noxious. Very intense stimuli provoked a generalized defence reflex (mass reflex). Grasping mechanisms were well developed in both hands and feet; they could be clearly observed during trophotropic activities, such as sleep and feeding. Functions of mime and vocal expression were well developed: contortions of the trunk, vermicular movements of the head and limbs, sometimes certain facial expressions of affective pleasure reactions with stretching, extension of the arms, yawning, and sighing. Passive extension of the leg induced, for example, a Moro reflex, with deflexion of the head, extension of the arms, especially the right arm, opening of the mouth, and sighing. As to vocal reactions, they were limited to a sort of hiccough and stridor. The functions of extension and of lifting against weight remained rudimentary: reactions of extension and abduction of the arms (stage 1 of Moro's reflex) with lifting of the trunk. As regards functions of active orientation of the head in space, they were limited to mechanisms of buccal prehension (prehension of fingers or bottle with lips, lifting of the head under the influence of proprioceptive excitation from the stretched nape of the neck or from the vestibular apparatus). The lifting of the trunk in sitting position by passive extension of the legs can also be considered an elementary lifting mechanism.

In this type of anencephalic we were able to observe in the course of weeks the transformation of an inadequate reaction (turning of the head towards a noxious stimulus: prick of a needle) into an adequate flight reaction. This adequate reaction appeared seven weeks after birth; it was at times so intense that it even took the place of buccal prehension behaviour; the mouth moved away from the finger presented instead of seizing it [4].

Mesencephalic anencephalic

In the anencephalic of pure mesencephalic type, described by Gamper [1], all the vegetative functions are well regulated, especially respiration and circulation. There is a distinct alteration between periods of sleep and waking activity. General spontaneous activity is more intense (movements of the tongue, contortions). Locomotor paths are highly developed; they consist mainly of reflexes of crossed extension, automatically released, and very clear successive induction phenomena in sitting position (epileptoid trembling). The functions of facial and vocal expression are better elaborated: smiles and tears. The Moro reaction, induced by a puff of cold air, is shown again by extension of the arms, but also by deflexion of the head, with a yawning reaction, whereas in the rhombencephalic anencephalics we had mostly a head-flexion reaction. The functions of protection and defence are well developed. Extension and lifting functions are definitely better developed than in the preceding anencephalic types. The same is true of the tonic neck reflexes, the reflexes of lifting of head and trunk, and the reactions to vestibular stimulation of rotatory or linear acceleration. This is also the case with all the functions of orientation of the head and upper body in space. The paths of oral prehension are so well developed that they produce in the anencephalic an effect of an automaton, which always directs its mouth towards the finger that touches it. Here too one can say that the development and maturation are characterized by greater spontaneous activity, mainly pre-locomotor, by better differentiated functions of facial expression, giving the impression of affective reactions, better elaborated functions of lifting and motor orientation and especially by a closer and more adequate adaptation of reactions to objective [1].

I would like now to discuss the question of reactive patterns changing with the development of the nervous system. During the first six weeks of life, the mesorhomboencephalic anencephalic infant turned the head towards a source of nocive stimulation (prick of a needle); thereafter, the head was turned away from the stimulus. This latter protective reaction could be elicited chiefly from the seventh week after birth. Ipsiversive and contraversive patterns of head turning were probably both integrated in the brain at birth, but the threshold of the two systems was different: low threshold for ipsiversive turning during the first weeks (tegmental reaction), higher threshold for contraversive turning (protective reaction). The threshold of the latter decreases only seven weeks after birth, as a sign of greater maturation of the brain. [Thus] I should like now to define growth and maturation as a process which locates, which circumscribes a reaction, instead of spreading it. Diffusion and generalization are expressions of an immature nervous system. During growth the reaction becomes more adequate, better adapted to its purpose. I gave as an example the meso-rhombencephalic anencephalus, which showed a better adaptation of the head reaction to various stimuli seven weeks after birth; head turning away from the nocive stimulus. In this regard, we have to consider the notion of threshold. We know in the tegmentum of the brain stem there are pre-configurated systems for ipsiversive and contraversive head turning. These systems must have at different times different thresholds. During the first six weeks, we elicited chiefly ipsiversive patterns; during the second month, as maturation of the brain progressed, the contraversive reaction of the head, away from the nocive stimulus, became more prominent. There was even a kind of rivalry between ipsiversive responses (turning of the head with sucking) and contraversive responses (flight reaction). It was sometimes even difficult to feed the baby, since the flight reaction of the head was too strong, so that the nurse could not get near the lips with the bottle. This rivalry was typical for the transition state.

What other conclusions can we draw from our observations in relation to the problems of psychobiological development? We may say that in the lowest rhombencephalic type of anencephaly, the protective patterns of flexion type are predominant. The surface of the body is reduced in order to escape nocive stimuli. At a higher integrative level (meso-rhombencephalic type) some elementary mechanisms of standing and righting postures develop. On the other hand, the mime changes with maturation; it becomes more elaborate, sighing appears with contortions of the body, which have sometimes an expression of pleasure or displeasure. We do not know, of course, if a psychological experience occurs behind these various expressions.

References

1. GAMPER, E. (1926). *Z. ges. Neurol. Psychiat.* **104**, 49.
2. MONNIER, M. (1946). *Schweiz. Arch. Neurol. Psychiat.* **56**, 233, and **57**, 325.
3. ── and WILLI, H. (1947). *Ann. Paediat.* **169**, 289.
4. ── and ── (1953). *Mschr. psychiat. Neurol.* **126**, 239 and 259.

10 Ontogenesis of sleep cycles

HOWARD P. ROFFWARG, JOSEPH N. MUZIO, AND WILLIAM C. DEMENT†

WITHIN the last decade new discoveries have forced extensive modification of traditional concepts of sleep. In the past there was always considerable interest in mechanisms of sleep [1, 2], but its function was largely taken for granted. The view prevailed that the role of sleep is self-evidently allied to the need for restitution or, at least, for rest.

Since the demonstration that there are two distinct phases of sleep [3–5] we realize that more than a simple parallelism between rest and sleep is required to elucidate the role of sleep in our biological economy. As a matter of fact, it is probably begging the question of function to discuss *sleep* as a totality at all. For the physiological characteristics of the alternating states within behavioural sleep are so different that it is questionable whether a single designation, purporting to apply meaningfully to the normal condition of the individual when not awake, is any longer adequate. Currently, a 'dualistic' hypothesis about sleep mechanisms is widely, though not universally [1, 6], accepted, in which the two major types of sleep are viewed

† From 'Ontogenetic development of the human sleep–dream cycle'. *Science* **152**, 604–19 (1966). Copyright © 1966 by the American Association for the Advancement of Science. Reprinted by permission of the authors and the Association.

as qualitatively distinct states [7–9]. It is likely that a dichotomy will and should apply to the question of function as well.

Owing to its singular properties and recent discovery, the sleep stage accompanied by rapid eye movements (REM sleep) has received a greater share of investigative attention [3–5] than the non-rapid-eye-movement stages (NREM sleep). Most studies have been concerned with the physiological attributes of REM sleep or with the factors that influence its percentage of total sleep. In an attempt to assess the factor of age we began a series of observations on the proportions of REM and NREM sleep in various age groups. Another reason for our interest in the REM sleep process in pre-adult groups was the wish to determine the onset of dreaming. Since Aserinsky, Kleitman, and Dement [3, 4] first demonstrated a relationship between REM sleep and dreaming, confirmations of the association have been numerous [10–15]. We therefore thought it might be possible to designate when dreaming begins by determining the age when REM sleep first appears. Surprisingly, we found that pre-school children had a higher percentage of REM sleep than adults. We also observed REMs in apparently sleeping newborn infants [16]. Such unexpected findings suggested the need for a thorough poly-graphic investigation of sleep in human neonates.

In this article we shall attempt a new synthesis of current information about the REM state, dream phenomena, and the relationship between sleep pattern and maturation; present our findings in newborns which carry implications with regard to a 'functional consequence' of REM sleep; and explore some of the data which lead us to suggest that REM sleep plays an important role in the ontogenetic development of the central nervous system.

Typical pattern in sleep

A normal adult, upon falling asleep, exhibits a typical succession of elec-tro-encephalographic (EEG) changes [5, 16]. After fragmentation and dis-appearance of alpha activity, the waves diminish slightly in frequency as their amplitudes grow (descending stage 1). High-voltage, notched slow waves, 'K complexes', and character-istic trains of 14-cycle/s 'sleep spindles' invade the background activity (stage 2). Tall 'delta' waves (1 to 2 cycles/s) progressively fill the record (stage 3) and finally dominate it in virtually un-broken sequence (stage 4). The dis-tinguishing criteria of these EEG 'stages' are arbitrary but the stages are all considered phases of NREM sleep [7, 17, 18].

Approximately 50 to 70 min after onset of sleep, the initial REM period of the night begins. Appearing just before the first REMs are manifest and persisting until the last terminate, the characteristic low-voltage, rela-tively fast, non-spindling EEG of stage 1 sleep resumes, encompassing an interval termed a stage 1-REM period, or REM sleep. Short trains of 'sawtooth' waves (2 to 3 cycles/s) invade the stage 1 EEG, presaging or coinciding with the REM clusters [12, 19, 20]. The periods recur every 80 to 90 min and comprise 20 to 25 per cent of the conventional night's sleep of young adults. Short early in the night and longer towards morning, they average 20 min in length. Spindle and high-voltage EEG patterns re-appear between the REM periods.†

Although the nocturnal sleep cycle of an individual on a consistent diurnal schedule tends to be fairly constant from night to night [4], it may vary under conditions such as apprehension or anxiety (the 'first night effect' in the laboratory) [21], hypnotic sug-gestion [22], the effects of certain drugs and their withdrawal [20, 23–25], compensation from experimental interruptions of REM sleep [8, 26, 27], and acute and chronic psychotic states [24, 28]. Age is also an im-portant variable [16].

The state of the adult in REM sleep is singularly distinct from that in NREM sleep. Hence REM sleep has been classified as a 'third' state along-side NREM sleep and waking [7, 8, 29]. The physiological characteristics

---

† From this point on we will employ the terms 'REM sleep' and 'NREM sleep' to dis-tinguish the two primary divisions of sleep activity. Depending on the author, the terms 'paradoxical sleep', 'rhombencephalic sleep', 'stage 1-REM sleep', 'activated sleep', 'fast sleep', 'deep sleep', and 'low-voltage fast (LVF) sleep' have been used instead of REM sleep. We believe that whatever the designation employed or the aspects studied all the terms probably describe a homologous neuro-physiological state. REM sleep seems its most inclusive designation since all animals evincing this state show REMs. It should be emphasized, however, that the term 'REM sleep' is de-scriptive and is not meant to ascribe any causal or primary function to the rapid eye move-ments themselves.

of the REM state have already been extensively reviewed by Jouvet [9], Snyder [7, 29], and Dement [18]. We shall attempt here only to summarize the basic phenomena, focusing our attention on the events in the central nervous system.

Whereas respiratory rhythm, heart rate, and blood pressure tend to be basal in NREM sleep, they display greater activity and greater variability during REM phases [3–5, 11, 12, 31]. The fine muscles of the face and extremities contract frequently, though there are few gross body displacements [14]. In the absence of movement, however, muscle tone measured from the head and neck virtually disappears in REM periods [20, 31]. The extrinsic ocular muscles are an exception to this rule. Before and during shifts of eyeball position, tone may be sustained in uninvolved and antagonist muscles [32]. Penile erections are specific to the REM periods, detumescence occurring as NREM sleep ensues [33]. Basal skin resistance, which should fall with heightened arousal, has been reported to rise in REM sleep by some investigators [34] but not by others [11, 29]. In view of the eye activity and oneiric phenomena during REM sleep, it is intriguing that the REM sleep EEG is remarkably similar to that of a subject awake under circumstances of visual imaging or stimulation, when alpha activity is blocked. Furthermore, cortical responses evoked during the waking state are extremely similar to those evoked in REM sleep [35].

An unexpected finding has been that motor-response and arousal thresholds are no higher in deep NREM sleep than in REM sleep [5, 36]. This seems to fit with the finding in cats that during REM sleep there is a high response threshold in the mesencephalic reticular formation to auditory [37] as well as to direct stimulation [38, 39]. In spite of the lowered responsiveness to stimulation, however, there is greater spontaneous activity in the reticular formation during REM sleep [38]. (It is precisely this aspect of brain functioning in REM sleep which renders 'depth of sleep' so difficult to designate.) Huttenlocher has speculated that in REM sleep evoked responses may be *occluded* because of this high level of spontaneous activity. Recently, however, Adey *et al.* [40] were not able to demonstrate higher response thresholds in the mesencephalic reticular formations of chimpanzees during REM sleep.

Studies in animals

A dual neurophysiological organization of sleep is not specific to human beings. Every species of mammal so far studied exhibits rhythmically alternating periods of REM and NREM activity which are marked by vegetative alterations similar in most respects to those that are found in man [12, 40–51].

Moreover, animal experimentation has greatly extended our knowledge of the active processes occurring in the central nervous system during the REM state, such as: increase in blood flow to the cortex [46]; rise in brain temperature [51]; elevation in frequency of spontaneous neuronal firing in the MRF [39], medial and descending vestibular nuclei [52], pyramidal tract [53, 54], and occipital cortex [55]; development of monophasic wave aggregates in the pons, lateral geniculate body, and other subcortical areas; continuous theta activity in the hippocampus (even more regular than during arousal) [9, 50, 56–59]; and evidence of facilitatory influences at the somatic afferent [60, 61] and visual afferent (lateral geniculate body) thalamic relays [62]. During REM sleep, excitability as measured by the evoked-response technique in motor cortex is higher than, and in sensory cortex is at least as high as it is during NREM sleep [39]. In both regions, excitability is greater than it is in the waking state [4, 61, 62]. A shift in cortical and subcortical direct-current potentials towards the level in arousal and away from that during NREM sleep has also been demonstrated.† In general, we find, surprisingly, that during REM sleep, thalamic and cortical neurons are more responsive than they are in the waking state. Many of the changes noted are most marked during actual REM bursts. Accordingly, there are both phasic and tonic components to REM-state activity.

Seemingly contrary to the direction of all these changes is a sharp attenuation of spinal reflexes and resting muscle tone in REM sleep, but these phenomena are probably due to an active inhibitory system [12, 63–64]. Therein lies the unique quality of REM sleep, that it is a time of considerable excitation within the brain which is largely blocked at the periphery [9, 54, 64–66]. Perhaps it is this inhibition of motor and reflex activity that allows perpetuation of behavioural sleep when many areas of the brain are discharging at frequencies approximating those during alert wakefulness [52–55].

The exhaustive studies of Jouvet and his colleagues have provided some understanding of the mechanism of REM sleep. These investigators have demonstrated an indispensable region for REM sleep in the rostral pons (nucleus pontis caudalis) which appears to be crucial for the entire range of REM phenomena [9]. A cat with this area ablated no longer exhibits REM phases or low-voltage fast EEG activity in sleep. It shows only two states, NREM sleep and wakefulness which may gradually progress to insomnia leading to death. Conversely, a decorticated cat shows no evidence of NREM sleep. The mesencephalic EEG never deviates from the low-voltage, fast tracing. However, REMs, myoclonic twitches, respiratory irregularity, and diminished muscle tone continue to appear regularly, in precise periods associated with discharges in subcortical structures identical to the discharges in intact animals during REM sleep. In between the episodes of REM sleep, the decorticate animal appears for the most part awake. Accordingly, Jouvet suggests that the pontine mechanism is both necessary and sufficient for REM sleep, whereas NREM sleep requires the presence of cortical tissue. His studies in decorticate and decerebrate humans indicate that in man there is an analogous dependence of REM sleep upon brain-stem and of NREM sleep upon cortex [12, 67]. Rossi *et al.* [68] have disagreed with

---

† KAWAMURA, H. and SAWYER, C. H. (1964). *Am. J. Physiol.* **207**, 1379; Wurtz R. H. (1965). *Electro-encephalog. Clin. Neurophysiol.* **18**, 649; The d-c potential shifts in REM sleep are opposite in sign in cat and rabbit, but in each species the REM shift is the reverse of the NREM shift. In the rat, early work showed the d-c shifts to be in the same direction in the two stages of sleep [Caspers, H. in *Brain Function* (Brazier, M. A. B. (Ed.)) (Univ. of California at Los Angeles, Forum on Medical Science, 1964), vol. 1, p. 177], but a recent study has demonstrated the shifts to be in opposite directions [Wurtz, R. H. (1965), *Electro-encephalog. Clin. Neurophysiol.* **19**, 521].

Jouvet as to specific nuclei but have validated his basic finding of an essential area for REM sleep in the pons. There is still some doubt concerning the specific connecting pathways from the pontine centre to the midbrain [50, 58, 69]. More extensive studies are necessary before we can be certain that, in cats, the exact site of initiation of the REM state discharges is the mid to rostral pontine reticular nuclei or that the mechanism is applicable in every detail to higher forms [46].

REM sleep and dreaming

It is now widely acknowledged that dreaming sleep and REM sleep are identical, though ideational material and poorly defined imagery can apparently persist through the entire range of sleep stages [11, 13, 70]. Numerous associations between dream hallucinations and alterations in physiological systems have been observed in the REM state. Although such correspondences are by no means always demonstrable or precise, they may reach a high order of specificity in the visual system. For example, REMs in abundance are observed at times of frequent alterations of gaze in the dream, whereas the presence of few REMs, or a total absence of REMs (during dreaming sleep), is correlated either with staring at immobile objects or with breaks in the pictorial imagery [10]. Roffwarg *et al.* [71] have shown that the number and direction of REMs may be predicted with reasonable accuracy by treating the dream scene as a visual event that the dreamer has scanned as he would the same event when awake. The fact that sequences of REMs associated with visual dream events can be correctly predicted through reference to

the REMs expected in replicated waking experience renders the old notion of the instantaneous dream extremely unlikely. Dement and Wolpert [10] fixed particular points in the flow of time in dreams by provoking incorporations of identifiable stimuli into the dream sequence and demonstrated a close correspondence between actual time and the sense of time in dreams. Dream events evidently have a dimension in real time, though intermediary steps in an action may be skipped ('telescoping') [71].

Additional psychophysiological relationships have been suggested by Wolpert's finding [72] of a correlation between dreamed limb excursions and action potentials in wrist muscles. Moreover, when sleep talking takes place in REM sleep (it usually does not), it may relate to the situation in the dream [73]. Hobson *et al.* [74] have shown that major respiratory irregularities (such as periods of apnea) are frequently linked to concurrent dream experiences such as talking, laughing, or choking. And penile erections, though typically present in the REM state, show size fluctuations in association with specific dream content (such as sexual activity, anxiety, attack) [33]. A single experience in Snyder's laboratory dramatically highlights these correlations. In the middle of a REM period a subject's respirations and heartbeat began to race. When awakened a few minutes later, he recalled that he was dreaming of participating in sexual intercourse. He had experienced a nocturnal emission just prior to the arousal [29].

Other physiological 'windows into the dream' may become available as new parameters are studied. The recently reported elevations of gastric hydrochloric acid in peptic-ulcer patients and the increases of adrenal corticoids in normal subjects during REM sleep [75] may turn out to vary in magnitude in relation to simultaneous dream content. It has already proved possible to derive crude inferences about dream content from variations in physiological activity during the REM period. Additional indirect support for existence of a biological relationship between mind and body events during the REM state is contributed by the finding of heightened vividness of imagery at moments of greatest physiological variation [29, 71, 74, 76]. There can no longer be any doubt that a dream, far from being merely a diaphanous and elusive creature of mind, is the sensate expression of a fundamental and rhythmically repetitive, and enormously active neurophysiological state. Hence dreaming, heretofore knowable only via subjective report and intuitive conjecture, is now accessible to more objective investigation.

Hallucinatory activity

There is general agreement that, with the exception of certain delirious states, dream hallucinations are more encompassing than other hallucinatory events, most of which are merely superimposed on a background of uninterrupted sensory input from the environment. In the dream the total perceptual field is hallucinated. Though predominantly visual, the imagery may include realistic components from most if not all sensory systems simultaneously [77]. It is common experience that every nuance of emotion as well as of perception—the full world of our experience—may be reduplicated in dreams. A sub-

stantial portion of the brain must be active during this state.

Dement [78] has suggested that dream hallucinations may constitute the only 'true' hallucinations because the sensory material in dreams does not depend upon external input at the time of dreaming (although concurrent stimulations may be incorporated into a dream in progress) [10, 77]. During REM sleep, the brain appears to be 'in business for itself'. Blinded individuals continue to experience visual imagery in dreams [19]. And input to the central nervous system from the body environment, as for example from a parched throat [10] or an empty stomach [80], does not seem to elicit overtly drive-reducing dream content, at least not in short-term laboratory experiments. These findings are easily reconciled with data from animal studies. During the REM state the optic tract of intact cats does not exhibit the sharp elevations in discharge frequency that are seen in the lateral geniculate body and occipital cortex [81], and firing in the geniculate body does not diminish as a result of acute enucleation of the eye-ball [82]. These findings suggest that visual 'information' supplying the dream appears to originate within the brain-stem and 'feeds' into the visual afferent pathway at some intermediary point along its route [8]. The fact that the spike discharges in the lateral geniculate body are synchronous with those in both the pontine reticular formation [56, 57] and visual cortex [8, 82] further supports this view.

Just as the dreamer, as an observer of the dream, is confronted by (hallucinated) sensory 'percepts', he is also involved as a participant in the dream action in responding to them with (hallucinated) motor activity. The dreamer may experience the appearance and proprioceptive sense of his arm moving to brush away a bee that he hears in flight and sees alighting on his nose. Hence hallucinatory experiences occur not only of sensory objects but also of sensory components of motor performance 'evoked' by the hallucinated object. As mentioned above, in REM sleep, upper motor-neuron activity is markedly increased, spikes in the extraocular muscles are co-ordinated with discharges in the visual afferent system, and phasic bursts of muscle potentials may accompany hallucinated movements [72]. We may conjecture, therefore, that impulses are introduced from within the central nervous system into motor as well as sensory pathways, and that the recordable motor discharges may be correlated with hallucinated 'percepts' of, or 'intentions towards', movement.

Not only, then, is the brain highly activated during REM sleep from a physiological point of view, but as we have just speculated, it seems to be 'perceiving' and 'reacting' to its percepts much as an awake brain does. If the dreaming brain is in any sense 'awake', however, it seems attuned primarily to the compelling phenomena originating and being perceived within itself. On the other hand, under conditions such as direct suggestion (hypnotic or otherwise) or threat of negative reinforcement, subjects in REM sleep can increase their reactivity to exogenous stimuli to levels greater than during any other stage of sleep [83, 84]. Inattention, therefore, may to some extent explain the high arousal thresholds in REM sleep [37, 38, 40]. When external events compete with internal events for significance, however, attention may be diverted from the latter [84, 85].

Approaches to function

Speculations concerning the role of the REM state have risen mainly from two previous lines of study: phylogenetic and deprivational. Because of the location of the pontine REM sleep mechanism, Jouvet first considered REM sleep to be a phylogenetically archaic state. The findings that in the newborn cat the behavioural and EEG characteristics of the REM state mature earlier than those of NREM sleep or waking, and that sustained periods of REM sleep appear directly after arousal without intermediary NREM sleep, initially seemed to confirm the more 'primitive' quality of the REM state [43].

Correspondingly, Jouvet believed NREM sleep to be a state which depends on a functioning neocortex, acquired in the course of phylogenetic telencephalization. He therefore referred to it as 'neo-sleep' [12]. A corollary of this scheme is that species having less neocortical tissue would be expected to manifest greater proportions of REM sleep. However, studies on the rat [41, 50], opposum [41], sheep [44, 47], goat [45], cat [12], and monkey [41] have not shown a consistent trend in that direction. The most primitive vertebrates polygraphically demonstrated to have REM sleep are birds, in which the periods are exceedingly brief (0·3 per cent) [47]. Among the reptiles, the tortoise has been studied but the REM state has not been demonstrated [86]. Therefore, only in the ontogenetic sense can REM sleep be considered a 'primitive' state [48]. More data are needed concerning the phylogeny of REM sleep, but if it is borne out that

REM sleep developed later in evolution than NREM sleep, phylogenetic studies may still clarify two important questions: (1) What functional requirement was met by the development of REM sleep? (2) Why did the rhombencephalon become the site of the REM sleep mechanism?

The attempt to study the function of REM sleep by experimentally eliminating it was first made by Dement [26]. By awakening subjects at the commencement of each REM period he effectively reduced the amount of REM sleep. After a series of consecutive 'deprivation' nights the subjects were allowed uninterrupted sleep, and almost all exhibited a dramatic rise in amount and percentage of the REM phase. This was regarded as evidence of a physiological 'need' for REM sleep. Additional experiments in humans and animals have confirmed the tendency to compensate for lost REM sleep after artificial interruptions of sleep [8, 27, 87-89].

Suppression of REM sleep by experimental destruction of the nucleus pontis caudalis causes hyperirritability and hallucinating-like behaviour in animals [12]. These changes are reversible if only small amounts of REM sleep reappear, whereas cats who do not recover any capacity for REM sleep may progress to a state of insomnia and agitation and eventually die. These animals have brain-stem lesions, and thus to implicate loss of REM sleep exclusively for these difficulties may not be warranted. In contrast, studies of *functional* deprivation of REM sleep in cats currently being pursued by D. Jouvet *et al.* [87] and Dement [90] reveal surprisingly few overt behavioural changes in the animals even after lengthy periods of complete deprivation, though persistent tachycardia [87] and a faster auditory-recovery cycle [91] have been demonstrated during the deprivation. Hypersexuality is also a feature of the deprived cats, but when awake the animals may appear remarkably unaffected by the deprivation. Behavioural changes in humans have been observed only after the 15th day of continuous deprivation of REM sleep in recent studies [9, 27]. Therefore, it appears that the function of REM sleep in the intact adult organism is not so immediate that the consequences of REM sleep deprivation are soon apparent or necessarily fatal.

Evolution of sleep patterns

Because of the inconclusiveness of phylogenetic and deprivational approaches to the function of REM sleep, we [16, 92] and others [93-97] have begun to examine its role in human ontogenetic development. These observations, as well as those in newborn and immature animals [43-45, 47-49], reveal that REM sleep assumes a high proportion of total sleep in the first days of life and that its amount and ratio diminish as maturation proceeds (Fig. 10.1). Earlier work in our laboratory with infants and children pointed to certain relationships among maturation, daily behaviour, and evolving sleep patterns [16].

In infancy, when the proportion of time awake is smaller than in any other period of life, there is a large amount of REM activity. REM periods appear soon after sleep begins and are of random duration at any time of the night. Later, when the developing infant spends protracted intervals awake in increasingly active involvement with the environment (particularly when locomotive capacity is attained), the

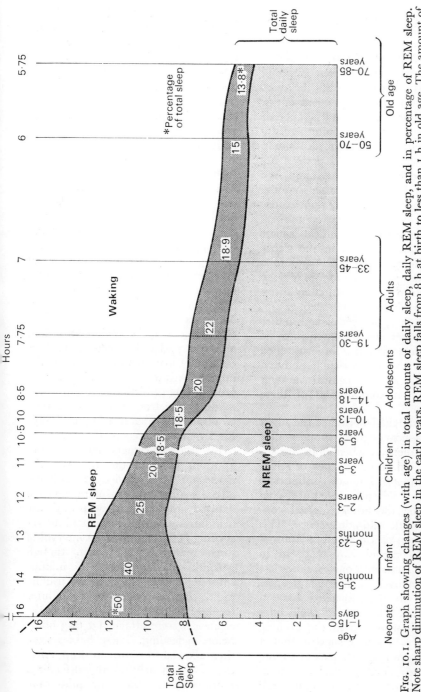

FIG. 10.1. Graph showing changes (with age) in total amounts of daily sleep, daily REM sleep, and in percentage of REM sleep. Note sharp diminution of REM sleep in the early years. REM sleep falls from 8 h at birth to less than 1 h in old age. The amount of NREM sleep throughout life remains more constant, falling from 8 h to 5 h. In contrast to the steep decline of REM sleep, the quantity of NREM sleep is undiminished for many years. Although total daily REM sleep falls steadily during life, the percentage rises slightly in adolescence and early adulthood. This rise does not reflect an increase in amount; it is due to the fact that REM sleep does not diminish as quickly as total sleep. Work in progress in several laboratories indicates that the percentage of REM sleep in the 50- to 85-year group may be somewhat higher than represented here. Data for the 33- to 45- and 70- to 85-year groups are taken from Strauch [139] and Lairy [140], respectively.

total amount as well as the percentage of REM sleep diminishes.

This evolution in the relative proportions of the sleep stages continues through the period when napping terminates. Long stretches of deep NREM sleep occupy the first hours. Correspondingly, the first REM period in children past the napping age appears much later and is shorter than in children who nap. REM periods become longer towards morning. We have considered it probable that the child's progressively closer approximation of a diurnal pattern of uninterrupted daytime wakefulness causes corresponding changes in the sleep-stage pattern. Post-nappers ($4\frac{1}{2}$ to 7 years) average 110 to 120 min of deep NREM sleep (stage 4) in comparison to 75 to 80 min in the pubescent group. It is, of course, not yet clear whether these changes are a consequence of lengthening periods of sustained arousal, increased muscular activity, maturation of the central nervous system, or a combination of these factors.

The first REM period of the night usually appears 50 to 70 min after sleep commences, whereas in the $4\frac{1}{2}$- to 7-year-old group, latency of REM onset is 3 to 4 h. Latency continues to shorten as children mature but it does not assume the adult interval consistently until mid-adolescence. This phenomenon of a delayed or 'missed' first REM period may reappear in adults under conditions of sleep loss [98]. Moreover, nocturnal sleepers who nap in the afternoon have a shorter REM latency in their naps than those who nap in the evening [99]. These findings suggest that a condition ('fatigue', for lack of a more exact term) develops under circumstances of prolonged arousal (and possibly intensive activity) which tips the normal balance between REM and NREM sleep mechanisms, augmenting temporarily the 'need' for deep NREM sleep and antagonizing REM sleep processes. We speculate that the immature central nervous system is more vulnerable to 'fatigue', though youngsters are unquestionably more active than adults.

Studies of neonates

Electro-encephalograms and electro-oculograms from 14 normal full-term newborns were recorded by the usual technique for registration of protracted sleep [5, 71]. All but one of the infants, aged 9 days, were under 5 days old and three were only 5, 9, and 29 h old, respectively, when monitored. Newborns in the Columbia-Presbyterian Nurseries are fed every 4 hours. Their environment lacks major variation, and one period between feedings is essentially like all the others. All the infants had received a high Apgar [100] rating at birth. No attempt was made to select according to the type of obstetrical anaesthesia employed. Each infant was recorded once.

Electrode placement required 30 to 45 min. In 9 of the 14 cases the electrodes were applied immediately after a feeding, and the infant was then allowed uninterrupted sleep until the next feeding. In these instances the recording period followed an interval of some manipulation which, though generally undisturbing to the infants, caused a postponement of the usually rapid commencement of sleep after feeding. In the remaining infants the electrodes were attached 2 to 3 hours before a feeding. These babies were then allowed to return to sleep. After the next regularly scheduled feeding, there was no need for additional

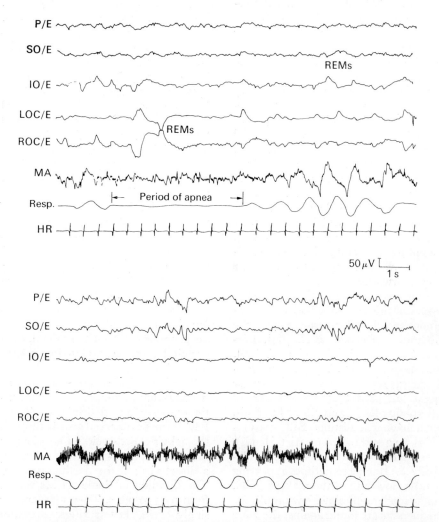

Fig. 10.2. Recordings of 30-s intervals from the two stages of sleep in a newborn. Top REM sleep; bottom, NREM sleep. EEG lead: P/E, parietal referred to both ears. Eye-movement leads: (vertical) SO/E, supra-orbital ridge to ears; IO/E, infra-orbital ridge to ears; (horizontal) LOC/E, left outer canthus to ears; ROC/E, right outer canthus to ears; MA, resting muscle activity (recorded submentally); Resp., respirations; HR, pulse. The electro-encephalogram is low-voltage and fast in REM sleep and higher-voltage, with frequent 1- to 2-cycle/s waves, in NREM sleep. There are short trains of saw-tooth waves in upper EEG tracing just preceding sharp vertical and horizontal REMs. Note the absence of muscle activity, the rapid respiratory rate, and the changing respiratory amplitude in REM stage.

experimental manipulations. This procedure made it possible to achieve a truer picture not only of post-feeding sleep onset but of the full feeding-to-feeding sleep pattern. Resting muscle activity was recorded with submentally placed electrodes [30] and respiratory rate by means of a 0·5 mm thermocouple placed just inside a naris known to be unobstructed. A precordial electrode was used for heart rate. Heart and respiratory rates were tallied during either the first or second half of each minute of recording, whichever contained less muscle artifact. Half-minutes during which gross body movement occurred were not counted. Counting was stopped during small body movements and not resumed for 10 s afterwards.

Our observations of the sleep EEG cycles of full-term newborns are consistent in all major respects with the findings of Delange *et al.* [93], Parmelee *et al.* [94], Monod *et al.* [96], and Weitzman *et al.* [97]. The sleep tracings, whether recorded day or night, all consist of a succession of alternating REM and NREM periods, each having a distinct EEG pattern (Figs. 10.2 and 10.3, see parietal leads). The REM EEG is a low-voltage, relatively fast tracing sometimes appearing a little slower than the waking EEG. Some moderately slow, low-amplitude frequencies are found against the more rapid, low-amplitude background. Amplitude averages 15 to 25 μV and reaches a maximum of 40 μV. Brief sequences of 3-cycle/s 'saw-tooth' waves appear over central areas, often just preceding or in conjunction with REMs.

The NREM EEG, by contrast, is characterized by frequent notched, high amplitude slow waves (2 to 3 cycles/s), seen best in frontal leads, against a low-voltage background. Moderately slow frequencies (3 to 8 cycles/s) are often interspersed between the 2- to 3-cycle activity. The NREM EEG has an amplitude averaging 40 to 75 μV. Bursts of 13- to 15-cycle/s waves were seen in most of the infants over postfrontal and parietal areas. Though lacking the typical 'spindle' form and duration, they often follow high-voltage slow waves, having much the same relationship to them as spindles to K complexes in adult stage-2 recordings.

The major distinguishing features of the NREM EEG are the slow, high-amplitude elements and 13- to 15-cycle/s bursts. High-amplitude (delta) waves of 1 to 2 cycles/s are occasionally seen, but they are never a continuous or predominant waveform. The NREM EEG of the newborn resembles the adult NREM stage-2 sleep tracing. Frontal parietal, and occipital areas are all in phase with respect to EEG shifts.

The low-voltage, fast EEG pattern is invariably accompanied by discontinuous ocular deflections. These REMs can be observed grossly through the baby's closed eyelids. Occasionally the eye is open wide enough to allow a direct view of the darting eyeballs. The duration of single REMs ranges from 0·05 to 0·2 s. They may appear singly or in clusters (Figs. 10.2 and 10.3) and are predominantly vertical. We have never observed a uniform NREM EEG pattern accompanied by REMs in a newborn.

When all sleep onsets are aligned at a point in time (Fig. 10.4), it is clear that periodic re-emergence of REM sleep adheres to a rhythm for the group of newborns as a whole. The sequence from wakefulness to sleep is the reverse of that in adults. An almost direct transition from the awake state to REM sleep marks sleep onset in newborns. Only after the initial REM period terminates does NREM sleep emerge for any appreciable duration. Conversely, in adults the eventual debut of the first REM period waits upon a 50-to-70 min period of NREM sleep.

As in the records of older individuals, the EEG of the first REM period (and sometimes of the second) may show some intermingling of high-voltage, slow waves. However, the change

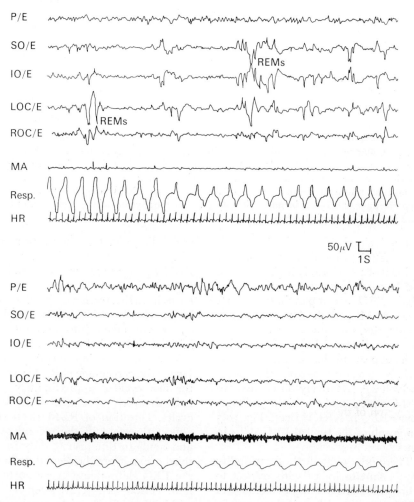

FIG. 10.3. Recording of 12-s intervals from the two stages of sleep in a newborn. Top, REM sleep; bottom, NREM sleep. Symbols as in Fig. 10.2. The SO/E lead picks up the EEG in addition to vertical REMs because of its prefrontal placement. Note the absence of REMs. MA baseline is wavy because of respiration, but resting tone is clearly higher in REM sleep. Apneic periods, as in the above tracing, are common in the REM stages.

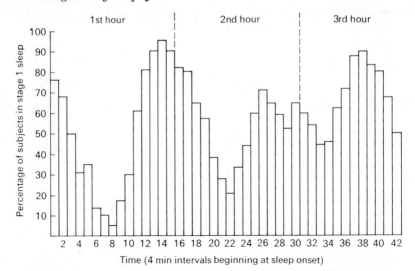

FIG. 10.4. Bar graph representing the ratio of subjects wholly in REM sleep (stage 1) during successive 4-min intervals. All times of onset of sleep have been aligned. If subjects were in REM sleep during a portion of a 4-min interval, percentage was prorated. Hence, in the first 4 min of sleep, because of fragmented or slightly delayed REM periods, the percentage of subjects in stage 1 is only 76. Note the rhythmical re-emergence of REM periods across the entire group.

in stage is clearly identifiable inasmuch as the EEG of the first-cycle NREM period is of considerably higher voltage and lower frequency than the rather mixed EEG accompanying the first cycle REM period. After the early sleep cycles, subsequent cycles exhibit the more distinct EEG differentiation with respect to REM and NREM periods described above—that is, a low-voltage, relatively fast EEG in REM sleep, and a higher-voltage, slower EEG in NREM sleep. Fig. 10.5 is a graph of the typical EEG shifts in a newborn.

There is a great deal of variability from infant to infant with respect to sleep-cycle duration and percentage of REM sleep. This is particularly true in the first cycle. The findings for the group as a whole are represented in Table 10.1. The mean REM percentage is 48·8.† As an illustration of

variability, Fig. 10.6 shows the record of a newborn whose feeding-to-feeding REM percentage approached 65. Usually the first sleep cycle in newborns has a shorter mean duration than later cycles. Even if the lengths of sleep cycles are taken into account, the initial REM period is proportionately briefer than ensuing REM periods. Hence the percentage of REM sleep in the first cycle is approximately one-half that in subsequent individual cycles. Duration of REM sleep rises almost threefold in the second cycle and tends to diminish slightly in the third cycle. From the second cycle on, the EEG shifts phase every 20 to 35 min. Periods of NREM sleep remain within these limits fairly consistently, but REM periods exhibit greater

† Recent 24-hour recordings in this laboratory confirm this as the daily percentage of REM sleep.

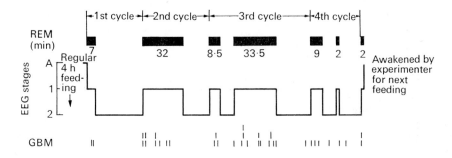

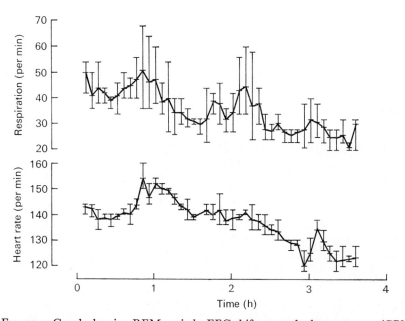

Fig. 10.5. Graph showing REM periods, EEG shifts, gross body movement (GBM), and respiratory and heart rates during a 3-h 35-min period of sleep between feedings in a 4-day-old infant. Each cycle begins with a REM period (stage 1) and ends with a NREM period (stage 2) longer than 15 min. Sleep onset is directly from waking to REM sleep (stage 1). Gross body movements occur predominantly at the beginning of and during REM periods. Vertical lines represent successive 5-min spans of respiration and heart-rate recording. Top of each line indicates the fastest per-min rate, and bottom of each line, the slowest per-min rate, in each 5-min portion. The connecting lines join points designating mean per-min rates for each 5-min span. Note, particularly with respiration, the usual increase in rate and widening of range of per-min rates, commencing with and sustained throughout each REM period. There is an over-all slowing of respiratory and cardiac rates as the sleep period progresses. Note that the latter two REM periods are fragmented by NREM intervals of less than 15 min. This occurs in one fifth of all REM periods recorded in this series. Total time of REM sleep is 1 h 32 min (43·2 per cent).

deviation about the mean (two REM periods exceeding 50 min have been recorded). In general, second and third cycles are split almost evenly between the REM and NREM phases, and REM percentage is fairly constant from the second cycle on.

Physiological characteristics

Except for an occasional gross body twitch and the respiratory excursions of the chest cavity, NREM sleep may be considered essentially devoid of muscular activity. The infant lies passive and motionless, in marked

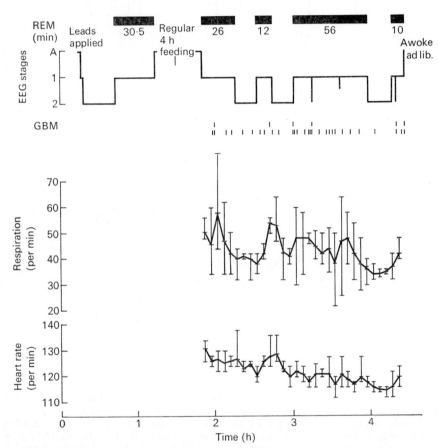

FIG. 10.6. Graph of another sleep record in a 2-day-old infant, showing REM periods, EEG shifts, gross body movements (GBM), respiration rate, and heart rate. Stage 1 = REM sleep; stage 2 = NREM sleep. As in Fig. 10.5, vertical lines represent 5-min spans of respiratory and heart rate recording, and connecting lines join the mean rates/min for each 5-min interval. Leads were attached during previous sleep period and infant returned to sleep until feeding. The first REM period is unusually long (26 min) after feeding in this infant. Note the higher and more variable respiratory rates during REM periods. This point is less clear for heart rate but both rates show slight decrease during sleep period. Note 56-min REM period. REM sleep is 64·4 per cent of total (2 h 36 min) sleep.

contrast to the almost continuous muscle contractions during the REM state. Grimaces, whimpers, smiles, twitches of the face and extremities are interspersed with gross shifts of position of the limbs. There are frequent 10- to 15-s episodes of tonic, athetoid writhing of the torso, limbs, and digits. Bursts of REMs commonly accompany the generalized muscle contractions, and approaches isoelectric levels (0 to 10 μV) in REM sleep. Whenever muscle contractions occur, electromyographic potentials appear and disappear instantaneously as the contraction terminates. The activity may be only as brief as 1 to 2 s. Hence, there is a fascinating confluence of two skeletal muscle phenomena during REM sleep: suppression of muscle

TABLE 10.1. *Mean Duration of Sleep Cycles and REM Periods and Mean Percentages of REM Sleep, in 14 Human Neonates. Standard Deviations appear in Parentheses.*

Sleep cycle	Duration of cycle (min)	Length of REM period (min)	Percentage REM
1st	43·4 (11·4)	12·6 (10·7)	29·1† (15·2)
2nd	61·2 (17·8)	33·9 (15·2)	55·0† (12·6)
3rd	54·1 (13·3)	29·8 (8·4)	57·0† (6·6)
All cycles			48·8‡ (10·3)

† Weighted means.
‡ Four infants fell asleep before all leads were in place. Data for their first sleep cycle are hence incomplete and have been omitted. Because percentage of REM is appreciably less in the first cycle than in subsequent cycles, omission of these infants' first-cycles slightly raises the ratio of REM to total sleep for the whole group. If all data for these infants are dropped, REM sleep is 46·4 per cent (S.D. 6·9) of total sleep.

but the former are also present in the absence of other body movements. We have also observed that in the REM state, newborns display facial mimicry which gives the appearance of sophisticated expressions of emotion or thought such as perplexity, disdain, scepticism, and mild amusement. We have not noted such nuances of expression in the same newborns when awake.

Though phasic muscular contractions are extremely numerous during the REM sleep of neonates, we have found a striking reduction in resting muscle activity (RMA) occurring in conjunction with each REM period emergence (Figs. 10.2 and 10.3). The amplitude of RMA is greatest in the awake state (40 to 60 μV), is slightly lower in NREM sleep (10 to 30 μV), tone punctuated by frequent muscle contractions.

Muscle tone is always present during the body of the NREM periods. But between the well-defined stages of sleep there are transitional phases of approximately 1 to 5 min. Usually after an extended period of NREM sleep, RMA amplitude gradually ebbs, though the NREM EEG persists for a few minutes. At the same time there is a sharp increase in frequency of gross body, facial, and sucking movements. Finally, after one of the body movements, the RMA will remain below its pre-movement base line and, at virtually the same moment, breathing becomes uneven. The EEG then flattens to the characteristic REM pattern and REMs appear. This

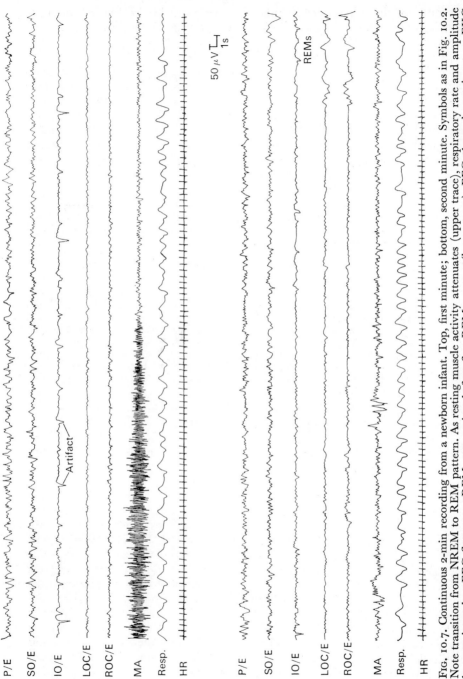

FIG. 10.7. Continuous 2-min recording from a newborn infant. Top, first minute; bottom, second minute. Symbols as in Fig. 10.2. Note transition from NREM to REM pattern. As resting muscle activity attenuates (upper trace), respiratory rate and amplitude become irregular. EEG flattens to REM pattern just before first REMs appear (lower trace). EEG channel contains some EKG artifact. MA in lower trace shows some irregularity and increased amplitude during sucking.

sequence—increase in body move-ment, gradual reduction and the complete suppression of RMA, com-mencement of respiratory irregularity, appearance of a lower-voltage, faster EEG, and finally REMs—describes the transition stage which heralds (or con-stitutes) the onset of REM sleep. Fig. 10.7 shows such a transition period. At the termination of a REM period, RMA may not immediately return to the prior NREM level. Even when slow waves have returned to the EEG and REMs have ceased, RMA may remain low for several minutes before a twitch, suck, or other muscular contraction seemingly triggers its in-stantaneous increase.

The diminution of RMA at sleep onset serves as a specific indicator in newborns that sleep has commenced in spite of an almost negligible change in the EEG from the waking state. If it were not for this substantial reduction, the moment of passage from waking to sleep would still defy exact designa-tion. RMA may be inhibited abruptly or gradually diminish over the course of a few minutes as sleep supervenes, depending on whether the infant has passed directly into the REM phase or through a brief interval (1 to 3 min) of NREM sleep. In either case, the diminution definitely establishes onset of sleep. As long as the baby is awake, RMA remains relatively high.

Figs. 10.2 and 10.3 demonstrate some differences between the respira-tory patterns in the two phases of sleep.† In REM sleep, respiratory rate is 18 per cent greater than in NREM sleep. More critical, however, is the very irregular breathing, which results in significantly greater minute-to-

† Statistical data on respiratory rate, heart rate and their respective variabilities will be published by us in a separate report.

minute variation. Infants commonly display periods of apnea, usually but not exclusively associated with REM bursts, lasting up to 10 s (Fig. 10.3). Contrary to the even respirations during NREM sleep, wide fluctuations in chest expansion characterize REM sleep.

With the advent of REM sleep, res-piratory rate increases. With the transition to the next NREM period the rate falls to a new low. Hence rate elevations accompanying REM periods embark from a progressively diminishing base, and there is thus a systematic decrease in rate (Figs. 10.5 and 10.6).

As with respiration, there is a cycle-to-cycle decrease in heart rate, though not nearly as sharply defined (Figs. 10.5 and 10.6). Mean heart rate is 3·4 per cent higher during REM sleep. This difference, though statistically significant, is not so striking as the disparity in respiratory rates. Heart-rate variability is not clearly greater in REM sleep. Analysis of heart rate when the muscular activity of each stage is taken into consideration reveals that the former may not be a truly independent discriminator of REM and NREM stages. During REM sleep the frequent body movements, REMs, and irregular, rapid respira-tions may account for the apparent elevation in REM heart rate.

Just as a gradual diminution in muscle tone heralds a REM period, so do progressive increases in mouth movements (resembling sucking). This activity may be observed 5 to 10 min before a shift to REM sleep. It reaches a crescendo at the commencement of the REM period but continues to be evident throughout the period. At termination, there is again a brief augmentation of sucking which trails off quickly as the NREM phase is definitively established. Hence, sucking activity seems to be connected mainly with the onset of REM sleep.

We have often noted an exception to this general pattern in the sleep cycle just before a feeding. During this cycle, frequent mouth movements persist during the NREM period. This is interesting in light of studies on resumption of gastric ('hunger') contractions in infants after nursing. Gastric contractions resume 150 to 160 min after a feeding [10], almost exactly the interval before the appearance of sustained NREM sucking. Sucking in sleep may be a manifestation of REM activation, but it continues into the NREM phase under conditions of physiological hunger. Aserinsky and Kleitman had previously reported that spontaneous awakenings in infants generally occur at commencement of REM phases [102]. We have confirmed this finding and have further noted that the awakenings generally occur in the REM period that just follows the breakthrough of persistent NREM sucking. Past a certain threshold of activity, therefore, the REM period appears to give way to arousal.

Discussion

The EEG is one of the most widely used criteria for determining change in state of consciousness. However, there has been considerable disagreement with regard to the differentiation of the

† By the time NREM sleep ensues in the first sleep cycle, the infant appears unquestionably asleep by behavioural criteria. However, the appearance of the second cycle REM period must have posed a new dilemma. On the basis of only the unadorned EEG tracing, which is difficult to distinguish grossly from the waking pattern, especially when accompanied by an increase in behavioural activity, earlier workers were probably compelled to

EEG patterns of wakefulness and sleep in the newborn. Some investigators [10, 104] reported finding determining criteria, but others [105] could not demonstrate fundamental alterations between sleep and waking patterns. With one exception (see [106]), most observers had concurred that the neonate's sleep EEG cannot be divided into specific stages.

The reason for this confusion is now apparent in light of the discovery that one of the EEG stages of sleep in newborns closely resembles the waking EEG. The stage in question is the relatively low-voltage, high-frequency pattern of REM sleep described above. Previous disagreements with respect to EEG differentiation of the stages of sleep and of sleep from waking in the newborn were undoubtedly fostered by the fact that REM sleep directly succeeds waking at sleep onset (unlike the normal adult pattern in which NREM sleep always precedes REM sleep). Infants generally close their eyelids when passing into sleep, but this was probably of little assistance to previous investigators attempting to specify sleep onset, since REM sleep brings with it transient eyelid openings, frequent twitches, body and eye movements, irregular respiration, and vocalizations. Thus actual commencement of sleep, which can now be easily identified in neonates with the assistance of electromyography, was no doubt frequently mistaken for a continuation of the awake state.†

decide that the infant had either awakened, or (if it were felt on behavioural grounds that the baby was still asleep) that the sleep EEG is extremely variable and unstable, often looking like an awake record. Now, with the help of EMG and REM recordings in the neonate, both stages of sleep can be distinguished clearly from the awake state as well as from each other.

'Dreaming' in the newborn

There can be little question that the stage of sleep in newborns that manifests REMs and a low-voltage, relatively fast EEG is related to adult REM sleep. Therefore the REM state must originate from inborn neurophysiological processes, as opposed to being engendered by experience. Important as this finding is, the fact of most significance is that the neonate spends fully one-half of its total sleep, or one-third of its entire existence, in this unique state of activation. In view of this, new questions must be considered. For instance, does REM sleep fulfil a vital function in the newborn? Does the sharp reduction of REM sleep in the first few years of life indicate that its most important function is related to early development?

In order to explore the implications of these questions, we must first deal with certain ambiguities. Since it has been previously established that REM sleep constitutes the time of dreaming in children and adults, does the *de facto* presence of a REM stage at birth indicate that newborns dream? And, if the REMs of adults are related to dream imagery, to what, if anything, are the REMs of newborns related?

If by dreaming one means a succession of vivid, discrete yet integrated, hallucinated images, it is hardly likely that newborns, who have extremely crude patterned vision [107], 'dream'. Though a most convincing demonstration of the relation of REM sleep to dreaming in adults has been the correlation of the REMs with the spatiotemporal aspects of visual imagery [71], REMs are certainly not unfailing

counterparts of visual imagery under all circumstances. REM sleep is not necessarily associated with the presence of either visual imagery or a functioning cerebral cortex. For example, REMs in sleep have been reported in congenitally blind individuals [108], functionally decorticate humans [67], decorticate cats [109], and newborn kittens [43, 48]. Rather than indicating that neonates experience patterned visual dreams or that REMs and imagery cannot be related in the dreams of older individuals, the fact that neonates and decorticates have REM activity indicates that absence of visual phenomena, due to immaturity of the ascending sensory pathways and visual cortex, need not preclude REM-state functioning of the oculomotor apparatus. The REMs, as well as all other phenomena of REM sleep, have been shown to result from activity in the pons. Hence, if the pontine-oculomotor pathways are not cut, the REMs persist [9, 68, 110].

Because the spike potentials in the lateral geniculate body, occipital cortex, and extraocular muscles have the same pontine source [56, 57, 82], it is not surprising that phasic activity in the geniculate body and occipital cortex is synchronous with REM bursts [55, 82]. The sensory-motor discharges occurring during REM sleep in the visuo-oculomotor system may therefore be thought of, in their barest essentials, as arising in the pontine sleep centre and travelling simultaneously over separate motor and sensory pathways, eventually reaching the oculomotor nuclei† and

† We do not intend to imply either a necessarily direct route from the pons to the oculomotor nuclei or a lack of influence from other centres upon the eye movements. The work of Jeannerod, Mouret, and Jouvet [110]

indicates a 'complexification' of pontine-triggered REMs at the mesencephalic level because of the actions of the occipital cortex, frontal cortex, superior colliculus, and other subcortical structures.

visual receiving areas, respectively. As long as the common pontine source of stimulation is intact, the sensory routes may be interrupted (as after decortication) or be relatively inoperative (as is probably the case in infancy) without interrupting the functioning of the motor route. It would also be true that interruption of the motor pathways for eye movements should not, in itself, interfere with visual imagery in REM sleep. Accordingly, though the common centre subserving a link between visual imagery and REMs is operative before birth, actual visuo-motor correlations must await maturation of the neurophysiological apparatus for vision and visual memory.

The question of whether memory traces are established in humans at such an early age and, if so, whether they are highly transient or permanent is not currently accessible to investigation. It is known that learning, of the conditioned response variety, may be demonstrated at birth and even before [111]. Hence, it is not out of the question to speculate that even in foetal life the REM state may provide the neurophysiological setting for hallucinatory repetition of accumulated experience. Prior to the infant's acquisition of visual perception and visual memory, rudimentary hallucinations might be expressed in sensory modalities in which intrauterine experience had occurred. Speculations aside, however, whether or not 'dreaming' understood as subjective sensation exists in the newborn, 'dreaming' understood as physiological process certainly does.

REM sleep in newborns

If we dismiss the 'dream experience' as the vital attribute of REM sleep in the newborn period, we are in a position to consider the possible physiological significance of the great abundance of REM sleep in early life. Parmelee *et al.* [112] have confirmed our finding of approximately 50 per cent REM sleep in the newborn at term [92]. In premature infants, the percentage of REM sleep is 58 at 36 to 38 weeks, 67 at 33 to 35 weeks, and 80 (one infant) at 30 weeks gestational age. The direction of the data supports the contention that the proportion of REM sleep nears 100 per cent before the 30th week [112], but as yet little is known about what processes are responsible for the profusion of REM sleep in the immature organism or, for that matter, for the regulation of the proportion of REM sleep at any age. Nevertheless, at least two possible systems of regulation may be considered: (1) the amount of REM sleep is a 'passive' consequence of the relative presence or absence (possibly due to cortical immaturity) of restraining influences on the REM centre; (2) the amount of REM sleep is a product of an 'active' system which responds to the specific requirements of the central nervous system for that state in foetal and neonatal periods of development just as it responds to the requirements in later maturational periods.

With regard to the first possibility, the cortex is known to send inhibitory impulses to many subcortical areas. Recently, Koella and Ferry [113] have demonstrated that the brain-stem stimulates both cerebral hemispheres and that each hemisphere feeds back restraining forces upon the brainstem. Such inhibitory regulation may be operative with respect to brain-stem centres for REM sleep. And, accordingly, the large proportions of REM sleep in the neonatal period may be 'passively' determined by a lack of restriction on the pontine centre because of insufficient cortical super-imposition.

Data on evoked responses [104, 97, 114] indicate that the human cortex at birth has achieved at least some degree of functional maturity. Furthermore, given such a 'passive' mechanism, it should follow that 'passive' release of REM sleep processes would be a prominent finding after a mature organism had been subjected to decortication or interference with the NREM sleep mechanism. The fact is, however, that the totally decorticated cat manifests less REM sleep (15 to 20 per cent) than the intact animal (25 per cent), and the partially decorti-cated cat shows no change from the normal percentage [9]. Where record-ings have been possible in decorticate humans [12, 67, 109] the proportion of REM sleep is said to be in the range of 20 per cent of the total registration period [67], but because no 24-h recordings have been published we do not know whether this figure allows for diurnal variation. Still, the over-all results are certainly not what would be expected if REM ratios were estab-lished solely as a result of the degree of cortical inhibition of the REM mechanism. It has also been demon-strated that when NREM sleep is cut owing to lesions in the basal forebrain area, the time formerly occupied by NREM sleep is henceforth taken up by alert patterns. The percentage of REM sleep does not increase [115]. Hence, there is obvious inadequacy in an ontogenetic explanation of high percentages of REM sleep, based en-tirely on an early paucity of cortical inhibition. It is nevertheless likely that as the brain matures, the REM centre

may have to 'compete for time' in reciprocal interplay with other centres and that it may be subject to some type of regulatory feedback. We have by no means fully ruled out the possibility that the REM centre, like other excitatory mechanisms, may achieve functional capacity before auxiliary inhibitory mechanisms and, hence, that the high percentages of REM sleep in early life merely reflect a failure of the pontine system to be turned off or to turn itself off. Our emphasis, however, is not on why the REM mechanism operates so prolific-ally in the foetus and newborn, but on the functional effects of that pro-lificacy in terms of the central nervous system.

To turn to the second possibility, there are strong reasons for considering that the pontine mechanism is at least partially autonomous. To put it another way, the output of the REM mechanism may not be subject solely to greater or lesser degrees of cortical dominance, but may be dynamically reactive to the organism's need for the REM state. As an example, the paroxysmal attacks of sleep in narco-lepsy have been identified as REM sleep [116] and may be interpreted as episodes of pathological overactivity or premature triggering of the pontine sleep mechanism. Furthermore, new-borns and REM-deprived adults as well as narcoleptics show a forward displacement of the first REM period to the moment of sleep onset [116, 8]. Substantial evidence is accumulating that the REM mechanism can com-pensate for specific losses of REM sleep by means of subsequent increases in REM time [26, 27, 8, 87–89]. Recent studies of cats placed on vary-ing sleep-loss or sleep-excess schedules demonstrate that their REM percentages increase or decrease to effect adjustments towards baseline values [88]. Moreover, quantitative alterations may be only part of the readjustment, in that REM phenomena have been shown to be qualitatively more 'intense' under circumstances of restricted REM time [92]. It is also pertinent to the notion of an 'active' mechanism that a number of drugs such as lysergic acid diethylamide (LSD) [25] and butyrolactone [117] apparently exert a specific stimulating effect on the REM mechanism.

Of course, if the REM state is an expression of a process, autonomous in the sense that it is not completely under cortical control, to what is it responding? Jouvet [9] and Dement [8] have both proposed that the REM mechanism is triggered by a neurohumoral substance which accumulates to a critical threshold level and is then released. This hypothesis would account for the heightened REM percentages following deprivation of REM sleep, on the basis of over-accumulation or 'back-up' of the specific agent. Correspondingly, the effects of pharmacologic substances on REM sleep could be treated as instances of blockage, neutralization, early release, or enhancement of the action of the endogenous agent.

Evidence for a neurohumoral process is scant. Nevertheless, such a mechanism is suggested by the finding that short stimulations of the nucleus pontis caudalis can induce long periods of REM sleep followed by intervals of temporary refractoriness to further triggering [9]. The study of Dement *et al.* [118], demonstrating that the compensatory increase in REM time following REM deprivation may be delayed but not vitiated, also lends support to a hypothesis that allows for

accumulation and storage of some substance. Preliminary data reveal that a specific agent may be found in the cerebrospinal fluid of cats subjected to long REM-deprivation schedules [119]. There is as yet little information about the chemical properties of the proposed agent, whether it accumulates intracellularly or extracellularly, and what type of transport is involved. Of course, any hypothesis which purports to account for the regulation of REM sleep will eventually have to explain the great quantities of REM sleep during early development.

Function of REM sleep in early development

Between the newborn period and young adulthood, mean REM sleep diminishes approximately 80 per cent (8 h to 1 h 40 min), whereas mean NREM sleep diminishes only 25 per cent (8 to 6 h); that is, of the total reduction in all sleep in that period, 75 per cent is in the REM portion (Fig. 10.1). Accordingly, in answer to the possible contention that there may be more REM sleep in infancy merely because infants sleep longer, it might well be argued that the sleep requirement in infancy is a function of the requirement for the REM stage. As stated earlier, we believe that the diminution of REM sleep in ontogenesis does not reflect merely a maturation of inhibiting centres. Rather, the drop-off may signify a reduced requirement for REM sleep after one of its most important early functions has been fulfilled.

Irrespective of the processes regulating proportions of REM sleep, the functional consequences of the protracted REM upheavals in the immature organism must be considered. Accordingly, we have suggested [16] that in early infancy, when waking life is limited in time and scope and offers little occasion for stimulation, the REM periods may allow a substantial (and necessary) discharge of activity. Now we would like to develop this formulation further.

Has it not formerly been our tendency to think of the foetus as receiving only those stimuli which are available to it from the protected uterine environment, and of the newborn as exposed to sensory excitation only by virtue of the provocations provided by waking life? Have we not traditionally considered the sleep of babies as well as of adults to constitute a surcease from excitation, a time of rest, a reversal of fatigue, and an opportunity for metabolic restitution? In this conventional view the infant either sleeps and is separated from external stimulation, or he is awake and receptive to it.

But we now are aware that during REM sleep brain activity is vigorous. Spontaneous electric discharge is at peak rates in many and diverse areas of the central nervous system [39, 53–58]. Reports that intense hallucinations are experienced in various sensory modalities indicate excitation over widely separate cortical regions. It is not likely that these hallucinatory phenomena simply result from spontaneous and unprovoked discharges in an excitable cortex during the REM phase, for recent data do not indicate a great increase in the excitability of sensory cortex during REM sleep over that during NREM sleep [60–62]. Hence consideration of more specific pathways of cortical activation seems justified.

Indeed, the hallucinatory activity and heightened discharge frequencies may be comparable to the active perceptual and processing activities taking place in the awake brain in response to large volleys of incoming impulses. Already there is evidence that the normal neuro-anatomical routes to the cortex are travelled by REM-state impulses in the visual sensory system after they arrive at the lateral geniculate body from the pons [56, 57, 81, 82, 8], and that they do not descend from suprapontine structures but travel only in an ascending direction [57, 82]. There is other evidence which suggests that the thalamus is the site of introduction of brainstem influences on their way to higher sensory centres during REM sleep [60, 61]. We believe, consequently, that the active discharges in diverse brain sites during REM sleep originate in the phasic and tonic impulses which emanate from the pontine REM centre; some ascend to the thalamus and course along the primary thalamo-cortical projection pathways traversed by environmentally induced impulses until they reach the cortical sensory receiving areas. Dement has suggested elsewhere that once this 'internal sensory input' is 'substituted' in the 'stimulus-response chain', higher centres interpret and react to it as if it were a set of true percepts impinging on the central nervous system from without [78, 8]. The pontine REM centre also appears to have important links to excitatory and inhibitory efferent centres for eye movement, motor activity, muscle tone, spinal reflexes, respiration, heart rate, and probably others [9]. It apparently sends excitations into sensory channels directly, and into motor channels directly as well as indirectly (in that some motor responses may result from typical reactions in higher centres to the receipt of 'sensory' material).

On the basis of this scheme we hypothesize that REM sleep affords intense stimulation to the central nervous system, stimulation turned on periodically from within it by a mechanism capable of stimulating the rest of the central nervous system. This is probably the pontine REM mechanism which functions largely independently of factors external to the central nervous system. The intervals of intense activity during sleep would be available in great quantity to the developing organism *in utero* and later in its early extra-uterine life when stimuli are limited. Measures of the systematized qualities of this activity are the sustained, realistic, and sequential attributes of dream images [10, 71] and the seemingly purposeful associated activity in motor and autonomic systems [75] which it can provide.

The REMs of neonates, which likely have no counterpart in patterned vision, are extraordinarily similar to those of sleeping adults (though they are somewhat more clustered and vertical). In view of this fact, we wonder whether the eventual development of dream imagery may involve a process by which the cortex 'fits' sensory images to discharge patterns of brainstem origin established before the accumulation of sensory experience. The cortex may develop some modulating influence over these pontine discharges, but the basic discharge rhythm probably has a brainstem genesis. In this sense, the dream would truly appear to be born in the brainstem but clothed in the cortex.

Structural growth, and REM sleep

Although nerve tissue is able to differentiate somewhat in the absence of any external input [120], many studies *in vivo* have demonstrated that structural maturation and maintenance are seriously impaired by lack of stimulation [121, 122]. Moreover, there is considerable evidence that functional stimulation potentiates structural growth in the nervous system; that, for instance, activity may precede myelinization [121, 123–125]. This is extremely significant, we believe, in that functional stimulation commences in foetal life and may result not only from actual sensory stimulation but perhaps also from the REM sleep process, which begins to operate at some point in foetal development. The ascending impulses originating in the pons during the REM state may be useful in assisting neuronal differentiation, maturation, and myelinization in higher centres. In addition, the downward discharges from the REM centre, such as those found by Gassel *et al.* [66] to be activating the peripheral musculature, may provide activation to the neuromuscular apparatus. Could these downward discharges account for Langworthy's curious early finding that ventral root nerves display myelinization before dorsal root nerves [124]?

The demonstration in the foetus of myelinization in tactile, auditory, gustatory, and proprioceptive pathways comes as no surprise, because a degree of sensory stimulation and development in these systems can be assumed during the intra-uterine period. But why, if stimulation and development are linked, should there be substantial myelinization in the visual system before birth without exogenous stimulation to the retina save that from physical pressure [124]? And why before birth should the sensory neurons of the striate cortex be second in development only to the Betz cells of the pyramidal tract [126] ? We would contend that structural building has occurred in the visual sensory system in response to the afferent or afferent-like excitations periodically provided to it by the pontine REM mechanism.

Romanes's conclusion [127], growing out of his finding that myelinization begins in the visual pathways of the sheep 50 days before birth, seems germane to our proposal: 'It may be that the development of myelin in the optic system is initiated by factors quite different from those found elsewhere in the nervous system, but it is clear that the transmission of impulses resulting from light reaching the retina is *not* a factor in the sheep or in man. . . .' Structural maturation in the other sensory systems during foetal life may also substantially depend on discharges emanating from the pontine centre.

If we accept the concept of 'stimulus-induced' development, to use Riesen's term, we should not overlook REM sleep as a prime source of cortical stimulation in early ontogenesis. Its hypothesized role may offer a new approach to the processes of growth and maturation in higher brain centres. It makes all the more meaningful the somewhat unspecific but undoubtedly true suggestions of Carmichael [128], Dodgson [129], Riesen [125], and others that the immature central nervous system can 'anticipate' or 'prepare' for its future active role long before such functions are called into play. The abundance of REM sleep in early development also fits with the tremendous growth of the central nervous system during the first year or two of life. We conjecture that the REM mechanism became necessary in phylogenetic evolution at the time that extensive telencephalization began because of the need for maintenance of large masses of neural tissue not directly involved in motor and sensory reactions taking place during the progressively longer periods of sleep manifested by evolving species.

It is noteworthy that the areas in the central nervous system which are myelinated *in utero* either receive afferent fibres directly from subcortical centres or are principally related to them.† Conel's descriptions of cortical histology in the newborn place the most differentiated and mature cells in the brain within the primary sensory receiving areas, principal motor areas, limbic system, and rhinencephalon [126]. All these areas are intimate participants in the neurophysiology of the REM state. Therefore it is plausible that the REM mechanism is responsible for the first appearance, in ontogenetic development, of a 'state' of the central nervous system which recurs throughout life. The mechanism may then function to bring higher brain centres to an operational capacity requisite to handling the rush of external stimulation in waking experience.

If REM sleep delivers significant functional stimulation to the cortex in infancy, then it probably maintains this role throughout life. It might even be conjectured, on the basis of the large reduction in REM sleep and the augmentation of time awake in the adult, that the need for endogenous stimulation becomes negligible, owing either to the maturity of the cortex or to a surfeit of exogenous input. On the other hand, many would argue that dreaming, the epiphenomenon of the

† For a brief summary of Flechig's findings in English, in addition to a bibliography, see Dodgson, [129], pp. 162–64.

REM state, is not a process without a purpose, and that it, indeed, serves a necessary psychological function in the adult. A physiological system that remains active throughout life probably continues to execute physiological as well as other functions. It is known that deprivation of REM sleep induces certain behavioural and (in humans) psychological aberrances [26, 27, 8, 90, 91]. This information, however, does not clearly indicate the natural physiological function, if any, of REM sleep in the adult. One possibility we are considering is that frequent excitation of higher brain centres during sleep, accruing from periodic activation of the REM process, serves to maintain the central nervous system in a state of physiological readiness so that it may react swiftly to the exigencies of the real world. Extended interruptions of excitation may be injurious to optimal responsiveness of neural structures. (It is interesting that accuracy of depth perception is considerably weakened after one eye has been covered for a matter of hours [130].) In this sense, then, the stimulating function of the REM mechanism may remain important to the organism throughout life.

We hope that embryologists and experimental neurophysiologists will give consideration to the possibility that REM sleep plays a role in stimulating structural maturation and maintenance within the central nervous system. If our hypotheses have any validity, then a developing foetus should show critical failures or lags in maturation of certain neural systems if deprived of the REM state. Another corollary of our proposal is that a significant reduction of external sensory input to the developing central nervous system might, by means of a feedback system, retard the rate of diminution of the REM moiety. However, if the normal fall-off of REM sleep were programmed by an autonomous REM sleep mechanism, lack of external sensory input and a failure of nervous tissue to develop during critical growth periods might not substantially affect proportions of REM sleep. Certainly, further experimentation is required in order to distinguish, separate, and quantitatively assess the specific part played by REM sleep in the maturation of central nervous structures.

Summary

When the means for physiologically identifying rapid-eye-movement (REM) or 'dreaming' sleep became available and sleep–dream patterns were first investigated, it was totally unexpected that more REM sleep would be found in younger individuals than in adults. However, this fact has been demonstrated in both humans and animals. We have presented data indicating that normal newborns spend one-third of their day and one-half of their sleep in the REM state. This high ratio diminishes progressively with maturation. The early large percentages of REM sleep compel us to look to early development for the most important function of REM sleep.

This activated phase of sleep is a state during which the central nervous system is functioning at intensities as great as or greater than during arousal and in which vivid hallucinations (dreams) are experienced. Accumulating data suggest that centres in the pons constitute the REM mechanism and that the pontine area sends impulses to motor as well as to sensory areas of the brain. After reaching the thalamus from the pons, the impulses appear to traverse the usual pathways to cortex.

We have hypothesized that the REM mechanism serves as an endogenous source of stimulation, furnishing great quantities of functional excitation to higher centres. Such stimulation would be particularly crucial during the periods *in utero* and shortly after birth, before appreciable exogenous stimulation is available to the central nervous system. It might assist in structural maturation and differentiation of key sensory and motor areas within the central nervous system, partially preparing them to handle the enormous rush of stimulation provided by the postnatal milieu, as well as contributing to their further growth after birth. The sharp diminution of REM sleep with development may signify that the mature brain has less need for endogenous stimulation. Proof that the critical function of the REM sleep mechanism during development is the one of 'autostimulation' of structural and responsive capacity in the central nervous system must await future experimentation.

References

1. KLEITMAN, N. (1939, 1964). *Sleep and wakefulness.* University of Chicago Press, Chicago.
2. FOSTER, H. H. (1901). *Am. J. Psychol.* **12**, 145.
3. ASERINSKY, E. and KLEITMAN, N. (1955). *J. appl. Physiol.* **8**, 1.
4. DEMENT, W. C. and KLEITMAN, N. (1957). *J. Exp. Psychol.* **53**, 339.
5. —— (1957). *Electro-encephalog. Clin. Neurophysiol.* **9**, 673.
6. HERNANDEZ-PEON, R. (1964). *Electro-encephalog. Clin. Neurophysiol.* **17**, 444; —— (1965). *In Aspects anatomo-fonctionnels de la physiologie du sommeil* (Colloque International Centre National de Recherche Scientifique, Paris).
7. SNYDER, F. (1963). *Arch. Gen. Psychiat.* **8**, 381.
8. DEMENT, W. C. (1964). *In* (Masserman, J. (Ed.)) *Science and psychoanalysis.* Vol. 7. Grune and Stratton, New York, p. 129.
9. JOUVET, M. (1962). *Arch. Ital. Biol.* **100**, 125.
10. DEMENT, W. C. and WOLPERT, E. A. (1958). *J. exp. Psychol.* **55**, 543; WOLPERT, E. A. and TROSMAN, H. (1958). *Arch. Neurol. Psychiat.* **79**, 603; GOODENOUGH, D. R., SHAPIRO, A., HOLDEN, M., STEIN-SCHRIBER, L. (1959). *J. abnorm. Soc. Psychol.* **59**, 295.
11. KAMIYA, J. (1961). *In* (Fiske, D. W. and Maddi, S. R. (Eds.)) *Functions of varied experience.* Dorsey, Homewood, Ill., p. 145.
12. JOUVET, M., MICHEL, F., and MOUNIER, D. (1960). *Rev. Neurol.* **103**, 189.
13. ORLINSKY, D. (1962). Psychodynamic and cognitive correlates of dream recall, Ph.D. dissertation, University of Chicago.
14. ANTROBUS, J. S., DEMENT, W. C., and FISHER, C. (1964). *J. abnorm. Soc. Psychol.* **69**, 341.
15. BERGER, R. and OSWALD, I. (1962). *Science* **137**, 601.
16. ROFFWARG, H. P., DEMENT, W. C., and FISHER, C. (1964). *In* (Harms, E. (Ed.)) *Problems of sleep and dreams in children.* Pergamon, New York.
17. OSWALD, I. (1962). *Proc. R. Soc. Med.* **55**, 910.
18. DEMENT, W. C. (1965). *In* (Newcomb, T. (Ed.)) *New directions in psychology.* Vol. 2. Holt, Rinehart, and Winston, New York, p. 135.
19. BERGER, R. J., OLLEY, P., and OSWALD, I. (1962). *Quart. J. Exp. Psychol.* **14**, 183; SCHWARTZ, B. A.

and FISCHGOLD, H. (1960). *Vie Med.* **44**, 39.

20. DEMENT, W. C. (1964). *In* (Bender, M. B. (Ed.)) *The oculomotor system.* Hoeber, New York, p. 366.

21. KEITH, C. R. (1962). *Bull. Menninger Clin.* **26**, 248; DEMENT, W. C., KAHN, E., and ROFFWARG, H. P. (1965). *J. nerv. Men. Dis.* **140**, 119.

22. TART, C. T. (1963). Effects of post-hypnotic suggestion on the process of dreaming, Ph.D. dissertation, University of North Carolina; STOYVA, J. M. (1965). *Arch. gen. Psychiat.* **12**, 287.

23. WHITMAN, R. M., PIERCE, C. M., and MAAS, J. W. (1960). *In* (Uhr, L. and Miller, J. (Eds.)) *Drugs and behavior.* Wiley, New York, p. 591; WHITMAN, R. M., PIERCE, C. M., MAAS, J. W., and BALDRIDGE, B. (1961). *Comp. Psychiat.* **2**, 219; OSWALD, T. and THACORE, V. R. (1963). *Brit. Med. J.* **2**, 427; GRESHAM, S. C., WEBB, W. B., and WILLIAMS, R. L. (1963). *Science* **140**, 1226; KAUFMAN, E., ROFF-WARG, H. P., and MUZIO, J. N. (1964). Paper presented to the Association for Psychophysiological Study of Sleep, Palo Alto, California; RECHTSCHAFEN, A., and MARON, L. (1964). *Electro-encephalog. clin. Neurophysiol.* **16**, 438; TOYODA, J. (1964). *Folia Psychiat. Neurol. Japan,* **18**, 198; FEINBERG, I. (1964). Paper presented to the Association for Psychophysiological Study of Sleep, Palo Alto, California; FISHER, C. (1965). *J. Am. Psycho-anal. Ass.* **13**, 197; YULES, P., CHANDLER, L. A., and FREEDMAN, D. X. (1965). Paper presented to the Association for Psychophysiological Study of Sleep, Washington D.C.

24. OSWALD, I., BERGER, R. J., JARAMILLO, R. A., KEDDIE, K. M. G., OLLEY, P. C., and PLUNKETT, G. B. (1963). *Brit. J. Psychiat.* **109**, 66.

25. MUZIO, J. N., ROFFWARG, H. P., and

KAUFMAN, E. (1964). Paper presented to the Association for Psychophysiological Study of Sleep, Palo Alto, California.

26. DEMENT, W. C. (1960). *Science* **131**, 1705.

27. —— and FISHER, C. (1963). *Can. Psychiat. Ass. J.* **8**, 400; DEMENT, W. C. (1965). *In Aspects anatomo-functionnels de la physiologie du sommeil* (Colloque International Centre National de Recherche Scientifique, Paris); KALES, A., HOEDE-MAKER, F. S., JACOBSON, A., and LICHTENSTEIN, E. L. (1964). *Nature* **204**, 1337.

28. FISHER, C. and DEMENT, W. C. (1963). *Am. J. Psychiat.* **119**, 1160; GULEVICH, G. and DEMENT, W. C. (1964). Paper presented to the Association for Psychophysiological Study of Sleep, Palo Alto, California; FEINBERG, I., KORESKO, R. I., and HELLER, W. (1965). *Am. J. Psychiat.* **121**, 1018; FEINBERG, I., KORESKO, R. I., GOTTLIEB, F., and WENDER, P. H. (1965). *Comp. Psychiat.* **6**, 21.

29. SNYDER, F. (1965). *In* (Greenfield, N. S. and Lewis, W. C. (Eds.)) *Psychoanalysis and current biological thought.* University of Wisconsin, Madison, p. 275.

30. SNYDER, F., HOBSON, J. A., and GOLD-FRANK, F. (1963). *Science* **142**, 1313; SNYDER, F., HOBSON, J. A., MORRI-SON, D. F., and GOLDFRANK, F. (1964). *J. appl. Physiol.* **19**, 417.

31. BERGER, R. (1961). *Science* **134**, 840; JACOBSON, A., KALES, A., LEH-MANN, D., and HOEDEMAKER, F. S. (1964). *Exp. Neurol.* **10**, 418.

32. MICHEL, F., RECHTSCHAFFEN, A., and VIMONT-VICARY, P. (1964). *Rev. Neurol.* **158**, 106.

33. FISHER, C., GROSS, J., and ZUCH, J. (1965). *Arch. gen. Psychiat.* **12**, 29; FISHER, C. and GROSS, J. (1965). Paper presented to the Association for Psychophysiological Study of Sleep, Washington D.C.

34. HAWKINS, D. R., PURYEAR, H. B., WALLACE, C. D., DEAL, W. B., and THOMAS, E. S. (1962). *Science* **136**, 321; FRESSY, J. (1964). *Rev. Neurol.* **110**, 306.

35. WILLIAMS, H. L., TEPAS, D. I., and MORLOCK, JR., H. C. (1962). *Science* **138**, 685; WEITZMAN, E. D. and KREMEN, H. (1965). *Electro-encephalog. clin. Neurophysiol.* **18**, 65; KHAZAN, N. and SAWYER, C. H. (1964). *Psychopharmacologia* **5**, 457.

36. WILLIAMS, H. L., HAMMACK, J. T., DALY, R. L., DEMENT, W. C., and LUBIN, A. (1964). *Electro-encephalog. clin. Neurophysiol.* **16**, 269.

37. HUTTENLOCHER, P. R. (1960). *ibid.* **12**, 819; WINTERS, W. D. (1964). *ibid.* **17**, 234.

38. —— (1961). *J. Neurophysiol.* **24**, 451.

39. HODES, R. and SUZUKI, J.-I. (1965). *Electro-encephalog. clin. Neurophysiol.* **18**, 239.

40. ADEY, W. R., KADO, R. T., and RHODES, J. M. (1963). *Science* **142**, 932.

41. DEMENT, W. C. (1958). *Electro-encephalog. clin. Neurophysiol.* **10**, 291; JOUVET, M. (1961). *In* (Wolstenholme, G. E. W. and O'Connor, C. M. (Eds.)) *The nature of sleep.* Little, Brown, Boston, p. 188; WEITZMAN, E. D. (1961). *Electro-encephalog. clin. Neurophysiol.* **13**, 790; MICHEL, F., KLEIN, M., JOUVET, D., and VALATX, J. L. (1961). *Compt. Rend. Soc. Biol.* **155**, 2289; CANDIA, O., FAVALE, E., GUISSANI, A., and ROSSI, G. F. (1962). *Arch. ital. Biol.* **100**, 216; SWISHER, J. (1962). *Science* **138**, 1110; FAURE, R. (1962). *Rev. Neurol.* **106**, 190; ROLDAN, E., WEISS, T., and FIFKOVA, E. (1963). *Electro-encephalog. clin. Neurophysiol.* **15**, 775; SNYDER, F. (1964). Paper presented to the Association for Psychophysiological Study of Sleep, Palo Alto, California; GASSEL, M. M., GHELARDUCCI, B., MARCHIAFAVA, P. L., and POMPEIANO, O.

(1964). *Arch. ital. Biol.* **102**, 530; KHAZAN, N. and SAWYER, C. H. (1964). *Psychopharmacologia* **5**, 457; WEISS, T. and FIFKOVA, E. (1964). *Physiol. Bohemoslov.* **13**, 242; REITE, M. L., RHODES, J. M., KAVAN, E., and ADEY, W. R. (1965). *Arch. Neurol.* **12**, 133; WEITZMAN, E. D., KRIPKE, D. F., POLLAK, C., and DOMINGUEZ, J. (1965). *Arch. Neurol.* **12**, 463; GUAZZI, M. and ZANCHETTI, A. (1965). *Science* **148**, 397.

42. SHIMAZONO, Y., HORIE, T., YANAGISAWA, Y., HORI, N., CHIKAZAWA, W., and SHOZUKA, K. (1960). *Neurol. Medicochir.* **2**, 82.

43. JOUVET, D., VALATX, J. L., and JOUVET, M. (1961). *C. r. Soc. Biol.* **155**, 1660.

44. JOUVET, D. and VALATX, J. L. (1962). *ibid.* **156**, 1411.

45. RUCKEBUSCH, Y. *ibid.*, p. 867.

46. KANZOW, E., KRAUSE, D., and KUBNEL, H. (1962). *Pfluegers Arch. Ges. Physiol.* **274**, 593.

47. RUCKEBUSCH, Y. (1963). *Arch. ital. Biol.* **101**, 111.

48. VALATX, J. L., JOUVET, D., and JOUVET, M. (1964). *Electro-encephalog. clin. Neurophysiol.* **17**, 218.

49. KLEIN, M., MICHEL, F., and JOUVET, M. (1964). *C. r. Soc. Biol.* **158**, 99.

50. BRUGGE, J. F. (1965). *Electro-encephalog. clin. Neurophysiol.* **18**, 36.

51. RECHTSCHAFFEN, A., CORNWALL, P., and ZIMMERMAN, W. (1965). Paper presented to the Association for Psychophysiological Study of Sleep, Washington D.C.

52. BIZZI, E., POMPEIANO, O., and SOMOGYI, I. (1964). *Science* **145**, 414; —— (1964). *Arch. ital. Biol.* **102**, 308.

53. ARDUINI, A., BERLUCCHI, G., and STRATA, P. (1963). *Arch. ital. Biol.* **101**, 530; EVARTS, E. V. (1964). *J. Neurophysiol.* **27**, 152.

54. MARCHIAFAVA, P. L. and POMPEIANO, O. (1964). *Arch. ital. Biol.* **102**, 500.

55. EVARTS, E. V. (1962). *J. Neurophysiol.* **25**, 812.

56. BROOKS, D. C. and BIZZI, E. (1963). *Arch. ital. Biol.* **101**, 648.

57. BIZZI, E. and BROOKS, D. C. *ibid.*, p. 666.

58. PARMEGGIANI, P. L. and ZANOCCO, G. *ibid.*, p. 385.

59. GRASTYAN, E. (1959). *In* (Brazier, M. A. B. (Ed.)) *Central nervous system and behavior.* Josiah Macy, Jr., Foundation, New York, p. 119; CADILHAC, J., PASSOUANT-FONTAINE, T., and PASSOUANT, P. (1961). *Rev. Neurol.* **105**, 171.

60. FAVALE, E. and MANFREDI, M. (1963). *Boll. Soc. ital. Biol. Sper.* **39**, 435; FAVALE, E. LOEB, C., MANFREDI, M., and SACCO, G. (1965). *Electro-encephalog. clin. Neurophysiol.* **18**, 354.

61. ALLISON, T. (1965). *Electro-encephalog. clin. Neurophysiol.* **18**, 131.

62. DAGNINO, N., FAVALE, E., LOEB, C., and MANFREDI, M. (1965). *J. Neurophysiol.* **28**, 443; PALESTINI, M., PISANO, M., ROSADINI, G., and ROSSI, G. F. (1964). *Exp. Neurol.* **9**, 17; WALSHE, J. T. and CORDEAU, J. P. (1965). *ibid.* **11**, 80.

63. HODES, R. and DEMENT, W. C. (1964). *Electro-encephalog. clin. Neurophysiol.* **17**, 617; GIAQUINTO, S., POMPEIANO, O., and SOMOGYI, I. (1964). *Arch. Ital. Biol.* **102**, 245; KUBOTA, K., IWAMURA, Y., and NIIMI, Y. (1965). *J. Neurophysiol.* **28**, 125; GASSEL, M. M., MARCHIAFAVA, P. L., and POMPEIANO, O. (1965). *Arch. ital. Biol.* **103**, 1, 25; HISHIKAWA, Y., SUMITSUJI, N., MATSUMOTO, K., and KANEKO, Z. (1965). *Electro-encephalog. clin. Neurophysiol.* **18**, 487.

64. GIAQUINTO, S., POMPEIANO, O., and SOMOGYI, I. (1964). *Arch. ital. Biol.* **102**, 282.

65. GASSEL, M. M., MARCHIAFAVA, P. L., and POMPEIANO, O., *ibid.*, p. 471.

66. —— *ibid.*, p. 449.

67. JOUVET, M., PELLIN, B., and MOUNIER, D. (1961). *Rev. Neurol.* **105**, 1.

68. ROSSI, G. F., MINOBE, K., and CANDIA, O. (1963). *Arch. ital. Biol.* **101**, 470.

69. CARLI, G., ARMERGOL, V., and ZANCHETTI, A. (1963). *Science* **140**, 677; HOBSON, A. (1965). *Electro-encephalog. clin. Neurophysiol.* **19**, 41.

70. FOULKES, W. D. (1962). *J. abnorm. Soc. Psychol.* **65**, 14; —— (1964). *Psychol. Bull.* **62**, 236; RECHTSCHAFFEN, A., VOGEL, G., and SHAIKUN, G. (1963). *Arch. gen. Psychiat.* **9**, 536; RECHTSCHAFFEN, A., VERDONE, P., and WHEATON, J. (1963). *Can. Psychiat. Ass. J.* **8**, 409.

71. ROFFWARG, H. P., DEMENT, W. C., MUZIO, J. N., and FISHER, C. (1962). *Arch. gen. Psychiat.* **7**, 235.

72. WOLPERT, E. A. (1960). *ibid.* **2**, 231.

73. RECHTSCHAFFEN, A., GOODENOUGH, D. R., and SHAPIRO, A. (1962). *ibid.* **7**, 418.

74. HOBSON, J. A., GOLDFRANK, F., and SNYDER, F. (1966). *J. psychiat. Res.* **3**, 79–90.

75. WEITZMAN, E. D., SCHAUMBERG, H., and FISHBEIN, W. (1965). Paper presented to the Association for Psychophysiological Study of Sleep, Washington D.C.

76. SHAPIRO, A., GOODENOUGH, D. R., BIDERMAN, I., and SLESER, I. (1964). *J. appl. Physiol.* **19**, 778.

77. RAMSEY, G. (1953). *Psychol. Bull.* **50**, 432; KAHN, E., DEMENT, W. C., FISHER, C., and BARMACK, J. (1962). *Science* **137**, 1054.

78. DEMENT, W. C. (1965). *In* (Hoch, P. H. and Zubin, J. (Eds.)) *Psychopathology of perception.* Grune and Stratton, New York.

79. FOULKES, D. and RECHTSCHAFFEN, A. (1964). *Percept. mot. Skills.* **19**, 983.

80. Discussion by RECHTSCHAFFEN, A., of paper by DEMENT, W. C. (1964). *In* (Masserman, J. (Ed.)) *Science and Psycho-analysis.* Vol. 7. Grune and Stratton, New York, p. 162.

81. BENOIT, O. (1964). *J. Physiol. Paris* **56**, 259.

82. MICHEL, F., JEANNEROD, M.,

MOURET, J., RECHTSCHAFFEN, A., and JOUVET, M. (1964). *C. r. Soc. Biol.* **158**, 103.

83. COBB, J. C., EVANS, F. J., GUSTAFSON, L. A., O'CONNELL, D. N., ORNE, M. T., and SHOR, R. E. (1964). Paper presented to the Association for Psychophysiological Study of Sleep, Palo Alto, California; TART, C. T. (1964). Paper presented at 72nd meeting, American Psychological Association, Los Angeles, California; ANTROBUS, J. S., ANTROBUS, J. S., and FISHER, C. (1965). *Arch. gen. Psychiat.* **12**, 395.

84. WILLIAMS, H. L., MORLOCK, JR., H. C., and MORLOCK, J. V. (1963). Paper presented to the American Psychological Association, Philadelphia, Pennsylvania.

85. BERGER, R. (1963). *Brit. J. Psychiat.* **109**, 722.

86. HERMANN, H., JOUVET, M., and KLEIN, M. (1964). *C. r. Soc. Biol.* **258**, 2175.

87. JOUVET, D., VIMONT, P., DELORME, F., and JOUVET, M. (1964). *C. r. Soc. Biol.* **158**, 756.

88. FERGUSON, J. and DEMENT, W. C. (1965). Paper presented to the Association for Psychophysiological Study of Sleep, Washington D.C.

89. KHAZAN, N. and SAWYER, C. H. (1963). *Proc. Soc. exp. Biol. Med.* **114**, 536.

90. DEMENT, W. C. (1965). Paper delivered to the American Psychiatric Association, New York.

91. DEWSON, J. H. III, DEMENT, W. C., WAGONER, T., and Nobel, K. (1965). Paper presented to the Association for Psychophysiological Study of Sleep, Washington D.C.

92. ROFFWARG, H. P., DEMENT, W. C., and FISHER, C. (1963). Paper presented to the Association for Psychophysiological Study of Sleep, New York; ROFFWARG, H. P., MUZIO, J. N., and DEMENT, W. C. (1964). *Electro-encephalog. clin. Neurophysiol.* **17**, 611.

93. DELANGE, M. M., CASTAN, P., CADILHAC, J., and PASSOUANT, P. (1962). *Rev. Neurol.* **107**, 271.

94. PARMELEE, JR., A. H., WENNER, W. H., AKIYAMA, Y., and FLESCHER, J. (1967). *In The regional maturation of the nervous system in early life.* Blackwell, Oxford.

95. DELANGE, M. M., CASTAN, P., CADILHAC, J., and PASSOUANT, P. (1961). *Rev. Neurol.* **105**, 176; PASSOUANT, P., CADILHAC, J., DELANGE, M., CALLAMAND, M., and KASSABGUI, M. E. (1964). *ibid.* **110**, 303.

96. MONOD, N., DREYFUS-BRISAC, C., MOREL-KAHN, F., PAJOT, N., and PLASSARD, E., *ibid.*, p. 304.

97. WEITZMAN, E. D., FISHBEIN, W., and GRAZIANI, L. (1965). *Pediatrics* **35**, 458.

98. BERGER, R. J. and OSWALD, I. (1962). *J. ment. Sci.* **108**, 455.

99. MARON, L., RECHTSCHAFFEN, A., and WOLPERT, E. A. (1964). *Arch. gen. Psychiat.* **11**, 503.

100. APGAR, V. (1953). *Current Res. Anesthes. Analges.* **32**, 260.

101. GINSBURG, H., TUMPOWSKI, I., and CARLSON, A. J. (1915). *J. Amer. Med. Soc.* **64**, 1822; TAYLOR, R. (1917). *Am. J. Dis. Children* **14**, 233.

102. ASERINSKY, E. and KLEITMAN, N. (1955). *J. appl. Physiol.* **8**, 11.

103. SMITH, J. R. (1937). *Proc. Soc. Exp. Biol. Med.* **36**, 384; —— (1938). *J. Genet. Psychol.* **53**, 431, 471; HUGHES, J. G., EHEMANN, B., and BROWN, U. (1948). *Am. J. dis. Children* **76**, 503, 626; HUGHES, J. G., EHEMANN, B., and HILL, F. S. (1949). *ibid.* **77**, 310; KELLAWAY, P. and FOX, B. J. (1952). *J. Pediat.* **41**, 262.

104. ELLINGSON, R. J. (1958). *Electroencephalog. clin. Neurophysiol.* **10**, 31.

105. GIBBS, F. A. and GIBBS, E. L. (1950). *Atlas of electro-encephalography.* Vol. 1. Addison-Wesley, Cambridge, p. 90; SUREAU, M., FISCHGOLD, H., and CAPDEVIELLE, G. (1949). *Rev. Neurol.* **81**, 543; —— (1950). *Elec-*

tro-encephalog. clin. Neurophysiol. **2**, 113; Fois, A. and Low, N. L. (1961). *The electro-encephalogram of the normal child.* Charles C. Thomas, Springfield, Ill., pp. 12, 25.

106. Dreyfus-Brisac, C. (1962). *World Neurol.* **3**, 5.

107. Fantz, R. L. (1963). *Science* **140**, 296; —— (1964). *ibid.* **146**, 668; Haynes, H., White, B. L., and Held, R. (1965). *ibid.* **148**, 528.

108. Amadeo, M. and Gomez, E. *J. Can. Psychiat. Ass.*, in press.

109. Jouvet, M., Dechaume, J., and Michel, F. (1960). *Lyon Med.* **204**, 479.

110. Jeannerod, M., Mouret, J., and Jouvet, M. (1965). *Electro-encephalog. clin. Neurophysiol.* **18**, 554.

111. Mann, M. (1946). *In* (Carmichael, L. (Ed.)) *Manual of child psychology.* Wiley, New York, pp. 370–449.

112. Parmelee, A. H., Akiyama, Y., Wenner, W. H., and Flescher, J. (1964). Paper presented to the Association for Psychophysiological Study of Sleep, Palo Alto, California.

113. Koella, W. P. and Ferry, A. (1963). *Science* **142**, 586.

114. Hrbek, A. and Mares, P. (1964). *Electro-encephalog. clin. Neurophysiol.* **16**, 575; Barnet, A. B. and Goodwin, R. S. (1965). *ibid.* **18**, 445.

115. Knauss, T. and Clemente, C. D. (1965). Abstract submitted to American Association of Anatomists and personal communication.

116. Rechtschaffen, A., Wolpert, E. A., Dement, W. C., Mitchell, S. A., and Fisher, C. (1963). *Electroencephalog. clin. Neurophysiol.* **15**, 599; Hishikawa, Y. and Kaneko, Z. (1965). *ibid.* **18**, 249; Hishikawa, Y. *ibid.*, p. 487; Dement, W. C., Rechtschaffen, A., and Gulevich, G. *Neurology*, in press.

117. Jouvet, M., Cier, A., Mounier, D., and Valatx, J. L. (1961). *C. r. Soc. Biol.* **155**, 1313.

118. Dement, W. C., Greenberg, S., and

Klein, R. (1965). Paper presented to the Association for Psychophysiological Study of Sleep, Washington D.C.

119. Henry, P., Cohen, H., Stadel, B., Stulce, J., Ferguson, J., Wagener, T., and Dement, W. C. (1965). Paper presented to the Association for Psychophysiological Study of Sleep, Washington D.C.

120. Crain, S. M. and Peterson, E. R. (1963). *Science* **141**, 427; Crain, S. M. and Bornstein, E. M. (1964). *Exp. Neurol.* **10**, 425.

121. Hyden, H. (1947). *Symp. Soc. Exp. Biol.* **1**, 152; (1943). *Acta Physiol. Scand.* **6** (Suppl. 17), 1.

122. Nissen, H., Chow, K., and Semmes, J. (1951). *Am. J. Psychol.* **54**, 485; Brattgard, S. (1952). *Acta Radiol. Suppl.* **96**; Chow, K. L., Riesen, A. H., and Newell, F. W. (1957). *J. Comp. Neurol.* **107**, 72; Hess, A. (1958). *ibid.* **109**, 91; Weiskrantz, L. (1958). *Nature* **181**, 1047; Rasch, E., Swift, H., Riesen, A. H., and Chow, K. L. (1961). *Exp. Cell. Res.* **25**, 348; Rosenzweig, M. R., Bennett, E. L., and Krech, D. (1964). *J. comp. Physiol. Psychol.* **57**, 438; Bennett, E. L., Diamond, M. C., Krech, D., and Rosenzweig, M. R. (1964). *Science* **146** 610.

123. Westphal, A. (1897). *Arch. Psychiat.* **29**, 474; Walls, G. L. (1942). *The vertebrate eye and its adaptive radiation.* Cranbrook, Bloomfield Hills, N.J.; Kennard, M. A. (1948). *In Problems of Early Infancy.* Josiah Macy Jr., Foundation, New York, pp. 78–81; Hamburger, V. (1955). *In* (Waelsch, H. (Ed.)) *Biochemistry of the developing nervous system.* Academic Press, New York, pp. 52–71; Edds, M. V. Jr., (1950). *J. comp. Neurol.* **93**, 259.

124. Langworthy, O. R. (1933). *Contrib. Embryol.* **24**, 1; see particularly discussion on pp. 52, 53.

125. Riesen, A. H. (1961). *In* (Fiske, D. W.

and Maddi, S. R. (Eds.)) *Functions of varied experience*. Dorsey, Homewood, Ill., p. 57.

126. CONEL, J. L. (1939). *The postnatal development of the human cerebral cortex*. Vol. 1. Harvard University Press, Cambridge, p. 104.

127. ROMANES, G. J. (1947). *J. Anat. London* **81**, 64.

128. CARMICHAEL, L. (1951). *In* (Stevens, S. S. (Ed.)) *Handbook of experimental psychology*. Wiley, New York, p. 281.

129. DODGSON, M. C. H. (1962). *The growing brain*. Wright, Bristol, England.

130. WALLACH, H. and KARSH, E. B. (1963). *Am. J. Psychol.* **76**, 413.

131. STRAUCH, I. H. (1963). Paper presented to the Association for Psychophysiological Study of Sleep, New York.

132. LAIRY, G. C., COR-MORDRET, M., FAURE, R., and RIDJANOVIC, S. (1962). *Rev. Neurol.* **107**, 188.

Influence of 'state' upon responsivity to stimulation

S. J. HUTT, H. G. LENARD AND
H. F. R. PRECHTL†

Reflexes

The ubiquity of the state variable is clearly seen in studies of spinal reflexes. These may be categorized as monosynaptic or as polysynaptic, and it appears that the two types of reflex are differentially affected by state. By repeatedly evoking a reflex during polygraphic recording, its relationship to state may be clearly seen. In one study [17] comparison of the effect of state on the tendon knee jerk (a monosynaptic reflex) and on the exteroceptive skin reflex of the distal part of the tibia (a polysynaptic reflex) was made. The babies were studied under physiologically neutral conditions for periods of 1 to 2 h between feeds. Recordings were made of respiration, heart rate, EEG, and EMG from eight sites. Reflexes were elicited manually at regular intervals of either 15 or 30 s. Responses to both kinds of eliciting stimuli were scored on a four-point scale using EMG criteria. The baby's state was monitored by an observer and substantiated by reference to the polygraph. Only states I–IV were studied.‡ Motor responses after exteroceptive stimulation of the skin were absent or weak in state I. Positive reactions occurred more frequently and were more strongly expressed in state II. Negative responses in states III and IV were rare. In contrast, the knee jerk was regularly obtained in both states I and III, but was either weak or totally absent in state II.

The lip-tap reflex [15] is of particular interest since it contains both monosynaptic and polysynaptic components. On applying an abrupt but gentle tap with the finger upon the baby's philtrum, there occurs first short-lashing jerk (the monosynaptic component) followed by a prolonged protrusion of the lips (the polysynaptic component). In a study of the effects of regular and irregular sleep, the lip-tap reflex was elicited repeatedly at 15- to 30-s intervals in a group of 11 full-term babies, aged 4 to 8 days [16]. The babies were studied under physiologically neutral conditions for 1 to 2 h between feeds. Polygrams were recorded of respiration, heart rate, EEG, and eye movements, together with an EMG from the obicularis oris. The lip jerk could be clearly seen in the EMG record as a high voltage phasic response, and the lip protrusion as a large tonic response. The two reflex components were seen to vary in intensity with respect to the two sleep states. In state I, the lip jerk was consistently elicited and was of high

---

† From 'Psychophysiological studies in new-born infants'. *In Advances in child behavior and development* (Lipsitt, L. P. and Reese, H. (Eds.)). Vol. IV. Academic Press, New York, pp. 127–72 (1969). Reprinted by permission of the publishers.

‡ For definitions of these states see p. 83.

amplitude, whereas lip-protrusion responses were rare. In state II, lip-jerk responses were significantly smaller, but lip-protrusion responses now occurred frequently.

Sensory thresholds

If a constant stimulus can have such variable effects, depending upon the baby's state, it is to be expected that to elicit responses of similar magnitude in each state, quite different stimulus intensities will be required. Similarly, it will be expected that the minimum stimulus magnitude required to produce a response on 50 per cent of occasions (the absolute threshold for the stimulus) will be a function of the baby's state.

Data on auditory thresholds in neonates are contained in a report by Bartoshuk [4] on the relationship between stimulus intensity and heart-rate change. Tones of 1000 cycles/s and of 1 s duration were presented through a loudspeaker. Four intensities, varying from 38 dB to 67·5 dB above the ambient noise level, were presented consecutively in first ascending then descending order for five complete cycles. The amount of change in heart rate, plotted on a logarithmic scale, was found to be linearly related to intensity in decibels. This is consistent with Stevens' [21] power law relating sensory magnitude and physical intensity.

Responses to tones 47·5 dB above noise level were significantly greater than the 'spontaneous' changes observed when the loudspeaker was disconnected. Responses to a tone only 38 dB above noise level did not, according to Bartoshuk, differ significantly from the spontaneous changes, showing that for this tone the absolute threshold for cardiac acceleration was between 38 and 48 dB above the ambient noise level. While the design of the experiment is valid for demonstrating Stevens' power law, it is not an appropriate design for investigating sensory thresholds, if these are state-dependent. (If they are not, the finding is so important that it should be reported.)

Using a 2-s sine wave tone at 1000 cycles/s and 75 dB (25 dB above the ambient noise level), we found that cardiac change, as computed by Bartoshuk's [4] method, was significantly greater when the baby was in state III than when he was in states I and II. To produce an equivalent heart-rate change in regular sleep required an increase in the intensity of the stimulus of approximately 20 dB. It is important, therefore, that studies of thresholds specify the behavioural state of the babies during stimulation. Without such specification, the results can, at best, be regarded only as an approximation for all states, and not in any sense indicative of absolute thresholds.

Several authors [8, 11, 13] have studied changes in sensory thresholds during successive days of the baby's life. Here again, the question of state is neglected and the details of procedure are not sufficiently explicit to make accurate inferences possible. While this in no way affects the validity of the results, it does make interpretation difficult. Moreover, when quite contrary results are obtained in two studies of the same phenomenon, it is not unreasonable to look at considerations of state as one possible source of such differences. For example, in the Gullikson and Crowell study, increasing electrotactual thresholds were found in tests conducted at approximately 24, 48, and 72 h after birth.

While the apparatus is described in detail, no information is given as to whether the babies were asleep, awake, or crying. Since, generally, the intensity of stimulus required to produce a behavioural response varies directly with state, one possible interpretation of the results might be that the babies were spending progressively longer periods in state I on successive days. This would be in accord with what is known of the development of sleep states in the neonate—the amount of state I sleep being smallest on day 1 and thereafter increasing on successive days. The fact that the threshold of the control group, tested on the third day of life, did not differ significantly from that of the experimental groups on day 1 should have been a convincing argument against this interpretation. Unfortunately, here again we are told nothing of the behavioural state of the control group. Thus, while the authors' own interpretation that the experimental infants developed an habituation to the shock is plausible, Kagan and Henker [10] have been tempted to suggest: 'An alternative interpretation is that the control babies did not have the experience of being brought into a strange room and manipulated and, as a result, may have been in a higher state of arousal.' Transport of the control babies to the laboratory and attachment of the electrodes would have been a valuable control.

A decrease in electro-tactual threshold is reported by Lipsitt and Levy [13] and Kaye and Lipsitt [11]. It is possible, as Gullikson and Crowell suggest, that their quite contrary findings are due to differences in procedure. It is equally possible, however, that the differences may have been due to differences in the babies' states. In the report of Lipsitt and Levy, the state of the babies on stimulation is not recorded, but, interestingly, the authors suggest as one of four possible explanations of their results that 'thresholds are higher when the baby is asleep, the child tends to be awake an increasing amount of time on successive days, and the baby has a higher probability of being tested during an awake state with increasing age'. In the later report [11] a clearer account is given of the conditions under which stimuli were presented: 'after at least 10 s of record had passed in which there was no stabilimeter or leg movement, and in which the breathing record was smooth and rhythmic (p. 309 of [11]).' As it is not possible to decide whether the babies were predominantly in state I or in state III, the possibility that the results could be partly accounted for in terms of state is not excluded. To give credit, Kaye and Lipsitt are obviously aware of this fact, but it is regrettable that the variable was not more diligently examined in an otherwise admirable study.

It may seem somewhat *ad hoc* to proffer an interpretation of one set of findings in terms of an increase in regular sleep and the other in terms of an increase in wakefulness. The point is, however, that because state is not consistently treated as an experimental variable, we are always left in doubt as to whether a significant amount of the variance could have been accounted for by this factor. Moreover, the amount of time spent in any state is, in part, a function of the environmental conditions under which the experiment is conducted. In one study, the environment may be conducive to producing regular sleep, in another wakefulness. Wolff [22], for instance, has shown that continued stimulation with noise results in prolonged periods of regular sleep, which are nevertheless atypical in certain respects. It is thus desirable that reports should contain a statement of temperature, humidity, ambient illumination, noise, the use of drugs, etc. Even more informative would be a description of state in relation to stimulation. Alternatively, state could be varied as an experimental variable. In the absence of such treatments, we would have to regard the threshold measurements obtained in the studies quoted as very approximate.

Nevertheless, the direction of the serial measurements made by Lipsitt and his colleagues, are biologically of considerable interest as they show a rapid increase in the sensitivity of a sensory system during the first few days of life. These results also agree well with another threshold study of olfaction by Lipsitt, Engen, and Kaye [12]. This study is highly informative; the precise environmental conditions are reported, together with adequate descriptions of the baby's state at the time of stimulation, i.e. regular sleep. Olfactory thresholds, measured in terms of the concentration of a solution of asafetida in diethylphthalate required to produce a response, fell steadily during the first 4 days after delivery. It is quite clear in this study that the threshold measurements are relative to one state only, regular sleep; thus the results cannot be explained by variability in the baby's state on successive days. This enables us to reduce the number of interpretations. Unfortunately, this is one case in which more details of maternal medication during labour would have been most relevant. That decreasing sensory thresholds during the first 4 days of life may be a biological

phenomenon is nevertheless an intriguing possibility.

State cycles

In a previous paper, Prechtl *et al.* [14] discussed the serial changes in state that occur in an unstimulated baby between two feeds. Failure to take cognizance of these changes may lead to difficulties of interpretation in studies in which the time course extends across such endogenous changes. An investigation in which state cycles should have been a crucial variable, since it purported to study 'arousal level', is the interesting re-examination by Brackbill, Adams, Crowell, and Gray [5] of Salk's findings [18, 19]. Salk had presented a recording of a heartbeat (at 72 beats/min and 85 dB) through a loudspeaker in a newborn nursery for 4 days. Seventy per cent of the 102 newborn infants exposed to this stimulation had gained weight at the end of the 4 days, compared with 33 per cent of a control group of 112 babies not thus exposed. The control group cried 60 per cent more than the experimental group. Food intake was almost identical in the two groups. In a later study with 2-year-old institutionalized children, Salk compared the relative effectiveness in inducing sleep of the heartbeat sound, a metronome at 72 beats/min, and lullabies. The study by Brackbill *et al.* [5] was in two parts: the first examined the relative efficacy of four stimulus conditions in producing sleep in nursery school children, and the second studied their effects upon crying, movement, heart rate, and respiration in neonates. The stimuli were: no sound, lullaby, metronome, and heartbeats. For the older children, the mean number of minutes taken to fall asleep was 20·04, 17·96,

17·95, and 14·64, respectively, for the four conditions, which were presented on different days for different subgroups. For the neonatal study, the four sound conditions were presented consecutively, each for 15 min. Eight orders of presentation were used, the no-sound condition appearing twice in each of the four possible positions, the position of the remaining three stimuli being randomly determined. The resulting experimental design is of

What is surprising, therefore, is not that by analysis of variance the heartbeat condition was not significantly different from the other two sound conditions, but that the rank order of the various experimental conditions, in terms of their effects upon each parameter, should so consistently have favoured heartbeats. On both measures of 'crying rate', the lowest values were obtained under the heartbeats condition. Despite its over-representa-

TABLE 11.1 *Design of Neonatal Study* †

| | 15-min period | | | |
Stimulus	First	Second	Third	Fourth
Heartbeats	4	2	1	1
Lullaby	1	2	2	3
Metronome	1	2	3	2

† From Brackbill *et al.* [5].

interest. Omitting the no-sound condition, which appears equally often in each 15-min period, the frequency of occurrence of the stimuli in each position was as shown in Table 11.1.

Irrespective of stimulation, babies will be in a more active state in the period immediately following fixing of the electrodes than in subsequent periods. By the beginning of the third period, most babies will be in state I.

We would therefore predict over-representation of the heartbeats condition during the first period and its under-representation in the third and fourth periods would militate against the association of heartbeats with a low activity state, the heartbeats condition having a higher probability of being associated with fast and irregular heart rate and irregular respiration. In short, the experiment was unintentionally biased against Salk.

tion during the period of greatest endogenous activity, the heartbeat condition produced heart-rate and activity level values that were no higher than those for lullaby and metronome. Thus, the heartbeat condition was producing values that were better (in the sense of producing lower activity scores) than would be predicted on the basis of endogenous changes only. Since the experimental design placed the heartbeat condition at a particular disadvantage, the absence of a statistically significant effect is not strong evidence against the Salk phenomenon.

The greatest effect of state changes is likely to be manifested in studies of habituation because of the relatively long period of time over which they extend. A particularly interesting example is presented by Bartoshuk [2]. One-second trains of 50 clicks were presented via a loudspeaker to babies aged 1 to 4 days. The intensity of the stimuli was 85 dB above adult auditory threshold. Forty signals were presented with interstimulus intervals of 15, 30, or 60 s in each of three subgroups. Changes in heart rate were measured by comparing rates computed from the five beats before and the five beats after the stimulus. The differences between pre- and post-stimulus rates were then expressed as percentages of the response obtained on the first stimulus presentation (appropriate corrections having been applied to take into account the law of initial value). Repetitive stimulation produced a gradual decrement in heart-rate response over the 40 stimulus presentations. While the actual heart-rate changes were not given, it is possible to infer that the response decrement between the second and fortieth presentation must have been about two to three beats. The inter-stimulus interval did not significantly affect the rate of decline. Bartoshuk interprets his results as evidence for habituation of tonic arousal and points out the similarity of his findings to those of Sharpless and Jasper [20] on acoustic habituation in cats. He rejects the possibility that his results can be accounted for by a 'gradual over-all reduction in activation level during the experiment because mean heart-rate was higher before the fortieth than the first stimulus'. Unfortunately, this increase in pre-stimulus heart rate neither supports nor refutes the author's claim that the results were not due to a change in activation level. With a 15-s separation between successive stimuli, the experimental session would last for 10 min, and with a 30-s separation, for 20 min. Bartoshuk gives no information regarding his environmental conditions or the timing

of his experiment, making comparisons with our own data difficult. Nevertheless, assuming that his babies were studied shortly after a feed—for nursing convenience, a usual procedure— and in conditions approximating physiological neutrality, we would (from the paper by Prechtl *et al.* [14]) expect heart rate to increase for approximately the first 30 min of experimental time and then to decrease even if no stimuli were applied. It is interesting that with a 1-min inter-stimulus interval, heart rate before the fortieth stimulus did not differ significantly from that before the first stimulus. Again, we are given no information about the state of the babies at any time during recording. Their pre-stimulus heart-rate levels lead one to suppose, however, that the babies were certainly not in regular sleep at the beginning of the experiment. From our own natural history studies of normal unstimulated babies we would expect that most babies who were awake at the beginning of the experiment would have passed into irregular sleep, even during the shortest experiment, and that babies who were originally in irregular sleep would have certainly passed into regular sleep in the longer experiments. Since level of behavioural responsivity to sound is lower in regular than in irregular sleep, and lower in irregular sleep than during waking, any decrease in responsivity could be accounted for by a state change.

Using both electromyographic activity and heart-rate changes as their measure of responsivity to repeated sounds, Hutt *et al.* [9] were unable to demonstrate a decremental process other than one arising from a change of state. Their stimuli consisted of 2-s square wave or sine wave tones and human voices, all calibrated to produce a sound pressure reading of 75 dB at the baby's ear when delivered from a loudspeaker 40 cm away. Each stimulus was presented 60 times with an inter-stimulus interval of 30 s. Polygraphs of respiration, heart rate and EKG, EEG, eye movements, and EMG (6 channels) were recorded. The EMG channels were first independ-

ing behavioural responsivity during different states and that what he construed as habituation may represent only a diminution of response contingent upon a 'downward' state change.

The point at issue is not the validity of the findings but their interpretation. Without adequate monitoring of the state and of the presence or absence

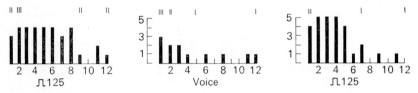

FIG. 11.1. Typical half-hour records from babies showing number of electromyographic responses per block of five stimuli. The state changes are shown above each histogram. In each case, decrements in response are accompanied by downward changes of state.

ently assessed by two experimenters, for the presence or absence of any of four specific types of response within 10 s of each stimulus. With the EMG channels covered, another experimenter then assessed the state of the baby from the remainder of the polygraph. Only states I, II, and III were considered: regular sleep, irregular sleep, and waking. The state assessments were then matched with the EMG data. A typical sample of the records thus obtained is shown in Fig. 11.1. For convenience the stimuli are grouped in blocks of five.

There is a decrease in EMG responsivity in those blocks during which the state changes from III to II and from II to I. In our data as a whole (10 babies were studied for periods varying from 2 to 6 h each), no decrement in responsivity could be demonstrated within a steady state. The heart-rate data showed a similar pattern. The possibility arises, therefore, that Bartoshuk was measur-

of behavioural changes, such results are always open to at least one other interpretation, namely, that the experiment is merely reflecting endogenous changes in an 'ultra stable' system [1].

A similar problem of interpretation arises in considering the phenomena of dishabituation, i.e. the reappearance of a response when an habituated stimulus is changed. In a study by Bartoshuk [3], a 500 cycles/s square wave tone of 80 dB was presented 17 times, at 1-min intervals. As in his earlier study [2], heart-rate change was computed as a percentage of stimulus change on the first trial. A decrease in responsivity was again observed; and again we would predict that a change of state of at least one downward step would have occurred in most babies. On the eighteenth trial the stimulus intensity was increased to 91 dB, producing an increase in heart rate of 50 per cent above that of the first trial. This phenomenon was interpreted as evidence of dishabituation. Our own experience with sound stimuli has shown that, if the baby is in regular sleep, broad-band signals (such as square wave pulses) of this intensity generally produce a startle (again, Bartoshuk gave no behavioural data) followed by a period of irregular sleep or by waking. Following the intense

Further evidence suggesting that state changes may account for much of the response decrement regarded as habituation, particularly to acoustic stimulation, is provided by the study of Eisenberg, Coursin, and Rupp [7]. Eight normal newborns, three rated as 'suspect' and two as 'at high risk' of developmental disorders of communication, were stimulated repeatedly

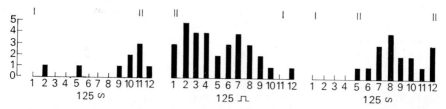

FIG. 11.2. Three successive half-hour records from one baby showing successively an increase in responsivity accompanied by corresponding state changes. Note apparent 'dishabituation' on presentation of the 125 cycle/s sine wave tone. The state has already begun to change, however, in the two preceding blocks.

stimulus, the responses to all six subsequent stimuli were greater than those to the six stimuli preceding the intense stimulus, again suggesting that the babies' state had changed. Although this interpretation does not invalidate that of the author, it does change the point of emphasis.

Evidence regarding dishabituation was also obtained from the study of Hutt *et al.* [8]. If iterative stimulation was continued after 'habituation' had occurred, a sudden increase in responsivity frequently occurred. When state changes were entered on the polygraphs, it was found that these response increases invariably corresponded with a state change upward. Changes in the properties of the 'habituated' stimulus did not produce dishabituation unless such a change had already begun. An example of 'dishabituation' in one baby is shown in Fig. 11.2.

with a modulated tone falling in pitch from 5000 cycles/s to 200 cycles/s in 4 s. The mean intensity of the stimulus was approximately 80 dB. Stimuli were repeated at intervals of 10 s, until ten consecutive failures to respond had been obtained. The sound pattern was then presented in reverse order 10 s later. Habituation was considered to have occurred when ten non-responses were followed by a clear-cut response to the reverse pattern sound. Responses were motor, visual, or vocal events, which were carefully distinguished from non-stimulus behaviours. In addition to specific stimulus-bound responses prior to each stimulus, observers recorded the baby's state using a seven-point scale varying from deep sleep to extreme excitation. The relation between behavioural responsivity and state is an interesting one. Following presentation of the first three signals, all normal subjects showed upward changes in state, attaining 'peak arousal within 7–8 trials'. Thereafter there was a gradual decline in response to the stimulus. This was accompanied by one or more downward changes of state until the pre-stimulus state was regained within 16 to 20 trials. Stimulation was then continued until the criterion for habituation had occurred. In eight cases (including two rated as 'suspect'), the baby's state at this point was one or more steps lower than its pre-stimulus state: 'infants who were wakeful during the pre-stimulus period either were sleeping or approaching that state when stimulation was terminated; those who were dozing went to sleep; those who were sleeping returned to sleep'. When there were fluctuations in responsivity, these were accompanied by almost parallel changes of state. We would therefore suggest that it may be physiologically both more meaningful and more parsimonious to talk of changes of state than of habituation. Certainly, in our own experiment we were unable to demonstrate any systematic decline in responsivity within a stable state, and the findings of Eisenberg *et al.* are essentially in agreement with ours.

It is of interest that two of the subjects of the Eisenberg *et al.* study did not show habituation; both showed upward changes of state following onset of stimulation and remained effectively in that state for the duration of the experiment. The babies were those described as at 'high risk' for developmental disorders of communication. Again, it may be more parsimonious to say that risk babies stay in the more active behavioural states longer than normals. That the endogenous behavioural cycles of neurologically abnormal babies are deviant has recently been shown in our work. The states of irregular sleep were prolonged in such babies and the regular sleep states foreshortened. It may be more helpful to look at their abnormality in terms of the functional perversion of a biological clock, than in terms of a 'learning' process such as failure to habituate.

Conclusion

In the human newborn, the probability and magnitude of a response to a given stimulus is almost without exception a function of state. Here again, however, there is no regular progression in responsiveness from state to state. This was most clearly seen in the case of spinal reflexes. Some reflexes could be elicited strongly in regular sleep, but not during irregular sleep. Other reflexes showed the converse relationship; yet others could be elicited only during intense behavioural activity; while a further group could be evoked irrespective of the baby's state. While, therefore, we would regard specification of the baby's state as a *sine qua non* of psychophysiological studies, we do not consider that the physiological evidence requires that these states be placed on a continuum. Rather, they may better be regarded as qualitatively different neurophysiological conditions with specific functional organization.

Although state is a variable of the utmost importance in determining the degree of response to a stimulus, it is often remarkably little affected by the stimuli applied. In our own studies of the effect of repetitive elicitation of monosynaptic and polysynaptic reflexes [17] and auditory stimulation [9] at the state cycles showed similar durations to those observed in unstimulated babies [17]. Moreover, the heart rate showed the same saw-toothed pattern of fluctuations as in the unstimulated baby, the different stimuli having little apparent effect. Whatever the nature of the physiological mechanism that regulates the newborn infant's state cycles, it clearly has great stability. This does not mean that it is impervious to all environmental influences. Dressing, environmental temperature, and possibly humidity influence both the duration and stability of the state cycles. Wolff [22] has claimed that ambient noise and light also affect the baby's state. Pending further research on the effects of environmental influences upon state, it is important that the fullest details of recording conditions be given in reports of newborn psychophysiological studies.

References

1. ASHBY, W. R. (1957). *An introduction to cybernetics*. Chapman and Hall, London.
2. BARTOSHUK, A. K. (1962). Human neonatal cardiac acceleration to sound: Habituation and dishabituation. *Percept. mot. Skills.* **15**, 15–27.
3. —— (1962). Response decrement with repeated elicitation of human neonatal cardiac acceleration to sound. *J. comp. physiol. Psychol.* **55**, 9–13.
4. —— (1964). Human neonatal cardiac response to sound: A power function. *Psychon. Sci.* **1**, 151–2.
5. BRACKBILL, Y., ADAMS, G., CROWELL, D. H., and GRAY, L. M. (1966). Arousal level in neonates and pre-school children under continuous auditory stimulation. *J. exp. Child Psychol.* **4**, 178–88.
6. EISENBERG, R. B., GRIFFIN, E., and COURSIN, D. B. (1964). Auditory behavior in the human neonate: A preliminary report. *J. speech hear. Res.* **7**, 245–69.
7. EISENBERG, R. B., COURSIN, D. B., and RUPP, N. R. (1966). Habituation to an acoustic pattern as an index of differences among human neonates. *J. aud. Res.* **6**, 239–48.
8. GULLIKSON, G. R. and CROWELL, D. H. (1964). Neonatal habituation to electrotactual stimulation. *J. exp. Child Psychol.* **1**, 388–96.
9. HUTT, C., LENARD, H. G., VON BERNUTH, H., HUTT, S. J., and PRECHTL, H. F. R. (1968). Habituation in relation to state in the human neonate. *Nature* **220**, 618–20.
10. KAGAN, J. and HENKER, B. A. (1966). Developmental psychology. *A. Rev. Psychol.* **17**, 1–50.
11. KAYE, H. and LIPSITT, L. P. (1964). Relation of electro-tactual threshold to basal skin conductance. *Child Dev.* **35**, 1307–12.
12. LIPSITT, L. P., ENGEN, T., and KAYE, H. (1963). Developmental changes in the olfactory threshold of the neonate. *Child Dev.* **34**, 371–6.
13. —— and LEVY, N. (1959). Electro-tactual threshold in the neonate. *Child Dev.* **30**, 547–54.
14. PRECHTL, H. F. R., AKIYAMA, Y., ZINKIN, P., and KERR GRANT, D. (1968). Polygraphic studies of the full-term newborn infant. I. Technical aspects and qualitative analysis. *In* (Bax, M. C. O. and MacKeith, R. C. (Eds.)) *Studies in infancy. Clinics in developmental medicine No. 27.* Heinemann, London, pp. 1–25.
15. —— and BEINTEMAN, D. J. (1964). *The neurological examination of the full-term newborn infant. Clinics in developmental medicine No. 12.* Heinemann, London.
16. —— KERR GRANT, D., LENARD, H. G., and HRBEK, A. (1967). The lip-tap reflex in the awake and sleeping newborn infant. *Exp. Brain Res.* **3**, 184–94.
17. —— VLACH, V., LENARD, H. G., and KERR GRANT, D. (1967). Exteroceptive and tendon reflexes in various behavioural states in the new-

born infant. *Biologia Neonat.* **11**, 159–75.

18. SALK, L. (1960). The effects of the normal heart beat sound on the behaviour of the newborn infant: Implications for mental health. *World mental Health* **12**, 168–75.

19. —— (1962). Mother's heart beats as an imprinting stimulus. *Trans. N.Y. Acad. Sci.* **24**, 753–63.

20. SHARPLESS, S. and JASPER, H. (1956). Habituation of the arousal reaction. *Brain* **79**, 655–80.

21. STEVENS, S. S. (1961). To honor Fechner and repeal his law. *Science* **133**, 80–6.

22. WOLFF, P. H. (1966). The causes, controls, and organization of behavior in the neonate. *Psychol. Issues* **5**, (1, Whole No. 17).

IV Perceptual capacities

THE fact that an infant responds to the same signals as an adult does not mean that he employs the same underlying mechanisms. This caution is especially important in relation to visual perception, where there is already an abundance of animal evidence regarding the bases on which visual discriminations are made. Fantz's claim (Chap. 12), that babies have an innate capacity for discrimination of visual form, is based upon the finding that newborn infants appear to show preferential fixation upon 'complex' visual patterns relative to simpler patterns, when total luminous flux is controlled. Though undoubtedly important—not least for the impetus it has given to research on infant perception in the last decade—Fantz's work is open to question on both methological and theoretical grounds. What this and studies by other authors may have demonstrated is not *form* perception, but *brightness* discrimination.

Animal studies employing surgical procedures have demonstrated that true form perception—the discrimination of orientation, shape, and pattern —demands the functional integrity of the striate cortex. Schneider [6] working with the hamster, and Barnes [1] with the rat have demonstrated that what we loosely refer to as pattern perception consists of at least two perceptual processes: orienting and discrimination, the former being mediated by sub-cortical structures, such as the superior colliculus and the latter by the striate cortex. Monkeys with bilateral lesions of the striate cortex are able to distinguish figures which differ in number of light–dark gradients, or 'edginess', though they cannot distinguish figures containing the same number of light–dark gradients in differing orientations (Weiskrantz [8]). Humphrey and Weiskrantz [4] demonstrated that movement provides a powerful cue to monkeys with striate lesions, and more recently Humphrey [3] has reported successful discrimination learning in a striate monkey employing size and brightness cues. In effect, contour, or edginess may itself be resolved into size and brightness components [2]. It appears therefore that the only stimulus variables to which striate animals respond—flux, size, contour, and movement—are ones capable of generating variable quantities of retinal stimulation. The over-all picture is well accounted for by Weiskrantz's suggestion that striate animals respond to visual patterns on the basis of 'the integral of all retinal ganglionic activity' [8].

In babies, as we saw in Part III, the striate cortex is the least developed of all the sensory receiving areas until about the sixth month of life. Thus, it seems more parsimonious to suggest that they respond to the *quantitative* than to the qualitative properties of stimuli, i.e. they orient to that part of the visual field which evokes the greatest amount of retinal activity. This hypothesis is the more likely since, under the conditions of Fantz's experiments, the patterns presented were almost certainly out of focus. Haynes *et al.* (Chap. 13) show that in the earliest weeks of life the baby can focus his eye on targets only at a distance of about 8 in. Fantz's targets were presented at a distance of 12 in from the eye. His scoring criteria too are of some concern since the reflection of a target in either eye was recorded as a 'hit'. However, Wickelgren (Chap. 14) shows that convergence, as well as accommodation, develops only slowly. During the neonatal period, the reflection of a target in one eye does not exclude the possibility that the other eye is engaged upon a second stimulus. The difficulties of judging *what* stimulus an infant is fixating are also exemplified by the studies of Salapatek and Kessen [5], which furnish further evidence for the notion that visual behaviour in the neonatal period is governed by brightness gradients. Visual fixations were directed not towards the figure as a whole or to its centre, but only to selected elements, mostly to the apices (double brightness gradients) and less to the sides (single brightness gradients).

Further evidence for the argument that responsivity in the neonatal period is governed by gross quantity of neural input, rather than by specific qualitative features of stimuli, is provided by Hutt *et al.* (Chap. 15). The authors demonstrate that what at first sight appears to be a highly sophisticated neonatal behaviour—differential response to the sound of an adult's voice—can be accounted for by a relatively simple subcortical mechanism controlled by the total amount of basilar membrane excitation elicited by an auditory stimulus. The apotheosis of the argument is provided by a recent essay by Schneirla [7], based primarily upon consideration of the behaviour of non-human species. Its argument, however, is clearly adumbrated in a earlier paper, which is more concerned with human infants. The present reading (Chap. 16) is based upon excerpts from this earlier study.

References

1. BARNES, P. J., SMITH, L. M., and LATTO, R. M. (1970). Orientation to visual stimuli and the superior colliculus in the rat. *Quart. J. exp. Psychol.* **22**, 239–47.

2. HECHT, S. (1935). A theory of visual intensity discrimination. *J. gen. Physiol.* **18**, 767–89.

3. HUMPHREY, N. K. (1970). What the frog's eye tells the monkey's brain. *Brain Behav. Evol.* **3**, 324–37.

4. —— and WEISKRANTZ, L. (1967). Vision in monkeys after removal of the striate cortex. *Nature* **215**, 595–7.

5. SALAPATEK, P. and KESSEN, W. (1966). Visual scanning of triangles by the human newborn. *J. exp. Child Psychol.* **3**, 155–67.

6. SCHNEIDER, G. E. (1967). Contrasting visuomotor functions of tectum and cortex in the golden hamster. *Psychol. Forschung* **31**, 52–62.

7. SCHNEIRLA, T. C. (1965). Aspects of stimulation and organisation in approach/withdrawal processes underlying vertebrate behavioural development. *In* (Lehrman, D. S., Hinde, R. A., and Shaw, E. (Eds.)) *Advances in the study of behaviour.* Vol. 1. Academic Press, New York.

8. WEISKRANTZ, L. (1963). Contour discrimination in a young monkey with striate cortex ablation. *Neuropsychologia* **1**, 145–64.

12 Pattern vision in newborn infants

ROBERT L. FANTZ†

I T is usually stated or implied that the infant has little or no pattern vision during the early weeks or even months, because of the need for visual learning or because of the immature state of the eye and brain, or for both reasons.‡ This viewpoint has been challenged by the direct evidence of differential attention given to visual stimuli varying in form or pattern [1]. This evidence has shown that during the early months of life, infants: (1) have fairly acute pattern vision (resolving $\frac{1}{8}$-in stripes at a 10-in distance); (2) show greater visual interest in patterns than in plain colours; (3) differentiate among patterns of similar complexity; and (4) show visual interest in a pattern similar to that of a human face.

The purpose of the present study was to determine whether it was possible to obtain similar data on newborn infants and thus further exclude visual learning or post-natal maturation as requirements for pattern vision. It is a repetition of a study of older infants which compared the visual responsiveness to patterned and to plainly coloured surfaces [2]. The results of the earlier study were essenti-

ally duplicated, giving further support for the above conclusions.

The subjects were 18 infants ranging from 10 hours to 5 days old. They were selected from a much larger number on the basis of their eyes remaining open long enough to be exposed to a series of six targets at least twice. The length of gaze at each target was observed through a tiny hole in the ceiling of the chamber (Plate 6) and recorded on a timer. The fixation time started as soon as one or both eyes of the infant were directed towards the target, using as criterion the superposition over the pupil of a tiny corneal reflection of the target; it ended when the eyes turned away or closed.§ The six targets were presented in random order for each infant, with the sequence repeated up to eight times when possible. Only completed sequences were included in calculating the percentage of total fixation time for each target.

The targets were circular, 6 in in diameter, and had non-glossy surfaces. Three contained black-and-white patterns—a schematic face, concentric circles, and a section of newspaper

† From *Science* **140**, 296–7 (1963). Copyright © 1963 by the American Association for the Advancement of Science. Reprinted by permission of the author and the Association.

‡ See, for example, DEWEY, EVELYN, (1935), *Behavior Development in Infants*, Columbia Univ. Press, New York; PRATT, K. C. (1945). In *Manual of Child Psychology* (Carmichael, L. (Ed.)), Wiley, New York; SPOCK, B. (1957), *Baby and Child Care* Pocket Books, New York.

§ High reliability of a similar technique, using the same criterion of fixation, was shown with older infants. Since eye movements are less coordinated and fixations less clear-cut in newborn infants, a further check of the response measurement is desirable; I plan to do this by photographic recordings.

TABLE 12.1. *Relative Duration of Initial Gaze of Infants at Six Stimulus Objects in Successive and Repeated Presentations.*

| Age group | N | Mean percentage of fixation time | | | | | | $P\dagger$ |
		Face	Circles	News	White	Yellow	Red	
Under 48 hours	8	29·5	23·5	13·1	12·3	11·5	10·1	0·005
2 to 5 days	10	29·5	24·3	17·5	9·9	12·1	6·7	0·001
2 to 6 months‡	25	34·3	18·4	19·9	8·9	8·2	10·1	0·001

† Significance level based on Friedman analysis of variance by ranks.
‡ From an earlier study [1].

containing print $\frac{1}{16}$ to $\frac{1}{4}$ in high. The other three were unpatterned—white, fluorescent yellow, and dark red. The relative luminous reflectance was, in decreasing order: yellow, white, newsprint, face and circles, red. Squares containing the patterns or colours were placed in a flat holder which slid horizontally into a slightly recessed portion of the chamber ceiling to expose the pattern or colour to the infant through a circular hole in the holder. The chamber and underside of the holder were lined with blue felt to provide a contrasting background for the stimuli, and to diffuse the illumination (between 10 and 15 ft-candles) from lights on either side of the infant's head. The subject was in a small hammock cot with head facing up directly under the targets, 1 ft away.

The results in Table 12.1 show about twice as much visual attention to patterns as to plainly coloured surfaces. Differences in response to the six stimulus objects are significant for the infants both under and over 2 days of age; results from these groups do not differ reliably from each other, and are similar to earlier results from much older infants. The selectivity of the visual responses is brought out still more strikingly by tabulating the longest-fixated target for each newborn infant: 11 for face, 5 for concentric circles, 2 for newsprint, and 0 for white, yellow, and red. For comparison, the first choices of infants 2 to 6 months were distributed as follows: 16, 4, 5, 0, 0, 0.

Three infants under 24 h could be tested sufficiently to indicate the individual consistency of response. Two of these showed a significant (0·005 and 0·05) difference among the targets in successive sets of exposures, one looking longest at the face pattern in 7 or 8 exposures, the other looking longest at the 'bull's-eye' in 3 of 6 exposures. The third infant 10 h after birth looked longest at the face in 3 of 8 exposures.

It is clear that the selective visual responses were related to pattern rather than hue or reflectance, although the latter two variables are often thought to be primary visual stimuli. Specification of the pre-potent configurational variables is unwarranted at this time. The results do not imply 'instinctive recognition' of a face or other unique significance of this pattern; it is likely there are other patterns which would elicit equal or greater attention.† Longer fixation of

† I chose the targets for their expected attention value for the older infants of the earlier study; this may be different for newborn subjects: response to the newsprint may be decreased by less acute vision (although

the face suggests only that a pattern with certain similarities to social objects also has stimulus character-istics with considerable intrinsic interest or stimulating value; whatever the mechanism underlying this in-terest, it should facilitate the develop-ment of social responsiveness, since what is responded to must first be attended to.

---

some patterning would be visible without resolution of individual letters); 'bull's-eye' elicited strong differential attention only over 2 months of age in another study [2]; and blue is preferred to red and yellow by new-borns. The face pattern might for these reasons have a relative advantage for newborns.

Substantiation for the visual selec-tion of patterned over unpatterned objects is given in an independent study of newborn infants in which more visual attention was given to a coloured card with a simple figure, when held close to the infant, than to a plain card of either colour [3].

The results of Table 12.1 demon-strate that pattern vision can be tested in newborn infants by recording differential visual attention; these and other results call for a revision of traditional views that the visual world of the infant is initially formless or chaotic and that we must learn to see configurations.

References

1. FANTZ, R. L., ORDY, J. M., and UDELF, M. S. (1962). *J. comp. physiol. Psychol.* **55**, 907; FANTZ, R. L. (1958). *Psychol. Rec.* **8**, 43.

2. FANTZ, R. L. (1961). *Scient. Am.* **204**, No. 5, 66.

3. STIRNIMANN, F. (1944). *Ann. Paediat.* **163**, 1.

Development of visual accommodation

HAROLD HAYNES, BURTON L. WHITE,
AND RICHARD HELD†

INCREASING interest in the vision of newborn infants is demonstrated by the growing amount of research on their acuity, form discrimination, preferences, and other visually controlled behaviours [1]. In all such studies the focus of the retinal image limits the fineness of discrimination. Moreover, changes in focus may be confounded with other conditions that determine responses to visible objects. Nevertheless, in practically all research on infant vision, focal length has been an uncontrolled variable. Whereas accommodation of the lens in the eye of the young adult automatically focuses the retinal image for target distances ranging from 10 cm to optical infinity, we cannot assume comparable behaviour in very young infants. The fragmentary data that are available suggest limited accommodative capacity, at best, in the newborn human [2].‡ Even if an infant's eyes are oriented towards a target, his optical system may be focused for any distance along his line of sight. The blurring of the retinal image that results from inadequate focusing may interact significantly with the effects of experimental variables. We now report the first data known to us on the course of acquisition of accommodative ability in human infants.

Changes in accommodation are largely accomplished by involuntary contraction or relaxation of the ciliary muscle which in turn changes the shape of the crystalline lens. Retinoscopic studies performed with the ciliary muscle immobilized by atropine (cycloplegia) have suggested that the normal infant is hyperopic (farsighted) for all target distances [2]. On the other hand, Elschnig found a significant difference between responses measured during cycloplegia as opposed to nondrugged conditions in 2-day-old infants.‡ He concluded that the newborn infant is capable of some degree of accommodation. Aside from these reports we know of no others on dynamic accommodative behaviour in human infants.

Dynamic retinoscopy is a technique for measuring accommodative responses without immobilizing the lenticular system [3]. A sharply focused streak or spot of light is projected into the subject's eye through the pupillary opening. Modifications in the reflected image are used as an index of the refractive state of the eye. These modifications are quantitatively

† From 'Visual accommodation in human infants'. *Science* **148**, 528–30 (1965). Copyright © 1965 by the American Association for the Advancement of Science. Reprinted by permission of the author and the Association.

‡ Cited in FELDMAN, W. M. (1920). *Principles of antenatal and post-natal child Physiology, pure and applied.* Longmans Green, New York.

assessed by means of lenses of known power. Refraction is measured while the subject fixates nearby objects and also while he tracks an object moving towards and away from his eye. Although this technique has been employed with considerable success with adults it has been less useful with children because it requires a co-operative subject. Children of 1 or 2 years of age can rarely be induced to attend persistently to a prescribed target. Fortunately, we have found that infants between 2 and 5 months of age make good subjects for this task. Unlike older children, they will stare at appropriate targets steadily enough to allow measurement. In fact, by occasionally moving the target one can often induce the young infant to maintain fixation for several minutes. This type of performance is not at all unusual in infants during the first half year of life. Both McGraw and Ling have cited several instances of comparable 'stimulus-bound' behaviour in such subjects [4].

A white cardboard shield, 11·4 by 13·3 cm, was mounted on a Reid streak retinoscope to shield the major portion of the examiner's head from the infant's view. A 0·95-cm hole was cut in the centre to allow the beam of the retinoscope to shine into the subject's eyes. Centred around this aperture a red annulus with an outside diameter of 3·8 cm was painted. Black marks and dots were inked into this red area in a random manner to increase the complexity of the stimulus.

The study was performed at a state institution on 22 normal infants ranging in age from 6 days to 4 months. Their time at the institution varied as a consequence of several factors, including adoption. Consequently, some subjects were available for examination only once, whereas others were tested repeatedly for several months. On the average, each subject was tested five times. Sample size for the 4 months varied from 7 to 13 (Fig. 13.1). The children were examined in a supine position under standardized conditions. One examiner did the retinoscopy while the other measured the distance between the retinoscope target and the eye of the infant. To assure 'on axis' retinoscopy [3] both examiners had to agree that the child appeared to be fixating within the 3·2-cm target area before an observation was acceptable.

The examination procedure was as follows. To capture the infant's attention, the retinoscope and attached target were moved back and forth horizontally at approximately 2·5 cm^{-1} across the infant's line of sight. The examiner did not place his eye to the retinoscope until after pursuit fixations were obtained from at least one eye. (Infants less than 1 month of age did not exhibit sustained fixations on the target. With these subjects the examiner simply placed the retinoscope at several points along the line of gaze.) Retinoscopic measurements were taken whenever possible within each of four ranges of distance: (i) 8 to 15 cm; (ii) 15 to 25 cm; (iii) 25 to 51 cm; and (iv) 51 to 100 cm. The typical sequence of testing was (iii)–(ii)–(i)–(iv). The accommodative response was measured by briefly introducing lenses of known power in front of the fixating eye. By moving the retinoscope in depth, thereby inducing accommodative tracking, we then determined the range of distance over which each infant could maintain accommodation on the target within 0·5 diopter. In subjects who had

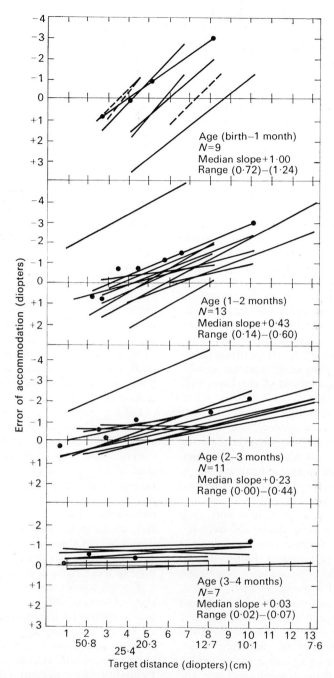

Fig. 13.1 Four stages in the development of accommodation in the first 4 months of life. The heavy lines fitted to the filled circles illustrate both the progress of a typical infant and also the closeness of fit of the lines to the plotted points. During the first month, the data that were estimated are represented by dashed lines. Plus values indicate myopic performance. Minus values indicate deviations in the hyperopic direction.

developed convergence responses prior to testing, each eye was observed alternately. For each distance the average response was recorded. Since the examiner's eye was not placed exactly at the plane of the target the data were corrected for the resultant error, as described previously [3]. Repeated measurements were taken routinely on many of the infants. They rarely varied more than 0·5 diopter. Whenever an infant had been examined more than once in a particular month, measurements taken at replicated distances were averaged.

The corrected and averaged data for the multiple-distance retinoscopy taken during each of the 4 months were plotted for each infant. The best-fitting straight line was then drawn for each subject (see Fig. 13.1). Each line typically represents six points compiled from these separate examinations. The extent of the lines indicates the range of distance over which data were actually collected. The lines do not always extend over the full range, since subjects often turned away from the target when it was presented nearer than 10 cm or further than 38 cm from the eye. A slope value was calculated for each subject at each test age. Median slope values and their ranges were then calculated from the group data for each month, starting at birth and ending at 4 months of age. The group performance for each month is shown in Fig. 13.1.

Perfect adjustment to changing target distance would be represented by a slope of 0·00, whereas the complete absence of accommodative change would be indicated by a value of +1·00. Prior to 1 month of age, the infant's accommodative response did not adjust to changes in target distances. The system appeared to be locked at one focal distance whose median value for the group was 19 cm. This is indicated by a slope value for the group of +1·00. Occasionally, infants of this age did not remain alert long enough to allow complete calibration of their responses. In these few instances, the magnitude of error was estimated (see Fig. 13.1). Flexibility of response began at about the middle of the 2nd month and performance comparable to that of the normal adult was attained by the 4th month, as shown by a median slope value of 0·03.

For infants less than 1 month of age it might be assumed that the accommodative system is incapable of any change whatever. We therefore tested 11 sleeping infants, opening their lids in order to take readings. In every case, the lenticular system was relaxed and measured on the average 5 diopters less than when the infant was awake and alert.

During the 2nd month of infancy, the accommodative system began to respond adaptively to change in target distance. By 3 months of age, the median magnitude of hyperopia for targets at 20 cm was 0·75 diopter, a degree of accuracy comparable to the emmetropic (normal) adult. By the time the infants began to look at their own hands and make swiping motions at nearby objects [5] their eyes were able to focus sharply on such targets.

Knowledge of the developmental state of the accommodative system is a prerequisite for measuring the limits of visual discrimination in infants, because resolution is limited by the sharpness of the retinal image. Although accurate accommodation is a first step in achieving clear vision, there is not a simple relation between the capacity to focus an image on the retina and the ability to see clearly (visual acuity). Even when the image is optically focused on the retina, visual acuity in the infant is unlikely to be equivalent to that of the adult until the visual receptor mechanisms and neural pathways are sufficiently mature. The results of this study provide a basis for the design of studies of the vision of human infants.

References

1. GORMAN, J. J., COGAN, D. G., and GELLIS, S. S. (1957). *Pediatrics* **19**, 1088; FANTZ, R. L. (1963). *Science* **140**, 296; STECHLER, G. (1964). *ibid.* **144**, 315; HERSHENSON, M. (1964). *J. comp. physiol. Psychol.* **58**, 270; DAYTON, JR., G. O., JONES, M. H., IAU, P., RAWSON, R. A., STEELE, B., and ROSE, M. (1964). *Arch. Opthalmol.* **71**, 865.
2. SLATAPER, F. J. (1950). *Arch. Ophthalmol.* **43**, 466; DUKE-ELDER, W. S. (1949). *Textbook of Ophthalmology.* Vol. 4. Mosby, St. Louis.
3. PASCAL, J. I. (1930). *Modern Retinoscopy.* Hatton, London; HAYNES, H. M. (1960). *Optom. Wkly.* **51**, 43.
4. McGRAW, M. B. (1943). *Neuromuscular maturation of the human infant.* Columbia University Press, New York; LING, B. C. (1942). *J. genet. Psychol.* **61**, 277.
5. WHITE, B. L., CASTLE, P. W., and HELD, R. (1964). *Child Dev.* **35**, 349.

14 Development of convergence

LYN W. WICKELGREN†

RECENT studies of ocular orientation in newborn infants have used human observers to judge direction of orientation [2, 3]. A reflection of any part of the stimulus over the approximate pupil centre in either eye has been used as the operational definition of orientation towards the stimulus. Such judgements of orientation may be inaccurate if the newborn's eyes are not directed towards the same place at a given moment (lack of convergence) or if the eyes do not move together (lack of conjugation).

It is possible for the two eyes to move together in conjugation without converging on the same spot while resting. Dayton, Jones, Steele, and Rose [1] have demonstrated electro-oculographically that newborns can look at and follow a series of targets with relatively close conjugation of eye movements. Hershenson [5] observed some degree of newborn conjugation and convergence, while White [8] did not find convergence in the newborn. Thus, although evidence indicates that conjugate eye movements occur in newborn infants, the evidence for convergence is less clear.

The present study consisted of two experiments. The first experiment was designed to assess colour-brightness preference in newborns. In large part

† From *J. exp. Child Psychol.* **5**, 74–85 (1967). Reprinted by permission of the author and the publishers, Academic Press, Inc.

the Ss' two eyes were not directed towards the same stimulus at a given moment, and therefore preference could not be determined unambiguously. Consequently, a second experiment was designed specifically to study convergence. As previous experiments have shown preferences for patterns in newborns [3, 4], Experiment 2A paired a distinctive striped stimulus with a neutral grey one. Experiment 2B used a single centre stimulus to test the possibility that stimulus competition with the paired stimuli might have accounted for the lack of convergence in Experiment 1.

Method

Subjects

Subjects for the experiments were 28 awake newborn infants from 2 to 5 days of age in the nursery of the Yale-New Haven Community Hospital. In Experiment 1 were 16 Ss, 9 males and 7 females. In Experiment 2 were 12 Ss, 8 males and 4 females. An additional 34 babies were seen, but observations of these babies could not be used either because they fell asleep during the observation or because their film records were unscorable.

Apparatus

The experiments were conducted in a small room on the maternity ward of the hospital. Fig. 14.1 shows a diagram of the apparatus. The S was placed facing upward in a head-restraining crib on a table. Two ground-glass stimulus screens were mounted 14 in above *S*'s head, one to each side of midline. The screens were 6-in squares and were 6 in apart. The total stimulus field, from the left edge of the left screen to the right edge of the right screen, subtended approximately 60° of visual angle. Two 500-W slide projectors were mounted so as to project

lus panels but did not obstruct the field photographed by the camera. Kodak high-speed infra-red film (HIR 417) was used for photographing the eyes. The camera was fitted with an 85-mm Pentax lens and an S II adaptor ring. Photographs were made with f/8·0 and a focal distance of 27 in. The field of the photographs encompassed *S*'s head. Photographs were made once per second with an exposure of $\frac{1}{6}$ s. A

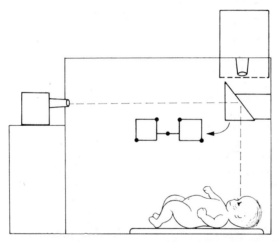

Fig. 14.1. Side view diagram of the apparatus with inset of stimulus panels as seen by *S*s.

stimulus images from slides on to the screens when the projector beams were bent 90° by two front surface mirrors above the screens. Four Bausch and Lomb Nicholas illuminators fitted with Kodak Wratten 87C and Corning 7·69 filters were used as marker lights for the stimulus panels. The filters eliminated all visible light except a barely visible reddish beam above 800 mμ.

An Automax model G-2 35-mm variable-speed sound-proofed camera was mounted above the stimulus panels behind a wire screen. The camera lens was centred between the two stimulus panels. A small white light was mounted between the stimu-

counter provided a record of the number of frames of film exposed.

Stimuli

Experiment 1. The four stimuli were squares of uniform light provided by filters placed between Kodak B351 glass slide covers. Two red stimuli, bright and dim, and two grey stimuli, bright and dim, were used. The bright red stimulus was a Wratten 25 filter. The dim red stimulus was a Wratten 25 filter plus a Wratten ND 1·30 filter. The bright grey stimulus, equated with the bright red for physical intensity, was a Wratten ND 0·70 filter. The dim grey, equated for physical intensity with the dim red stimulus, was a Wratten ND 2·00 filter. The dim stimuli were clearly visible, and the bright ones did not cause *S*s to close their eyes. The stimuli were grouped into four pairs: bright red versus dim red, bright red versus dim grey, bright grey versus dim grey, and bright grey versus dim red. Each member of a pair was presented in both left and right positions to balance out any position preference. Thus each *S* saw a total of eight stimulus pairs.

Experiment 2A. One of the two stimuli used was the dim grey stimulus of Experiment 1, a Wratten ND 2·00 filter. The second stimulus was a panel of vertical black and white stripes, each of which subtended a visual angle of about 3°. The stripes panel was bright enough to cause some potential *S*s to close their eyes. All *S*s saw each member of the stimulus pair in both left and right positions.

Experiment 2B. The single stimulus was the small light centred above *S*'s head, which blinked on for $\frac{1}{2}$ s every second. The light was moderately bright and led no *S*s to close their eyes.

Procedure

The same general procedure was followed for all *S*s. Subjects were observed about 30 min before feeding, at 9.00 am or at 1.00 pm. A nurse brought each *S* to the observation room from the nursery and placed him in the cot. The *S* was then given a pacifier. The room lights were turned off, and the small centre light began blinking above *S*. The observation began as soon as *S* was judged to be looking towards the blinking light.

Experiment 1. Each *S* received successive presentations of all eight stimulus pairs in the experiment, according to a predetermined random sequence. All stimulus pairs were shown at least 30 s to permit 30 photographs of the eyes. In order to bring *S*'s orientation back to mid-line, the blinking light was on for 5 to 10 s between stimulus presentations, i.e. while slides were being changed. The procedure seemed quite effective; *S*'s turned their heads back to midline as soon as the light began blinking. If *S* began crying or closed his eyes, the camera was stopped while *S* was quieted or roused. If possible, the experiment was then continued until at least 30 frames were photographed for each stimulus pair. There was a total stimulus-on time of 4 min, and the experimental session lasted at least 5 min.

Experiment 2. Both parts of Experiment 2 were run during the same observation period. Each *S* received successive presentations of the three stimuli in the experiment according to a predetermined random sequence. Each stimulus presentation was at least 30 s to permit 30 photographs of the eyes. In addition, in order to bring *S*'s orientation to midline, as in Experiment 1, the blinking light was on for 5 to 10 s between the three stimulus presentations. The stimulus-on time was 90 s, and the session lasted about 2 min.

Scoring and analysis

No *S*'s film was scored unless a preliminary check indicated that there was a minimum of ten scorable frames for each stimulus. A film frame was scorable if the marker lights were clearly visible and if the position of the centre of the pupil could be determined. Films were projected on to a wall, and each eye was scored independently for each film frame of each stimulus. In both experiments each eye was scored as oriented towards the left panel, the centre, or the right panel. The criterion of orientation was that the centre of the pupil fell within any part of a stimulus region as defined by the infrared marker lights. Thus the eye in Fig. 14.2 would be scored as

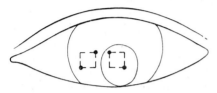

Fig. 14.2. Diagram of *S*'s right eye. The four dots represent reflections of the infra-red marker lights on the cornea; dotted lines indicate relative positions of the stimulus panels. The eye is scored as looking at the left stimulus panel.

looking left since the pupil centre falls within the left stimulus panel. Film records of an adult who was instructed to look left, centre, and right, scored on a Vanguard motion analyser, indicated little or no film distortion. Several strips of film were scored independently by two people. The correlation between their judgements of joint orientation of both eyes was +0·94.

Convergence. In order to determine the degree to which both eyes were oriented towards the same part of the stimulus field, a matrix was constructed for each *S* with the orientation of each eye as the marginals and the total number of film frames for each joint orientation as the entries. The right eye could be oriented left, centre, or right on a film frame where the left eye was oriented left, centre, or right. Each *S*'s orientation totals were reduced to proportions, and for each

experiment the *S*s' proportions were averaged together. The left-left, centre-centre, and right-right proportions were summed to indicate the over-all proportion of convergence for each experiment.

Interpupillary distance. A Vanguard motion analyser was used to score each *S*'s interpupillary distance (distance between the pupil centres) for 20 film frames per stimulus. Intrascorer reliability for the scoring of interpupillary distance was +0·96. The interpupillary distance which represented exact convergence of the two eyes on one point at the stimulus plane was measured and subtracted from each *S*'s mean interpupillary distance. The resulting difference score was converted into its corresponding distance at the stimulus plane, which indicated how far apart at the stimulus plane each *S*'s pupil centres were, i.e. the extent of pupil divergence. The mean distance between pupil centres at the stimulus plane and the mean within-subject standard deviation in interpupillary distance were computed for each experiment.

Results
Convergence
Mean proportions for joint orientations of the two eyes in Experiment 1 (colour-brightness stimuli) are given in Table 14.1. The matrix shows that in no cases did the two eyes cross between panels; all instances of between-panel non-convergence were in the direction of flare. For example, the right eye looked at the right stimulus while the left eye looked at the left stimulus 22 per cent of the time. The most frequent orientation was for both eyes to look right. Proportions representing convergence on a stimulus

panel or on the centre are along the left-left to right-right diagonal of the matrix. These proportions are not a true indication of convergence; they include instances in which *S*s' eyes were in fact looking at different parts of the same panel and thus did not converge on one point.

Mean proportions for joint orientations of the two eyes in Experiment 2A (stripes versus grey stimulus pair) are given in Table 14.2. As in Experiment 1 there were no cases of the two eyes crossing between panels, and the most frequent orientation was for both eyes to look right.

Table 14.3 gives the mean propor-

tions for joint orientations of the eyes in Experiment 2B (single centre stimulus). In this situation the most frequent orientation was for the right eye to look right and the left eye to look left; there were again no instances of the eyes crossing.

The mean proportion of convergence (left-left, centre-centre, and right-right orientations combined) in Experiment 1 was 0·42; that for Experiment 2A was 0·70. Convergence of *S*s in Experiment 1 was significantly less than that in Experiment 2A ($t=3·66$, $df=26$, $p<0·001$). The mean proportion of convergence in Experiment 2B was 0·09. Statistical assess-

TABLE 14.1. *Mean Proportions of Orientation for Left Eye by Right Eye with Colour-Brightness Stimuli*

		Right eye orientation		
		Left	Centre	Right
Left eye	Left	0·16	0·14	0·22
orientation	Centre	0·00	0·01	0·22
	Right	0·00	0·00	0·25

TABLE 14.2. *Mean Proportions of Orientation for Left Eye by Right Eye with Stripes versus Grey Stimulus Pair*

		Right eye orientation		
		Left	Centre	Right
Left eye	Left	0·31	0·12	0·11
orientation	Centre	0·00	0·01	0·07
	Right	0·00	0·00	0·38

TABLE 14.3. *Mean Proportions of Orientation for Left Eye by Right Eye with Centre Stimulus*

		Right eye orientation		
		Left	Centre	Right
Left eye	Left	0·01	0·12	0·50
orientation	Centre	0·00	0·01	0·29
	Right	0·00	0·00	0·07

ment of the differences in convergence between *S*s seeing the centre stimulus and *S*s seeing the paired stimuli is inappropriate because there was greater opportunity to meet the criteria of convergence with the paired stimulus

presentation than with the single stimulus presentation.

Interpupillary Distance

Fig. 14.3 shows schematically the range of interpupillary distance as

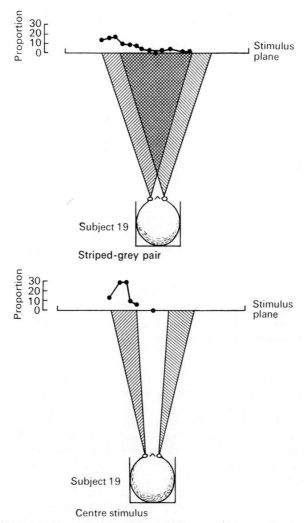

FIG. 14.3. Range and mean of interpupillary distance as reflected at the stimulus plane for one *S* in Experiment 2. The upper diagram represents the *S*'s range when he looked at the stripes versus grey stimulus pair, and the lower diagram represents his range when he looked at the centre stimulus. Frequency distributions of the interpupillary distances are shown above the left eye.

reflected in distance at the stimulus plane for one S in Experiment 2. The upper half of the diagram represents the S's range of interpupillary distance when he looked at the stripes versus grey stimulus pair. The lower half represents the same S's range when he looked at the centre stimulus. In the figure, the width of one stimulus panel equals one-third the distance across the stimulus plane drawn. The figure

from S 19's eyes to the stimulus plane represent his extreme deviations from convergence. The frequency distributions above the left eye represent frequency of the various interpupillary distances. The S's eyes, like those of other Ss, generally diverged but with a much smaller range for the centre stimulus than for the stripes versus grey stimulus pair. Subject 19's eyes crossed within a stimulus panel when

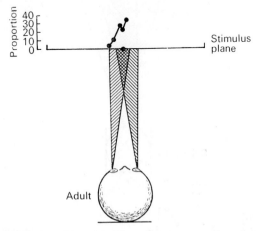

FIG. 14.4. Range and mean of interpupillary distance as reflected at the stimulus plane for an adult. The range is drawn about an assumed convergence point centred above the eyes. The frequency distribution is shown for the left eye.

is drawn about an assumed convergence point at the centre of the stimulus plane. Although the figure is drawn about an assumed convergence point, cases in which one eye looked straight ahead and the other looked to one side are included.

To determine the range of interpupillary distance, the interpupillary distance which represented exact convergence on the centre point was subtracted from S's actual interpupillary distances. The resulting difference scores were converted into corresponding distances at the stimulus plane of the figure. The outer and inner lines

he looked far to one side of it. Even though S 19's eyes rarely converged on one point, his interpupillary distances were often within one stimulus panel. Fig. 14.4 shows that, unlike the newborn S's eyes, an adult's eyes converged on one point with a high frequency. The adult's range in interpupillary distance was smaller than that of the newborns.

In Experiment 1 (colour-brightness stimuli) the mean distance between the pupil centres was 1·50 in, 0·06 in greater than the interpupillary distance representing exact convergence of the two eyes. The corresponding mean pupil divergence at the stimulus plane was 5·22 in. The mean within-subject standard deviation of inter-pupillary distance was 0·025.

In Experiment 2A (stripes versus grey stimulus pair) the mean distance between the pupil centres was 1·47 in, 0·03 in greater than the interpupillary distance representing exact convergence of the eyes. The corresponding mean pupil divergence at the stimulus plane was 2·61 in. The mean within-subject standard deviation of inter-pupillary distance was 0·037.

In Experiment 2B (centre light) the mean distance between the pupil centres was 1·49 in, 0·05 in greater than the interpupillary distance representing exact convergence of the eyes. The corresponding mean pupil divergence at the stimulus plane was 4·35 in. The mean within-subject standard deviation of interpupillary distance was 0·014.

There was no significant difference among the experiments in the mean distance between pupil centres. The mean within-subject standard deviation for Ss seeing the stripes versus grey stimulus pair was significantly greater both than that when the same Ss were seeing the centre stimulus ($t = 2·14$, $df = 11$, $p < 0·03$) and than that for Ss seeing colour-brightness stimuli ($t = 1·85$, $df = 26$, $p < 0·05$). The difference between the mean within-subject standard deviation for centre and colour-brightness stimuli was not significant. A single assessment of all differences could not be made since the same Ss were run in Experiments 2A and 2B.

Discussion

Stimulus preferences were masked in most instances by dominant position preferences, which made the magnitude of individual stimulus preferences negligibly small. When preferences were assigned to individual Ss, extreme individual differences in the order of stimulus preference precluded the establishment of an over-all order of stimulus preference. Moreover, stimulus preference tendencies could not be interpreted meaningfully since they were based on cases in which Ss' eyes often were not looking at the same panel. Examination of those data based only upon cases of convergence upon one panel did not yield any consistent preferences in either experiment.

In both experiments newborns sometimes did converge on a single stimulus; that is, both eyes were directed towards one stimulus at a particular moment. Such nominal convergence on a stimulus panel often occurred, however, when the two eyes were actually directed to *different parts* of that panel. Furthermore, Ss' eyes often did not even converge upon the same stimulus panel. Convergence upon a stimulus panel was significantly greater with the stripes versus grey stimulus pair than with colour-brightness stimuli. Lack of convergence might indicate lack of a well-perceived stimulus on which to converge, stimulus competition, physical inability to converge, or some combination of these possibilities. The differences between the experiments in amount of non-convergence may have reflected in part some kind of differential stimulus perceptibility. Stimulus competition did not completely account for non-convergence since marked divergence occurred with the single stimulus. The structure of the newborn's eye may make convergence difficult. During embryonic development the eyes swing inward from the side of the head towards the front [6]. It may be that further growth is necessary before newborns can bring the eyes inward enough to converge consistently on a stimulus. Finally, the lack of convergence in Experiment 1 may have partly reflected a fatigue effect from the long session.

The mean extents of pupil divergence for the two experiments were not significantly different, suggesting that the newborns' eyes were diverging a similar amount regardless of stimuli at the particular distance used. Yet the within-subject standard deviation in interpupillary distance differed significantly among stimulus situations. Probably the amount of variability in interpupillary distance is influenced by direction of looking since divergence is limited when one looks far to one side of midline. One also might postulate that amount of variability in interpupillary distance reflects attention to the stimulus. Yet, although the least variability was with the centre stimulus, the most variability was with the stripes versus grey stimulus pair, presumably a distinctive stimulus pair. Another possible interpretation is that variability reflects amount of competition between stimuli. The centre stimulus, with no stimulus competition, elicited the least response variability, while the stripes versus grey stimulus pair may have elicited more stimulus competition and response variability than the colour-brightness stimuli.

Differential duration of ocular orientation has been assumed without question to reflect stimulus discrimination and preference. If non-convergence is the general phenomenon it appears to be with newborns, then observer judgements based on one eye, particularly when both eyes are open, are unlikely to be a meaningful indication of newborn stimulus discrimination and preference. Photographing the eyes is necessary for accurate knowledge of the exact place towards which the newborn's eyes are orienting. Salapatek and Kessen [7] have presented data which indicate that one eye is a stable indicator of ocular orientation, and it may be that only monocular vision should be used in studies of newborn visual responses. Finally, it may be that variability rather than duration of ocular orientation towards a stimulus is the more accurate index of visual preference or attention.

References

1. DAYTON, G. O., JONES, MARGARET H., STEELE, B., and ROSE. M. (1964). Developmental study of co-ordinated eye movements in the human infant. II. An electro-oculographic study of the fixation reflex in the newborn. *Arch. Opthal.* **71**, 871–5.
2. FANTZ, R. L. (1966). Pattern discrimination and selective attention as determinants of perceptual development from birth. *In* (Kidd, Aline H. and Rivoire, Jeanne L. (Eds.)) *Perceptual development in children*. Int. Univ. Press, New York.
3. —— (1963). Pattern vision in newborn infants. *Science* **140**, 296–97.
4. —— ORDY, J., and UDELF, M. S. (1962). Maturation of pattern vision in infants during the first six months. *J. comp. physiol. Psychol.* **55**, 907–17.
5. HERSHENSON, M. (1964). Visual discrimination in the human newborn. *J. comp. physiol. Psychol.* **58**, 270–6.
6. MANN, IDA (1964). *The development of the human eye.* Brit. Med. Assoc., London.
7. SALAPATEK, P. and KESSEN, W. (1966). Visual scanning of triangles by the human newborn. *J. exp. Child Psychol.* **3**, 155–67.
8. WHITE, B. L. (1963). The development of perception during the first six months of life. Paper read at Amer. Assoc. Advance Sci., Cleveland, Ohio.

15 Auditory discrimination at birth

S. J. HUTT, CORINNE HUTT,
H. G. LENARD, H. V. BERNUTH, AND
W. J. MUNTJEWERFF†

ELECTROMYOGRAPHIC, autonomic, and electro-encephalographic responses were recorded from human neonates during stimulation with sine and square wave tones and with human voices. This communication will concentrate on the analysis of the electromyograms, both because of their importance in reflecting behavioural changes, and because changes in autonomic activity, such as heart-rate acceleration, are associated with movements. The 'artificial' sounds were chosen so as to have certain structural similarities to the 'biological' sound: they were either sine wave components of it or selected fundamentals with superimposed high frequencies. Sine wave and square wave tones of the following frequencies, rising by octaves, were selected: 125, 250, 500, 1000, and 2000 Hz. Further sine and square wave tones at 70 Hz were added because preliminary studies had suggested that responses to sound frequencies lower than 100 Hz may have especially interesting properties. Recordings of a male and of a female voice saying 'baby' were also included.

Twelve newborn infants, between 3 and 8 days old, were studied for 2–3 h between feeds; they were undressed

† From 'Auditory responsivity in the human neonate'. *Nature* **218**, 888–90 (1968). Reprinted by permission of Macmillan Journals Ltd.

and placed in a bassinet in a climate chamber at neutral temperature (32° C, 50–60 per cent humidity); the ambient noise level of the chamber was $50 \pm 2 \cdot 5$ dB. Each baby was placed on his side so that one ear only was exposed. The sounds were presented through a loudspeaker, 40 cm from the ear, its axis in the same straight line as that of the external auditory canal. The artificial sounds were generated by an electronic oscillator and the voices were reproduced from tape-loops. All sounds were calibrated to a sound pressure level of 75 dB ($0 \cdot 0002$ μbar) at the baby's ear.

Continuous polygraphic recordings were made of respiration, heart rate, EEG, eye movements, and muscle activity. In order to obtain a reliable measure of muscular activity, electromyograms were recorded from six sites using surface electrodes [1]: right and left biceps brachii, right and left triceps, and right and left quadriceps. Each subject was stimulated in the three following states [2]: state 1: regular sleep; state 2: irregular (REM) sleep; state 3: quiet wakefulness.

The experimental procedure was as follows: within a steady state the stimuli were produced in a randomized order; the duration of each stimulus was 2 s. Intervals between stimuli ranged from 30 s to 60 s. Each subject was presented with no fewer than four stimuli of each type in each state, the exact number of stimuli being determined by the state durations. The response period chosen was 10 s from stimulus onset.

Because muscle activity periodically occurs in unstimulated infants, any assessment of response to stimulation must take into account a measure of this background activity. Each stimulus period was therefore paired with a 10 s interval between stimuli, selected by a random sampling procedure. Fig. 15.1 summarizes the EMG response criteria employed. Fig. 15.2

similar in each state; with the sine waves the interaction between frequency and state was highly significant, the frequency-specific effects being only clearly manifest in state 3. Individual comparison of means [3] showed the 125 Hz and 250 Hz stimuli of both square and sine wave tones to be significantly different ($p = 0.01$) from all other frequencies in all states, with the following exceptions: (a) not different from 70 Hz square wave in state 1; (b) not different from 1000 Hz sine wave in state 2; and (c) 250 Hz

TABLE 15.1. *Analysis of Variance of Transformed and Corrected Response*

Source	S.o.s.	D.f.	V.r.	F
A, Square waves				
Between states	0·878	2	0·439	3·99**
Between frequencies	5·675	5	1·135	10·32**
Interaction	1·024	10	0·102	0·98
Residual	9·963	90	0·110	
Total	17·540	107		
B, Sine waves				
Between waves	0·143	2	0·071	10·14**
Between frequencies	0·326	5	0·065	9·28**
Interaction	3·529	10	0·353	50·43***
Residual	0·616	90	0·007	
Total	4·614	107		

shows the probability of obtaining activity in any of the six EMG leads during and between stimulations in states 1, 2, and 3. Because the probabilities of baseline EMG activity differed significantly between states, response levels were 'corrected' for state by subtracting each subject's baseline scores from the corresponding response scores in each state. The resulting data were then normalized and submitted to analysis of variance (Table 15.1). With both types of artificial sounds, frequency and state had significant effects. With square waves the frequency effects were

not different from 500 and 1000 Hz sine waves in state 1.

Startles were most commonly elicited by the 70 Hz square wave tone. Startles to sine wave stimulation were less common, but again, of all startles elicited, most were to 70 Hz. Other behavioural evidence suggests that this tone elicits distinctly aversive responses. In general, responses to the stimuli varied with state, the infant being least responsive in regular sleep. The exception was the response to the square wave 70 Hz which was the same in all three states.

At birth the human cochlea is

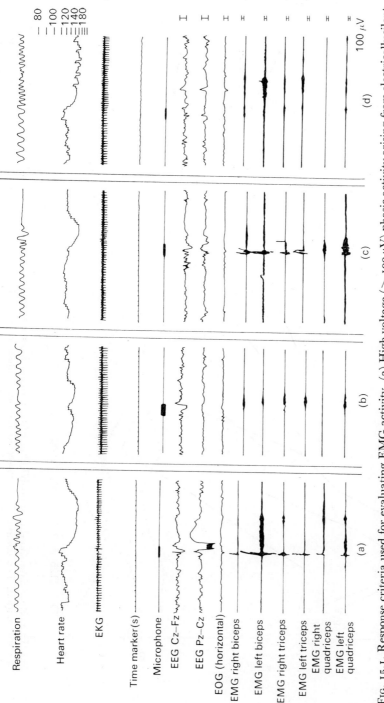

Fig. 15.1. Response criteria used for evaluating EMG activity. (a) High voltage (> 100 μV) phasic activity arising from electrically silent background (accompanied in this case by a startle); (b) bursts of activity, minimum duration 1 s, average voltage ⩾ 50 μV arising from electrically silent background; (c) high voltage (> 100 μV) phasic activity arising from tonic background activity (see left quadriceps); (d) bursts of increased (twice that of background), voltage activity, minimum duration, 1 s, superimposed upon already present tonic activity (see left biceps).

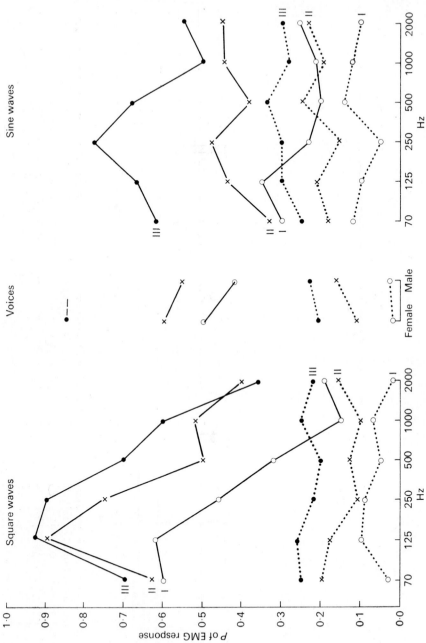

Fig. 15.2. Raw data showing probability of EMG response in each behavioural state, with and without three types of auditory stimulation. For computations corrected response values were used: these were obtained by subtraction of the no-stimulation response probabilities (. . .) from the response-to-stimulation probabilities (———). The number of male voice stimuli presented in state 3 was insufficient for meaningful representation.

structurally fully mature [4]; this contrasts with other species in which the auditory apparatus is in a less developed state at birth [5, 6]. No satisfactory explanation appears to have been adduced for the survival value of this difference. A possible explanation is suggested by this work. The mechanical properties of a structurally mature cochlea would ensure at least rudimentary discrimination between different stimuli, even if no 'inhibitory' processes [7] were present at birth to 'sharpen' frequency discrimination. The lower the frequency of a stimulus, the greater the length of basilar membrane which will be displaced by a travelling wave; hence the greater excitation elicited by the stimulus. Still greater excitation will be produced by a broad-band stimulus with a low frequency fundamental and high energy peaks at several different points in the frequency spectrum. In the absence of further evidence relating to the neurophysiological maturation of later stages of the auditory pathway, it is not clear how different degrees of membrane excitation are transformed into behavioural responses. Assuming, however, that such transformation does take place, we would predict that a broad-band noise with a low frequency fundamental would elicit maximum response. Thus greatest responsivity would be expected to the 70 Hz square wave tone. In fact response to this stimulus was less than to the corresponding 125 Hz and 250 Hz stimulus; this was due to the low intensity of the first harmonic in this sound, resulting in inconsistent reproduction. Nevertheless, the fact that this tone was so frequently accompanied by startles suggests that excitation throughout the length of the basilar membrane may elicit defensive reflexes, accompanied perhaps by protective adjustments of the middle ear muscles. This would be adaptive, for, at least at high intensities, very low frequency sounds may produce shearing forces which could damage the membrane.

The rest of the data agree with the proposed model. The stimuli eliciting behavioural responses were, in order of increasing effectiveness: low frequency sine waves, the human voice and low frequency square waves. Evidence that the brain may receive signals of the predicted magnitude from the peripheral sense organ is provided by a recent study of acoustic evoked responses (our unpublished work). Changes in the amplitude of the cortical evoked response (N_2 wave) exactly parallel the changes in behavioural responsivity described here.

The patterned sounds clearly elicited more response than the pure tones, and within both categories the most effective stimuli were those the fundamental frequencies of which were within the range of the fundamentals of the voice. Thus the structure of the human auditory apparatus at birth ensures both that there is a limit of basilar membrane excitation beyond which defensive reflexes are evoked, and that the voice at normal intensities is nonaversive and prepotent. The survival value of this differential responsivity may lie in the part it plays in the development of the affectional bond between parent and child.

References

1. PRECHTL, H. F. R., AKIYAMA, Y., ZINKIN, P., and KERR GRANT, D. (in the press). *Dev. Med. child Neurol.*
2. PRECHTL, H. F. R. and BEINTEMA, D. (1964). *The neurological examination of the full-term newborn infant.* Heinemann, London.
3. TUKEY, J. W. (1949). *Biometrics* **5**, 99.
4. BAST, T. H. and ANSON, B. J. (1949). *The temporal bone and the ear.* Charles C. Thomas, Springfield, Ill.
5. ANGGARD, L. (1965). *Acta Oto-Laryngol.*, Suppl. 203.
6. MIKAELIAN, D. O. and RUBEN, R. J. (1964). *Arch. Otolaryngol.* **80**.
7. VON BEKESY, G. (1960). *In* (Rasmussen, G. L. and Windle, W. F. (Eds.)) *Neural mechanisms of the auditory and vestibular systems.* Charles C. Thomas, Springfield, Ill.

16 Biphasic processes in early behaviour

T. C. SCHNEIRLA†

THE aspect of towardness or awayness is common in animal behaviour. Our problem is to consider, from the phylogenetic and the ontogenetic approaches, the question of how animals generally manage to reach beneficial conditions and stay away from the harmful, that is, how survivors do this. Although this valuable series of conferences has by now covered nearly all phases of the motivation problem, the evolutionary and developmental aspects are perhaps the ones touched on lightly in evidence and theory. My purpose is to discuss some promising theoretical ideas and evidence bearing on these questions.

Motivation, broadly considered, concerns the causation and impulsion of behaviour. The question here is what impels the approach and withdrawal reactions of very different animals from protozoans to man and how each level develops its characteristic pattern. Have these levels anything in common, or does each have a basis very different from the others?

In studying this broad problem of behaviour, an objective methodology is indispensable. To be specific, I submit

† From 'An evolutionary and developmental theory of biphasic processes underlying approach and withdrawal'. In *Nebraska symposium on motivation* (Jones, Marshall R. (Ed.)) Univ. of Nebraska Press, Lincoln, pp. 1–42 (1959). Copyright © 1959 by the University of Nebraska Press. Reprinted by permission of the publishers.

that approach and withdrawal are the only empirical, objective terms applicable to all motivated behaviour in all animals. Psychologically superior types of adjustment are found, but only on higher psychological levels and after appropriate individual development.

As elementary definitions, an animal may be said to approach a stimulus source when it responds by coming nearer to that source, to withdraw when it increases its distance from the source. This point is not sufficiently elementary, however, to escape confusion. Confusion is indicated when the term 'approach' is combined with 'avoid', as if these were opposite concepts for motivation. This practice, common in the literature, is indulged in even by psychological dictionaries. But however conventional, it is psychologically wrong, for withdrawal is the conceptual opposite of approach, and the opposite of avoidance is seeking, which means 'to look or search for' something. Seeking and avoidance are of a higher evolutionary and developmental order than approach and withdrawal, and these terms should not be mismated.

To put it differently, whereas all behaviour in all animals tends to be adaptive, only some behaviour in some animals is purposive. Behaviour is adaptive when it contributes to individual or to species survival, especially the latter. . . . How then, does behaviour in surviving animals, even the lowliest, come to have the character of adaptiveness, centring around efficient approach and withdrawal responses? The main reason seems to be that behaviour, from its beginning in the primitive scintilla many ages ago, has been a decisive factor in natural selection. For the haunts and the typical niche of any organism must depend on what conditions it approaches and what it moves away from—these types of reaction thereby determine what future stimuli can affect the individual, its life span, and the fate of its species.

The principle may be stated roughly as follows: Intensity of stimulation basically determines the direction of reaction with respect to the source, and thereby exerts a selective effect on what conditions generally affect the organism. This statement derived from the generalization that, for all organisms in early ontogenetic stage, low intensities of stimulation tend to evoke approach reactions, high intensities withdrawal reactions with reference to the source [41]. Doubtless the highroad to evolution has been littered with the remains of species that diverged too far from these rules of effective adaptive relationship between environmental conditions and response. . . .

Much evidence shows that in all animals the species-typical pattern of behaviour is based upon biphasic, functionally opposed mechanisms insuring approach or withdrawal reactions according to whether stimuli of low or of high intensity, respectively, are in effect. This is an oversimplified statement; however, in general, what we shall term the A-type of mechanism, underlying approach, favours adjustments such as food-getting, shelter-getting, and mating; the W-type, underlying withdrawal, favours adjustments such as defence, huddling, flight, and other protective reactions. Also, through evolution, higher psychological levels have arisen in which through ontogeny such mechanisms can produce new and qualitatively advanced types of adjustment to environmental conditions. Insects are superior to protozoans, and mammals to insects, in that ontogeny progressively frees processes of individual motivation from the basic formula of prepotent stimulative-intensity relationships. . . .

Whatever their equipment of specialized neurones may be, the nervous systems of multi-cellular animals are all capable of discharging differentially according to afferent intensity. The general formula supported by much neurophysiological research on both invertebrates (e.g. [21]) and vertebrates is that, with increasing stimulus intensity in any modality, successive increases are evoked not only in the volley rate of discharge into the central nervous system but also in the number of neurones conducting [6]. Consequently, instead of type-A actions, predominant at lower stimulus intensities, type-W actions of higher threshold can be aroused increasingly.

Primary to all such phenomena is a dependence of the neural discharge on the quantitative aspects of stimulation. For particular types of discharge, Sherrington [46] remarked that 'The accuracy of grading within a certain range of intensities is so remarkable that the ratio between stimulus intensities and response-intensity has by some observers been assigned mathematical precision.' From Sherrington's pioneer work on the differential arousal of flexion and extension reflexes through the spinal cord, with his associates [9] he derived the principle of 'half centres', which may be characterized as reciprocally functioning ganglionic subcentres. This principle outlines the functional differentiation of partially overlapping neurone groups adjacent to each other in the same neural centre, differing in their arousal thresholds and capable of working reciprocally in the excitation of antagonistic effector systems. The view that such reciprocally related neurone groups normally operate to oppose the strong arousal of A-type and W-type effectors simultaneously, but favour the predominance of one or the other type in a smoothly working pattern, is well supported [16]. This principle, first demonstrated for antagonistic neurone groups in the cord, may have a considerably wider application to neural correlation in the control of biphasic effector systems.

A finding of significance for mammalian ontogeny is that of Adrian [1], that impulses from deep or protopathic and impulses from epicritic or superficial cutaneous receptors, selectively aroused according to stimulus intensity, may take different paths and have typical discharge-pattern differences, as in the lesser opportunities for summation in epicritically aroused than in protopathically aroused patterns. The quantitative aspects of stimulation and of conduction therefore would tend to favour a routing of impulses in the first case predominantly through that neurone group in the spinal level discharging to A-type effectors, and in the second case through its antagonist discharging to W-type effectors. This may be considered the paradigm for neural discharge to common centres in early ontogeny, dependent on stimulus energy delivered to any modality.

Although most of the research on the functions of the autonomic nervous system has been done with adult mammals, and the evidence is understandably complex, the generalization seems justified that, according to stimulus magnitudes acting upon the central nervous system, the two principal sections of the autonomic system are selectively aroused to characteristically different functions. Through the cranial and sacral regions of the central system, the parasympathetic outflow tends to arouse visceral and skeletal functions of an A-type of vegetative character; through the thoracic and lumbar regions the sympathetic outflow arouses functions of a W-type of interruptive nature. The antagonism of these systems may be illustrated by Kuntz's [28] description of the selective arousal by weak stimuli of impulses over a dorsal cord depressor path of long fibres and low resistance, associated with the parasympathetic system and arousing vasodilatation, and by strong stimuli of impulses over a ventral cord pressor relay of short fibres and high resistance, associated with the sympathetic system and eliciting vasoconstriction.

Significantly, although the autonomic nervous system is old in vertebrates, in its full biphasic function in higher mammals it is highly specialized. Recently, Pick [37] has concluded that whereas primitively in vertebrates the dorsal-outflow (parasympathetic) system is the predominant system of visceral arousal from the cord, the ventral outflow, although at first negligible, from amphibians to man increases steadily in potency and specialization as the sympathetic system, and becomes progressively more effective as the antagonist of the parasympathetic.

Evidence concerning metabolic processes effected largely through smooth muscles and the autonomic nervous system widely supports the Cannon–Langley theory of antagonistic functioning dependent on opposition of the parasympathetic and sympathetic autonomic divisions. As Darling and Darrow [10] demonstrated, the biphasic character of human visceral function shows through even in the adult in blood pressure and other physiological aspects of emotional reactivity, notwithstanding certain exceptions (e.g. galvanic skin response) in which the divisions of the autonomic tend to reinforce each other. Starting with Cannon's research, the patterning of opposed function has been revealed in all types of visceral actions, including smooth muscle and the neurohumoral. Neurophysiological research gives a familiar picture of vegetative (A-type) changes (homeostatic, smooth-running processes occurring within a range characteristic of species and developmental stage), aroused characteristically by low-intensity stimulation through the parasympathetic system, and of interruptive (W-type) changes supported by secretion of adrenalin and aroused characteristically by high-intensity stimulation through the sympathetic system. With experience, the functional relationships of these systems become more complex and varied, perhaps often to the point of cancelling or reversing aspects of their basic antagonistic, reciprocal relationship.

The effectors, also, seem to function biphasically in all animals. In the earthworm, under weak stimulation the circular muscles are dominantly aroused, thinning and extending the body and facilitating movement towards the source; under strong stimulation the longitudinal muscles are dominant, thickening the body and facilitating withdrawal from the source. A striking interruption of normal smooth reciprocal function of the two systems occurs when high-intensity stimulation causes the body to contract suddenly backward through a rapid maximal innervation of the W-system via giant-fibre conduction. In other invertebrates, through corresponding mechanisms in tentacles and other local structures, the mobile part typically swings towards the side of weak stimulation, away from that of strong stimulation, and through comparable synergic action the entire organism may react equivalently.

For vertebrates, the principle of differential and antagonistic systems in skeletal muscle function was established by Sherrington [46], who demonstrated it in the action of sets of muscles working against each other at the same joint or on different joints of the same limb. Between extensor dominance with weak stimulation and flexor dominance with strong stimulation, a gradation of functional combinations was demonstrated both by myographic recordings and by direct palpation of muscles to intact limbs. In the developing organism, relationships of threshold may be stated conveniently in terms of the Lapique concept of chronaxie, as a measure of arousal threshold. Bourguignon [3] found that adult mammalian extensors tend to have a low chronaxie and flexors a high chronaxie, particularly in the limbs. These two muscular systems commonly act concurrently in the general behaviour of animals [31]; however, summaries of the evidence (e.g. [19, 22]) leave no question that their antagonistic function in synergic patterns is a primary fact in mobility and action, and that their reciprocal arousal is essential to the development of co-ordinated patterns of behaviour [25]. For research on vertebrates generally, flexion of a limb to strong stimulation is a response taken for granted as available for conditioning from early stages. Although Sherrington described extension as postural and flexion as a 'reflex to noxious stimulation', their biphasic function, as we shall see, constitutes a mechanism of expanding relationships basic to ontogeny.

In sum, diverse biphasic mechanisms of the receptors, central and auxiliary nervous systems, and effectors are fundamental to ontogeny in all animals. They have in common, generally, the property of A-type arousal by weak stimuli, facilitating local or general approach to the source, and W-type arousal by strong stimuli, facilitating local or general withdrawal. Recently Kempf [26] has reviewed the evidence for such antagonistic functional systems in man, in relation to problems of conflict and neurosis. The thesis here is that relationships between stimulus magnitude and the degree and direction of response, although different on the various psychological levels as to their form and the extent to which their function may be modified, are always critical for the determination in ontogeny of what conditions may attract and what may repel members of a given species. These matters must not be oversimplified, of course, as many conditions besides experience, including adaptation, fatigue, and health, may affect the potency and directness of the biphasic processes.

The property of differential thresholds in biphasic systems may take a more specific origin in early ontogeny when the probing termini of developing neuroblasts react selectively to the biochemical properties of tissue fields near by, and may influence their environs in turn. Threshold differences evidently progress throughout the organism along biphasic lines. Many types are as yet little understood, as for example that involved in Eccles' [16] distinction between 'fast' and 'slow' muscles in the cat. Such differences, paralleling biphasic differences in afferent, visceral, and neural systems, underlie the rise of specialized patterns of approach and withdrawal, the detailed character of which is a matter of phyletic level and ontogenetic attainments.

. . . Doubtless, as Bousfield and Orbison [4] state, the infant mammal is 'essentially precorticate at birth'. Also, as a perceptually naive animal, his emotional–motivational processes seem diffuse and dominated by stimulus magnitude swaying autonomic-visceral susceptibilities. But, contrary to impressions that seem general in the child-psychology literature, there is significant evidence that at birth the infant mammal already has a crudely dichotomized organic basis for his perceptual – motivational – emotional ontogeny. In this context, however, the question, 'Are there any innate emotions?' should be dismissed as posing the false alternatives of finding or not finding adultlike patterns in psychologically barren early stages.

This interpretation differs sharply from that of Bridges [5], that an 'undifferentiated excitement' prevails for the human neonate, differentiated only later into conditions of 'delight' and 'distress'. Textbook writers who adopt this conclusion seem to have overlooked the fact that Bridges' research on infant emotionality did not involve intensive research on neonates. Many psychologists seem also to have been influenced in their views by a conventional rejection of Watson's [49] theory of infant emotions. Watson, as many will recall, concluded from studies with neonate infants that their emotions may be differentiated as 'love', 'fear', and 'rage', arousable by stimuli such as stroking and patting, loud noises, and restraint, respectively. Sherman [44], however, found competent judges unable to distinguish the fear and rage patterns without knowing the stimuli, and Taylor [48] reported that Watson's conditions did not initiate 'constant-pattern responses' in infants he tested. Watson would have been well advised to call his emotional reactions X, Y, and Z (as he himself once suggested), differentiating them by effective stimulus intensities rather than arousal patterns, for then the differentiation can be made of X as relatively unexcited responses of A-type from XY as excited responses of W-type, to weak and strong stimuli, respectively (Fig. 16.1). With gentle tactual stimulation of neonates Pratt et al. [38] obtained pacifying reactions and relaxation of limbs; with stroking Watson obtained extension of limbs and quiescence as a rule; with intense light Canestrini [7] observed typically an intake of breath and sudden contraction of the abdominal wall, rising fenestral and breathing curves, and external signs of 'fear'; with strong contact Peiper [36] noted a withdrawal of the part affected, general action, and crying; with

sudden intense auditory stimuli the Shermans [45] noted arm flexion, crying, and signs of visceral disturbance or 'colic'; with intense stimuli a 'startle pattern' is obtained involving strong general limb flexion and signs of visceral disturbance [34]. In the general evidence, the biphasic aspects of neonate reactions, and their general correlation with stimulus intensity, seem clearly indicated.

The conclusion seems warranted that in neonate mammals generally these early biphasic processes of a physiological order, aroused according to stimulus magnitude, furnish a basis for individual perceptual, motivational, and emotional development. The theory is schematized in Figs. 16.1 and 16.2. The foregoing discussion, in this sense, supports Leeper's [29] position that the processes of emotion and motivation are fundamentally related. The socialization of early physiologically given biphasic excitatory states and the specialization of motivation and emotion seem to advance hand in hand in the education of the infant mammal in perceptual processes and action. To suggest the relevance for human psychological development of the theory of biphasic processes sketched in this article, I shall outline evidence bearing on the ontogenetic course of two adjustive processes unquestionably crucial in man's perceptual and motivational adjustment to his world: smiling and reaching.

After Darwin, the general recognition advanced the primate evolution must have involved concurrent organic changes admitting an upright posture, an increase in visual range, a freeing of the limbs for specialized prehension and the face for social expression, and a specialization of the brain admitting conceptual plasticity. These superior human assets for perceptual–motivational development may be considered marks of a stage in natural selection far advanced beyond that at which lower vertebrates with far less advanced properties for cephalic dominance are limited to the simple lunge as an approach. Significant also in this impressive evolutionary progression are changes such as Pick [37] has described, underlying a steady specialization of the parasympathetic autonomic division, an energy-conserving system, correlated with an even more rapid advance of its antagonist, the sympathetic system, an energy-expending system in adjustive behaviour. In the organismic setting available on the human level, emphasizing adaptive plasticity, the potential ontogenetic relevance of the autonomic divisions, as with that of other biphasic processes, reaches far beyond an elementary status of simple antagonism.

Consistent with Darwin's [11] concept of antithesis in mammalian emotional expression, anatomists find evidence for the rise of two antagonistic systems of facial muscles in mammals, one elevating the lip corners, the other pulling them down, in close correlation with progressive elaboration of the trigeminal or facial-cutaneous sensory system [24]. Significantly, physiological and behavioural evidence indicates that the levator system has a lower arousal threshold than the depressor system. With low-intensity shocks to cheek or mastoid regions of adult human subjects, Dumas [14, 15] noted a mechanical 'smile' resembling that of hemiplegics; with higher intensities, a different grimace involving facial musculature more widely.

Now Koehler [27] represents the view of many who consider smiling innate as a social pattern in man, pointing out that a semblance of this reaction can occur in premature and neonate infants. Strictly considered, however, this early response is a grimace, a physiologically forced response to low-intensity stimulation, and the 'smile' is a specialized social adjustment appearing only after much perceptual–motivational development. Although light facial contact, particularly near the lip corners, is generally most effective in producing the neonate grimace, Dennis [13] obtained it with other weak stimuli such as light patting of the chest and asafetida released at the nostrils. In the early neonate this action is infrequent and has a fleeting character, occurring 'incidentally with other facial activities in an overflow reaction', according to Spitz and Wolf [47]. A concurrence with vegetative visceral conditions is indicated by its appearance when the infant is calming down, relieved from disturbance, or recently satiated.

Neither Dennis nor Spitz and Wolf, however, reported any 'unconditioned' stimulus for this reaction. The difficulty seems to have been that they looked for a specific unconditioned stimulus. For there is evidence, including their own, that although a variety of stimuli can arouse this reaction, all have in common the property of low intensity. Even interoceptive changes after feeding may be effective, as suggested by the traditional 'gas smile', which seems more often a response to a gentle stomach pressure (as during 'burping') than to 'belly-ache' as Spitz and Wolf maintain. The conclusion seems in order that this action first specializes through a gradual conditioning process, in which the unconditioned stimulus is a facial-nerve arousal by low-intensity stimulation. Such a process, elicited most frequently by tactual stimuli when the neonate is in a vegetative organic condition, would later be available for control by visual stimuli of low intensity, when visual centring of stimuli has improved sufficiently.

A diffuse, generalized conditioning process is indicated initially. Although within the first two months Spitz and Wolf obtained few grimace reactions to visual stimuli, these came increasingly after the third month, when Dennis noted also a growing reactivity by grimacing to a face presented over the crib. The face as such cannot be credited for this effect, as Spitz and Wolf obtained the response with a variety of stimuli, including sounds and horror masks. The visual effect evidently is initially very general and diffuse, but in time becomes more specific. A crude contiguity-conditioning process is indicated, through the concurrence of certain visual effects with satiation or relief from disturbance. By six months, as a rule, Spitz and Wolf observed definite advances in the specificity of stimulus control, 'in the direction of increased discrimination', with the response not only elicited selectively by faces rather than masks, but also changed in pattern from the 'fleeting grimace' of the first three months, 'not well differentiated from general facial action', to a 'more definite expression'.

Next indicated is a discriminative 'social smile', to familiar as against unfamiliar faces. That the 'smile' comes about through a progressive perceptual–motivational learning process dependent on the developmental situation to an important extent is indicated by Spitz and Wolf's finding that this response developed precociously in infants who had the 'best relations with attentive mothers', but was delayed, infrequent, and unspecialized in infants who had experienced poor relations with indifferent mothers. From its initial status as a crude reaction forced through low-intensity arousal, under optimal conditions this response appears to specialize simultaneously in its afferent, organic, and motor aspects, first with a general set to associated stimuli, then with a rudimentary perceptual anticipation of more specifically 'desirable' stimuli. It is difficult to fit these results within the framework of contiguity conditioning alone; rather, from the circumstances of development, it is probable that a process of selective learning underlies the metamorphosis of this and related aspects of the infant's expanding repertoire of 'seeking' adjustments.

The reach, another significant approach response, seems to develop concurrently in the infant with the 'smile' as a related adjustment. These early stages, as Frank [18] has pointed out, involve a progressive self-contact process of individual adjustment, which, as Nissen, Chow, and Semmes [35] demonstrated for chimpanzees, progresses badly without adequate opportunities for tactual experience through limb mobility. The matrix of this process in earlier stages evidently consists in the characteristically variable and diffuse reactions of relaxation and local limb extension to gentle limb contact, when a vegetative organic condition prevails. These types of reaction occur characteristically with low-intensity stimulation of many kinds, usually tactual but also at times auditory or olfactory. The local reactions typically elicited by such stimuli stand in definite contrast to the mass-action type obtained with strong stimulation. To stimulation of the foot with a needle, termed 'pain', the Shermans [45] usually obtained a 'pulling away of the leg or the face, associated with movements of the arms and crying'. Although neonate behaviour seems chaotic and often unpredictable, limb flexion is typically obtained with strong stimulation, and this was the unconditioned response used both by Wenger [50] and by the Wickens [52], who conditioned it to previously ineffective stimuli within the first ten post-natal days. Watson, who noted limb flexion as a typical response to loud sounds or dropping, conversely identified arm extension as a frequent response to gentle stroking of the neonate's arm or cheek.

The infant's approach or A-type reactions normally seem to change from soon after birth in a more regular manner than do the more episodic, excited W-type reactions. At first the face takes the lead, with close functional relationships between sucking, lip-contact, and hand movements. As Davis [12] concluded, the initial afferent control seems to be tactuo-postural, with vision entering gradually into a steadily more dominant role. A progressive self-communication through tactuo-motor channels, emphasized by Holt [23] as basic to motivation and learning, underlies gradually developing integrations between proximal sensory control and visual control in early space perception.

Initially the infant gets his arm out incidentally, as part of a forced overt A-type response to low-energy stimulation. One significant aspect of the tactuo-visual integration that gradu-ally assumes control of this reaction is the concurrence of head-turning to the side of gentle stimulation with progressive efficiency in centring the eyes on the focal area. McGinnis [33] reported for the first 6 weeks an increased frequency of head turning towards small objects seen in motion. Centring objects in the visual field, as it improves, elaborates into an eye-following of both the infant's hand and objects.

Advancing the anterior body or its parts extends the infant's 'space', as Werner [51] puts it, and in its early posturo-tactual basic may relate to reactive trends begun *in utero*. Progress through tactuo-visual integration represents complex psychological developments in which maturation and experience factors are doubtless interrelated inextricably [42]. A dependence of progress in learning and motivation on the trophic aspects of reciprocal stimulative exchanges with self and environs is emphasized by Spitz and Wolf's finding that smiling is likely to be retarded when infants have an inferior maternal adjustment, and without much doubt this is also true of the closely related response of reaching.

Halverson's [20] studies on grasping and reaching began with the infant at about 12 weeks, supported in a chair with a small cube of white sugar on the table before him. At this stage the infants tended to 'regard' this stimulus or centre it variably in the visual field, with frequent head-bending forward. Responses were quantified in terms of the nearest approach of the hand to the cube in each trial. Early deviations were large, as the infant's arms moved in various directions from his vertical axis but not particularly towards the exciting stimulus. From the data, these responses may be interpreted as crude arm extensions forced by low-intensity stimulation, a getting-out-the-arm reaction rather than a reaching for something. Significantly, in infants from 12 to 24 weeks there was an actual increase in the average digression from the stimulus, evidently due mainly to an accelerated maturation of shoulder muscles, so that the arm struck out laterally rather than forward in the trials.

It is significant that during this period the infant continued to respond to the stimulus by extending and abducting his arms, although he seldom touched or grasped the object and hardly ever got it into his mouth. But, as Castner [8] noted, in these months the duration of visual 'regard' increases steadily, along with the frequency of arm extensions to visually centred stimuli. Daily life of course offers many experiences to the infant, in which he handles just-seen objects in A-type situations, as when the waving hand is seen, then gets into his mouth and stays there after feeding. It is a question of equivalent processes facilitating one another in the learning of related adjustments, and Halverson's results show steady progress after about 24 weeks in arm extension through elbow straightening, paralleled by increasing efficiency in getting the hand to the pellet. In the test situation the infant progressed steadily in directing his arm to a seen object, rather than just extending the limb as at first. Around 6 months, therefore, as the infant starts his reach, we may infer the presence of a simple anticipation of having the object in hand, then a different anticipation of mouthing it.

The significant point is that fore-limb extension, the local adjustment central to the infant's perceptual–motivational development in the first year, begins as an incidental response to low-energy stimulation, but, through progressive integrations of vision with pre-existing tactuo-proximal adjustments, becomes first a specific approach response, then a perceptually directed seeking response (Fig. 16.2).

Motivation and learning theory meet difficulties here, of course, partly through insufficient evidence and partly through logical short-comings. It is plain that research on infant perception and motivation has taken us beyond the stage of Watson's kinaesthetic-motor theory and Holt's reflex-circle theory. But for reasons advanced before, S–R or connectionistic theories seem limited to early stages, when events are dominated by what contiguities of stimuli and A-type processes are sufficiently experienced. Such occurrences might explain attainment of a simple visually directed arm approach based on earlier tactuo-proximal adjustments. But to understand progress into the stage of perceptually directed reaching, we must postulate qualitatively new processes of selective learning developing through the situation-altering effect of action [32]. Related aspects concern relevance of stimulus properties to the optimal organic condition [30], changing relationships between action and its organic consequences [32, 43] and qualitative differences between non-perceptual and perceptual learning [39].

Reaching may well be the most significant indicator of early approach-responsiveness in man. Fundamental to processes changing incidental limb extension to perceptual seeking is an intimate relationship to A-type organic

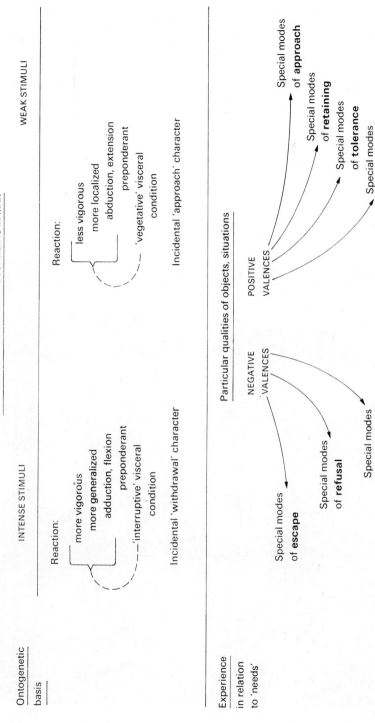

Fig. 16.1. Scheme of theory basing approach and withdrawal reactions on biphasic processes dependent in early stages (*top*) on effective stimulative intensity, subsequently (*bottom*) on developmental processes related particularly to experience.

		High intensities	Low intensities
INITIAL STAGES	**Adequate stimuli**	Focal to disturbing situations	Focal to 'gratifying' situations
Incidental 'approach—withdrawal'	**Reaction:** Somatic component	Vigorous mass action Flexion, adduction Crying, tension	Pacified, local action Extension, abduction Turning-to, 'smile'
	Visceral component	'Interruptive' effects Sympathetic-autonomic predominant	'Vegetative' effects Parasympathetic-autonomic predominant
SOCIAL ADAPTATION	**Adequate stimuli**	Focal to disturbing situations	Focal to 'gratifying' situations
Purposive approach—withdrawal	**Reaction:** Perceptual adjustment	Specialized withdrawal: pulling . . . walking **off** Indirect modes of escape, negation, aggression 'Sulk', gestures, sounds symbolizing NO	Specialized approach: reaching . . . walking **to** indirect modes of approval, acquisition Social smile, gestures, sounds, symbolizing YES
	Visceral background	Condition interruptive patterns Sympathetic-automatic facilitation	Conditioned vegetative patterns Parasympathetic-autonomic facilitation

Fig. 16.2. Scheme of theory outlining biphasic functional conditions basic to the ontogeny of early approach or withdrawal and of related subsequent perceptual and emotional differentiation in man.

processes, first as concomitant events, then in versatile roles influencing the plastically utilized relationships of selective learning (Figs. 16.1 and 16.2).

In these ways, the human infant normally acquires in his first half-year an anticipative way of dealing with objects at a distance. Anticipative reaching, in its turn, is basic first to approach and then to seeking by crawling and walking, respectively. These developments themselves provide a perceptual–motivational basis for approaches and seeking of the conceptual type. What earlier stages may contribute to the more vicarious forms of reaching is suggested by the difficulties experienced in completing approach reactions in the period when 'the infant must touch everything'. Richardson's [40] study of infant learning showed that infants must pass through many months of progressive toil before they can perceive a string and lure as related, with the former a means of getting the latter. From Fischel's [17] tests it appears that dogs never deal with such relationships as well as do young children.

Early progress in motivated reaching, providing a basis for perceiving and using the arm as an extension of the body towards incentives, thereby leads in some primates to the use of objects as means to increase still more the scope of approaching and seeking responses. Such attainments are limited in monkeys, but accelerate from chimpanzee to man. This view of motivated problem-solving is supported by Birch's [2] evidence that chimpanzees achieve few insight solutions in the Kohler stick-combination test unless sticks have been handled previously in play. After the animal has perceived a stick in an arm-extending pattern, a reasoned combining of sticks evidently can arise through anticipating further extensions of a single held stick. Dependence of this indirect seeking response on the animal's motivated condition was demonstrated when Birch made the subjects' hunger excessive before tests, whereupon chimpanzees capable of insight solutions limited themselves to reaching directly for the distant food with the arm alone.

By means of comprehensive rules of conduct, inhibitive procedures and the like, man is capable of extending his motivated approach adjustments under conditions of stress beyond the limitations of direct response. But even man, schooled as he can be in ways of seeking what may lie in hyperspace, at times follows the wrong rules or for other reasons reaches short through petty motivation.

References

1. ADRIAN, E. D. (1935). *The mechanism of nervous action*. University of Pennsylvania Press, Philadelphia.
2. BIRCH, H. (1945). The relation of previous experience to insightful problem-solving. *J. comp. Psychol.* **38**, 367–83.
3. BOURGUIGNON, G. (1929). Classification fonctionnelle des muscles par la chronaxie. *Traite physiol. norm. Path.* **8**, 157–238.
4. BOUSFIELD, W. A. and ORBISON, W. D. (1952). Ontogenesis of emotional behavior. *Psychol. Rev.* **59**, 1–7.
5. BRIDGES, KATHARINE M. B. (1931). *The social and emotional development of the pre-school child*. Kegan Paul, London.
6. BRINK, F., JR. (1951). Excitation and conduction in the neuron. Chap. 2, pp. 50–93 and Synaptic mechanisms. Chap. 3, pp. 94–120. *In*

(Stevens, S. S. (Ed.)) *Handbook of experimental psychology*. Wiley, New York.

7. CANESTRINI, S. (1913). Uber das sinnesleben des Neugeborenen. *Monogr. neurol. Psychiat.* No. 5, Springer, Berlin.

8. CASTNER, B. M. (1932). The development of fine prehension in infancy. *Genet. psychol. Monogr.* **12**, 105–93.

9. CREED, R. S., DENNY-BROWN, D., ECCLES, J. C., LIDDELL, E. G. T., and SHERRINGTON, C. S. (1932). Reflex activity of the spinal cord. Oxford University Press, London.

10. DARLING, R. and DARROW, C. W. (1938). Determining activity of the autonomic nervous system from measurements of autonomic change. *J. Psychol.* **5**, 85–9.

11. DARWIN, CHARLES. (1873). *Expression of the emotions in man and animals*. Appleton, New York.

12. DAVIS, R. C. (1943). The genetic development of patterns of voluntary activity. *J. exp. Psychol.* **33**, 471–86.

13. DENNIS, W. (1935). Experimental test of two theories of social smiling in infants. *J. soc. Psychol.* **6**, 214–23.

14. DUMAS, G. (1922). L'expression des emotions. *Revue philosoph.* **47**, 32–72, 235–58.

15. —— (1948). *Le sourire, psychologie et physiologie*, 3me ed. Presses niver, Paris.

16. ECCLES, J. C. (1953). *The neurophysiological basis of mind*. Clarendon Press, Oxford.

17. FISCHEL, G. (1950). *Die Seele des Hundes*. Parey, Berlin.

18. FRANK, L. (1957). Tactile communication. *Genet. Psychol. Monogr.* **56**, 209–55.

19. FULTON, J. F. (1926). *Muscular contraction and the reflex control of movement*. Williams and Wilkins, Baltimore.

20. HALVERSON, H. M. (1937). Studies of the grasping response of early infancy. *J. genet. Psychol.* **51**, I, 371–92; II, 393–424; III, 425–49.

21. HARTLINE, H. K. (1935). The discharge of nerve impulses from the single visual sense cell. *C. Spr. Harb. Symp. Quant. Biol.* **3**, 245–50.

22. HINSEY, J. C. (1934). The innervation of skeletal muscle. *Physiol. Rev.* **14**, 514–85.

23. HOLT, E. B. (1931). *Animal drive and the learning process*. Holt, New York.

24. HUBER, E. (1930). Evolution of facial musculature and cutaneous field of trigeminus. *Quart. Rev. Biol.* **5**, 133–88, 389–437.

25. HUDGINS, C. V. (1939). The incidence of muscular contraction in receirocal movements under conditions of changing loads. *J. genet. Psychol.* **20**, 327–38.

26. KEMPF, E. J. (1953). Neurosis as conditioned, conflicting, holistic, attitudinal, acquisitive avoidant reactions. *Ann. N.Y. Acad. Sci.* **56**, 307–29.

27. KOEHLER, O. (1954). Das Lacheln als angeborene Ausdrucksbewegung. *Z. mensch. Vererb.-u. Konstitutionslehre* **32**, 390–8.

28. KUNTZ, A. (1929). *The autonomic nervous system*. Lea and Febiger, Philadelphia.

29. LEEPER, R. W. (1948). A motivational theory of emotion to replace 'emotion as disorganized response'. *Psychol. Rev.* **55**, 5–21.

30. LEUBA, C. (1955). Toward some integration of learning theories: the concept of optimal stimulation. *Psychol. Rep.* **1**, 27–33.

31. LEVINE, M. G. and KABAT, H. (1952). Cocontraction and reciprocal innervation in voluntary movement in man. *Science* **116**, 115–18.

32. MAIER, N. R. F. and SCHNEIRLA, T. C. (1942). Mechanisms in conditioning. *Psychol. Rev.* **49**, 117–34.

33. McGINNIS, J. M. (1930). Eye-movements and optic nystagmus in early infancy. *Genet. Psychol. Monogr.* **8**, 321–430.

34. McGRAW, M. (1937). The Moro reflex. *Am. J. dis. children*, **54**, 240–51.

35. NISSEN, H., CHOW, K. L., and SEMMES, JOSEPHIEN (1951). Effects of restricted opportunity for tactual, kinesthetic, and manipulative experience on the behavior of a chimpanzee. *Am. J. Psychol.* **64**, 485–507.

36. PEIPER, A. (1926). Untersuchungen uber die Reaktionzeit im Sauglingsalter: II. Reaktionzeit auf Schmerzreiz. *Monatschr. Kinderheilk.* **32**, 136–43.

37. PICK, J. (1954). The evolution of homeostasis. *Proc. Am. Phil. Soc.* **98**, 298–303.

38. PRATT, K. C., NELSON, A. K., and SUN, K. H. (1930). The behavior of the newborn infant. *Ohio State Univer. Stud., Contr. Psychol. Mo.* 10.

39. RAZRAN, G. (1955). Conditioning and perception. *Psychol. Rev.* **62**, 83–95.

40. RICHARDSON, H. M. (1932). The growth of adaptive behavior in infants: An experimental study of seven age levels. *Genet. Psychol. Monogr.* **12**, 195–359.

41. SCHNEIRLA, T. C. (1939). A theoretical consideration of the basis for approach–withdrawal adjustments in behavior. *Psychol. Bull.* **37**, 501–2.

42. —— (1957). The concept of development in comparative psychology. (Harris, D. B. (Ed.)) *The concept of development.* University of Minnesota Press, Minneapolis, pp. 78–108.

43. SEWARD, J. P. (1952). Introduction to a theory of motivation in learning. *Psychol. Rev.* **59**, 405–13.

44. SHERMAN, M. (1927). The differentiation of emotional responses in infants. I. Judgments of emotional responses from motion picture views and from actual observation. *J. comp. Psychol.* **7**, 265–84.

45. —— and SHERMAN, IRENE C. (1925). Sensory-motor responses in infants. *J. comp. Psychol.* **5**, 53–68.

46. SHERRINGTON, C. S. (1906). *The integrative action of the nervous system.* (1923 ed.). Yale University Press, New Haven.

47. SPITZ, R. and WOLF, K. M. (1946). The smiling response: a contribution to the ontogenesis of social relations. *Genet. Psychol. Monogr.* **34**, 57–125.

48. TAYLOR, J. H. (1934). Innate emotional responses in infants. *Ohio State Univer. Stud., Contrib. Psychol.,* No. 12, 69–81.

49. WATSON, J. B. (1919). *Psychology from the standpoint of a behaviorist.* Lippincott, Philadelphia.

50. WENGER, M. A. (1936). An investigation of conditioned responses in human infants. *Univer. Iowa Stud. Child Welfare* **12**, 8–90.

51. WERNER, H. (1940). *Comparative psychology of mental development.* Harper, New York.

52. WICKENS, D. D. and WICKENS, C. A. (1939). A study of conditioning in the neonate. *Psychol. Bull.* **36**, 599.

V · Development of attachment

WE have argued that the mechanisms subserving early behaviour may be illuminated through study of the anatomical and physiological development of the central nervous system. Not merely *what* an organism learns at a particular age, but *how* it learns is limited by what neural networks are mature. In human ontogeny we may distinguish three critical periods in the first year. During the first month, the pre-corticate infant is limited to learning by classical conditioning; from the second month, instrumental learning becomes possible, and from 6 months, perceptual or insightful learning is conceivable. All three forms of learning probably play a part in the development of 'attachment' behaviour in human infants. Attachment refers to those processes by which proximity between an infant and his main caretaker—usually his mother—are maintained. It appears that most vertebrates have developed some patterns of behaviour whose special function is to ensure the success of this attachment.

But how does attachment take place? Essentially, there are two groups of theories, which stress the maturational and the learned components, respectively, of the behaviours involved in attachment. Protagonists of the first theoretical position ([1, 3, 9] and Chap. 17 of this book) tend to stress the initiative taken by the infant in determining its parents' behaviour, while protagonists of the second position place more importance upon the reinforcement contingencies provided by mothering ([8] and Chap. 18 of this book). Clearly, both processes must play a part in attachment and the differences between the two theoretical positions may often be seen as differences in emphasis than in substance. In Part I we mentioned the importance of genetic factors in determining the availability of social responses, presumably by regulating the maturation of the neural networks mediating these behaviours. Reciprocally, the strengthening and maintenance of the behaviours in the infant's repertoire demands feedback from the environment.

In the first month of life proximity is ensured by the baby's nursing needs, or by those infant responses which have a *signal* rather than an *executive* function [3]. A question we have left unanswered (Chap. 15) is that of the biological function of the enhanced development of the subcortical structures involved in sound reception in the human neonate in contrast with other mammals. One possible answer is that the human voice plays a part in attachment. It seems reasonable to suppose that the constellation of arousal–reducing stimuli we call 'mothering'—removal of pain stimuli, feeding, rocking, providing warmth, and contact comfort—will frequently be preceded by the sound of the mother's voice. Bronson's model (Chap. 8) suggests that the voice may thus become, through classical conditioning, a stimulus for 'de-arousal' and will itself acquire secondary reinforcing properties. However, it must be remembered that the voice is also a prepotent stimulus—it is the most effective stimulus for non-social smiling [7] and, in the form of a cry, facilitates the cries of newborns more than other sounds of comparable intensity and complexity [11]. Thus, it may be more consistent with the facts if we regard the voice as one component in a positive feedback system rather than solely as a conditional stimulus.

As the direct caretaking role of the mother weakens, a behaviour appears whose function has been characterized as 'to put her (the mother) in a mood to be with her infant' [2], namely gaze-fixation or eye-contact (Chap. 19). Steady eye contact only becomes possible at four weeks of age and clearly presupposes the development both of efficient accommodation and convergence (Part IV) and of the rapid myelination of some subcortial areas concerned with the control of visual orienting behaviour. The human eye is a biological curiosity which is particularly well adapted to elicit visual fixation in infants. It contains a central dark spot, surrounded by a large white area which is visually useless, in contrast to other primates who have a much smaller 'signal–noise' ratio. It is to this potent visual signal that the baby of four weeks directs his gaze.

Non-social smiling is present from birth [7]. But social smiling, i.e. the synchronization of smiling with eye contact, only appears about the sixth week and can be considerably modified by contingent events [5]. Here again it is interesting to note that the human voice is a powerful reinforcer.

As long as the conditional stimulus is identified in terms of brightness gradients, smiling is generalized to all conspecifics. During the second to fifth months, however, the baby gradually learns to discriminate the specific features of this immediate caretakers from those of strangers—a degree of pattern discrimination which has been shown to demand participation of the striate cortex. This is the period of 'indiscriminate attachment' [10] when discrimination may be adequate but differential responsiveness is yet not apparent.

By the time the baby is 6 months old, the striate cortex is well developed and perceptual learning is taking place. Specific attachments are now manifest; smiling-to-strangers disappears, to be replaced by staring, and eventually by fear responses. Since smiling to caretakers is followed by intermittent primary and secondary reinforcement, the strength of this response to them is increased, whereas smiling to non-reinforcers (strangers) gradually wanes. This conditioning process is reflected in the temporal course of smiling to a stranger in Ambrose's study (Chap. 20). The de-arousal produced by the presence of a familiar adult will reciprocally inhibit the increment of arousal generated by a novel stimulus, thereby enabling the infant to begin exploring his environment (Part VII).

One of the striking findings of the Schaffer and Emerson study was that in most cases the primary attachment was to the individual who was the main source of stimulation for the infant. Many animal experiments too have demonstrated that the strength of infantile attachment is proportional to the intensity of stimulation occurring in the critical period. More recently it has been shown that for adequacy in certain types of cognitive perform-ance, particularly those mediated by change in cholinergic activity, variety of stimulation is more critical than intensity of stimulation [6]. It is possible then that during the first few months of human life, intensity of stimulation is the salient variable in the formation of social attachments, whereas later on, for adequate cortical development, variety of stimulation is a more important factor. This topic is considered in Part VI.

References

1. AINSWORTH, M. D. (1963). The development of infant–mother inter-action among the Ganda. *In* (Foss, B. (Ed.)) *Determinants of infant behaviour*. Vol. II. Methuen, London.

2. AMBROSE, J. A. (1963). Theory and evidence on the significance of very early experiences. Mimeographed report.

3. BOWLBY, J. (1958). The nature of the child's tie to his mother. *Int. J. Psycho-anal.* **39**, 350–73.

4. —— (1969). *Attachment and Loss*. Vol. I. *Attachment*. The Hogarth Press, London.

5. BRACKBILL, Y. (1958). Extinction of the smiling response in infants as a function of reinforcement schedule. *Child Dev.* **29**, 114–24.

6. BROWN, C. P. and KING, M. G. (1971). Developmental environment: vari-ables important for later learning and changes in cholinergic activity. *Dev. Psychobiol.* **4**, 275–86.

7. FREEDMAN, D. G. (1964). Smiling in blind infants and the issue of innate versus acquired. *J. Child Psychol. Psychiat.* **5**, 171–84.

8. GEWIRTZ, J. L. (1961). A learning analysis of the effects of normal stimulation, privation and depriva-tion on the acquisition of social motivation and attachment. *In* (Foss, B. (Ed.)) *Determinants of infant behav-iour*. Vol. I. Methuen, London.

9. SCHAFFER, H. R. (1963). Some issues for research in the study of attach-ment behaviour. *In* (Foss, B. (Ed.)) *Determinants of infant behaviour*. Vol. II. Methuen, London.

10. —— and EMERSON, P. E. (1964). The development of social attachments in infancy. *Monogr. Soc. Res. Child Dev.* **29**, No. 3.

11. SIMNER, M. L. (1971). Newborn's response to the cry of another infant. *Dev. Psychol.* **5**, 136–50.

17

Patterns of attachment

MARY D. AINSWORTH†

SINCE this paper is concerned with attachment, perhaps I should begin with a definition. According to the Oxford Concise Dictionary, attachment is 'the act of fastening oneself to another, binding in friendship, making devoted'.

The implications of this definition are as follows: (1) attachment implies affection, (2) attachments are specific, and imply discrimination, (3) attachment is an act; it is behavioural and thus observable, (4) attachment is an active process; it does not come about merely through being a passive recipient of stimulation, (5) the act of attachment affects the response of the object. Attachment is a two-way process. It implies interaction.

Let us now attempt our own definition of attachment behaviour. Attachment behaviour is behaviour through which a discriminating, differential, affectional relationship is established with a person or object, and which tends to evoke a response from the object, and thus initiates a chain of interaction which serves to consolidate the affectional relationship.

The material that I am going to present is selected from a short-term longitudinal study of 28 babies in interaction with their mothers, visited

† From 'Patterns of attachment behavior shown by the infant in interaction with his mother'. *Merrill-Palmer Quart.* **10**, 51–8 (1964). Reprinted by permission of the author and the editor of *Merrill-Palmer Quarterly*.

in their own homes at intervals of approximately 2 weeks. The age-span best represented in the study is from 2 to 15 months of age.

These babies happened to be all African—all Baganda. But for our purposes here I urge you to consider my sample as merely one of human infants and disregard the fact that they were African (for I believe the same principles of development apply to infants regardless of specific racial or cultural influences).

These African babies, however, may have been somewhat more accelerated in their development of attachment than babies in our culture. There are three reasons for this opinion: (1) they were generally accelerated in their development, according to Gesell developmental schedules, (2) they were breast-fed, with one exception, and this may have facilitated the development of infant–mother attachment, (3) they experienced more interaction with adult figures than many infants in our culture. The modal pattern of infant care among the Baganda was that a baby was never alone when awake. Characteristically, he is held on someone's lap, most frequently his mother's lap, but he is offered to the visitor to hold, as a courteous gesture. As soon as he can sit unsupported he may be placed on the floor, in the midst of the gathering, for everyone sits on mats on the floor. As soon as he can crawl, he is free to move about, and to initiate contacts or to withdraw from them at will.

At the beginning of my study I was interested in the strength and quality of the infant's attachment to his mother, once formed, rather than in the behaviour patterns which mediated attachment. This interest led me

at which the pattern was commonly observed. Since some of these patterns were identified after the observations were completed, rather than before, and since these observations were therefore unsystematic, it may well be that the earliest and common ages indicated for these items are later than

TABLE 17.1. *Patterns of Attachment Behaviour Shown by the Infant in Interaction with his Mother*

Behaviour	Earliest observation	Commonly observed
Differential crying	8 weeks	12 weeks
Differential smiling	(9 weeks)	(32 weeks)
Differential vocalization	(20 weeks)	?
Visual-motor orientation	(18 weeks)	?
Crying when mother leaves	15 weeks	25 weeks
Following	17 weeks	25 weeks
'Scrambling' over mother	(10 weeks)	(30 weeks)
Burying face in mother's lap	(22 weeks)	(30 weeks)
Exploration from mother as a secure base	28 weeks	33 weeks
Clinging	25 weeks	40 weeks
Lifting arms in greeting	(17 weeks)	(22 weeks)
Clapping hands in greeting	(28 weeks)	(40 weeks)
Approach through locomotion	(26 weeks)	(30 weeks)

to attempt to establish criteria of attachment. At first I looked for reactions to separation and to threat of separation—crying when the mother left, following and clinging, especially. But there were some babies, who seemed clearly attached to their mothers, who did not dependably cry, follow or cling when their mothers showed signs of leaving. What, then, gave such a clear impression that they were nevertheless strongly attached to their mothers? In an attempt to answer this question, I examined my field notes exhaustively, and the catalogue of attachment behaviour shown in Table 17.1 is the result.

For each item, the earliest age at which the behaviour pattern was observed is shown, as well as the age

they should be. The data for those patterns are indicated in parentheses.

A catalogue of patterns of attachment behaviour

At the outset may I say that this catalogue of thirteen patterns of attachment behaviour omits behaviour associated with feeding—the rooting response, sucking and, later, search for the breast—because I wanted to distinguish attachment to the mother as a person from mere attachment to the breast as a need-satisfying object. This does not imply that I consider behaviour implicit in the feeding relationship to be irrelevant to attachment, particularly in the case of babies such as these who were breast-fed for most of the first year of life or longer.

The first three patterns, listed in Table 17.1, imply little more than discrimination of the mother from other people, and differential responsiveness to her.

Differential crying. The baby cries when held by someone other than the mother, and stops when taken by the mother. Or he cries and continues to cry when someone else attempts to comfort him, but stops crying immediately when taken by the mother. It was difficult to judge at first whether the object of attachment was the mother as a person, or a part-object—the breast—for the first act of many of these mothers after picking up a crying baby was to offer the breast.

Differential smiling. The baby smiles more readily and more frequently in interaction with his mother than in interaction with another person.

Differential vocalization. The baby vocalizes more readily and more frequently in interaction with his mother than in interaction with other people.

The next group of patterns have in common a concern on the part of the infant for the whereabouts of his mother—a concern that implies the use of distance receptors, especially vision.

Visual-motor orientation towards the mother. The baby, when apart from his mother but able to see her, keeps his eyes more or less continuously oriented towards her. He may look away for a few moments, but he repeatedly glances towards her. When held by someone else, he can be sensed to be maintaining a motor orientation towards his mother, for he is neither ready to interact with the adult holding him, nor to relax in her arms.

Crying when the mother leaves. The baby cries when the mother leaves his visual field and cannot be brought back into it through his own visual-motor adjustments. The usual occasion is when the mother leaves the room, in contrast with times when she merely moves to another part of the same room.

Following. The baby, once able to crawl, not only cries when his mother leaves the room, but attempts to follow her, by crawling after her, or, when he is older, by walking after her. By about 8 or 9 months, following tended to occur without crying; the baby follows, but cries only if frustrated by being held back, by a closed door, or by the mother going so fast as to outdistance him hopelessly.

Even before the baby is able to crawl and hence to follow, he can nevertheless take the initiative in making contact with his mother when on her lap or when placed on the floor beside her. There are two such patterns, scrambling over the mother, and burying the face in her lap. (I am excluding here behaviour that may obviously be interpreted as a search for or a demand for the breast.)

Scrambling. This pattern differs from clinging in that there is no apparent effort to preserve a close and continuous physical contact. The baby climbs over his mother, exploring her person, and playing with her face, her hair, or her clothes. On occasion, he may explore another person in this way, but since he much more frequently scrambles over his mother, this differential response is included in our catalogue.

Burying the face. The baby, whether in the course of scrambling over the mother, or having returned to her after exploring the world at some distance from her, buries his face in her lap. This behaviour was observed only in relation to the mother.

As Harlow [4] has observed with infant monkeys and Arsenian [2] with pre-school children, the baby, once attached to his mother, can use her as a secure base from which to explore the world, or as a 'haven of safety' from which he can face an external threat without panic.

Exploration from a secure base. Now that the baby is able to crawl, he does not always keep close to his mother, but rather makes little excursions away from her, exploring other objects and interacting with other people, but he returns to her from time to time. He may even go outside the room altogether if he is permitted to do so. His confidence in leaving the secure base is in remarkable contrast to his distress if the secure base gets up and moves off on *her* own initiative.

Clinging. The clinging pattern which is so conspicuous in infant monkeys was not observed in these infants until 25 weeks at the earliest. The most striking instances of clinging in the first year of life were clearly associated with fright. The only clear-cut fear-arousing stimulus which we observed was the stranger. If already in his mother's arms when faced by a stranger, the baby clings to her tightly; if apart from her, he scuttles to her as quickly as possible and then clings. From the safety of his mother's arms he can eye the stranger warily and without crying. If the mother tries to hand him to the stranger, however, the baby screams and clings desperately, resisting all efforts to disengage him. This panicky clinging in response to strangers was not observed in any child younger than 40 weeks of age. A less intense kind of clinging was seen in somewhat younger children. In one 6-month-old child, for example, the cause seemed to be separation anxiety, for he wanted to be with his mother the whole time, and sometimes clung to her, but in an intermittent way and not so desperately and tightly as did the infants who were frightened by a stranger. Another child clung to his mother in the same intermittent way during a period of illness at about 32 weeks of age. Marked clinging was also manifested by some children for a period immediately following weaning.

Finally, greeting responses are classed as attachment behaviour. Some infants, who had become accustomed to being put down by their mothers and left alone to sleep, showed their attachment more by the enthusiastic greeting they gave her when she returned after an absence than by a protest when she departed.

Lifting arms in greeting. The baby greets the mother after an absence by lifting his arms towards her, by smiling, and by vocalization that might be described as a 'crow' or delighted shout.

Clapping hands in greeting. This response is similar to the previous one except that instead of lifting his arms, the baby, while smiling and vocalizing, claps his hands together in a gesture of obvious delight.

Approach through locomotion. After the child is able to crawl, he characteristically terminates his greeting responses by crawling to the loved person as quickly as he is able. Smiling and vocalization usually accompany this response, as they do the other greeting responses. And of course, as described earlier, the infant, if apart from his mother when frightened, crawls to her as quickly as possible and then clings.

These then, together with responses associated with feeding, constitute a catalogue of behavioural components of attachment to the mother as a special person. Let us now consider the development of attachment as a whole.

Development of attachment

During the first year of life these infants passed through four main phases in regard to social behaviour, one phase leading to another with no sharp boundary between them. First there is a phase of undiscriminating responsiveness to people. Next there is a phase of differential responsiveness to the mother, with continuing responsiveness to other people. Then there is a phase of sharply defined attachment to the mother, with striking waning of undiscriminating friendliness. This is followed quickly by, and overlaps with, a phase of attachment to one or more familiar figures other than the mother.

The second phase, in which discrimination of the mother from other people emerges, began in this sample between 8 and 12 weeks of age, with differential crying as the chief criterion. In this sample, however, it was impossible to determine how much of this earliest attachment was to the mother as a whole person and how much to the breast. During the second quarter-year of life, differential responsiveness to the mother became much more clear-cut, and included differential smiling, differential vocalization, and

greeting responses. Crying when the mother left the room was common but inconsistent; infants who were used to being left with other people were more likely to cry if left alone or with a stranger than if left with a familiar figure. As soon as locomotion was attained the following response occurred, in some babies before 6 months of age, in others shortly afterwards. Following was not invariable or consistent at first; it was most likely to occur when the baby was judged to be hungry, tired, ill, or otherwise unhappy, and if the baby was left alone or with strangers rather than if he was left with a familiar person.

The third phase seemed to begin between 6 and 7 months of age, but without any abrupt transition. Following the mother became more and more consistent, as though the attachment to her were becoming stronger and better consolidated. Protest at the mother's departure became more consistent too—although increasingly protest was not simultaneous with following, and tended to occur only if following was frustrated. Greeting responses became more conspicuous, and babies began to use their mothers as a secure base from which to explore the world.

The fourth phase, as I mentioned earlier, overlapped with the third. Babies who were used to care from adults other than the mother never completely lost tolerance for this care, even though they might initially protest the mother's departure. Very shortly after the baby showed a clear-cut attachment to the mother he began to display attachment to other figures, often the father, chiefly through greeting responses. Sharp preferences were shown; for example, one sibling might be greeted joyously while other siblings were not. After nine months of age the baby, when left with a familiar figure, would follow it about, no longer reserving following solely for the mother. Soon after there was discrimination and attachment to figures other than the mother, fear of strangers appeared, as early as eight months with some babies.

Summary and discussion

I now wish to summarize and discuss these findings, drawing your attention to some considerations that seem important to me. I have identified thirteen patterns of behaviour which seem to mediate the attachment of the infant to his mother and soon afterwards to other favourite figures. This catalogue is probably incomplete, although it goes beyond Bowlby's [3] list, which was limited to sucking, crying, smiling, following, and clinging. The behavioural components of these attachment patterns are clearly unlearned—crying, smiling, vocalization, following with the eyes, reaching for an object, locomotion, and so on. These unlearned components become tied into attachment patterns, however, only when they become differentially directed towards different figures, and in the human infant this discrimination does not seem to emerge abruptly.

Although the various patterns of attachment behaviour that I have catalogued tend to become organized together with the mother as object, not all of them need be included in a particular attachment. The attachments of some infants seemed chiefly mediated by crying when mother leaves, by following, and later by clinging. This attachment of others seemed more conspicuously mediated by greeting, smiling, vocalization, and

visual-motor orientation. Perhaps no one of these components is essential; for example, the behaviour associated with the breast-feeding relationship is not essential to attachment in our culture.

I should like to close by emphasizing three features of attachment behaviour which I believe to be clearly apparent in the findings of this study.

First, I was struck with the active part the baby himself plays in the development of attachment. All of these behaviour patterns, as well as the seeking responses in feeding, show initiative. The striking part played by the infant's own activity in attachment leads me to the hypothesis that it is largely through his own activity that the child becomes attached, rather than through stimulation, or through the passive satisfaction of creature-comfort needs.

I attach a great deal of importance to the active initiative implicit in attachment behaviour. I view inter-action between the infant and his mother as a chain of behavioural inter-change, which may be initiated either by behaviour of the mother to which the infant responds, or by the infant's behaviour—at first his signals and later his actual attachment overtures —which evokes a response in the mother.

Hence, as I have stated elsewhere [1], I believe that maternal deprivation may best be defined as insufficient interaction between the infant and a mother-figure, and not as mere lack of stimulation. In deprivation the infant also lacks response of an adult to the behaviour he initiates, including his attachment behaviour.

Secondly, attachment behaviour is not necessarily terminated by a state of close physical contact between infant and mother. Although some attachment patterns imply physical contact as an end phase, others maintain proximity and interaction without requiring actual contact—vocalization, visual-motor orientation, following, exploring from a secure base, and so on. However important actual physical contact may be to the human infant, it is clear that some of the components of attachment and much important interaction between infant and mother involve distance receptors, rather than tactual and kinaesthetic modalities. Even in infancy, attachment can be sustained through a middle distance in which seeing of expression, movement and gesture, and hearing of vocalization, may form the basis of interaction.

I will not set forth in this present discussion my reasons for believing so, but I believe that it is the anxious infant who requires close physical contact with his mother, and who is not content to maintain interaction through a middle distance at least part of the time.

Third, this study suggests strongly that attachments to other figures tend to follow attachment to the mother very quickly, provided that the infant has adequate opportunity to interact with people other than his mother. Scarcely has the infant passed the phase of undiscriminating social responsiveness and formed a specific attachment to his mother than he begins to expand his capacity for attachment to other figures—the father, other adults, or selected older siblings. At the same time that his attachment to his mother grows in depth and strength, his general capacity for attachment grows in breadth. One interesting feature of such attachments is that they can be to figures who take no part in the routine care of the infant, and who therefore do not satisfy his creature-comfort needs but merely play with him and interact with him, smiling and vocalizing.

In final summary, I have made three points. First, the baby is active and takes initiative in forming attachments. Second, attachment does not necessarily imply close physical contact, for it can be maintained through a middle distance through distance receptors. Third, the baby becomes attached not only to the mother-figure who feeds him and satisfies his creature-comfort needs, but also to others who merely play with him and interact with him.

Taken together, these three points offer support to Bowlby's [3] challenge to the so-called secondary-drive theory of attachment which assumes that the infant becomes attached to a mother-figure solely because she is instrumental in the satisfaction of his primary visceral drives.

References

1. AINSWORTH, MARY D. (1962). The effects of maternal deprivation: a review of findings in the context of research strategy and controversy. *Public Health Papers* No. 14. World Health Organization, Geneva.
2. ARSENIAN, J. M. (1943). Young children in an insecure situation. *J. abnorm. soc. Psychol.* **38**, 225–49.
3. BOWLBY, J. (1958). The nature of the child's tie to his mother. *Int. J. Psycho-anal.* **39**, 1–34.
4. HARLOW, J. F. (1960). Primary affectional patterns in primates. *Am. J. Orthopsychiat.* **30**, 676–84.

Supplementary readings

AINSWORTH, M. D. (1963). The development of infant–mother interaction among the Ganda. *In* (Foss, B. M. (Ed.)) *Determinants of infant behaviour II.* Wiley, New York, pp. 67–112.

AMBROSE, J. A. (1963). The concept of a critical period for the development of social responsiveness. *In* (Foss, B. M. (Ed.)) *Determinants of infant behaviour II.* Wiley, New York, pp. 201–25.

CALDWELL, B. M. (1963). Infant interaction in monomatic and polymatic families. *Am. J. Orthopsychiat.* **33**, 653–64.

SCHAFFER, H. R. (1963). Some issues for research in the study of attachment behaviour. *In* (Foss, B. M. (Ed.)) *Determinants of infant behaviour. II.* Wiley, New York, pp. 179–99.

SCHAFFER, H. R. and EMERSON, P. E. (1964). The development of social attachments in infancy. *Monogr. Soc. Res. Child Dev.* **29**, No. 3.

WALTERS, R. H. and PARKE, R. D. (1965). The role of the distance receptors in the development of social responsiveness. *In* (Lipsitt, L. P. and Spiker, C. C. (Eds.)) *Advances in child development and behavior.* Vol. 2. Academic Press, New York, pp. 59–96.

18

A social learning model of attachment

S. W. BIJOU AND D. M. BAER†

Development of the discriminative function of mother for reinforcing events

A newborn baby is a thoroughly helpless creature. Without consistent care, he certainly will not survive. All of the frequent and consistent care he requires must be provided by others. In our culture (as in many) it is usually the mother who does most of this; the father does some, too, and other relatives, like grandparents and older siblings, may take a hand. We shall refer to the person providing the care as the 'mother', whoever the person may be on any specific occasion.

The essential function of the mother is to provide positive reinforcers to the infant and remove negative ones. This is not the ordinary description a mother gives of her duties, but it is a technical one—a functional and fairly comprehensive specification of her behaviour as a mother. Thus, she feeds her infant six to eight times a day at first, frequently ensures that his skin temperature is neither too hot nor too cold, holds him to her and strokes him, rescues him from any situation which she thinks is hurting him, adds toys to his crib, moves him and the objects

† From 'Socialization—the development of behavior to social stimuli'. In *Child development II*, Appleton–Century–Crofts, New York, pp. 122–41 (1965). Copyright © 1965. Reprinted by permission of the publishers.

in his world about, and puts him to bed for rest and sleep.

In doing these things and many others, the mother herself will, as a stimulus object, become discriminated as a 'time' and a place for either the addition of positive reinforcers to the baby's environment or the subtraction of negative reinforcers from it. Thus she is discriminative, as a stimulus, for the two reinforcement procedures which strengthen operant behaviour. Thereby, she acquires positive reinforcing function, and lays the foundation for the further social development of her infant.

The mother is discriminative for some reinforcement procedures by necessity, and for others by accident or through common cultural practice. To illustrate this, we consider a number of reinforcers separately, noting the discriminative role of the mother for each.

Food and water

The mother feeds the infant several times a day, every day for many months. If she is breast-feeding the child, then she is a stimulus that appears just before the receipt of milk (and sucking stimulation, too) and one that remains throughout the nursing period. If she is bottle-feeding him, she accompanies the initial presentation of the bottle, and the insertion of the nipple into the infant's mouth. Typically, she holds both infant and bottle throughout the feeding, thus remaining discriminative for milk throughout the ingestion process. Occasionally, she may prop up infant and bottle and leave for a time; even so, she has been discriminative for the first milk's presentation.

Even as the infant develops increasing competence to feed himself, the mother still retains much of her discriminative function for reinforcement derived from feeding. She typically prepares the food and places it before the infant or hands it to him. Indeed, long into his later life, when he is capable of preparing for himself, she continues to engage in the cultural practice of feeding him.

Taste stimuli

The nearly universal behaviour of giving candy to children may be singled out (somewhat arbitrarily) from the other feeding behaviours of the mother. Candy certainly is a food, but it often is given to children when they are fairly satiated with other foods, and presumably is consumed primarily for its taste. Cookies and fruit juices are also instances of distinctive tastes given to children by mothers. Thus the mother is discriminative for taste reinforcement too. However, the infant encounters some tastes without the help of the mother, since he sucks on nearly every object which can be fitted into his mouth. Some of these objects will have a taste that may be reinforcing. Some of these will be positive reinforcers, but some will be negative. Tastes of objects given by the mother, however, are almost always positive ones (except when she must give the child evil-tasting medicines).

Skin temperature

The infant's internal temperature is self-regulating. His skin temperature, however, depends on the temperature of his surroundings and the kinds and numbers of layers of clothing and blankets covering his body. For the regulation of external temperature change, he must at first depend upon his mother. By removing layers of clothing when he is hot, and adding them when he is cold, she marks an occasion of removal of a negative reinforcer and return of a positive one. Later, as part of the baby's increase in motor skills, he learns to dress and undress himself and adjust his own blankets, whereupon the mother loses much of her discriminative function from this source. Until then, however, her role is definitely discriminative.

Rest and sleep

The very young infant typically rests and sleeps most of his day. Many infants can drop off to sleep anywhere and any time, and the sight of an infant sleeping in a grocery cart, stroller, car seat, on a store counter, or in the aisle is not uncommon. Thus no help from the mother is consistently needed to mark occasions of rest and sleep reinforcement. However, cultural practices may give the mother a role in the infant's rest and sleep routines that would make her discriminative for rest and sleep. It is common in our society for a baby (or older child) to be 'put to bed'. This practice may consist of a change of clothes (usually into sleeping garments), placing the child in his cot, covering him with blankets, and sometimes, singing a lullaby; alternatively, it may consist of rocking and perhaps singing until the baby is asleep or shows signs of drowsiness. Through this feature of child-rearing practice the mother gratuitously acquires a discriminative function for rest and sleep reinforcers.

Tactual stimulation

It is a common practice in our society for mothers to hold their infants. For one thing, this is often the only way to transport them; moreover, it sometimes quiets them and, thirdly, it is often reinforcing to the mother. Another common practice of mothers in our society is to pet and stroke their infants, to kiss them, to tap them on the 'tummy', and to ruffle their hair (however sparse). These customs, too, seem to provide some reinforcement for the mother, possibly because of the tactual stimulation provided by the baby and his responses to such stimulation. At any rate, such practices provide tactual stimulation to the baby. If this type of tactual stimulation is reinforcing, and it seems to be in most instances, then the mother is discriminative for it. However, it is a discriminative function she shares with a variety of other stimuli, such as the baby's blanket, his clothes, his teddy bear, the cat, etc. In other words, the mother may be a significant source of tactual reinforcement, but she is by no means the only source, especially as the baby grows older.

Opportunity to breathe

The infant does his own breathing, of course. On infrequent occasions breathing may prove difficult for him, as when he has croup or asthma, or has managed to get his nose and mouth thoroughly covered by something he cannot remove by his own actions. On the occasions of internal obstructions brought about by physiological disturbances, mother may rescue him, perhaps by taking him into a warm, moist place (the bathroom with a hot shower running, seems a favourite prescription); or possibly by holding him upright, a position in which congested respiratory passages drain better. When breathing has been obstructed accidentally by such things as pillows or clinging sheets of plastic, it is necessary for the mother to remove them since the baby cannot. Thus there are scattered times when the mother takes on a discriminative role for the opportunity for the infant to breathe better. These occurrences are quite rare, but when they do occur they may be urgent (highly aversive) from the infant's point of view. Thus it is worth while to note these kinds of contributions to the mother's discriminative role.

Negative reinforcers

Despite meticulous care, negative reinforcers manage to act upon the infant from time to time. He may, for example, roll upon hard toys, pinch himself between mattress and crib bars, bang his head into the headboard, be exposed to hot, bright sunlight, have gastric pains, cut a tooth, and be manhandled by an older sibling or a house pet. From some of these accidents, the mother must rescue him, thereby functioning as a stimulus discriminative for the removal of negative reinforcers. She can, for example, roll him off the hard object, free him from the clutches of the mattress and crib, move him into the shade, 'burp' him, massage his gums, and drive off the older sibling or pet.

In many situations she can do little about removing negative reinforcers, since they have had their full impact before she can get into effective action. Yet even in these instances, she often plays something of a discriminative role by virtue of the nature of the course of a hurt. When an infant experiences a negative reinforcer, he usually cries. This respondent signal of distress often attracts the mother, who, seeking that he has been hurt but that it is all over, nevertheless picks him up and comforts him. In so doing, she marks an occasion of the waning of the stimulus which hurt him. Speaking loosely, he is just starting to feel better and there he is in mother's arms. How is he to know it wasn't mother who actually reduced the intensity of the hurt?

Stimulus change

If stimulus change is reinforcing to an infant, then at least some stimulus change is provided by the mother. She picks him up and moves him from one place to another, she places new toys in his view; she speaks and sings to him; and she plays games with him, such as peek-a-boo, patty-cake, and making faces. Thus, her appearance on the scene frequently is discriminative for rather widespread stimulus changes. Indeed, the younger the infant, the less accomplished he is in arranging his environment to produce changes; hence long hours in his crib constitute a considerable deprivation of stimulus change, and the greater is his dependence upon the mother to make something happen. As the baby grows older, however, many more responses which produce such changes become available to him, and hence the mother will constitute a smaller source of stimulus change in his total environment. Thus mother's initial discriminative status for much of this kind of reinforcement will diminish during the course of development.

·　　·　　·　　·　　·

The stimulus components of the mother

The functional characterization of the mother presented thus far is that of a discriminative social stimulus. Having outlined what she is discriminative for, it is now appropriate to identify more precisely the stimuli involved.

The equation of a person to a stimulus is of course an oversimplification. There are innumerable ways of characterizing the stimuli which make up a human being. Many of these, however, will have little or no functional value for the behaviour of other people, especially of their children. For example, we might describe a mother by the number of calories of heat she radiated per hour. This is certainly one of her stimulus characteristics, but it is of little significance to her baby unless the mother provides a source of heat for the baby in an otherwise cold environment. Similarly, a mother could be characterized by the number of hairs on her head. Her baby may respond to the colour of her hair and the shape of its arrangement on her head, but he is not responsive to the number of discrete hairs.

The characteristics of a mother which are important stimuli for her baby clearly are those which are involved in her discriminative functions. In effect, they are the stimuli, in all their variety, which allow the mother to be discriminated from the rest of the house and the objects in it and from other people who are not caretakers, at least to some degree. To a great extent, these are visual stimuli; but auditory, tactual, and olfactory stimulus elements also play a part. The mother has the usual shape of *homo sapiens* plus her own individual biological differences. The shape is seen by the baby in a variety of wrappings and positions, some more often than others.

The baby's initial discriminations may be no more elegant than that reinforcement often follows the appearance of a certain shape wrapped in grey bending over him. The shape has a distinctive top, a face crowned with hair. The hair is of fairly constant colour (ordinarily), but is seen in a variety of arrangements about the face. The face has certain constant elements consisting of its basic lines, the shape of the nose, and so on. The variations on the patterns of the face are considerable, however, ranging from broad smiles to stormy frowns. Some of these arrangements, such as smiles, may be more discriminative for positive reinforcement than others, such as frowns. The shape has a voice which occasionally makes noise, and the frequencies and tenor of this noise are fairly consistent. It does, however, include coos, gurgles, shouts, and happy, angry, and placid tones. The happy sounds may be more reliable cues for positive reinforcers than the angry ones (which, in time, often will be clearly discriminative for negative reinforcers). The specific patterns of sound making up the mother's language will initially have little discriminative value for the infant. Later they will acquire this function, and after about five years of age these sounds will control a highly complex assortment of discriminated operants.

The mother also has a number of surfaces providing tactual stimulation which the infant might experience. These stimuli are provided by her skin (especially her hands), the clothes she wears, and her hair. The touch of the mother's hands may be discriminative for subsequent reinforcement. The

feel of the mother's face sometimes might be modified by a layer of cosmetics or of perspiration. The feel of her clothes obviously will be a frequently changeable stimulus.

The mother also might provide a number of odours. Some of these are eminently associated with her appearance; some are added from time to time by perfumes, cosmetics, mouthwashes and toothpastes, smoking, and the like. It is unlikely that any of the latter are particularly discriminative for any reinforcing consequences for the infant (except, possibly, that a highly perfumed and made-up mother is likely to leave soon and be replaced by another person (babysitter). The nature of this sequence of events is hardly systematic in its effects. It depends upon the types of care given by the mother and the substitute mother).

These are at least some of the stimuli, then, which contribute to the baby's recognition of the mother. They allow him to discriminate her from other parts of his environment which also have shapes, make sounds, and provide tactual and olfactory stimulation. But because so many stimuli from mother vary within wide limits, it is necessary to consider her not as a fixed class of stimuli, but rather as a continuously changing array of stimuli from many classes. The classes of stimuli from which the mother's samples of stimuli are drawn are, of course, shared by other people. Thus the positions of the mother's body relative to the baby are duplicated by many other bodies from time to time, and clothes on the mother are much like those of others who come and go. Perhaps no one else has quite the mother's nose, but the general shape and location of her nose relative to her eyes and mouth, and the variations of facial contours arranged by smiles, frowns, and the like, are like the facial expressions of others. The mother's voice may have a characteristic tenor and style of inflection, but the voices of many persons produce similar frequencies and inflections, and share much of the same language, idioms, and exclamations. Other individuals will feel much like the mother to the baby and, on occasion, will also provide similar odours.

In effect, the mother is a changing sample of stimuli, some of which are unique to her, but many of which are shared by other people. Thus stimuli from a mother which become discriminative for reinforcement may overlap with stimuli from other people, and the baby's behaviours which have become strengthened to mother's stimulation may be evoked by others who present the same or similar stimuli. Consequently, there are natural bases for both *discrimination* of the mother from all other people and for *generalization* from the mother to others. Thus, the baby can unfailingly pick out his parents when necessary; yet, just as he smiles at them, makes noises, waves, claps, and does other 'tricks' for them, so he may do the same for others, even without previous direct experience with them.

As the mother becomes a social re-inforcer for the baby, other people acquire a generalized reinforcing value (to the extent that they, as samples of stimuli, are like the mother). This process may be the basic learning operation which gives the child a social character and allows the figurative label of man as a 'social animal'. That is, man is an organism whose mother, in being discriminative for reinforcement, is sufficiently change-

able as a stimulus complex to be much like other people he meets later in his life; he will respond to them at least in part as he has responded to his mother. (It is often said that the child learns about society 'through the eyes of his mother'.) Basically, the mother has been discriminative for the pre-sentation of positive and for the removal of negative reinforcers; there-fore the child's mother, and, by generalization, others similar to her, will acquire the stimulus property of a positive acquired reinforcer, i.e. a social reinforcer.

It is now essential to analyse in more specific terms the stimuli of the mother which are discriminative for behaviours leading to reinforcement. So far, discussion has centred on stimuli which make it apparent that the mother is distinct from other parts of the baby's environment. But the mother provides cues which are a part of the reinforcement procedures she performs; she provides more detailed stimuli: her *proximity* or nearness, her *attention*, and her *affection* or warmth. These stimulus components of the mother are of special significance for the future development of the baby and child.

Proximity of the mother to the baby

The majority of reinforcement opera-tions the mother performs are adminis-tered in close physical relationship to the baby. Mother cannot feed the baby, adjust his temperature, rescue him from hurtful objects, hold him, or prepare him for sleep at a distance. Such caretaking functions require handling of the baby while providing reinforcers, and thus the mother, to reinforce, must be near the baby—within reaching distance, at least. As a consequence, mother at a distance is hardly discriminative for reinforcement, but mother nearby is discriminative.

The stimulus dimensions involved in reacting to objects at different distances away, or distance perception, have long been an interesting problem in visual perception and discrimination. For an adult, the cues reacted to in discriminating distance include at least: (1) the angle of convergence the eyeballs assume in fixating an object at various distances, (2) the disparity or differences in images falling on the two retinas, (3) the texture, brightness, and parallel line characteristics, and (4) the interposition of other objects between the viewer and the object [4]. An infant may not use all of these cues in discriminating distances; indeed, some of them may be learned during his early days in the child-rearing situations under discussion. In these situations, the mother in close proximity to the baby is more discriminative for reinforcement than the mother at a distance, and it follows that any stimuli marking these differences in distance will themselves become functional for the baby. If mother is close, reinforcement follows, sometimes after a short delay; if mother is far, reinforcement follows only after a long delay or not at all.

The nearness of the mother is one of the basic social discriminative stimuli. Closeness-to-the-mother thereby takes on positive reinforcing power, and behaviours of the baby producing proximity of the mother will be strengthened, while behaviours losing this proximity will be weakened. For the young baby who does not move about, certain responses often will produce the essential proximity of a mother. These include crying and fussing, calling 'Mummy', or any responses with objects that make noise of the sort that will attract a curious parent. Certain facial expressions of a 'cute' sort often will attract a distant adult, as may other tricks which mothers interpret as especially charming or advanced, such as playing patty-cake.

For the baby who moves about, creeping, crawling, toddling, walking, or running are some of the responses that can produce the proximity of the mother and maintain it as the mother moves about. Tagging along after the mother is clearly one of the most prominent behaviours of young children, and may be viewed as a set of discriminated operants maintained by the proximity functioning as a positive reinforcer. The contribution of this basic social reinforcer to increasing skill and speed in locomotor behaviours may be great; it has often been clinically described (frequently in terms of the baby's need for security) but has not as yet been experimentally analysed. However, Gewirtz [2] has made an analysis of the role of proximity in stimulating a number of social responses such as attention-seeking.

Proximity should be a less distinctive stimulus for babies reared in small living quarters than for those living in large houses. Where the environment is quite small, as in a cramped one-room apartment, the mother is rarely far from the baby. Thus the difference between a distant mother and a near one is minimal: the mother when she is giving reinforcers is hardly much nearer than when she is not. When the baby and mother live in a large room, however, the non-reinforcing mother ₋nay be much further away than when she is reinforcing, and the distance dimension is much more prominent. In a house with many rooms, the non-reinforcing mother may frequently be out of the child's sight, and the role of proximity as a distinctive cue for reinforcement is maximized.

Casual observation shows that many young crawlers and toddlers spend a considerable proportion of their waking day near the mother. Even when a special room has been equipped with attractive toys for the baby, the mother may find that these play objects are displaced to the vicinity of her feet as she stands washing dishes at the kitchen sink and that, in effect, her baby's recreation room is whatever room she is in at the time. Although proximity seems to be a rather simple pattern of stimuli, it is a potent social reinforcer for babies and young children.

Proximity may not remain potent. It may even reverse its function from being discriminative for positive stimulation to being discriminative for aversive stimulation under special circumstances. If, for example, a mother should become very punitive, giving more negative than positive reinforcers, her proximity becomes a discriminative stimulus for aversive stimulation or punishment. Proximity thereby acquires a negative reinforcing function which may override and displace its previously acquired positive function. The child may avoid her nearness. To put it simply, he cannot be spanked from a distance.

.　　.　　.　　.　　.

Affection towards the baby

Some mothers are prompted to display affection by the reinforcing occasions involved in child-rearing practices. On such occasions their affection takes the form of smiles, kisses, hugs, and pats, special crooning tones of voice, loving words, nuzzling, hair-ruffling, tickling,

and similar behaviours associated with delighted and effusive parents. Other mothers are, by contrast, inclined to provide affection most reliably only when they are in the midst of an affectionate display generated by conditions not directly associated with child-caring activities. In either situation there is a correlation between such stimuli and reinforcement which is sufficient to give the affectionate stimuli discriminative status. As with attention, the variability in individual mothers' styles of being affectionate will correspond to the kinds of affection which will prove maximally reinforcing for their children later. Thus, some children may be more responsive to smiles than to extravagant displays of hugging, kissing, and fondling; others may be more reinforced by an affectionate word or phrase; still others may be most susceptible to a pat on the head, and so on.

Few experimental studies have been conducted to provide specific information on affectionate stimuli, the range of their physical properties, the probable time of their initial effectiveness, etc. One study by Brackbill on smiling [1] is described because it is instructive for further research in this area.

Brackbill's study of smiling in 4-month-old infants was generated by her interest in the response in relation to its presumed social nature and its early role in social learning. The infants chosen were old enough to remain awake throughout the experimental sessions, young enough not to respond discriminatively to 'mother' versus 'others', placid enough not to cry too often during sessions and to lie on their backs for at least five minutes without struggling, and responsive enough to show an operant level of at least two smiles within a five-minute session. Brackbill does not give a verbal description of smiling, but reports that prior to the main study, she and another judge observed some 970 occasions of smiling or non-smiling in infants, and agreed in 97·5 per cent of their judgements.

Two limiting factors should be kept in mind in reviewing this study. First, smiling (like vocalization) is a lingering response in infants, which adds to the difficulty in perceiving changes in its rate. Second, limitations were imposed by the length of time it took to offer the social reinforcement given as a consequence of smiling: 'Five seconds were required for picking S up; 30 s for reinforcement; 5 s for putting S down; and 5 s for recording. Therefore, no more than six responses could occur and be reinforced during any 5-min interval.'

Despite these less than ideal conditions, the experimental conditions, which consisted of (1) an operant level period, (2) a conditioning period (of either continuous or intermittent reinforcement), and (3) an extinction period, produced differences in smiling frequencies. The operant level was taken as the rate observed through at least eight separate 5-min intervals, during which the investigator stood motionless over the infant (who lay on his back in his crib), and maintained an expressionless face at about 15 in from the infant's face. During conditioning sessions (consisting of ten to twelve 5-min intervals), the investigator reinforced smiling by smiling at, picking up, and cuddling the infant, using continuous reinforcement with one group and working steadily from continuous to variable ratios of 1, 2, 3, and 4 with another group. (These behaviours typify the activities of many affectionate mothers.) Extinc-

tion was similar to the operant level condition, and was observed over fifteen or more 5-min intervals.

The rate of smiling during the conditioning period was reliably higher than the rate during the operant level. During extinction, the intermittently reinforced group extinguished less rapidly; both groups fell below their previous operant level rate of smiling, and both displayed 'protest' behaviour to the unsmiling investigator, crying or turning away from her.

All subjects were studied immediately after nursing and following a nap. The mother in each case phoned Brackbill when her infant awoke, and Brackbill arrived at the infant's home to work with a freshly diapered infant just satiated with food. The mother cooperated to the extent of engaging in minimal contact with the infant prior to each experimental session. The study took place in the infant's own home and crib.

Returning to the general concept of affection, it seems that affection is a much more variable stimulus constellation than is either proximity or attention. It is variable to the point of being entirely absent in some mothers. It is clear that in order for a mother to reinforce, she must be both near and attentive, but she need not be affectionate. Some mothers are not characteristically affectionate, and their children should be quite unresponsive to affection. However, they may be well reinforced by both the proximity and attention of adults. The literature of clinical child psychology is rich in descriptions of children who are 'social', in that they are extremely sensitive to having an audience, but 'psychopathic', in that the respect or affection of that audience is entirely without value to them. Such a child might well have a history in which displays of affection were never discriminative for other reinforcers.

For children with mothers who have made their affection discriminative to the baby for the other reinforcers in caretaking activities, affection operates as a positive reinforcer. It serves as an important stimulus in the developing behaviour of these children because it is not ordinarily used to strengthen bad behaviour (as attention and proximity often are). The mother may not be able to avoid attending to the baby's undesirable behaviour, bringing herself in close proximity to him, but she is unlikely to meet it with affection. In fact, she is much more likely to cease all displays of affection on occasions that displease her. Because the withdrawal or loss of a positive re- inforcer acts to weaken any preceding operant behaviour, bad behaviours may be weakened more by the mother's withdrawal of affection than they are strengthened through her attention.

The ease of giving affection for good behaviour, and the natural tendency not to present it and to withdraw it when confronted with bad behaviour, set up situations which strengthen selectively those behaviours which please the mother, rather than those which displease her. This line of reasoning suggests that children who are maximally responsive to affection as a positive reinforcer are more readily influenced by the mother's goals for them than are children more responsive to her attention than to her affection.

References

1. BRACKBILL, YVONNE. (1958). Extinction of the smiling response in infants as a function of reinforcement schedule. *Child Dev.* **29**, 115–24.
2. GEWIRTZ, J. L. (1954). Three determinants of attention-seeking in young children. *Monogr. Soc. res. Child Dev.* **19**, No. 2.
3. —— (1961). A learning analysis of the effects of normal stimulation, privation and deprivation on the acquisition of social motivation and attachment. *In* (Foss, B. M. (Ed.)) *Determinants of infant behavior*. Wiley, New York.
4. GIBSON, J. M. (1950). *The perception of the visual world*. Houghton Mifflin, Boston.

19 The role of eye-contact in attachment

K. S. ROBSON†

AMONG clinicians and researchers in child development there is general agreement that the character and quality of one's earliest relationships will contribute significantly to, and even predict the nature of, many later behaviours. Consequently, increasing attention is being focused on the parameters of maternal–infant interaction in a search to define the more significant variables of this system. An eloquent attempt in this direction was made by Bowlby [8] in a paper devoted to 'The nature of the child's tie to his mother'. After reviewing the relevant aspects of both psychoanalytic and learning theories, Bowlby takes an ethological position in describing the growth of the infant's first relationship. He cites five behaviours —crying, smiling, following, clinging, and sucking—as innate 'releasers' of maternal caretaking responses.

The point of departure of the present report is to add another variable to Bowlby's list: eye-to-eye contact, an interchange that mediates a substantial part of the non-verbal transactions between human beings. This interaction (as will be noted later) is well known in the animal kingdom, and it is beginning to be studied by

observers of adult behaviour [5, 10, 11] but has received little consideration by child development researchers. In this report the viscissitudes of eye-to-eye contact will be followed through the first six months of life with an emphasis on attachment from the point of view of both mother and infant. The author's aim is to bring together a number of diverse but related observations in order to offer some ideas that can be subjected to experimental verification.

Some introductory comments on the visual mode

There are some unique peculiarities of the visual mode that favour its pre-eminence as a major vehicle of intrapsychic and inter-personal development. Greenman [18] states that of all the neonatal reflexes visual fixation and following are the only ones that do not drop out over time, but, on the contrary, demonstrate increasing facility. Rheingold [33] notes that this behaviour '. . . is all the more remarkable . . . because of its maturity relative to . . . other patterns of behaviour . . . (so that by the end of the second month) . . . it is already in the form it will keep throughout life'. Furthermore, following and fixation are among the first acts of the infant that are both intentional and subject to his control. Vision is the only modality which, by closure of the eyelids, gaze

† From 'The role of eye-to-eye contact in maternal–infant attachment'. *J. Child Psychol. Psychiat.* **8**, 13–25 (1967). Reprinted by permission of Maxwell Microforms International Marketing Corp.

aversion, and pupillary constriction and dilation is constructed as an 'on–off' system that can easily modulate or eliminate external sensory input, sometimes at will, within the first months of life. And finally, the appeal of the mother's eyes to the child (and of his eyes to her) is facilitated by their stimulus richness. In comparison with other areas of the body surface the eye has a remarkable array of interesting qualities such as the shininess of the globe, the fact that it is mobile while at the same time fixed in space, the contrasts between the pupil–iris–cornea configuration, the capacity of the pupil to vary in diameter, and the differing effects of variations in the width of the palpebral fissure.

Rheingold [33] has suggested that '. . . not physical, but visual contact is at the basis of human sociability . . .', and she adds '. . . (that the) basic and primary activity is the infant's visual exploration of his environment . . .'. In his observations of neonatal visual behaviour Greenman [18] makes the point that the importance of vision '. . . exceeds the essential role it plays in perception of the outside world and in differentiating the self from the non-self . . . (in that) . . . one of the primary ways in which human beings communicate at a non-verbal level is by looking at one another . . . (and) . . . when visual communication does not exist between humans, something deviant or pathological often exists in the relationship'.

The first comprehensive review of the functions of the distance receptors, vision and hearing, in the development of social responsiveness has been made by Walters and Parke [46]. As for vision, it is only recently that studies exclusively concerned with the role of this modality as an important avenue

for accomplishing the tasks of early development have appeared in the literature. These have tended to fall into the three categories, the first of which has been concerned with the evolution of perceptual and attentive capacities in the infant [12, 18, 22, 23, 28, 24, 44, 48, 49, 53, 54]. Another group of papers has described, primarily from the psychoanalytic point of view, the effects of blindness on maturational processes [9, 13, 32, 35, 50]. Although these efforts have been useful, a reconstruction of the functions of vision built upon the effects of its absence is fraught with difficulties, not the least of which is maternal disturbance secondary to the birth of a severely defective child. A third series of reports approaches behaviour, broadly speaking, from the ethological position [3, 14, 15, 19, 45, 52]. Of the latter type, three studies have particular relevance to eye-to-eye contact. Kaila [25], Spitz and Wolff [43] and Ahrens [1]—all of whom were exploring the infant's social responses to faces—have established an important fact: that one of the earliest and most effective stimuli for eliciting social smiling is a visual gestalt ('key stimulus' in ethological terms) consisting of the two eyes and forehead configuration *en face*, i.e. such that the eyes of the infant and those of the observer meet fully in the same vertical plane of rotation. Indirect confirmation for this finding is implicit in Watson's [47] work. Studying both smiling to, and fixation of, faces and face schemata, in infants from 7 to 26 weeks of age he found that both behaviours were maximal in the *en face* position. Watson also noted that this facial orientation was not the most frequent in routine caretaking but that when mothers addressed their infants 'socially', i.e.

to the face, they used the *en face* orientation. But none of these authors, including Spitz [42] in his recent text on the formation of early object relations, elaborate on the long-range significance of this eye-to-eye interaction in more than a passing way.

The first three months

The beginnings of maternal attachment. The development of maternal attachments in most non-human mammals requires a comparatively short time span, and the ties that result are rather abruptly terminated by active discouragement of the infant's approach behaviour. Rosenblatt [34] has recently summarized the course of these processes in a number of animal species. Even in those species where infancy is prolonged, these non-human mothers seem to need far less responsiveness from their offspring than would satisfy man. Eye-to-eye contact and precursors of the human smiling response (i.e. lip-retraction in dogs and cats and the 'grins' and 'grimaces' of primates) play a minimal part in sub-human attachments. When these behaviours serve a social function it is mainly to indicate fear, 'appeasement' or the intention to attack [4, 29]. 'Staring down' in man occurs in a similar context. Generally, however, the more usual pattern of intermittent gaze fixation between humans '. . . signifies a readiness to interact . . . (and) . . . little social interaction is possible without it' [20].

The human mother is subject to an extended, exceedingly trying and often unrewarding period of caring for her infant. Her neonate has a remarkably limited repertoire with which to sustain her. Indeed, his total helplessness, crying, elimination behaviour, and physical appearance frequently elicit aversive reactions. Thus, in dealing with the human species, nature has been wise in making both eye-to-eye contact, and the social smile that it often releases in these early months, behaviours that at this stage of development generally foster positive maternal feelings and a sense of payment for 'services rendered'. As others have suggested [1, 14, 45], there is no reason to believe that smiling and eye contact in human babies differ in origin from the primarily defensive functions they play in the animal world. Lorenz [29] views the human smile as a ritualized form of aggression comparable to the 'greeting' ceremonies which inhibit intra-specific fighting in many lower animals. Hence, though a mother's response to these achievements may be an illusion, from an evolutionary point of view it is an illusion with survival value.

Both Greenman [18] and Wolff [52] note the pleasure that new mothers take when their infants begin to 'see' them. The latter author notes that during the fourth week of life '. . . the baby now seems to focus on the observer's eyes as if there were true eye-to-eye contact . . . (and) . . . it appears to be specifically the contact between the eyes (of the infant and the observer) that is effective (in evoking a smile)'. Three of his mothers, who spent little time playing with their infants before the fourth week, suddenly began doing so within 2 or 3 days of his first recording eye-to-eye contact, yet these mothers had no idea of why this was so. Unlike the smiling response, which follows soon after eye contact is established, the infant's fixing of his mother's gaze seems rarely available to her for conscious recall.

One aspect of a longitudinal study in which the author is participating involves rather extensive post-natal interviews with 54 primiparous mothers. Most of these women describe some initial feelings of 'strangeness', 'distance', and unfamiliarity towards their offspring which persist for at least the first few weeks of life. When one inquires as to when the mother first felt love, when she ceased feeling 'strange' with her child and when he 'became a person' to her, the answer to these questions frequently involves the baby's 'looking', as if recognizing objects in the environment. A small number specifically articulate that eye-to-eye contact releases strong positive feelings. These feelings have something to do with 'being recognized' in a highly personal and intimate way.

The resolution of maternal anxiety

When one 'sees eye-to-eye' with another person, exclusive communication, 'resonance', and accord of a fundamental sort are implied. The often intense discomfort experienced in encounters with the blind or cross-eyed may indeed stem in part from a variety of unconscious fantasies. But the absence of eye-to-eye contact in these situations realistically leaves one feeling ill at ease, since it impedes the most usual form of mutual recognition, assessment and contact. Visual impairment interferes with the development of certain social responses that are derivatives of eye-to-eye contact. Freedman [14] comments that although fleeting spontaneous smiles emerge at the usual time in blind infants '. . . prolonged social smiling seems to require visual regard as a maintaining stimulus'. Selma Fraiberg (personal communication), in her observations of blind infants, has noted that she was unable to carry out

a normal 'dialogue' with her subjects, with one exception, a baby who was supposedly blind but demonstrated visual following. She also comments [13] that 'When the mother sought contact through her eyes, the child's eyes did not meet hers, which feels curiously like a rebuff if you do not know the baby is blind. All those ways in which the eyes unite human partners (are) denied this mother and baby.' In an attenuated form, the same situation—probably one of the sources of early maternal anxiety—obtains for a new mother before her infant establishes eye-contact with her. In the course of several home-observations, previously anxious and uncomfortable mothers have told the author that they feel somehow 'more at ease' and 'comfortable' with their infants. This shift coincides with the beginning of true eye-to-eye contact over a time span as brief as three days, but as in Wolff's [52] study these mothers were unable to specify why they felt differently.

The eye gestalt as a perceptual organizer

Though up to 3 months eye-contact has no true social relevance to the infant, it may fulfil another function. A baby of this age reacts to a wide variety of endogenous and exogenous stimuli. Yet in terms of orienting, attentive and discriminative capacities, his visual apparatus is manifestly advanced relative to other receptor systems. Eye-to-eye contact occurs either simultaneously with, or in close contiguity to, many non-visual stimuli. Furthermore, the eye gestalt is a highly discriminable stimulus configuration that can focus and hold the infant's attention more successfully than many competing internal and external per-

ceptual events. One could then speculate that in the first months of life many
forms of stimulation are experienced
by the infant as 'coming from' the
eyes of his caretakers. If this speculation were even partially true, and
relevant empirical data will be presented below, the vicissitudes of eye-
to-eye contact would provide one
starting point for examining the
origins and persistence of perceptions
in adults whereby internal experiences
are attributed to external events.

Many mothers report that as soon as
eye-to-eye contact is established it
often dominates the feeding situation,
so that their infants are totally dis-
tracted from sucking. Only much later
does the sight of breast or bottle evoke
excitement. Also, when an infant of
this age is spoken to he ignores the
mouth of the speaker and fixates the
eyes. According to Ahrens [1] the
mouth is not involved in eliciting the
smiling response until the fifth or sixth
month, and even then eye fixation
precedes the smile.

Though relatively little is known
about the development of body image,
if attention to eyes is dominant in early
development it should be reflected in
the emerging body concept of the
young child. Thus, despite the fact that
psycho-analytic theory has emphasized
the mouth as an early focal point of
body image [41] in terms of their
salience the eyes should have priority.
Shapiro and Stine [38] collected the
figure drawings of 3- and 4-year-old
children in order to test the primacy of
mouth perceptions. In their younger
sample, less than 46 months old, 89 per
cent drew eyes while 22 per cent drew
the mouth. Ninety-nine per cent of
children older than 46 months drew
eyes and 75 per cent the mouth. They
also found that eyes were represented

independently of the nose and mouth,
both of which tended to appear
simultaneously and usually later in
time. Some children, when asked to
draw a face, will represent the eyes
alone. As to whether figure drawings
in fact represent body image, a
definitive answer must await further
research. None the less, Shapiro and
Stine suggest that the earliest body
representations are taken from visual
experience while tactile experiences
are only later 'projected'. These drawings, of course, bear a strong resemblance to the 'two eyes' gestalt mentioned earlier, a fact that further supports the argument that this stimulus
configuration is selectively attended to
as the *'locus vitae'* of the infant's
primary caretakers, and as such serves
as an important organizer of his perceptual world.

Four to six months

By the fourth month an infant shows
differential reactions of anticipatory
excitement to his mother's approaching step, her voice, and for the present
purposes most important, her face, by
his selective smiling response. Up to
this time his smiles have been indiscriminate. Ahrens [1] states that the
'. . . absolute stimulus . . . which must
stand at the root of social behaviour
. . . (is) . . . the eye part (of a mask or
an observer's face)'. Rheingold [33]
has pointed out that the infant's
capacity to initiate physical contact
and clinging develop towards the end
of the first year of life. For sub-human
primates such 'contact comfort' [19]
is essential in establishing their first
relationships and can be sought out
from birth. Schaffer and Emerson
[37] found that 'non-cuddly' infants
displayed less intense social relationships in the first year of life when

compared with a 'cuddly' group; but by 18 months both populations were comparable in their attachment behaviours. Elsewhere [36] they observe that with increasing frequency during the first year of life, situations in which 'visually maintained contact' is interrupted are the most provocative of separation protest.

Eye-to-eye contact is one of the most intense and binding visual interactions for an infant at this age. And though visual scanning of other facial characteristics becomes an associated behaviour, the maternal eye gestalt retains its salience. Kagan *et al.* [24] found that 4-month-old infants smiled far more often to the presentation of a realistic face stimulus than to those where the features were either scrambled or lacking eye representations. Children from $4\frac{1}{2}$ to $10\frac{1}{2}$ years-of-age, given the task of identifying familiar peers from photographs showing isolated facial features, were far more successful when part or all of the two eyes and forehead configuration was displayed [17].

Through repeated visual scrutiny of his mother's face, more particularly its eye area, the infant of 4–6 months comes to single out his primary caretaker. In a sense, one might say that this face—the most discrete and localizable human point of reference in the infant's world—is 'mother'. Only gradually, over many months, does the rest of her body become an integral part of his scheme of things.

A fundamental two-way process of communication—looking at and being looked at [2]—is set in motion. In the normal course of events this process continues to operate in human relationships. The fulfilment of physical needs, and the experiencing of pleasurable stimulation through non-visual modes, are equally significant factors in the development of attachment. Eye-to-eye contact is one component in the matrix of maternal and infant behaviours that comprise reciprocal interaction. Yet the nature of the eye contact between a mother and her baby seems to cut across all interactional systems and conveys the intimacy or 'distance' characteristic of their relationship as a whole.

.　　.　　.　　.　　.

The quality of the relationship— contingent maternal behaviour

In his formulation of early social and attachment behaviour, Gewirtz [16] stresses that '. . . we must take account of the circumstances under which given stimuli are made available to (the baby) and in particular, whether these stimuli are functional, and with his behaviours enter into effective contingencies for learning'. He notes, in discussing the deprivation of institutionalized infants, that what is lacking in such an environment is not contact *per se*, but caretaking behaviour that is contingent upon the baby's signals. It would seem worth while to differentiate at least three dimensions of such contingency.

First, a mother's responses should follow the infant's signals within a period of time that is sufficiently short for him to causally associate his behaviours with her actions. Schaffer and Emerson [36] found that 'maternal responsiveness', the rapidity with which the mother responded to her infant's demands, yielded a positive and significant correlation with both choice of a favoured caretaker and attachment intensity. A second parameter is the degree to which maternal responses accurately meet the baby's immediate needs. For example, one can often see mothers who are preoccupied with food intake interpret every fuss or cry as a sign of hunger and act accordingly. As a result, they may force feeding and prolong distress, or waken a drowsy, full but fretful infant from sleep. Although neither the time nor 'need meeting' axes of contingent responses directly involve eye-to-eye contact, these two parameters apply to maternal behaviours which probably become associated through contiguity with the infant's 'gestalt' of his mother's gaze.

The third aspect of contingent behaviour is less refined but no less important than the preceding two. It has to do with the affective accompaniment of maternal eye contact. Behaviourally speaking, this might be defined as the degree of animation and modulation of facial expression, particularly around the upper half of the face. During the first months of life mothers utilize the eye-to-eye interchange for a variety of purposes: it can be used as a means of establishing pleasant social contact with the infant in a contented state; on other occasions it is used to 'figure out' what is going on with a fussy or distressed baby. Still another use of the eye-to-eye exchange is to activate a placid infant or calm a fussy one. In the latter case, it is interesting that a baby who is mildly upset can be quieted through eye-contact and the concomitant caretaking behaviours, but an infant who is fussing or crying either averts his gaze or, if he makes contact, often becomes more upset.

In all of these examples an observer senses an emotional 'climate' that is specifically apparent through the mother's facial expression. One sees a range of this behaviour: some mothers maintain a fixed and flat expression, others a fixed but unconvincing smile, and still others a highly animated face that reflects joy, anger, or anxiety. There is little data on the capacity of infants to perceive such differences, but both Benjamin [7] and Meili [31] note that from the fourth month onward, i.e. when the mother's face begins to be differentiated from others, infants are particularly sensitive to changes in the upper portion of her face. A sober maternal demeanour can produce a fearful reaction in the infant. Ahrens [1] observed that around the fifth month responsiveness to eyes diminishes and the mouth becomes more effective in eliciting smiling and attention. But after the mouth, the baby's eyes invariably fixate the eyes of an observer or a stylized 'dummy' face, and if the gaze of the former is averted or the eyes of the latter are missing, the smiling ceases.

One could easily rate the degree of animation of the maternal face. However, whether a mother modulates her expression to the particular circumstances of the infant so as to reassure rather than disrupt, or quiet rather than prolong distress, is also a critical dimension of the eye-to-eye exchange that should strongly influence the quality of the infant's face-tie. In optimal circumstances all three dimensions of contingent maternal behaviour should function in parallel, but they can and often do operate quite independently of one another.

For a particular infant one would like to dimensionalize the infant and maternal variables in predicting the intensity and quality of the face-tie. Yet, even then one is hard put to determine the direction of effects; that is, to what extent maternal behaviours are influenced by infant character-istics and vice versa. Currently, the work of Kagan and his associates [22, 23, 24, 28] offers a paradigm in which some of these dimensions can be assessed under laboratory conditions. Fixation time, frequency of smiling and vocalization, and cardiac deceleration to the presentation of face stimuli, have already proven to be differentiating measures. Even more productive

would be a combination of such studies with antecedent observations of the mother–infant pair from birth on-wards.

In any event, if the face-tie is not established, or if its quality fosters disruption and distress, the infant will experience varying degrees of inter-ference in forming his earliest—and probably future—human relation-ships.

References

1. AHRENS, R. (1954). Beitrag zur ent-wicklung des physiognomie und mimikerkennens. *Z. exp. angew. Psychol.* **2**, 412–54.
2. ALMANSI, R. J. (1960). The face–breast equation. *J. Am. psycho-anal. Ass.* **8**, 43–70.
3. AMBROSE, J. A. (1961). The develop-ment of the smiling response in early infancy. *In* (Foss, B. M. (Ed.)) *Determinants of infant behaviour.* Vol. II. Wiley, New York, 179–201.
4. ANDREW, R. J. (1965). The origins of facial expressions. *Scient. Amer.* **213**, 88–94.
5. ARGYLE, M. and DEAN, J. (1965). Eye contact, distance and affiliation. *Sociometry* **28**, 289–304.
6. BENJAMIN, J. D. (1959). Prediction and psychopathological theory. *In* (Jess-ner, L. and Pavenstedt, E.) *The psychopathology of childhood.* Grune and Stratton, New York.
7. —— (1963). Further comments on some developmental aspects of anxi-ety. *In* (Gaskill, H. (Ed.)) *Counter-point.* Int. Univ. Press, New York.
8. BOWLBY, J. (1958). The nature of the child's tie to his mother. *Int. J. Psycho-anal.* **39**, 350–73.
9. BURLINGHAM, D. (1964). Hearing and its role in the development of the blind. *Psycho-anal. Study Child* **19**, 95–112.
10. EXLINE, R. V. (1963). Explorations in the process of person perception: Visual interaction in relation to

competition, sex, and need for affiliation. *J. Personality* **31**, 1–20.
11. —— and WINTERS, L. (1965). The effects of cognitive difficulty and cognitive style upon eye-to-eye contact in interviews. Paper read at Eastern Psychological Association, Atlantic City.
12. FANTZ, R. L. (1958). Pattern vision in young infants. *Psychol. Rec.* **8**, 43–57.
13. FRAIBERG, S. and FREEDMAN, D. A. (1964). Studies in the ego develop-ment of the congenitally blind child. *Psycho-anal. Study Child* **19**, 113–69.
14. FREEDMAN, D. G. (1964). Smiling in blind infants and the issue of innate versus acquired. *J. Child. Psychol. Psychiat.* **5**, 171–84.
15. —— (1965). Hereditary control of early social behaviour. *In* (Foss, B. M. (Ed.)) *Determinants of infant behaviour.* Vol. III. Wiley, New York, 149–59.
16. GEWIRTZ, J. L. (1961). A learning analysis of the effects of normal stimulation, privation and depriva-tion on the acquisition of social motivation and attachment. *In* (Foss, B. M. (Ed.)) *Determinants of infant behaviour.* Vol. I. Wiley, New York, 213–99.
17. GOLDSTEIN, A. G. and MACKENBERG, E. J. (1966). Recognition of human faces from isolated facial features: a developmental study. *Psychon. Sci.* **6**, 149–50.
18. GREENMAN, G. W. (1963). Visual

behaviour of newborn infants. *In* (Solnit, A. and Provence, S. (Eds.)) *Modern perspectives in child development.* International Universities Press, New York.

19. HARLOW, H. F. (1961). The development of affectional patterns in infant monkeys. *In* (Foss, B. M. (Ed.)) *Determinants of infant behaviour.* Vol. I. Wiley, New York, 75–88.

20. HUTT, C. and OUNSTED, C. (1966). The biological significance of gaze aversion with particular reference to the syndrome of infantile autism. *Behav. Sci.* **11**, 346–56.

21. ISAKOWER, O. (1938). A contribution to the patho-psychology of phenomena associated with falling asleep. *Int. J. Psycho-anal.* **19**, 331–45.

22. KAGAN, J. (1965). The growth of the 'face' schema: theoretical significance and methodological issues. Paper presented at the annual meeting of the American Psychological Association, Chicago.

23. —— and LEWIS, M. (1965). Studies of attention in the human infant. *Merrill-Palmer Quart.* **11**, 95–127.

24. —— HENKER, B., HEN-TOV, A., LEVINE, J., and LEWIS, M. (1966). Infant's differential reactions to familiar and distorted faces. *Child Dev.* **37**, 519–32.

25. KAILA, E. (1935). Die reaktionen des sauglings auf des menschliche gesicht. *Z. Psychol.* **135**, 156–63.

26. KANNER, L. (1949). Early infantile autism. *Am. J. Orthopsychiat.* **19**, 416.

27. LEWIN, B. (1950). *The psychoanalysis of elation.* Norton, New York.

28. LEWIS, M., KAGAN, J., and KALAFAT, J. (1966). Patterns of fixation in the young infant. *Child Dev.* **37**, 331–41.

29. LORENZ, K. (1953). *Man meets dog* (translated by M. Wilson). Penguin Books, Baltimore.

30. —— (1966). *On aggression* (translated by M. Wilson). Harcourt, Brace, and World, New York.

31. MEILI, R. (1957). *Anfange der Charakterentwicklung.* Huber, Stuttgart.

32. NAGERA, H. and COLONNA, A. B. (1965). Aspects of the contribution of sight to ego and drive development. *Psycho-anal. Study Child* **20**, 267–87.

33. RHEINGOLD, H. L. (1961). The effect of environmental stimulation upon social and exploratory behaviour in the human infant. *In* (Foss, B. M. (Ed.)) *Determinants of infant behaviour.* Vol. I. Wiley, New York, 153–77.

34. ROSENBLATT, J. S. (1965). The basis of synchrony in the behavioural interaction between the mother and her offspring in the laboratory rat. *In* (Foss, B. M. (Ed.)) *Determinants of infant behaviour.* Vol. III. Wiley, New York, 3–45.

35. SANDLER, A.-M. (1953). Aspects of passivity and ego development in a blind infant. *Psycho-anal. Study Child* **18**, 343–60.

36. SCHAFFER, H. R. and EMERSON, P. E. (1964). *The development of social attachments in infancy.* Monog. No. 94, Vol. 29, Society for Research in Child Development.

37. —— and EMERSON, P. E. (1964). Patterns of response to physical contact in early human development. *J. Child Psychol. Psychiat.* **5**, 1–13.

38. SHAPIRO, T. and STINE, J. (1965). The figure drawings of 3-year-old children. *Psycho-anal. Study Child* **20**, 298–309.

39. SPITZ, R. A. (1946). Anaclitic depression: an enquiry into the genesis of psychiatric conditions in early childhood. *Psycho-anal. Study Child* **2**, 313–42.

40. —— (1950). Anxiety in infancy: a study of its manifestations in the first year of life. *Int. J. Psycho-anal.* **31**, 138–43.

41. —— (1955). The primal cavity: a contribution to the genesis of perception and its role for psychoanalytic theory. *Psycho-anal. Study Child* **10**, 215–40.

42. —— (1965). *The first year of life.* Inter-

national Universities Press, New York.

43. —— and WOLF, K. M. (1946). The smiling response. *Genet. Psychol. Monogr.* No. 34.

44. STECHLER, G. and LATZ, E. (1966). Some observations on attention and arousal in the human infant. *J. Am. Acad. child Psychiat.* **5**, 517–25.

45. SZEKELY, L. (1954). Biological remarks on fears originating in early childhood. *Int. J. Psycho-Anal.* **35**, 57–67.

46. WALTERS, R. H. and PARKE, R. D. (1965). The role of the distance receptors in the development of social responsiveness. *In* (Lipsitt, L. and Spiker, C. (Eds.)) *Advances in child development and behaviour.* Vol. 2. Academic Press, New York.

47. WATSON, J. S. (1965). Orientation-specific age changes in responsiveness to face stimulus in young infants. Paper presented at the annual meeting of the American Psychological Association, Chicago.

48. WHITE, B. L. and CASTLE, P. W. (1964). Visual exploratory behaviour following postnatal handling of human infants. *Percept. mot. Skills* **18**, 497–502.

49. —— —— and HELD, R. (1964). Observations on the development of visually directed reaching. *Child Dev.* **35**, 349–64.

50. WILLS, D. (1965). Some observations on blind nursery school children's understanding of their world. *Psycho-anal. Study Child* **20**, 344–64.

51. WOLFF, P. H. (1959). Observations on newborn infants. *Psychosom. Med.* **21**, 110–18.

52. —— (1963). Observations on the early development of smiling. *In* (Foss, B. M. (Ed.)) *Determinants of infant behaviour.* Vol. II. Wiley, New York, 113–38.

53. —— (1965). The development of attention in young infants. *Ann. N.Y. Acad. Sci.* **118**, 815–30.

54. —— and WHITE, B. L. (1965). Visual pursuit and attention in young infants. *J. Am. Acad. child Psychiat.* **4**, 473–84.

55. WOLFF, S. and CHESS, S. (1964). A behavioural study of schizophrenic children. *Acta. Psychiat. scand.* **40**, 438–66.

20

Temporal course of smiling

J. A. AMBROSE†

... THE smiling response in particular was selected for study because it was felt to be one of the various responses of an infant which clearly must perform a very significant function in this relationship. Also, as a jumping-off point in this area, it was felt to be an advantage to start with a response whose strength is relatively easily measurable and whose occurrence under natural conditions can be readily subject to some degree of control.

With regard to control it was apparent from previous studies, viz. those by Kaila and Spitz [3, 4], that smiling is elicited in the natural environment only by a very specific type of stimulation, namely the human face, at any rate from about 5 weeks of age; and that it remains subject to this external control for several months to come. These studies indicate that it is first elicited by the configurational property of any face and then after about the fifth month only by the faces of individuals who are not seen as strangers. More recently Ahrens [1] has shown how the effectiveness of various elements of the face in contributing to the elicitation of smiling grows only gradually over these

† From 'The development of the smiling response in early infancy'. In *Determinants of infant behaviour* (Foss, B. M. (Ed.)), Vol. I. Methuen, London (1959), pp. 179–201. Reprinted by permission of the Favistock Institute of Human Relations.

months, depending on the development of the infant's ability to fixate visually and to discriminate (Fig. 20.1).

These studies, however, were carried out largely on infants living in institutions separated from their mothers and, as the first analyses of the eliciting stimuli for smiling, they were concerned essentially only with whether the response did or did not occur to various different types of stimulation. The conception that responsiveness to external stimulation is much affected by the internal condition of the infant even in normal conditions is very little discussed; though it is acknowledged that the trends in smiling shown by the institutionalized infants studied probably occur somewhat later than with infants reared at home with their mothers. This one-sidedness resulted in little or no consideration being given to changes in response-strength: to measuring and explaining variations in this either between different individuals of the same age, or between the smiles of the same infant to a given stimulus on different occasions.

It was out of an interest in issues such as these that the results I wish to talk about now have come. ... The study was divided into three phases. In the first the aim was to see just how the smiling response varies once it has begun to occur in particular situations; and also how changes in other components of behaviour are related to these variations. This was done with institution infants because these provided greater initial freedom for exploration and experimental control. The second phase was concerned with how the smiling response changes over the weeks once it has become responsive to the face after about 6 weeks of age. The third phase involved a comparison of this long-term trend of smiling of institution infants with that of home infants.

From the outset it was known that one fact which causes variation in smiling during a social interaction is change in the external stimulus situa-

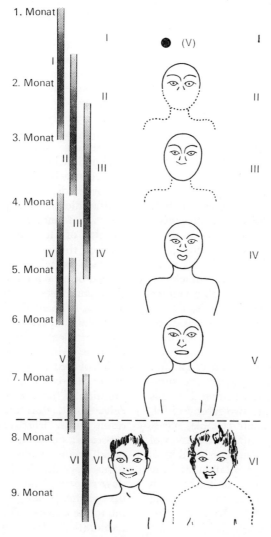

FIG. 20.1. Necessary and sufficient conditions for evoking smiling in infants up to eight months.

tion, and especially in the face being smiled at. This was clear from the work of Ahrens, which shows that the extent of the face exposed, the expression on it, and whether it is still or moving, do have an effect; although just how much effect at particular ages he did not study in detail. It was obvious therefore that, if variations in smiling other than those due merely to change in external stimulation were to be shown up, it would be necessary to standardize as far as possible the stimulus situation used for eliciting smiling. This was done, not by using masks, but by myself, as the observer, presenting my face to the infants as they lay in their cots after the lunch-time feed, and standing motionless beside the cot at a given distance of 4 ft from the infant and without smiling at him. Using this more or less constant stimulus with each infant studied, I observed his smiling for successive periods of half a minute at a time. These were interspersed with half-minute intervals during which I went to the other side of the cubicle or room and recorded the observations made during the previous half-minute. Such a series of stimulus presentations was continued either until smiling died out or until twelve successive presentations had been made, i.e. over 12 min.

... With regard to the measurement of smiling, it was found in this first phase that the two most fruitful, as well as adequately reliable, measures were the cumulative duration of smiling per half-minute, referred to as smiling time per presentation, and the latency of the first smile in each presentation, referred to as smiling latency. These both have a large range and are highly sensitive to any changes which take place outside or inside the infant. They are related to

each other, not directly, but in a special way that I will describe later, since it is of great interest for the interpretation of the long-term trends of smiling. The other two measures, rate of smiling and average breadth of smiling, were directly related to the smiling time measure and to each other, but as their range of variation was very much smaller they were not nearly so revealing. The measure 'smiling-time per presentation' was therefore used as the main indicator of the response-strength of smiling over a half-minute period.

The most general finding concerning this, in the standardized stimulus situation, was that over a run of such half-minute stimulus presentations smiling time nearly always commences at a relatively high level and, as the run proceeds, gradually declines until it either dies out or reaches a low level. This was found, for example, with a sample of ten institution infants between the ages of 13 and 26 weeks on each of whom three runs were carried out, each on different days. In all 30 runs response-strength waned in this way (Fig. 20.2). This waning may be explained partly in terms of habituation, or a learning not to respond to a stimulus which is not reinforcing, which of course is one of the characteristics of the constant standard stimulus situation. I have evidence, however, (Fig. 20.3), that the waning is the result of at least two decremental processes: one of these is subject to rapid recovery and is probably response-specific, the other is subject to slow recovery and is probably stimulus-specific. Strictly speaking, according to the usage of Thorpe and Hinde, habituation refers only to the second of these.

This phenomenon of response-wan-

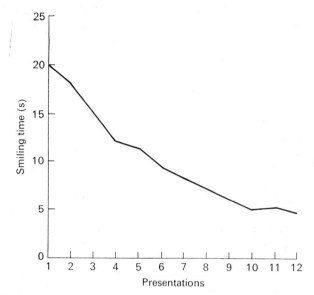

FIG. 20.2. Vincent curve of waning of smiling-time per presentation over a run. Sample of ten institutionalized infants. Three runs carried out on each, on different days.

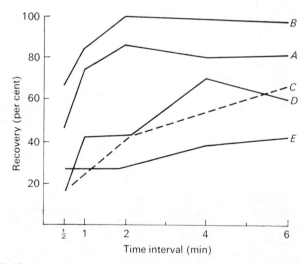

FIG. 20.3. Individual curves showing extent of recovery of smiling time with time interval for sample of five infants: smiling time per second series of five presentations as a percentage of that of first series, in relation to time interval between the two series. (Five infants: A, B, C, D, and E.)

ing over a run provided the basis for measuring variations in the response-strength of smiling over a long-term period of weeks. For at the point of complete waning the infant has ceased to smile not because of any change in the external stimulus situation but because of changes that have gone on inside him. If the smiling time of each presentation in a run is summed, this provides a measure called 'smiling-time per run'. This indicates the total amount of smiling which the infant is able to manifest in the particular situation at the particular time. It is the variation in the values of this measure over the weeks between the second and eighth months of life that I now want to consider.

In the second phase of the study a cross-sectional approach was used with institution infants with the object of measuring the response-strength of smiling of infants at varying ages between 8 and 26 weeks. In order to be sure that the level of response-strength would be uninfluenced by an infant having seen me on any previous occasion I measured smiling time on the first occasion on which I saw him. Using a sample of 48 infants I divided these into groups of 8, at 3-weekly age periods, 8–11 weeks, 11–14 weeks, and so on up to 26 weeks. The smiling time for the first run on each infant was taken and the average value and scatter for each age-group then calculated. These results were (Fig. 20.4) as follows. The youngest group showed no smiling at all. In the 11–14-week group hardly any infants smiled and the average smiling-time per run was only 0·1 s. From that age-group upwards all smiled, and the average values were: in the 14–17-week group, $9\frac{1}{2}$ s; in the 17–20-week group, a peak of $32\frac{1}{2}$ s; in the 20–23-week group

there was a decline to $29\frac{1}{2}$ s; and in the 23–26-week group it was down to $10\frac{1}{2}$ s. Another group in the 30–33-week age range, studied later, all showed no smiling whatever. There was a significant difference in group values between all groups except between the 17–20-week and 20–23-week groups. For institution infants, therefore, once smiling begins to occur in the experimental situation, it increases in response-strength over the weeks until it reaches a peak somewhere in the period 17–23 weeks, and then declines to reach a low level by 30 weeks.

In the third phase Mrs. Bernstein† set out primarily to compare the long-term trend of smiling of institution infants, in the experimental situation, with that shown by infants living at home with their mothers. For this purpose she used a longitudinal approach. Practical difficulties limited the number observed to four institutionalized infants and four home infants. Using her own face to elicit smiling, she adopted exactly the same method of standardized stimulation as had been used by me. This was carried out at weekly intervals between the ages of 6 and 36 weeks for all except two institution infants who could not be continued beyond 20 weeks.

. . . We will turn now to the main comparison of the long-term trends of smiling response-strength for the institution and the home infants. It was found that by and large the form of the trends was similar but that the equivalent characteristics of each trend occur significantly earlier in the case of the home sample than with the institution sample (Figs. 20.5 and 6). Thus smiling in the experimental situation starts earlier with the home infants: for them it starts within the 6–10-week range

† Dr. Ambrose's collaborator (Ed.).

compared with the 9–14-week range for the institution infants. The increase in response-strength reaches a peak earlier as well: whereas for the institution infants it occurs within the range 16–20 weeks, with the home infants it is between 11 and 14 weeks. Once this peak has been reached, in both groups response-strength declines to a low level. Thenceforth in individual cases it either remains low or else recovers to

First, let us take the general increase in response-strength of smiling over the weeks, from the time when it first begins to occur in the experimental situation to the time when it reaches a peak. Light is thrown on this by an experiment by Brackbill. . . . The effect of her responding to the infants was to bring about a gradual increase in the response-strength of smiling, measured by her in terms of the rate of

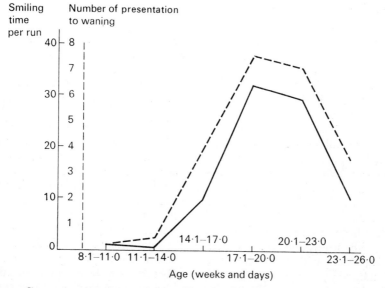

Fig. 20.4. Curve showing the average smiling-time per first run for each sub-sample of eight institutionalized infants in three-week age ranges from 8 weeks to 26 weeks. The dotted curve shows the average number of presentations to waning involved in the runs of each sub-sample.

some extent, though rarely to the level reached at the earlier peak.

Now how should we account for these findings, both the general trends and the differences shown in them between infants living in institutions and those living at home with their mothers? What light do they throw on the processes affecting the smiling of infants in real-life situations over these months? . . .

responding. The effect of her remaining unresponsive, however, was that the rate of smiling gradually declined until eventually the response died out. (She also found that smiling back, picking up the infant, etc., had a reinforcing effect even when carried out irregularly, e.g. at every fourth smile of the infant, and that with the infants treated in this way the response took much longer to extinguish.) It seems probable, therefore, that the increase in response-strength observed in both institution and home infants in our own experimental situation is to be explained in terms of such instrumental conditioning. This, of course, does not take place during the experiment itself but during the natural everyday life of the infant when he smiles at the mother-figure or figures who are caring for him. What is to be seen in the experimental situation are the effects of this natural reinforcement by the mother-figure being generalized on to the face of the experimenter. It seems that during this period of response-increase the faces of people other than the mother-figure are hardly or not at all discriminated by the infant, so that the expectations he learns in relation to the one face are generalized to all other faces. The peak to which the increasing trend of response-strength rises appears to mark the time at which such generalization ceases and discrimination begins.

What then is happening after the peak has been reached (at about 20 weeks with institution infants and about 13 weeks with home infants), when the trend of smiling in the experimental situation gradually declines? There is no reason to suppose that response-strength of smiling to the mother-figure begins to decline at this stage. . . . The decline of response-strength with increasing age in our experimental situation points unmistakably to the infant being able to discriminate between the face of the experimenter and that of the mother-figure. Now, it might be thought that the decline in response-strength is due to the fact that once this discrimination begins the experimenter comes to be seen as a stranger. This view would accord with that of most previous observers who have attributed the lack of smiling to strangers from about 5 or 6 months of age to a fear of strangers. In my opinion, however, the falling-off of smiling occurring in our experiments is not necessarily due either to fear or to strangeness in all cases. Our evidence suggests that it is more complicated than this.

I have already mentioned Mrs. Bernstein's finding that by 26 weeks, and probably before, the smiling of an infant at her is affected by his having learned not to respond to her the week previously. In other words, by this age, although she is discriminated from the mother-figure, she is not seen as a complete stranger. Yet in some cases the more weeks she continues to see the infant, and therefore the less strange she becomes, the less the infant smiles at her. What seems to be happening here is that, as the weekly runs are carried out, the process of learning not to respond to her each week comes to be associated specifically with her face, discriminated as a non-reinforcing one, so that eventually the infant may not smile at her at all even at the beginning of a run. The effect seems to be a long-term process of learning not to respond to a specific non-reinforcing stimulus. This is what I referred to earlier as habituation.

Nevertheless, there is evidence that the waning of the response during this age-period is not dependent only on a learning over the weeks that some particular face or person, viz. Mrs. Bernstein, is non-reinforcing in her behaviour. Thus, in the sample observed by me cross-sectionally, the 23–26-week age-group showed a significantly much lower response-strength than did the next younger group aged 20–23 weeks. Since no infant of either group had seen me before, the lower

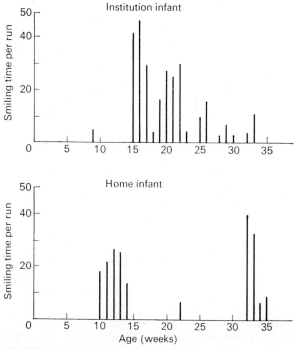

FIG. 20.5. Examples of long-term trends of smiling response-strength of individual infants responding to the face of the experimenter. Whereas the first peak of response-strength is reached at about 16 weeks or later in institutionalized infants, it is reached significantly earlier at about 13 weeks in home infants.

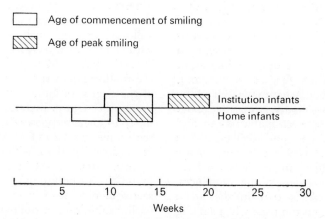

FIG. 20.6. Age-range of commencement of smiling and of peak response-strength in the experimental situation for samples of institution and home infants.

response-strength cannot have been due to their having learned in previous weeks that I was a non-reinforcing stimulus. It appears, therefore, that any face which is discriminated as different from that of the mother-figure in this period elicits smiling at lower response-strength simply by virtue of the fact that it is different. If this is so, it rather suggests that the lower smiling response-strength to me in this period is not due solely to my failure to respond to the infants during a run by behaviour of the sort which Brackbill [2] has shown to be re-inforcing. Instead, it seems, the dis-crimination of a face as being not that of the mother-figure may in itself be non-reinforcing. If this is so, it raises the question of whether perhaps the mere sight of the face of his mother-figure (or figures) has a re-inforcing effect, of itself. What I am suggesting is that the mere sight of the face of the mother-figure may come to have re-inforcing effects for an infant simply because it has become familiar to him over the weeks and not just because it is associated with being smiled back at and picked up. . . . Finally, I would like to consider why it is that the peak smiling-time per run is so much later for our samples of institu-tion infants, at around 20 weeks, than it is for the sample of home infants, at around 13 weeks (Figs. 20.5 and 20.6). Such consideration is made difficult by our lack of systematic knowledge about differences between maternal care and institutional care and their effects; as a result it is based at this stage mainly on two clinical impressions we have had regarding some of the differences. One of these is that in the home situation, from the time when smiling starts to occur to the face, it is both more frequently elicited and also re-inforced at a higher rate. From this at least, two consequences seem to follow. One is that with maternal care instrumental conditioning of smiling is likely to proceed at a faster rate than with institutional care and conse-quently the response-strength increases more rapidly. The other consequence is that with maternal-care condition-ing of the classical variety probably also takes place more rapidly than with institutional care, with the result that there is a more rapid learning of the characteristics of the face or faces which elicit smiling. If this is so, it means that the stage when relatively small details of the face are discrimin-ated will be achieved earlier. As a result it may be expected that the discrimination of faces as being differ-ent from that of the mother-figure will occur sooner with home infants.

The second difference between home and institution infants which must also contribute to the difference in peak smiling age is the fact that institution infants usually have many mother-figures and not just one or two. Now, if it is the case that with home infants discrimination between different faces commences earlier, then at any given age after this they will have become much more familiar with one face. In so far as the strange-ness of any face different from that of the mother-figure is partly a function of the degree of familiarity of that of the mother-figure, then such a face is likely to elicit responses incompatible with smiling, such as fear or curiosity, more strongly than with institution infants. Mrs. Bernstein has in fact found this to be the case, and so this seems to be a further reason for the earlier inhibition of smiling to people other than the mother-figure in the case of home infants. . . .

References

1. AHRENS, R. (1954). Beitrag zur Ent- wicklung des Physiognomie und Mimikerkennens. *Z. exp. angew. Psy- chol.* II, **3**, 412–54; II, **4**, 599–633.

2. BRACKBILL, Y. (1958). Extinction of the smiling response in infants as a func- tion of reinforcement schedule. *Child Dev.* **29**, 115–24.

3. KAILA, E. (1932). Die Reaktionen des Sanglings auf das Menschliche Ges- icht. *Ann. Univ. Aboensin. B. Humaniana.*

4. SPITZ, R. and WOLF, K. M. (1946). The smiling response: a contribution to the ontogenesis of social relations. *Genet. Psychol. Monogr.* **34**, 57–125.

Effects of early experience

WORK upon the effects of early experience has become one of the most rapidly advancing areas of psychology. Relatively little of this work has been carried out on humans and the degree to which the animal findings have any relevance to the development of human infants remains a matter of controversy. Studies of early experience may be classified in three ways. First, we may distinguish between those studies in which stimulation is applied from those in which it is withheld. Humanitarian considerations have generally precluded studies of the first type from being carried out on Man, so that until fairly recently, the validity of extrapolating findings from sub-human species to human infants has had to depend, at best, upon anthropological studies of diverse infant-rearing practices (e.g. [6, 10]), or at worst, upon anecdotes from Dr. Spock [5]. Unhappily, the need to provide for our social casualties in institutions has meant an abundant supply of research material on the effects of stimulus deprivation. Studies based upon this material have been generally more informative sociologically than biologically.

Secondly, we may classify according to whether the stimulation applied or withheld is specific or non-specific. In the case of stimulus application, this distinction generally refers to whether the stimulation is patterned or unpatterned. An example of the former would be provided by White and Held's [15] study of the effects of perceptual enrichment, while the same group's study of the effects of handling [16] would be an example of the latter. In the case of stimulus deprivation, separation from the mother would be an example of specific deprivation, while perceptual isolation would be an example of non-specific deprivation. This distinction is not very vigorous since the effects of one—maternal deprivation—have frequently been explained in terms of the other, perceptual deprivation. Moreover, perceptual deprivation is itself a relative term. Even the most impoverished early environments cannot be compared with the perceptual deprivation experiment.

Thirdly, studies may be classified in relation to the stage in ontogeny at which the subject is exposed to the particular experience in question. In Part III, Bronson identified three critical (or sensitive) periods circumscribed by the attainment of functional maturity at three levels of the central nervous system: level I (brain-stem) birth to one month; level II (sub-cortical forebrain) 2 to 6 months; level III (neocortex) 7 months onwards. Unfortunately, most studies of human infants cut across the boundaries between these three periods. Nevertheless, it may be conceptually helpful if we use Bronson's time scale as an heuristic framework.

Most work on the effects of early experience in humans has been concerned with institutionalization. The earliest studies, whose theoretical orientation was generally psycho-analytic, claimed that the roots of severe personality disorders and defective intelligence observed in institutionalized children, could be traced to the absence of a warm, loving relationship with a mother-figure in early life. These early studies were reviewed by Bowlby [2] in an important and influential monograph, an extract from which is included here (Chap. 21). Unfortunately, many of these studies were so redolent with methodological flaws, that it is often extremely difficult to isolate effects which reasonably may be attributed to maternal separation as opposed to other factors. (For critical reviews of these early studies, see [4, 11, 17].) It is a credit to Bowlby that he was one of the first to admit his overstatement of the case for maternal deprivation [2]. Several authors, such as Schaffer (Chap. 22) have suggested that the critical variable in institutionalization is relative deprivation of *perceptual stimulation* and that, at least in the first 6 months of life, it is in the provision of such stimulation, rather than in providing 'loving care' that mothering lies. In any case, the long term effects of institutionalization may be much more reversible, at least in the intellectual sphere, than has hitherto been suspected.

A most illuminating study by Dennis and Najarian (Chap. 23) of children brought up in two contrasting institutions in Beirut—one providing little perceptual stimulation in the traditional manner of such places, the other, with a higher caretaker/child ratio, offering much more variety of perceptual experience—showed that the sensory-motor deficits apparent at an early age in the truly institutionalized children appeared to be largely overcome by late childhood. In fact no *cognitive* deficit as such, was demonstrable in those children who were maternally deprived. There was much less cause for sanguinity with respect to their subsequent social adjustment. This is very much the situation which obtains with monkeys deprived of their mothers and peers in infancy [7–9]. It appears then that the absence of a suitable figure with whom an attachment bond may be formed results in damage to the personality but does not necessarily impair cognitive or learning abilities.

The functional equivalence often implied between 'arousing' experiences such as electric shock, and 'de-arousing' ones such as gentling [13] presents a particularly difficult problem of interpretation with respect to human infants. Is the maternal role one of producing gradual habituation to stressful stimuli in the pre-weaning period [14], or one of exposing the child to variable visual, and other stimulation [15], or both? And if both, are the two roles performed simultaneously? Korner and Grobstein (Chap. 24) are among the few authors who have acknowledged these questions. Their paper shows that at the time when level I networks are relatively more mature than higher levels of the nervous system, tactile contact between adult and child has effects (upon oculo-motor control) which are different from mere handling. It would appear that beneficial effects, in terms of increased visual alertness are associated with 'soothing' mothering experiences, or what in the previous section we categorized as 'de-arousing experiences'. From the second month of life, it seems that stimulation, more similar to that employed by animal workers, may have beneficial effects upon behavioural development. This is demonstrated by Casler's study [3] of the effects of tactile stimulation. It seems reasonable to suppose that such stimulation plays an important role in the development of level II networks, and the observation that postural and reflex development (largely midbrain functions) were not significantly affected by the stimulation procedure is especially pertinent. It is of interest that in White and Held's study [15] of the effects of 'enrichment', the babies who were exposed to a complex visual stimulus showed significantly greater visual alertness than controls only towards the end of this critical period. With the rapid increase in the maturity of the visual cortex level III networks from about the sixth month we would expect the infant to become more sensitive to the effects of visual novelty. Sayegh and Dennis [12] show that institutionalized infants of 7 months or more who are trained to engage in visual and manipulatory exploration of objects, gain more in developmental quotient over a one-month period than control subjects. As the authors admit, however, the study was not free from experimental contamination. Taking the last three papers in conjunction, there is some evidence: (1) that the kinds of stimulation to which babies are maximally sensitive differs according to age; and (2) that these differences correspond with 'critical periods' in neurological development. Bronson's (Chap. 8) conceptual model of the organization of the developing nervous system may be seen to perform an invaluable function in enabling an evaluation of the significance of particular experiences at different periods in ontogeny depending upon the functional maturity of cerebral structures at the time.

References

1. AINSWORTH, M. D. (1962). *The effects of maternal deprivation: a review of findings and controversy in the context of research strategy.* World Health Organization, Geneva.

2. BOWLBY, J. (1952). *Maternal care and mental health.* World Health Organization, Geneva.

3. CASLER, L. (1965). The effects of extra tactile stimulation on a group of institutionalized infants. *Genet. psychol. Monogr.* **71**, 137–75.

4. —— (1968). Perceptual deprivation in institutional settings. *In* (Newton, G. and Levine, S. (Eds.)) *Early experience and behavior.* Charles C. Thomas, Ill.

5. DENENBERG, V. H. (1966). Animal

studies on developmental determinants of behavioural adaptability. *In* (Harvey, O. J. (Ed.)) *Experience, structure, and adaptability.* Springer, New York.

6. GEBER, M. and DEAN, R. F. A. (1957). Gesell tests on African children. *Pediatrics* **20**, 1055–65.

7. HARLOW, H. F. (1961). The development of affectional patterns in infant monkeys. *In* (Foss, B. M. (Ed.)) *Determinants of infant behaviour.* Vol. I. Methuen, London.

8. —— (1962). Development of affection in primates. *In* (Bliss, E. L. (Ed.)) *Roots of behaviour.* Harper, New York.

9. —— HARLOW, M. K., and HANSEN, E. W. (1963). The maternal affectional system of rhesus monkeys. *In* (Rheingold, H. O. (Ed.)) *Maternal behavior in mammals.* Wiley, New York.

10. LANDAUER, T. J. and WHITING, J. N. M. (1954). Infantile stimulation and adult stature of human males. *Am. Anthrop.* **66**, 1007–28.

11. PINNEAU, S. R. (1955). The infantile disorders of hospitalism and anaclitic depression. *Psychol. Bull.* **52**, 429–62.

12. SAYEGH, Y. and DENNIS, W. (1965). The effect of supplementary experiences upon the behavioral development of infants in institutions. *Child Dev.* **36**, 81–90.

13. SCHAEFER, T. (1968). Some methodological implications of the research on 'early handling' in the rat. *In* (Newton, G. and Levine, S. (Eds.)) *Early experience and behavior.* Charles C. Thomas, Ill.

14. THOMPSON, W. R. and GRUSEC, J. (1970). Studies of early experience. *In* (Mussen, P. H. (Ed.)) *Carmichael's handbook of child psychology.* Wiley, New York.

15. WHITE, B. L. and HELD, R. (1966). Plasticity of sensorimotor development in the human infant. *In* (Rosenblith, J. F. and Allinsmith, W. (Eds.)) *The causes of behavior.* Vol. II. Allyn and Bacon, Boxton.

16. —— and CASTLE, P. W. (1964). Visual exploratory behavior following postnatal handling of human infants. *Percept. mot. Skills,* **18**, 497–502.

17. YARROW, L. J. (1961). Maternal deprivation: toward an empirical and conceptual re-evaluation. *Psychol. Bull* **58**, 459–90.

21

Maternal deprivation

J. BOWLBY†

Direct studies

Classes of evidence

Evidence that the deprivation of mother-love in early childhood can have a far-reaching effect on the mental health and personality development of human beings comes from many sources. It falls into three main classes:

(1) Studies, by direct observation, of the mental health and development of children in institutions, hospitals, and foster-homes—direct studies.

(2) Studies which investigate the early histories of adolescents or adults who have developed psychological illnesses—retrospective studies.

(3) Studies which follow up groups of children who have suffered deprivation in their early years with a view to determining their state of mental health—follow-up studies.

The extent to which these studies, undertaken by people of many nations, varied training and, as often as not, ignorant of each others' conclusions, confirm and support each other is impressive. What each individual

† From 'Review of evidence on effects of deprivation'. In *Maternal care and mental health.* World Health Organization, Geneva Monograph Series, No. 2 (1952). Reprinted by permission of the World Health Organization.

piece of work lacks in thoroughness, scientific reliability, or precision is largely made good by the concordance of the whole. Nothing in scientific method carries more weight than this. Divergent voices are few. Indeed, only three have come to light, all follow-up studies, but of a quality which bears no comparison with that of the research the conclusions of which they challenge.

The direct studies are the most numerous. They make it plain that, when deprived of maternal care, the child's development is almost always retarded—physically, intellectually, and socially—and that symptoms of physical and mental illness may appear. Such evidence is disquieting, but sceptics may question whether the retardation is permanent and whether the symptoms of illness may not easily be overcome. The retrospective and follow-up studies make it clear that such optimism is not always justified and that some children are gravely damaged for life. This is a sombre conclusion which must now be regarded as established.

There are, however, important features of the situation about which little is known. For instance, it is by no means clear why some children succumb and some do not. It may be that hereditary factors play a part, but, before resorting to a principle which has been so readily invoked as a universal solvent of biological problems, it is important to review what is known of the effects of such factors as the child's age, and the length and, especially, the degree of his deprivation, each of which there is reason to think is vital.

The three classes of evidence will now be reviewed, attention being paid throughout to data which may help towards an understanding of the role played by these three factors.

Direct studies

Direct observations of the ill-effects on young children of complete deprivation of maternal care have been made by a large number of paediatricians, psychologists, and child psychiatrists and have shown that the child's development may be affected physically, intellectually, emotionally, and socially. All children under about 7 years of age seem to be vulnerable and some of the effects are clearly discernible within the first few weeks of life.

Bakwin [2, 3] and Ribble [29] have each given detailed accounts of the adverse effects on physical health. Bakwin [3], who gives a valuable survey of the paediatric literature on the subject which goes back at least to 1909, summarizes his own observations thus:

Infants under 6 months of age who have been in an institution for some time present a well-defined picture. The outstanding features are listlessness, emaciation and pallor, relative immobility, quietness, unresponsiveness to stimuli like a smile or a coo, indifferent appetite, failure to gain weight properly despite the ingestion of diets which, in the home, are entirely adequate, frequent stools, poor sleep, an appearance of unhappiness, proneness to febrile episodes, absence of sucking habits.

These changes, he remarks, are not observable in the first 2–4 weeks of life, but can be seen any time thereafter, sometimes within a few days of the baby's separation from his mother. The failure of such babies to smile at the sight of a human face has been confirmed experimentally by Spitz and Wolf [33] while Gesell and Amatruda [13] have noted a diminished interest and reactivity to be characteristic as early as 8–12 weeks. A very careful study of the infant's babbling and crying by Brodbeck and Irwin [9] showed that babies from birth to 6 months in an orphanage were consistently less vocal than those in families, the difference being clearly discernible before 2 months of age. As will be seen, this backwardness in 'talking' is especially characteristic of the institution child of all ages.

This diverse evidence from reputable workers leaves no room for doubt that the development of the institution infant deviates from the norm at a very early age. If the regime is continued, the deviations become more pronounced. Gesell and Amatruda have listed their appearance. (See Table 21.1.)

Spitz [32], with Wolf, has more recently made a systematic study of the adverse effects which occur during the first year if the child is kept throughout in an institutional environment. They studied altogether four groups of children, in three of which the babies were with their mothers and one where they were not. Though the absolute levels of development, not unexpectedly, differed according to the social group the babies came from, there was on change of quotient during the year in the case of the babies, 103 in all, who lived with their mothers. The group of 61 brought up in an hygienic institution, on the other hand, showed a catastrophic drop of developmental quotient between the ages of 4 and 12 months. This shown in Table 21.2.

At the earlier age the average DQ was 124 and second in magnitude of the four groups. By 12 months it had

29 children aged from 6 months to $2\frac{1}{2}$ years (mostly 9 and 15 months) all of whom were awaiting adoption. All had been cared for by fostermothers; 15 with no other young children, the remainder with up to three others in the same foster-home. Those receiving all the foster-mother's attention were

TABLE 21.1. *Order of Appearance of Adverse Reactions in Institution Infants* (*Gesell and Amatruda*)

Adverse reactions	Time of appearance
Diminished interest and reactivity	8–12 weeks
Reduced integration of total behaviour	8–12 weeks
Beginning of retardation evidenced by disparity between exploitation in supine and in sitting positions	12–16 weeks
Excessive preoccupation with strange persons	12–16 weeks
General retardation (prone behaviour relatively unaffected)	24–28 weeks
Blandness of facial expression	24–28 weeks
Impoverished initiative	24–28 weeks
Channelization and stereotypies of sensori-motor behaviour	24–28 weeks
Ineptness in new social situations	44–48 weeks
Exaggerated resistance to new situations	48–52 weeks
Relative retardation in language behaviour	12–15 months

sunk to 72 and was by far the lowest. By the end of the second year it had sunk to 45. The last two figures indicate grave retardation.

In confirmation of earlier work, Spitz and Wolf's results show that most of the drop in DQ had taken place during the first 6 months of life.

It is true that these infants were living in conditions especially bad from the psychological point of view, as not only was there but one nurse to some 7 children, but, for reasons of hygiene, the children were kept restricted to cots and cubicles in what amounted to solitary confinement. However, studies such as those of Rheingold [28] and Levy [25] make it plain that retardation may occur in conditions which are far from being as adverse as these. Rheingold studied

on the average accelerated in development while those who had to share it with other babies were retarded to a statistically significant degree. Levy also studied infants awaiting adoption. Her main sample was composed of 122 babies, 83 cared for in an institution and 39 in foster-homes, all of whom had come into the agency's care within their first 2 months of life, and had been tested around 6 months of age. Those in the institution were in one large nursery, which had accommodation for 17 babies and was staffed by a total of 10 practical nurses, there never being fewer than two in attendance during the day. The DQs on Gesell tests are shown to be slightly above average for the foster-home children and slightly below for the institutionalized, a difference which is statistically significant. Unfortunately, neither Rheingold nor Levy give their results in a form comparable to those of Spitz and Wolf, but it is clear that the drop in DQ in Levy's institutional group is far less than that of the group studied by Spitz and Wolf, a result which no doubt reflects the better agreement between a number o different workers, among whom may be mentioned Gindl *et al.*, Goldfarb (who gave special attention to speech), Burlington and Freud, Simonsen, and Roudinesco and Appell.

Though there can be no mistaking the consistency of these findings, their

TABLE 21.2. *Mean Developmental Quotient of Infants at Beginning and End of First Year with Regard to Social Class and to Experience* (*Spitz*)

			Developmental quotient	
Social class	Presence or absence of mother	Number of cases	Average of 1st to 4th months	Average of 9th to 12th months
Unselected urban	absent	61	124	72
Professional	present	23	133	131
Peasant	present	11	107	108
Delinquent unmarried mothers	present	69	101·5	105

psychological conditions in which they lived.

So far only the over-all scores on tests of development (Hetzer-Bühler and Gesell) and of intelligence (Standford–Binet and Merrill–Palmer) have been used as criteria. Studies, however, show that not all aspects of development are equally affected. The least affected is neuromuscular development, including walking, other locomotor activities, and manual dexterity. The most affected is speech, the ability to express being more retarded than the ability to understand. (Speech retardation is sometimes made good remarkably quickly. Burlington and Freud [10] reporting that 'when children are home on visits . . . they sometimes gain in speech in one or two weeks what they would have taken 3 months to gain in the nursery'.) Midway in retardation between motor development and speech come social responses and what Gesell calls 'adaptivity'. Here again there is remarkable

import is frequently questioned on the grounds that many children in institutions are born of parents of poor stock, physically and mentally, and that heredity alone might well account for all the differences. Those who advance this objection do not seem to be aware that in the majority of the studies quoted care has been taken by the investigators to ensure that the control groups, brought up either in their own homes or in foster-homes, are of a similar social class and, as nearly as possible, spring from similar stock. Explicit data on this point are given by Brodbeck and Irwin [9], Levy [25], Spitz [32], and Goldfarb [21], while in the cases of Gindl *et al.* [14], Rheingold [28], Simonsen [31], and Roudinesco and Appell [30], sufficient care has been taken on the point to make it most improbable that heredity accounts for all the variation.

Positive evidence that the causative factor is maternal deprivation comes from innumerable sources. First, there are the very clear findings of Durfee and Wolf, of Spitz and Wolf, and of Roudinesco and Appell that the longer the deprivation, the lower falls the DQ. Secondly, there is experimental evidence that even if the child remains in the same institution, extra mothering from a substitute will diminish the ill-effects. Nearly twenty years ago Daniels studied two groups of two-year-olds living in the same institution. 'One group was given very little tenderness although adequately cared for in every other respect', while in the other 'a nurse was assigned to each child and there was no lack of tenderness and affection. At the end of half a year the first group was mentally and physically retarded, in comparison with the second'.†

Finally, there is the evidence of spectacular changes in the child's condition following restoration to his mother. Bakwin [2], after recording the views of the older generation of paediatricians, himself remarks:

The rapidity with which the symptoms of hospitalism begin to disappear when an afflicted baby is placed in a good home is amazing. It is convincing evidence of the etiologic relation of the emotionally arid atmosphere of the hospital to the symptoms. The baby promptly becomes more animated and responsive; fever, if present in the hospital, disappears in twenty-four to seventy-two hours; there is a gain in weight and an improvement in the colour.

The dramatic and tragic changes in behaviour and feeling which follow separation of the young child from his mother and the beneficent results of restoring him to her are in fact avail-

† Reported by Bühler in 1935. It is not clear whether in the second group each child had a separate nurse which the text implies, or whether each child was assigned to a nurse, which seems more likely.

able for all to see and it is astonishing that so little attention has been given to them hitherto. So painful, indeed, are the agonies which these children suffer on separation that it may well be that those who have their care shut their eyes in self-protection. Yet of their existence there can be no doubt, as distressingly similar pictures are given by numerous different investigators.

Bakwin's description of the typical separated infant—listless, quiet, unhappy, and unresponsive to a smile or a coo—has already been quoted. This clinical picture, in the age-range of 6–12 months, has been the subject of systematic study by Spitz and Wolf [33], who named it 'anaclitic depression'. And depression it undoubtedly is, having many of the hallmarks of the typical adult depressive patient of the mental hospital. The emotional tone is one of apprehension and sadness, there is a withdrawal from the environment amounting to rejection of it, there is no attempt to contact a stranger and no brightening if this stranger contacts him. Activities are retarded and the child often sits or lies inert in a dazed stupor. Insomnia is common and lack of appetite universal. Weight is lost and the child becomes prone to intercurrent infections. The drop in DQ is precipitous.

In what conditions, it may be asked, does this syndrome develop? In general, it is characteristic of infants who have had a happy relationship with their mothers up till 6 or 9 months and are then suddenly separated from them without an adequate substitute being provided. Of 95 children studied by Spitz and Wolf and on whom a diagnosis was made, twenty per cent reacted to separation by severe depression and another 27 per cent by mild depression making nearly 50 per cent in all.† Almost all those with a close and loving relation to their mothers suffered, which means that the depressive response to separation is a normal one at this age. The fact that a majority of those with unhappy relationships escaped indicates that their psychic development is already damaged and their later capacity for love likely to be impaired. The illness respected neither sex nor race—boys and girls, white and coloured, all being affected. Although recovery is rapid if the child is restored to his mother, the possibility of psychic scars which may later be reactivated cannot be disregarded, while, if the condition is permitted to continue, recovery is greatly impeded. Spitz and Wolf believe that there is a qualitative change after 3 months of deprivation, after which recovery is rarely, if ever, complete.

Spitz and Wolf report (verbal communication) that disturbances of development may also follow separation at an even earlier age. These disturbances are much less dramatic than in older babies and were at first described as 'mild depressions', but further observation made this term seem wholly inappropriate since it became evident that the condition was neither mild nor, in the view of Spitz and Wolf, could it properly be classified as depression. These disturbances, to which infants of the age-group 3–6 months are prone, are insidious in development and much less easily reversed by restoration to the mother.

† In the original paper another 28 children are shown as 'undiagnosed'. Subsequent study, it is understood, showed a large number of these cases to fall in the category of 'severe depression' so the figures quoted here are underestimates.

The DQ falls slowly but steadily (not precipitously as in the older babies), and recovery is only partial—perhaps 25–30 per cent of the drop—instead of almost complete.

These very adverse results, it must be emphasized, can be partially avoided during the first year of life by the children being mothered by a substitute. Hitherto many have thought that substitute care could be completely successful during most of this year. Ribble [29] has expressed doubts, however, and Spitz and Wolf (verbal communication) are now definitely of the opinion that damage is frequently done by changes even as early as three months. Nevertheless, all are agreed that substitute care, even if not wholly adequate, is indispensable and should on no account be withheld. In the second and third years of life, the emotional response to separation is not only just as severe but substitute mothers are often rejected out of hand, the child becoming acutely and inconsolably distressed for a period of days, a week, or even more, without a break. During much of this time he is in a state of agitated despair and either screaming or moaning. Food and comfort are alike refused. Only exhaustion brings sleep. After some days he becomes quieter and may relapse into apathy, from which he slowly emerges to make a more positive response to his strange environment. For some weeks or even months, however, he may show a serious regression to infantile modes of behaviour. He wets his bed, masturbates, gives up talking, and insists on being carried, so that the less experienced nurse may suppose him to be defective.‡

‡ Description based on unpublished observations of Robertson of the Tavistock Clinic, London.

Naturally there are very many variations of reaction in this age-group and not all children respond in the way described; and once again it appears to be the children who have had the most intimate and happy relationship with their mothers who suffer most. Those who have been brought up in institutions and have had no permanent mother-figure show no responses of this kind at all, the result of their affective life already having been damaged. Though the inexperienced nurse welcomes the child who regards one adult as being as good as another and criticizes the family baby who reacts violently as having been 'spoilt', all the evidence suggests that the violent reaction is normal and the apathetic resignation a sign of pathological development.

Retrospective and follow-up studies

Retrospective studies

Some of the immediately adverse effects of deprivation on young children and some of the short-term after-affects have now been discussed and note taken that those without training in mental health are apt either to deny the existence of such responses or to waive them aside as of no consequence. In this chapter, the tremendous weight of evidence will be reviewed which makes it clear that those who view these responses with concern, so far from 'crying wolf', are calling attention to matters of grave medical and social significance.

During the late 1930s and 1940s, at least six independent workers (Levy [25], Powdermaker *et al.* [27], Lowrey [26], Bowlby [6], Bender and Yarnell [5], and Goldfarb [16–18]) were struck by the frequency with which children who committed numerous delinquencies, who seemed to have no feelings for anyone and were very difficult to treat, were found to have had grossly disturbed relationships with their mothers in their early years. Persistent stealing, violence, egotism, and sexual misdemeanours were among their less pleasant characteristics. With monotonous regularity, each worker put his finger on the child's inability to make relationships as being the central feature from which all the other disturbances sprang, and on the history of institutionalization or, of the child's being shifted about from one foster-mother to another as being its cause.

Since these early communications there have been three major publications—a systematic clinical and statistical study by Bowlby [7, 8], a review by Bender [4] based on some hundreds of cases seen in the previous ten years, and a series of papers describing most carefully planned and executed research by Goldfarb [16–24]. Both Bender's and Bowlby's studies are retrospective in the sense that, as clinicians, they were called upon to examine and treat children showing neurotic symptoms and disturbances of behaviour and, by working back into the children's histories, unearthed the common factor of deprivation of maternal care—caused either by their being in institutions, or being posted, like parcels, from one mother-figure to another. The objection to these retrospective studies is, of course, that they are concerned only with children who have developed adversely, and fail to take account of those who may have had the same experience but have developed normally. This shortcoming, however, is made good in ample fashion by Goldfarb.

Bender's conclusions [4] are based

on the 5–10 per cent of the 5000 children whom she had under her care in Bellevue Hospital from 1935–1944 and who showed the characteristics already described. She gives a full

Bowlby [7, 8], besides giving fairly full case-histories, in some of which the child's response to the traumatic experience can be traced, lays especial emphasis on the tendency of these

TABLE 21.3. *Incidence of Separation and Affectionless Character in a Group of Thieves and a Control Group of Emotionally Disturbed Children Who Did Not Steal (Bowlby)*

	Thieves†			Controls
	Affectionless	Others	All	
Separation	12	5	17	2
No separation	2	25	27	42
Totals	14	30	44	44

† Both for the affectionless thieves versus the others, and for all the thieves versus controls, *P* is less than 0·01, which means that there is less than one chance in a hundred that the result is due to chance.

clinical description of the syndrome, which she terms 'psychopathic behaviour disorder of childhood'.

There is an inability to love or feel guilty. There is no conscience. The unconscious fantasy material is shallow and shows only a tendency to react to immediate impulses or experiences, although there often are abortive efforts to experience an awareness of the ego or to identify the personality. Their inability to enter into any relationship makes therapy or even education impossible. There is an inability to conceptualize, particularly significant in regard to time. They have no concept of time, so that they cannot recall past experience and cannot benefit from past experience or be motivated to future goals. This lack of concept is a striking feature in the defective organization of the personality structure . . .

Bender also reports a follow-up study of ten children referred to in her 1941 paper who were seen 5 years later. This showed that 'all remained infantile, unhappy and affectless and unable to adjust to children in the schoolroom or other group situation'.

children to steal. Dividing all the cases he had seen at a child-guidance clinic into those who had been reported as stealing and those who had not, he compares a group of 44 thieves with a control group, similar in number, age, and sex, who although emotionally disturbed did not steal. The thieves were distinguished from the controls in two main ways. First, there were among them 14 children whom Bowlby describes as 'affectionless characters', while there were none in the control group. Secondly, 17 of the thieves had suffered complete and prolonged separation (6 months or more) from their mothers or established foster-mothers during their first 5 years of life; only 2 of the controls had suffered similar separations. Neither of these differences can be accounted for by chance. Two further points of great importance were that there was a high and statistically significant degree of overlap between the 'affectionless characters' and those with a history of separation, and that the affectionless children were far more delinquent than any of the others Bowlby's results can be tabulated as in Table 21.3.

The overwhelmingly high incidence

Both Bender and Bowlby thus independently advance the hypothesis that there is a specific connection between prolonged deprivation in the early years and the development of an

TABLE 21.4. *Incidence of Adverse Genetic Factors in a Group of Thieves and a Control Group of Emotionally Disturbed Children Who Did Not Steal* (*Bowlby*).

	Thieves			
	Affectionless	Others	All	Controls
Bad heredity	3	16	19	18
Heredity not bad	11	14	25	26
Totals	14	30	44	44

of separation among the affectionless thieves stands out. When this is contrasted with the incidence of a bad heredity, there can be no doubting that for the affectionless thief nurture rather than nature is the pathogenic agent (see Table 21.4).

In assessing heredity the presence of neurosis, psychosis, or serious psychopathy in parents or grandparents is taken as the criterion. Evidence is admittedly most imperfect but equally so for the controls as for the thieves. Moreover, the internal clinical evidence in several cases of affectionless character makes it fairly clear that it was the experience of prolonged separation from the mother which was to blame. After reviewing evidence from the work of Burt [11], Glueck and Glueck [15], and others which is implicitly confirmatory, Bowlby concludes:

on the basis of this varied evidence it appears that there is a very strong case indeed for believing that prolonged separation of a child from his mother (or mother-substitute) during the first five years of life stands foremost among the causes of delinquent character development.

affectionless psychopathic character given to persistent delinquent conduct and extremely difficult to treat.

Follow-up studies

The inquiries so far described have the shortcomings inherent in the retrospective method; the follow-up studies of Goldfarb and others are therefore of especial value since they take a group of children institutionalized in infancy and seek to determine how they have developed.

The outstanding quality of Goldfarb's work derives from its having been scientifically planned from the beginning to test the hypothesis that the experience of living in the highly impersonal surroundings of an institution nursery in the first 2 or 3 years of life has an adverse effect on personality development. With this end in view he selected his samples so that, so far as is possible, they were similar in heredity, and thereby controlled a variable which has been the bugbear of most other investigations. Altogether he has done three main studies [17, 18, 21]. In each he has compared the mental development of children, brought up until the age of about three in an institution and then placed in foster-homes, with others who had gone straight from their mothers to foster-homes in which they had remained. In both samples the children

Their only contacts with adults occurred during these few hurried moments when they were dressed, changed, or fed by nurses.

Later they were members of a group of 15 or 20 under the supervision of

TABLE 21.5. *Differences Between Children Who Had Spent Their First Three Years in an Institution and Controls Who Had Not (Goldfarb)*

Function tested or rated	Test or rating method	Result expressed as	Results†	
			Institution group	Control group
Intelligence	Wechsler	mean IQ	72·4	95·4
Ability to conceptualize	Weigl	mean score	2·4	6·8
	Vigotsky	mean score	0·5	4·7
Reading	standard tests	mean score	5·1	6·8
Arithmetic	standard tests	mean score	4·7	6·7
Social maturity	Vineland scale completed by caseworkers	mean social quotient	79·0	98·8
Ability to keep rules ⎫ Guilt on breaking rules⎭	frustration experiment	⎧number of children ⎨number of children	3 2	12 11
Capacity for relationships	case-workers' assessment	number of children able to make normal relationships	2	15
Speech		number of children up to average	3	14
Number of children (total)			15	15

† In the case of all differences shown, *P* is less than 0·01.

had been handed over by their mothers in infancy, usually within the first 9 months of life. The sample most thoroughly studied consisted of 15 pairs of children who, at the time of the examination, ranged in age from 10 to 14 years [18]. One set of 15 was in the institution from about 6 months of age to 3½ years, the other set had not had this experience. Conditions in the institution conformed to the highest standards of physical hygiene but lacked the elementary essentials of mental hygiene:

Babies below the age of nine months were kept in their own little cubicles to prevent the spread of epidemic infection.

one nurse, who had neither the training nor the time to offer them love or attention. As a result they lived in 'almost complete social isolation during that first year of life' and their experience in the succeeding two years was only slightly richer. Goldfarb has gone to great pains to ensure that the foster-homes of the two groups are similar in respect of all observable criteria and demonstrates further that, in respect of the mother's occupational, educational, and mental status, the institution group was slightly superior to the controls. Any differences in the mental states of the two groups of children are, therefore, virtually certain to be the result of their differing experiences in infancy.

The two groups of children were studied by a great variety of tests and rating scales and all differences checked for the possible influence of chance. A few of the very numerous and striking

many of the direct observers. In this, he confirms the earlier observations of Lowrey [26].

Most of Goldfarb's findings in regard to personality disturbances are in line with those of Bender and Bowlby. There are, however, certain

TABLE 21.6. *Incidence of Problems in Children Who Had Spent Their First Three Years in an Institution and Controls Who Had Not (Goldfarb)*

Problem	Rated by	Result expressed as	Results† Institution group	Control group
Unpopular with other children	case-worker	number of children showing problem	6	1
Craving affection	,,	,, ,,	9	2
Fearful	,,	,, ,,	8	1
Restless, hyperactive	,,	,, ,,	9	1
Inability to concentrate	,,	,, ,,	10	0
Poor school achievement	,,	,, ,,	15	1
Number of children (total)			15	15

† In all cases but the first, *p* is less than 0·01. In the first case, it lies between 0·05 and 0·02.

differences are listed in Tables 21.5 and 21.6.

The number and consistency of these differences is truly remarkable. The disability in the cognitive field is striking and confirmed by several other tests. It is obviously connected with the lowered developmental and intelligence levels observed by those who have made direct studies, and makes it clear that, in some cases at least, the retardation of the institutionalized infant or toddler persists. Goldfarb's discoveries regarding the institution child's inability to conceptualize are particularly valuable as giving a clue to some of the psychological processes underlying the personality disturbances, a point discussed later. Another point which emerges from Goldfarb's work is the persistence of the speech disabilities, noted by so

differences which are not always easy to interpret (especially in the absence of case-histories, an omission which it is to be hoped Goldfarb will one day make good). The contrast between Goldfarb's finding that institution children 'crave affection' and Bowlby's observation of their being 'affectionless' is probably more apparent than real. Many affectionless characters crave affection, but none the less have a complete inability either to accept or reciprocate it. The poor capacity of all but two of Goldfarb's children for making relationships is clearly confirmatory of all other work. The fact that only one of this sample of Goldfarb's institution children stole and none truanted is, however, surprising in view of Bowlby's findings. The difference is probably valid and needs explanation.

The tenor of Goldfarb's summary of his findings in regard to personality disturbances will by now be familiar to the reader:

Briefly, the institution children present a history of aggressive, distractible, uncontrolled behaviour. Normal patterns of anxiety and self-inhibition are not developed. Human identifications are limited, and relationships are weak and easily broken . . . [24].

Finally, the fact that the personality distortions caused by early deprivation are not overcome by later community and family experience must be stressed. There is a continuity of essential traits as late as adolescence. If anything, there is a growing inaccessibility to change. [18]

One shortcoming in his discussion should, however, be noted—namely, his tendency to imply that all institutions and their products are the same. This will be referred to later. None the less, for skilful planning and care of execution, Goldfarb's work ranks high; not until a comparable piece of work has been done with different results can there be reason to doubt his findings.

There is one group of data which is sometimes quoted as casting doubt on these findings—that from the Jewish communal settlements in Israel known as Kibbutz (plural, Kibbutzim). In these settlements, largely for ideological reasons, children are brought up by professional nurses in a 'Children's House'. Babies are reared in groups of 5 or 6, and are later merged at the age of 3 years into larger groups numbering 12–18. The emphasis is throughout on communal rather than family care. Is not this, it may be asked, a clear example that communal care can be made to work without damaging the children? Before answering this question it is necessary to look more carefully at the conditions in which the children are raised. The following account is taken partly from the report of an American psychiatric social worker, Alt, who recently visited Israel, and partly from a personal communication from the Lasker Mental Hygiene and Child Guidance Centre in Jerusalem. Both describe life in certain of the non-religious Kibbutzim. Alt [1] remarks:

Separation is a relative concept and separation as it appears in the Kibbutz should not be thought of as identical with that of children who are brought up in foster-homes or institutions away from their parents . . . In the Kibbutz there is a great deal of opportunity for close relationship between child and parent.

Not only does the mother nurse the baby and feed him in the early months, but, to follow the Lasker Centre's description:

once the suckling tie between mother and child is abandoned, the daily visit of the child to the room of the parents becomes the focus of family life for the child, and its importance is scrupulously respected. During these few hours the parents, or at least one of them, are more or less completely at the disposal of the children; they play with them, talk to them, carry the babies about, take the toddlers for little walks, etc.

The time spent with the children 'may amount to as much as two to three hours on working days and many more on the Sabbath' [1].

Here, then, is no complete abandonment of parent–child relations. Though the amount of time parents spend with their young children is far less than in most other Western communities, the reports make it clear that the parents are extremely important people in the children's eyes, and the children in the parents'. It is interesting to note, too, that the trend is steadily towards parents taking more responsibility. Formerly parents had to visit the children in the Children's House—now the children come to the parents' room and the parents even prepare light meals for them; feasts are now celebrated in the parents' room as well as communally in the Children's House; mothers are asserting themselves and demanding to see more of their children.

Finally, it is by no means certain that the children do not suffer from this regime. While both observers report good and cooperative development in adolescence, the Lasker Centre think there are signs of 'a somewhat higher level of insecurity among Kibbutz children than among others, at least until some point in the latency period'. They also point out that the strong morale and intimate group life of the Kibbutz are of great value to the older child and adolescent and that these may offset some of the unsettlement of earlier years.

From this brief account it is evident that there is no evidence here which can be held to invalidate the hypotheses. The conditions provide, of course, unusually rich opportunities for research in child development, and it is to be hoped these will not be missed.

References

1. ALT, H. (1951). *Am. J. Orthopsychiat.* **21**, 105.
2. BAKWIN, H. (1942). *Am. J. dis. Child.* **63**, 30.
3. —— (1949). *J. Pediat.* **35**, 512.
4. BENDER, L. (1947). Psychopathic behaviour disorders in children. *In* (Lindner, R. M. and Seliger, R. V. (Eds.)) *Handbook of correctional psychology*. New York.
5. —— and YARNELL, H. (1941). *Am. J. Psychiat.* **97**, 1158.
6. BOWLBY, J. (1940). *Int. J. Psycho-anal.* **21**, 154.
7. —— (1944). *Int. J. Psycho-anal.* **25**, 19.
8. —— (1946). *Forty-four juvenile thieves, their characters and homelife.* London.
9. BRODBECK, A. J. and IRWIN, O. C. (1946). *Child Dev.* **17**, 145.
10. BURLINGTON, D. and FREUD, A. (1942). *Annual report of a residential war nursery.* London.
11. BURT, C. (1929). *The young delinquent.* London.
12. DURFEE, H. and WOLF, K. (1933). *Z. Kinderforsch.* **42**, 273.
13. GESELL, A. and AMATRUDA, C. (1947). *Developmental diagnosis: normal and abnormal child development. Clinical methods and pediatric applications,* 2nd ed. New York.
14. GINDL, I., HETZER, H., and STURM, M. (1937). *Z. angew. Psychol.* **52**, 310.
15. GLUECK, S. and GLUECK, E. T. (1934). *One thousand juvenile delinquents.* Cambridge, Mass.
16. GOLDFARB, W. (1943). *Am. J. Orthopsychiat.* **13**, 249.
17. —— (1943). *Child Dev.* **14**, 213.
18. —— (1943). *J. exp. Educ.* **12**, 106.
19. —— (1944). *Am. J. Orthopsychiat.* **14**, 162.
20. —— (1944). *Am. J. Orthopsychiat.* **14**, 441.
21. —— (1945). *Am. J. Orthopsychiat.* **15**, 247.
22. —— (1945). *Am. J. Psychiat.* **102**, 18.
23. —— (1947). *Am. J. Orthopsychiat.* **17**, 449.
24. —— (1949). *Am. J. Orthopsychiat.* **19**, 624.
25. LEVY, R. J. (1947). *J. Personality,* **15**, 233.
26. LOWREY, L. G. (1940). *Am. J. Orthopsychiat.* **10**, 576.
27. POWDERMAKER, F., LEVIS, H. T., and

TOURAINE, G. (1937). *Am. J. Orthopsychiat.* **7**, 58.

28. RHEINGOLD, H. L. (1943). *Am. J. Orthopsychiat.* **13**, 41.

29. RIBBLE, M. (1943). *The rights of infants: early psychological needs and their satisfaction.* New York.

30. ROUDINESCO, J. and APPELL, G. (1950). Sem. Hop. Paris, **26**, 2271.

31. SIMONSEN, K. M. (1947). *Examination of children from children's homes and day nurseries.* Copenhagen.

32. SPITZ, R. A. (1945). Hospitalism: an inquiry into the genesis of psychiatric conditions in early childhood. *In The psycho-analytic study of the child.* Vol. I, p. 53.

33. —— and WOLF, K. M. (1946). *Genet. Psychol. Monogr.* **34**, 57.

22

Maternal deprivation or perceptual deprivation?

H. R. SCHAFFER†

GENETIC explanations of personality tend generally to attach a great deal of importance to the period of infancy, and, mainly through the stimulus of psychoanalysis, much has been written about this stage of development. Direct empirical studies of infants, other than those concerned with the establishment of age norms for certain peripheral functions, are few, and our knowledge of psychological events taking place at this time is for the most part extremely scanty.

The main reason for the lack of data based on direct observation appears to arise from the difficulty of *access* to personality functioning at this age. In the present paper, however, we shall be concerned with a situation which does appear to lend itself to the isolation and study of some of the problems in this area. The observations arose in the course of a project on the effects of maternal deprivation in the first year of life as seen in a sample of hospitalized infants. Here we shall not, however, be concerned with the hospitalization issue as such, but rather with the light which it throws on the personality structure of the infants undergoing this experience. The empirical data of this project are

† From 'Objective observations of personality development in early infancy'. *Brit. J. med. Psychol.* **31**, 174–83 (1958). Reprinted by permission of the Editor of the *British Journal of Medical Psychology*.

presented in detail elsewhere [11], and only those parts of the study which are relevant to the present theme will therefore be mentioned here.

Subjects and methods

The subjects were 76 infants, admitted to a children's hospital for a variety of medical and surgical reasons. Their age at admission ranged from 3 to 51 weeks, and the length of hospitalization varied from 4 to 49 days, with a mean of 15·4 days. Most of the infants were in for periods between 1 and 2 weeks, and the median of the distribution is 12 days. Approximately half the children were visited daily, while of the rest only six were not visited at all. Developmental quotients were taken at the end of the hospitalization period with the Cattell Infant Intelligence Scale, and a range of 72 to 141 was obtained, with a mean of 100·7. All cases of possible brain injury and all premature and marasmic infants were excluded from the study.

The observations were focused on three points of the infants' experience —the period immediately following admission to hospital, the period immediately preceding discharge, and the period subsequent to return home. In order to rule out the effects of the illness factor on behaviour, only 'cold' cases were studied during the initial period, i.e. infants not affected by such factors as pain or fever and who were therefore not subjectively sick. There were 25 such cases on whom observations took place for the initial period of the first 3 days. The whole sample of 76 cases was studied for the last 3 days in hospital, by which time it could be assumed that the behavioural effects of their illnesses had disappeared for all babies.

the age of 29 weeks at discharge from hospital, while only 6 of the 28 showing the other syndrome appear above that cutting point. The characteristics of the syndromes are as follows:

The global syndrome

This pattern of behaviour was mainly shown by those under 7 months. When

TABLE 22.1. *Post-hospitalization Syndromes*

	Age in weeks at discharge from hospital														
	0–4	5–9	9–12	13–16	17–20	21–24	25–28	29–32	33–36	37–40	41–44	45–48	49–52	53–56	Total
Global	—	—	2	5	5	4	4	5	1	1	—	1	—	—	28
Overdependent	—	—	—	—	—	—	—	4	4	2	7	3	5	2	27
Miscellaneous	—	—	—	1	1	2	1	2	3	1	1	—	—	—	12
Unchanged	1	1	2	—	2	1	—	1	—	—	—	1	—	—	9
Total	1	1	4	6	8	7	5	12	8	4	8	5	5	2	76

Observation in the hospital took place in the context of a fixed daily observation session, and the data, collected under a standardized procedure, were subsequently analysed according to an infant behaviour schedule. This material is described in detail elsewhere [11].

All the infants were visited at home, always within 7 days after discharge from hospital and also subsequently, until the observer considered that all overt effects of their experience had disappeared. It is the information derived from these home visits which provides us with our point of entry for the present discussion.

The post-hospitalization syndromes

The main finding of this study, as shown in Table 22.1, is the emergence from the information obtained in the home of two distinct syndromes, each closely associated with a particular age range. The cutting point is at approximately 7 months, though there is some overlap. Thus one syndrome, shown by 27 cases, is not found at all below

these infants returned home they were, according to the reports of the mothers, 'strange' in their behaviour. The main feature of this 'strangeness' was an *extreme preoccupation with the environment*. For hours on end sometimes the infant would crane his neck, scanning his surroundings without apparently focusing on any particular feature and letting his eyes sweep over all objects without attending to any particular one. A completely blank expression was usually observed on his face, though sometimes a bewildered or frightened look was reported. In the extreme form of this syndrome the infants were quite inactive throughout, apart from the scanning behaviour, and no vocalization was heard though one or two were reported to have cried or whimpered. When confronted with a toy the infant disregarded it.

In the less extreme instances of the syndrome the preoccupation with the environment was again the central feature, but here the infant might not be completely subdued in his general activity, or there might be some vocalization, or he might momentarily show normal interest in toys before again returning to the unfocusing inspection of his surroundings. Seven of the 28 infants in this group showed such modifications.

Reactions to other people were also changed for the duration of the syndrome, and this applies equally to the familiar mother and to complete strangers. In some cases the infants were quite unheedful of all attempts on the part of the adult to make contact with them, as they appeared to be so absorbed in the scanning of their physical surroundings. In other cases the infants kept the head averted on being stimulated (almost as though deliberately avoiding the adult). In still other instances the infants gazed 'through' the adult with the same blank look that was used for the rest of the environment. Finally some infants were reported to respond to stimulation with a brief sign of interest such as a smile, usually after considerable delay, before again reverting to the scanning of the surroundings.

This pattern of behaviour was sometimes first observed in the waiting room off the ward where the mothers collected and dressed their children prior to leaving hospital, at times as the infants were carried out of the hospital into the street, and sometimes not until entry into their own home. The duration of this behaviour tended not to vary a great deal for the group as a whole—in the majority of cases it continued for the rest of the first day home, but in one or two cases it lasted only 20 or 30 min. In some others it continued for as long as 4 days.

Accompanying this pattern a somatic upset occurred in 61 cases. In a few instances this took the form of a feeding upset such as vomiting, but mostly it constituted a sleep disturbance, in which the infant would wake in the night crying and would not settle for several hours. In 3 instances, however, the upset took the form of excessive sleeping. In these cases the infant would fall asleep some time after discharge from hospital and continue sleeping for 1 or 2 days, waking only for feeds or even having to be wakened for them.

The somatic symptoms usually outlasted the environmental preoccupation, but if the time of disappearance of the last symptom is taken as the total length of upset on discharge from hospital, a mean of 2·96 days is found for this group. It is noteworthy that neither the total curation of upset nor the duration of the environmental preoccupation was found to be in any way dependent on any of the antecedent variables such as age, amount of visiting by the mother, or even length of hospitalization. Thus an infant hospitalized for 4 weeks would show the same phenomena for the same length of time as an infant hospitalized for 4 days (the minimum hospitalization in this group).

This pattern of behaviour has been named the 'global syndrome' because, first, it appears to be related to the total environment rather than any specific aspect of it (such as the mother, as in the following syndrome). Secondly it tends to involve the total organism, and somatic as well as psychological functions. Finally because it is believed to be indicative of a global, undifferentiated, syncretic stage of development. The first two points are, as we have seen, based on the observed data, whereas the last is a hypothetical point which will be elaborated later on.

The over-dependent syndrome

This pattern of behaviour, commonly found after the age of 7 months, presents a very different picture. The central feature here is overdependence on the mother after return from hospital, and it is thus of the same order as that described for older, pre-school children under similar circumstances [9]. The overdependence was shown in such ways as excessive crying when left alone by the mother, an almost continual clinging and a wish to be nursed by her, and a fear of strangers. Familiar figures, such as father or siblings, were sometimes regarded with suspicion. A somatic upset was found in 15 of these 27 cases, taking the form in most cases of a sleep disturbance. The mean duration of total upset is 14·69 days for this group, but there is a wide range (1–80 days).

Among the 27 cases in this group are 7 who showed a variation on this theme. These cases developed the global syndrome after discharge, and it was not till this had run its usual course that over-dependence manifested itself. There are no obvious reasons for the difference between this subgroup and the other 20 cases. Their age at discharge ranged from 29 to 47 weeks, and length of hospitalization, amount of visiting, and other relevant variables are not correlated with it.

While the above two groups may be taken to represent the main syndromes of post-hospitalization behaviour as seen by us, some infants were found who did not fit into this classification. There are two subsidiary groups.

Miscellaneous. The 12 infants in this group showed only such isolated symptoms as a sleep upset, or fear of strangers, or a decrease in their general activity. There were also 2 cases, both

approximately 8 months old, who were over-dependent on the mother before hospitalization and where after return home the only behavioural change observed referred to a marked lessening of the over-dependence.

Unchanged. Nine infants showed no reaction at all on return home, no change in their behaviour having taken place as compared with the pre-hospitalization picture. Four of these cases are the youngest of the sample, and here our observations on these infants suggested that visual awareness of the environment had not apparently sufficiently developed for them to have shown the global syndrome.

In general, apart from the 4 youngest in the 'Unchanged' group, it is difficult to see why the cases falling into the last two groups do not conform to the pattern set by the first two groups. None of the obvious antecedent variables can be adduced to account for the difference, and the behaviour of these infants in hospital was in all respects comparable to that of the others. In the remainder of this paper attention is paid, in the main, to the two main syndromes, for it is hoped that through an examination of the main sample we shall eventually arrive at an understanding of the reasons why some cases fail to conform.

Cognitive structure and the development of object relations

The main conclusion arising from the material presented above is that the same experience of hospitalization is reacted to very differently, according to the age of the subject. After 7 months the disturbance caused thereby is in the field of object relations, with particular reference to the relationship with the mother, and is thus continuous with that found generally in the pre-school age group. Before 7 months on the other hand, the disturbance is of a very different nature and appears to be related to the total environment rather than to any one aspect of it. The reason for this difference is to be found, we can assume, in certain developmental changes taking place soon after the middle of the first year, and the possible nature of these changes deserves to be examined in relation to the two different syndromes described.

The most useful way of approaching this problem appears to be through a consideration of the type of *cognitive structure* to be found in infancy, i.e. the way in which perceptions are organized and related to each other and to their external sources by the individual. This is a function about which Piaget [7, 8] has written most clearly, and his theoretical propositions will therefore be examined in relation to the material presented above. In the early months, according to Piaget, there is present a state of 'adualism', an undifferentiated absolute in which there is no distinction between the self and the environment. Objects at this stage do not exist in their own right but only as functional elements serving the infant's own activities, and are assimilated in terms of the present need of the individual. Moreover, once the object is out of the perceptual field the infant behaves as though it has ceased to exist. He is thus said to experience only a series of fleeting images which may be recognized but which have no continuity, permanence, or substance. There is consequently no conservation of the object, and the world is centred in the child's own activity. There is, furthermore, no appreciation of the

own body as one element among others, and it is thus not recognized as being part of a world of distinct, stable objects.

It is only in the second half of the first year that Piaget finds a new type of cognitive structure developing. It is only then that objects become detached from action and the first fundamental step taken in attributing to them a separate, independent existence. Though the individual must yet pass through many stages to reach the adult form of cognitive organization, the most important step may be said to take place at this point, for it is now that the body of the subject becomes appreciated as distinct from the environment and relationships to external objects can therefore be established.

This formulation has definite implications for studies on separation from the mother during the first year of life. As Anthony [1] has put it: 'It is only after the child has made a permanent object that he can lose it, search for it, or form a permanent relationship with it,' and from the theoretical formulations of Piaget he went on to deduce that the infant's reaction to separation from the mother must before 7 months lack the quality of separation feelings at a later stage. This is strikingly borne out by the present investigation, even in respect of the actual age stated. If we examine the initial reaction to hospitalization in the group of 'cold' cases, we find a very different pattern before 7 months from that occurring after this age. In the earlier period fretting as a protest to the separation does not occur, and apart from a sharp drop in the amount of vocalization (believed to be related to the general reduction of social stimulation) the infant's responsiveness to the strangers now caring for him is maintained at normal levels. After 7 months, however, one tends to find the classical separation picture, shown in particular by fretting, strong negative responses to the strange hospital staff, and clinging to the mother during her visits. This has been detailed elsewhere [11] and supports the conclusion suggested by the home data that separation from the mother becomes an experience manifestly and immediately affecting object relations only after the middle of the first year. (This does not, of course, prove that deficient mothering before this time cannot affect the development of the child in such a way as to influence later object-relationships.)

There is, however, another point suggested by the data, namely one referring to the speed with which the new development takes place. While these conclusions are admittedly based on cross-sectional material, it does seem remarkable that there is relatively little overlap between the two main syndromes, as though the new function comes into play quite suddenly around 7 months. What is more, there are indications that the intensity of the separation reaction does not increase gradually with age once this milestone has been reached, but that the upset is as great at the very beginning of the new phase of development as it is later on. There are three possible indices of the degree of upset caused by the separation.

The length of the fretting period

Basing conclusions on the 'cold' cases, a considerable range (1–22 days) was found. But as many of the infants were still fretting at discharge (including the 37-week-old infant who was still fretting after 22 days), no precise

statistics can be given. It is notable, however, that the very youngest in this group continued fretting for periods as long as those found at the older end of the age range. Thus of the two youngest, both 30 weeks at admission, one was still fretting when discharged on the 5th day, while the other ceased fretting only after the 6th day. One may compare such figures with those given for older children—for instance Robertson and Bowlby [10] mention periods ranging from a few hours to 7 or 8 days in the case of children 18–24 months old, and for a group of children aged between 1 and 4 years at the time of separation, Bowlby [2] describes the fretting period as lasting from 1 or 2 days to 17 days.

The intensity of fretting at the beginning of hospitalization

All infants were rated on a five-point rating scale for the amount of crying observed during each daily observation session. Studying the 'cold' cases again, it was found that the average rating for the first 3 days in hospital shows fretting to be as intense in the 7 and 8 months old infants as it is in those aged 11 and 12 months. Thus if the average ratings for the 7 infants aged between 29 and 40 weeks at admission are compared with those for the 8 infants aged between 41 and 52 weeks, mean figures of 3·68 and 3·55, respectively, are obtained. It would appear that at the very beginning of the new developmental phase protest at separation is as vigorous as it is for the oldest subjects of our sample.

Duration of upset after return home

Examining the group of 27 infants who were overdependent after discharge from hospital, a range of 1–80 days was found for this index. Again the very youngest infants in the group were no less affected than the oldest. Dividing the age range at 41 weeks, the mean duration of upset for those above and those below can be compared. The outcome is, however, influenced by the fact that in the older group three of the longest hospitalizations are found, whereas only one case of similar length is present in the younger group. As length of upset after discharge has in the literature generally been found to be directly related to the length of hospitalization (except in the case of those under 7 months), we felt justified in excluding these 4 cases for the sake of uniformity and comparability of the two groups. In this way a mean of 10–18 days was obtained for the 29–40 week old group, while the mean for the 41–52 week old group was 11·83 days. The difference between these means is not statistically significant.

It is implied by these figures that the intensity of separation upset is considerable at the very beginning of the new phase. Once an infant has reached the developmental stage where he becomes capable of showing a separation reaction his upset is likely to be as great then as it will be later on. The age range within which we have carried out comparisons is rather narrow, however, and the findings need therefore to be confirmed for a wider age range. Clinical impressions suggest in fact that the 7 or 8 months old infant frets at separation and clings after reunion just as intensely as the 2- or 3-year-old child, and if this can be confirmed by systematic studies a *stepwise* development is thus indicated.

It seems justified to assume that the intensity of the separation reaction is an indication of the strength of the child's libidinal attachment to the mother (as a special and unique person, rather than as a 'mothering agent'), and we thus have evidence that the 'common sense' view of a *gradual* development of the child–mother relationship in the course of the first year or so is a mistaken notion. The more likely hypothesis is that *permanent object relations (to specific persons) do not become possible until the cognitive structure of the child has developed to the point where others are seen as separate beings clearly distinguished from the self and from one another, that this occurs somewhere around 7 months, and that when this development does take place the attachment to a specific mother-figure is established relatively speedily and appears at once in its full intensity.*

It is significant that a similar theory of two-stage development emerges from a study of dogs by Scott [12], who found that despite the close association of the puppy with its mother during the first weeks of life, primary social relations cannot be established until certain maturational changes have taken place. These occur after 3 weeks of age, and it is only during the critical period for the process of socialization which begins at this time that the puppy becomes able to establish permanent social relations. From another point of view Bowlby in a paper [3] on the development of the child's tie to the mother, has also postulated a two-stage process of social development in infancy, according to which various instinctual components of the child's 'attachment behaviour' to the mother do not become integrated and focused on the one specific individual till the second half of the first year.

Analysis of the global syndrome

If we accept the view that an object relation to a specific person does not become established before approximately 7 months, it is understandable that in the earlier period hospitalization does not produce a manifest and immediate disturbance in the child–mother relationship. The problem arises, however, of why the global syndrome appeared after discharge from hospital, and what light it can shed on the processes underlying it.

In attempting to analyse this syndrome, we may take as our starting point the fact that this pattern of behaviour was elicited when the infants were moved from hospital to home. There are two possible explanations which must first be examined.

The first is that the global syndrome is the usual reaction at this age to all geographical displacement. All the mothers agreed, however, that the global pattern was quite unusual when compared with the infant's customary reaction to new surroundings, that it differed from the latter in its duration and intensity, in the inaccessibility of the infant, and in such other features as the unfocusing character of the environmental inspection and the quietness accompanying it. To check on this point the observations on the 'cold' cases at the time of their admission to hospital were examined, but no trace of any pattern of behaviour resembling the global syndrome could be found.

The second possible explanation is that the global syndrome is specific to the move from hospital to home. One may wonder, for instance, whether it is related to the return to a previously familiar environment, or to renewed handling by the mother. But this explanation too can be ruled out,

because it was found possible to elicit the global pattern actually within the hospital by merely moving the infant after a certain period of hospitalization from his customary place in the ward to another room. This is a development which has certain important implications to which we shall return later. In the present context, however, it indicates that the global syndrome is related to any change of environment following a period of hospitalization.

We may now ask how this effect could be brought about by hospitalization. The hypothesis suggested is that the operative factor in the infant's experience in hospital is one that can best be described as *perceptual monotony*, and that this factor is an essential precondition to the development of the global syndrome.

Close observation of the infants on whom this project is based vividly emphasized the considerable monotony of their perceptual experience. One may mention in this connection the following four aspects in particular.

(1) The child's illness necessitated his confinement to bed, so that he generally remained in the same environment for the whole period of hospitalization.

(2) The physical nature of the environment was often of a highly constrictive kind. The smallest infants were kept in solid-sided metal cots, others were isolated in cubicles or kept in side-rooms from which they could see or hear little of what went on outside, and only those in the busy general ward had the opportunity for greater perceptual variety.

(3) Even those in the general ward, however, were usually prevented by the limited perceptual-motor equip-

ment of infants in the first 12 months from making use of the greater amount of potential stimulation available. None of these infants could walk, few could stand, many could not sit up, and their sensory range tended in consequence to be limited.

(4) Due to factor (3), infants are generally very much at the mercy of others for the richness of their perceptual experience, yet in terms of human stimulation the experience of these infants was particularly deficient. Apart from the visiting hour (during which few mothers ever picked up their babies), the infants were rarely handled apart from the handling necessary for the relief of physical needs. Moreover, the feeding situation tended to be of very much shorter duration than in the home.

As a consequence of these four factors, there was considerable restriction in perceptual variation compared with the usual experience of infants cared for at home. While some variation in severity of perceptual monotony occurred from individual to individual, inspection of the data showed that the older infants (who later developed the overdependent syndrome) were also considerably affected, and that the more severe degrees of perceptual restriction occur among them as well as in the younger infants. If perceptual monotony is then to be regarded as an essential precondition for the formation of the global syndrome, it is necessary to account for the fact that it appears to play this part only within a certain age range. To do this, we must return to our discussion of the types of cognitive structure to be found in the first year, and advance the hypothesis, elaborated below, that *it is the interaction of perceptual monotony with the early type of cognitive structure which leads to the occurrence of the global syndrome.*

Given the early type of cognitive structure as described by Piaget (with its state of adualism, in which the self is merged with the environment in one functional whole), one may say that under normal conditions of child care the infant experiences a degree of environmental variation which will keep his perceptual field in a relatively 'fluid' state, for both the external boundaries and the internal characteristics of the field will fluctuate as a result of such stimulation.

Under condition of perceptual monotony, however, the rate of change is drastically reduced, and when an infant in whom the self has not yet emerged as a differentiated unit is confronted for a lengthy period with the same relatively static surroundings, the natural tendency to merge with the environment is thereby emphasized. It is as though under these conditions the perceptual field would tend to become 'set'. The boundaries of the field can be thought of as remaining constant for the relevant period, and the amount of variation in internal structure will be reduced more or less in proportion to the degree of sensory restriction.

The process of 'setting' which we have postulated becomes apparent when the infant is taken out of the accustomed environment and put into another. The 'set' perceptual field is disrupted and disintegrates, and such disintegration may be experienced as a stress situation—hence the somatic upset found in many of the infants. A new perceptual field must now be formed, and the infant's acute awareness of new sensations is reflected in the intense concentration with which he regards his new surroundings. It is this environmental preoccupation which forms the core of the global syndrome, and the various behavioural features of the syndrome may be said to stem from the disintegration of a perceptual field in which a 'setting' process has taken place and which must now be replaced by a new field.

That sensory deprivation even in adults can result in certain drastic changes of behaviour has been reported by several writers (e.g. [15]). Judging from the published results, however, it seems unlikely that the experimental conditions used bring about a state comparable to that described for the present sample. In the former case the self is a highly differentiated, independent unit, the dissolution of which could only be affected by the most extreme conditions. In young infants on the other hand, the global pattern can be regarded as an exaggeration of a process occurring all the time, a process of fusion of self and environment, and the complete restructuring of the perceptual field whenever the latter changes.

.   .   .   .   .

Conclusion

Two main syndromes, each associated with a particular age range, have emerged from this study of the effects of hospitalization in infancy. In this respect the findings parallel those of Spitz [13, 14], and they may be said to suggest the existence of two developmental stages—a *global stage* and a *differentiated stage*. The latter, centring around the differentiation of self and environment, appears to be essentially continuous with the adult form, and only when it has been attained can object relations to specific persons be established. The global stage, on the other hand, is of a very

different order, and certain life experiences may thus have quite a distinct meaning according to the developmental phase of the individual. The present study, for instance, suggests that the crucial factor in hospitalization at the differentiated stage is *maternal deprivation*, whereas at the global stage it is *perceptual deprivation*.

Stages of development in personality organization during infancy have been postulated by a number of different writers, and though terminology varies the overlap in meaning is considerable. One may in this connection mention Melanie Klein's [6] stages of part objects and of whole objects, Hartmann's [4] stages of the need satisfying object and of object constancy, and Hoffer's [5] stages of the object as part of the *milieu interne* and of the psychological object. Certain similarities exist between all these formulations and the two stages outlined here, but whereas the former have arisen from reconstructive data, the present approach is based on direct empirical observations. The controversy, for instance, about the age of change-over from one phase to the next has probably been due to the indirect nature of the evidence, but while some have postulated this important milestone of development to occur as early as 3 months and others as late as 10 months, the material presented in this paper suggests 7 months as the approximate time of graduation from one stage to the next.

The hospitalization situation has thus provided us with a means of 'diagnosing' the developmental phase of infants, and in the context of this situation it is possible to proceed to investigate the problems and to test the hypotheses formulated in this paper. These concern, among other things, the further characteristics of the two developmental phases, especially of the earlier one; the manner of passing from one stage to the other and the conditions, both organismic and environmental, for doing so; and the possibility of regression taking place once the later stage has been attained. Moreover, the stages may be regarded as a framework within which one can evaluate the varying effects of environmental influences on personality development and against which the growth of social relations may be assessed.

References

1. ANTHONY, E. J. (1956). The significance of Jean Piaget for child psychiatry. *Brit. J. med. Psychol.* **29**, 20–34.
2. BOWLBY, J. (1953). Some pathological processes set in train by early mother–child separation. *J. ment. Sci.* **99**, 265–72.
3. —— (1958). The nature of the child's tie to his mother. *Int. J. Psycho-anal.* **39**, 350–73.
4. HARTMANN, H. (1952). The mutual influences in the development of ego and id. *Psycho-anal. study Child* **7**, 9–30.
5. HOFFER, W. (1952). The mutual influences in the development of ego and id: earliest stages. *Psycho-anal. study Child* **7**, 31–41.
6. KLEIN, M., HEIMANN, P., ISAACS, S., and RIVIERE, J. (1952). *Developments in psycho-analysis.* Hogarth, London.
7. PIAGET, J. (1937). Principal factors determining intellectual evolution from childhood to adult life. *In* (Rapaport, D. (Ed.)) *Organisation and pathology of thought* (1951). Columbia University Press, New York.
8. —— (1950). *The psychology of intelligence.* Routledge and Kegan Paul, London.
9. PRUGH, D. G., STAUB, E. M., SANDS, H. H., KIRSCHBAUM, R. M., and LENIHAN, E. A. (1953). A study of the emotional reactions of children and families to hospitalization and illness. *Am. J. Orthopsychiat.* **23**, 70–106.
10. ROBERTSON, J. and BOWLBY, J. (1952). Responses of young children to separation from their mothers. *Courrier* **2**, 131–42.
11. SCHAFFER, H. R. and CALLENDER, W. M. (1958). Psychological effects of hospitalization in infancy. Unpublished paper.
12. SCOTT, J. P. (1958). Critical periods in the development of social behaviour in puppies. *Psychosom. Med.* **20**, 42–54.
13. SPITZ, R. (1945). Hospitalism. *Psycho-anal. study Child* **1**, 53–74.
14. —— and WOLF, K. M. (1946). Anaclitic depression. *Psycho-anal. study Child* **2**, 313–42.
15. WEXLER, D., MENDELSON, J., LEIDERMAN, P. H., and SOLOMON, P. (1958). Sensory deprivation. *Arch. Neurol. Psychiat.* **79**, 225–33.

23

How reversible are the effects?

WAYNE DENNIS AND PERGROUHI NAJARIAN†

RIBBLE [10, 11] and Spitz [12–16] have proposed that if certain stimulus deprivations occur in early childhood the consequences are drastic and enduring. These views have arisen largely from observation of infants in institutions. The supporting evidence has consisted in part of scores of institutional subjects on infant tests and in part upon general impressions of the emotional states of the children.

This report is concerned with behavioural development in an institution whose care of infants is in some respects identical with, and in some respects quite different from, that described in other studies.

The data were obtained in a foundling home in Beirut, Lebanon, which, because of inadequate financial support, is able to provide little more than essential physical care. We will report upon the developmental status of two age-groups of children in this institution: those between 2 months and 12 months of age, and those between $4\frac{1}{2}$ and 6 years of age. After describing the environmental conditions and presenting the data we will discuss the relationship of this study to previous studies, and to theories of child development.

† From 'Infant development under environmental handicap'. *Psychol. Monogr. gen. app.* **71**, No. 7 (whole no. 436) (1957). Reprinted by permission of the American Psychological Association. Copyright © 1957.

The Creche

The institution in which the study was conducted will be called the Creche, although this is not the formal name of the home. The Creche is a home for infants and young children operated by a religious order (of nuns). All children in the Creche are received shortly after birth. They arrive via two routes. The majority come from a maternity hospital operated by the religious order referred to previously. An unmarried woman being attended by this hospital may arrange to have her infant taken to the Creche. In so doing she relinquishes claim to the infant and may not see or visit it thereafter. The remainder of the Creche population consists of infants left upon the doorstep of the institution. Nothing is known definitely concerning their parents, but it is likely that the majority of these infants, too, are illegitimate.

The Creche is nearly 30 years old but it has a new building which was completed in the spring of 1955, and for which the order is still indebted. The building is an excellent one, being fireproof, sunny, and airy. The infant beds and other pieces of equipment are new and modern. The appearance of the institution fails to reveal that it exists month after month upon inadequate and uncertain contributions. The feeding, clothing, and housing of the children have the first claim upon the Creche's meagre income. The most stringent economy must be exercised in regard to expenditures for personnel. For this reason the number of persons taking care of the children is extremely limited. Understaffing is the direct cause of whatever deficiencies may characterize the child-care practices to be described later.

Naturally the number of children in the institution varies from time to time with the advent of new arrivals, and departures due to deaths, or to transfer to other institutions to which the children are sent at about six years of age. The size of the staff, too, is subject to some variations. However, estimates made at two periods separated by five months agree in showing that for each person directly concerned with the care of the children—i.e., those who feed the children, change diapers, bathe and clothe them, change their beds, nurse them when they are ill, supervise their play, and teach them—there are 10 children. This ratio of 1 to 10 includes those on night duty as well as on day duty. It does not, however, include personnel who work in the kitchen, laundry, and mending room, nor those who do the cleaning. It does not include the four nuns who constitute the administrative staff and who frequently assist in direct care. Clearly this is an extremely limited staff. The essential functions can be accomplished only by means of hurried procedures and long hours of work.

From birth to one year there is no assignment of individual children to particular attendants. Rather, a room of children is assigned jointly to several care-takers and observation showed no consist-ent relationships between attendants and children. At later ages, each group of children is assigned most of the day to a supervisor and an assistant.

During the first two months of life the infant is taken out of his crib only for his daily bath and change of clothes. He is given his bottle while lying on his back in his crib, because ordinarily no one has time to hold it. The nipple is placed in his mouth and the bottle is propped up by a small pillow. Bathing and dressing are done with a maximum of dispatch and a minimum of mothering.

In conformity with a widespread Near Eastern practice, the infant is swaddled from birth. Plate 2 illustrates the type of swaddling used. The baby has his arms as well as his legs enclosed in tight wrappings, and hence the scope of his movements is greatly restricted. During the early weeks the infant is bound as depicted except when being bathed and dressed. No fixed schedule is followed in regard to freedom from swaddling, but in general the hands are freed at about two months of age, and swaddling is ended at about four months. Swaddling is continued for a longer period during the winter months than during the remainder of the year because the wrap-pings of the child serve to keep him warm.

As shown in Plate 3, each crib has a covering around the sides. This is present to protect the child from drafts, but as a consequence the child can see only the ceiling and the adults who occasionally come near him.

The adults seldom approach him except at feeding times. When they feed him they do not usually speak to him or caress him. When two or three persons are feeding twenty infants, many of them crying, there is no tendency to dally.

At about four months of age, the child is removed to a room for older infants. He is placed in a larger crib, but for several further months his care remains much the same as it has been. A typical scene in the room is shown in Plate 3. A toy is usually placed in each crib, but it soon becomes lodged in a place inaccessible to the child and remains there. The child remains in this second crib until he begins to pull to the edge of the crib and faces some danger of falling out. At this point, he is usually placed during his waking hours with one or two other children in a play pen. This situation is illustrated in Plate 5. Some-times he is placed in a canvas-bottomed baby chair, as shown in Plate 4, but this is usually done only for short periods of time. The older child takes his daytime naps in the play pens. He is returned to his crib at night and tightly tucked in. The child graduates from room two to another room at one year of age or slightly thereafter. Some description of the care of older children will be given on later pages.

Until about four months of age the infant's food consists of milk, supplemented by vitamins. The feedings during this time are on a schedule of six feedings

gaining properly but again staff limitations make it difficult for an attendant to spend much time with any one child. The average weight during the first six months, based on records of the infants which we tested, is appreciably below what is ordinarily considered desirable (see Table 23.1). Comparable data are not available for other Lebanese children. No data are

TABLE 23.1. *Average Weights of Creche Infants*

Statistic	Birth	1 month	2 months	3 months	4 months	5 months	6 months
				Boys			
Average weight (gm)	2926	3233	3746	4365	4926	5555	5984
Number of cases	28	28	28	27	23	18	16
				Girls			
Average weight (gm)	2727	2985	3353	3858	4436	4910	5463
Number of cases	13	12	13	13	11	10	8

† In computing this average, for each child the record of weight taken nearest age 1·0 month was employed. A similar procedure was used at other ages.

per day at daytime intervals of three hours. After four months bottle feeding is gradually reduced in frequency. It ceases at about twelve months.

The introduction of cooked cereals begins at four months, and fruit juices, crushed bananas, apple sauce, and vegetables are begun at five months. Depending upon the preferences of an attendant a child is sometimes given these supplementary foods held in arms, sometimes while sitting in chairs, and sometimes lying down. Beginning at eight months, eggs and chopped meat are occasionally given. Feeding times are reduced to five times per day at four months and to four times per day at one year. Toilet training is begun between 10 and 12 months.

Children are weighed at weekly intervals. Serious efforts are made to give special feeding to infants who are not

available on children beyond six months of age at the Creche.

From about one year to about three years the children spend much of the day in play groups of about twenty children with a supervisor and an assistant. Equipment is limited to a few balls, wagons, and swings. From three to four years of age much of the day is spent seated at small tables. The children are occupied in a desultory way with slates, beads, and sewing boards. At about four years they are placed in kindergarten within the Creche where training in naming objects and pictures, writing, reading, and numbers is begun. Instruction is given in both Arabic and French.

Diet and medical care are under the supervision of a physician who devotes, gratis, about one hour per day to the Creche, whose population is about 140 children. During the winter months colds are common, and pneumonia occasionally occurs. The usual childhood illnesses occur. When a contagious disease enters the Creche it is likely to become widespread since there are no facilities for isolation of infectious cases. We do not have adequate statistics on mortality. It is our impression that it is high in the first three months of life, but not particularly high thereafter. Mortality seems especially high among those infants who are found on the doorstep, many of whom are suffering from malnutrition, exposure, or disease upon admission. In evaluating institutional mortality it should be noted that in some areas of Lebanon the crude death rate in the first year among children in homes is as high as 375 per 1000 [6].

The comparison group

For comparison with behavioural records of the Creche infants, data were obtained from children brought to the well-baby clinic of the American University of Beirut Hospital. All well babies of appropriate age who were brought to the clinic on certain days were tested. They were from among the poorer, but not the poorest, segments of the Beirut population.

All children tested were living at home and were brought to the clinic by their mothers. The majority were being breast fed. We did not obtain detailed data on swaddling, but typically the younger babies were brought in swaddled and the older ones unswaddled. It is our impression that swaddling customs among the poorer half of the Beirut population approximate those of the Creche. This conclusion is supported by a study by Wakim [17]. Other comparison data were provided by American norms and certain Lebanese norms to be described later.

The testing programme

For the subjects under one year of age the Cattell infant scale was employed [2]. This scale was selected because among available tests it seemed to offer the most objective procedures for administration and scoring. It provides five items for each month from 2 to 12 months of age, with one or two alternate items at each age level.

The procedures described in the test manual were carefully followed. They call for testing each infant at a level at which he passes all tests, at a level he fails all tests, and at all intermediate levels.

Several items on the test were not applicable to the Creche group because they require the examiner to obtain information from the mother or other caretaker. Among such items are babbles, anticipates feeding, inspects fingers, says 'dada', etc. Attendants at the Creche could not supply the information required by these items. For this reason, 'alternate' items provided by Cattell and based on direct observation were regularly substituted for these items. In the case of the comparison infants, all age-appropriate items, including all alternates, were administered; but in computing developmental scores for comparative purposes identical items were used for the Creche and the comparison groups.

At the 4½- to 6-year level the tests used were the Goodenough draw-a-man test, the Knox cube test, and the Porteus maze test. These were chosen because it was judged that they might be but little affected by the environmental handicaps of the Creche children. They have the further advantage of requiring a minimum of verbal instructions.

In giving and scoring the draw-a-man test, Goodenough procedures [5] were followed. For the other two tests the procedures and norms employed were those given in the Grace Arthur scale of performance tests, Revised form II [1].

Number of subjects

We tested all subjects who fell into our age categories upon two series of testing dates. The only exceptions consisted of children who were ill or

test. The Creche scores are shown by O-symbols, the comparison scores by X-symbols. Scores are grouped by step intervals of ten points. Thus, examining the figure by beginning at the top of column one, one finds that between 2·0 and 2·9 months of age one comparison infant had a developmental quotient between 140 and 149,

TABLE 23.2. *Individual Infant Scores by Age*†

Scores	Age (months)									
	2	3	4	5	6	7	8	9	10	11
140–149	X									
130–139	XX		X							
120–129	X	X					X			
110–119	OO		X		XX	XX		X		
100–109	OOXX	XXXX	X	XX		X	XX	X	XX	
90–99	OO	O		XX		OX				
80–89	OOX	OX	XXXXX			O		O		O
70–79		OO	OOX		OO			O	OO	
60–69		O	OOOOOO	OOOOO	O	X	O	O	O	O
50–59	X	OO	OOO	OO	O	O			OO	OO
40–49			O		OO	OOO		OO	O	

† Creche infant scores are indicated by O; comparison infants by X.

who had just undergone serious illness. The infant tests were given to 49 Creche infants and the 41 comparison cases. Since rather few of the Creche infants were above 6 months of age at the time of our first period of testing, during our second testing period we tested all infants who were 6 months of age and over even though this meant retesting in 13 cases. For this reason the number of *test scores* for the 49 Creche infants is 62.

In the 4½- to 6-year group, Goodenough tests were given to 30 subjects, and the Knox cube test and the Porteus maze test were each given to 25 subjects. None was retested.

Results

For the infants, Table 23.2 indicates by age levels the score earned on each

two comparison infants had quotients between 130 and 139, etc.

Examination of Table 23.2 shows that at the 2-months age-level there is little if any difference between the two groups. The mean of the Creche group is 97, that of the comparison group 107. These means, each based on only 8 cases, are not significantly different from each other or from the American norms. However, at all ages beyond 3·0 months the Creche infants score definitely lower than either the comparison or the normative groups, whose records are indistinguishable.

If all scores from 2 to 12 months are averaged, the Creche mean is 68, the comparison mean 102. For the 3- to 12-month period the mean of the Creche scores is 63, (S.D. 13), that of the comparison group 101 (S.D. 15), a difference of 38 points. This is a very large and highly significant difference ($p < 0.001$). In this age-range all of the comparison infants tested above the mean of the Creche subjects and all of the Creche subjects were below the mean of the comparison group. No

are concerned is unknown, here as elsewhere. According to the supervisory staff there have been no changes in child care within the past 6 years.

The results of the performance tests are shown in Table 23.3. It will be noted that the data there reported agree remarkably well in showing that

TABLE 23.3. *Results of Performance Tests*

Test	N	Various 'DQ' Scores			
		Range	Median	Mean	S.D.
Goodenough	30	58–136	93	93	20
Porteus maze†	25	69–150	89	95	20
Knox cube ‡	25	—	100		

† Four children earned fewer than 4 points, which is the minimum score for which Arthur gives a mental age. Since the lowest MA given by Arthur is 4·5, these children were arbitrarily given a mental age of 4 years and DQs were computed accordingly. Obviously these scores affect the mean and *S.D.* but not the median.

‡ On this test, 11 of the 25 subjects scored below the 4·5 MA, the lowest age for which Arthur gives norms. Because of the large number below 4·5 no arbitrary scores were given. Of the 14 subjects who earned MAs of 4·5 and above, one had a DQ of 80 and two of 100. The remaining scores ranged from 101 to 165. The median of 100 seems representative.

Creche baby between 3 and 12 months had a DQ above 95.

Before discussing the results of the infant tests we turn now to the tests given to Creche children between 4·5 and 6 years of age. We note first that there are reasons to believe that the subjects tested at 4·5 to 6·0 years of age performed, as infants, at the same level as did the children whose test results have just been presented. Because procedures of admission to the Creche have not changed in recent years the two groups of infants can be assumed to be genetically similar. Since practically all infants who enter the Creche remain for 6 years, there are no selective influences between admission and 6 years. The only qualification of this statement regards infant mortality, whose selective action so far as psychological tests

on these tests the development of the Creche children is only about 10 per cent below the norms of American home-reared children. In a separate report [3] it has been shown that on the Goodenough test Lebanese children at the 5-year level make scores equivalent to the American norms. No Lebanese norms are available for the Knox cube or Porteus maze tests but there is no reason to believe that they would be higher than the published standards. In other words, there is evidence that the environment of the Creche produces only a slight retardation among 4- and 5-year-olds on these tests.

In summary, the data show that, with respect to behavioural development, children in the Creche are normal during the second month of age, are greatly retarded from 3 to 12 months of age, and almost normal on certain performance tests between 4·5 and 6 years of age.

Interpretative discussion
To a reader acquainted with the numerous and often divergent opinions concerning the effects of early environment, the results just reported may, on the surface, only serve to confuse further the already unclear picture. We believe, however, that we can show that these data and others can be fitted into a coherent view.

Early normality of Creche infants
The fact that the Creche subjects had DQs of approximately 100 during the second month, and presumably during the first month also, should not be surprising. It has not been shown that any stimulus deprivation will affect infant behavioural development during the first 2 months. The twins reared under experimental conditions by Dennis and Dennis [4] made normal progress during this period. The infants tested by Spitz [12] had a mean developmental quotient of 130 during the second month. The supernormality of this score was probably due to the inadequacy of test norms rather than to institutional influence.

If it is true that restricted stimulation has little or no effect upon early behavioural development, this can be due to at least two different causes. One explanation would be in terms of maturation. Perhaps growth of the nervous system, apart from sensory stimulation, is alone responsible for postnatal behavioural growth during the first two months. A second explanation lies in the possibility that sensory experience is essential, but that for the tests presented to him the infant even when swaddled hand and foot and lying on his back obtains sufficient stimulation.

For the Cattell infant tests the second interpretation is not altogether unreasonable. Of the five tests which we employed at the two-months level, four are given to the infant while lying on his back and the responses required are visual. These are 'inspects environment', 'follows moving person', 'follows moving ring vertically', and 'follows moving ring horizontally'. Since the infants spend nearly 24 hours per day in a supine position in a well-lighted room, and some movement occurs near them, there is considerable opportunity to practice visual pursuit movements.

The fifth item among the two-month tests is lifting head when prone. The Creche infants are placed on the abdomen for a short time daily while being bathed, dried, and dressed. For this reason, lifting the head while in this position can be practiced and direct observation shows that it is practiced. Possibly the Creche infants respond normally to the items given them at two months because the required responses are well practiced. However, the possibility that maturation alone is sufficient for the development of the items is not ruled out.

Retardation between 3 and 12 months of age
Beyond the 2-months level the majority of items on the Cattell scale require that the infant be tested in a sitting position while being held on the lap of an adult. Sitting is a position to which the Creche infants under about 10 months of age are relatively unaccustomed. They are not propped up in their beds or placed in chairs before that age. The first occasion for placing the infants in a sitting position may come with the introduction of semisolid foods, but we have noted that some of the infants are given these while lying down. Perhaps as a consequence of inexperience in being held upright the infants as a group make a

poor record on the test item which involves holding the head erect and steady. This unsteadiness of the head, plus general unfamiliarity with sitting, may account in part for the low scores earned on certain purely visual items. These are 'regards cube', 'regards spoon', 'follows ball', and 'regards pellet'.

Many of the remaining items involve not only sitting but in addition manual skills directed by vision. Among the items are 'picks up spoon', 'picks up cube', 'grasps pellet', 'grasps string', 'lifts cup', 'takes two cubes', 'exploits paper', 'pulls out peg', etc. Between ages 5 and 7 months, the age placement given these items, the infants have little opportunity to practise visuo-manual co-ordinations in a sitting position and, further, visuo-manual co-ordinations are not required or encouraged even in a lying position.

Analysis of other items whose placement is between 3 and 12 months reveals that practically all of them require manual skills and require adjustment to visually presented objects. It is suggested that the relationship between the items and the environmental restrictions experienced by the children account for the low scores made by the Creche subjects.

We examined the records made by the Creche children aged 3 months and above on each item, expecting that one or two items might be found in regard to which their performance is normal. We were able to find none. But we were also unable to find an item in this age range on which the subjects were judged to receive a normal amount of relevant experience.

It is interesting to note two items on which the subjects are very deficient even though the motor component of the item is clearly present. These involve turning to sound. In one of these items, the child, sitting on the lap of an adult, is required to turn toward the experimenter who stands by the shoulder of the seated adult, and calls the infant's name. The second item is similar but a small hand-bell is used instead of the voice. The first item has an age placement of four months, the second, five months. Of 36 children tested between 4·0 and 10·0 months of age only one turned to the voice and only 4 turned to the bell.

Now all of the children turned to and followed a moving person in the field of view. The difficulty of the item apparently lies in the subject's lack of associations with sounds. We have noted that in approaching a child or providing services for a child the attendants seldom speak to him. This seems to be due partly to the fact that the attendants are too busy. A second relevant fact is that, with 20 children in a room, and the windows open to rooms containing 100 additional children, it is seldom quiet enough at feeding times and bathing times to encourage verbal greetings. So far as we could determine no event which happens to a Creche baby is consistently preceded by a sound signal. These conditions seem to explain the finding that the infants seldom turned to a voice or a ringing bell only a few inches from their ears.

From the preceding discussion it will be obvious that we tend to attribute the retardation of Creche subjects between 3 and 12 months of age to a lack of learning opportunities relative to the Cattell test items.

Relationship of the 3- to 12-month retardation to the findings of other studies

There seems to be a superficial, if not a basic, disagreement between the results here reported, and those of other studies, particularly those of Dennis and Dennis [4] and those of Spitz [12–16]. We wish to comment on the apparent divergences and to indicate how they can be reconciled.

In a study of a pair of twins named Del and Rey who were reared under experimentally controlled conditions until 13 months of age, Dennis and Dennis found that, while the subjects were retarded beyond the range of ordinary subjects in regard to the appearance of a few responses, the subjects' development in general equalled that of home-reared infants. The few specific retardations occurred on items in respect to which the infants could not engage in self-directed practice, namely, visually directed reaching, sitting without support, and supporting self with the feet. These retardations seem consonant with the behaviour of the Creche subjects. However, the prevailing normality of Del and Rey seems at variance with the Creche findings.

To begin with, certain differences between the environmental conditions of the subjects in the two studies should be noted. For one thing, the adult–child ratios in the two studies were very different. In the Del–Rey study there were two subjects and two experimenters, a one-to-one ratio. In the Creche, the adult–child ratio is one to ten, a greatly different situation. In the Del–Rey study the environmental restrictions in regard to learning were rather severe in the beginning, but were gradually relaxed as desired data were obtained. In the Creche, very limited opportunities for learning and practising responses continue throughout the first year. Certain specific contrasts may be mentioned: Del and Rey were kept in larger and deeper cribs, were less restrained by clothing and consequently probably had more opportunities for motor experimentation than did the Creche infants. Further, Del and Rey may have received more handling and more

varied exposure to stimuli than did the Creche infants. However, there can be no doubt that in several respects Del and Rey suffered as much a restriction of experience as did the Creche infants. Speech was not directed to Del and Rey nor did adults smile in their presence until they were 6 months of age. No toys were provided until the twelfth month. They were not placed in a sitting position until they were over 8 months of age.

But it is our belief that the difference between the normality of Del and Rey and the retardation of the Creche infants is due to the use of different indices of behavioural development rather than to real differences in behaviour. In the Del–Rey study no general scale of infant development was administered. The majority of the developmental data reported for Del and Rey consisted of noting when each of a number of common infant responses first appeared. That is, the observers recorded when each subject first brought hand to mouth, first grasped bedclothes, first vocalized to person, first laughed, etc. The initial date of occurrence of such responses cannot be determined by testing. The Del–Rey data are longitudinal and the Del–Rey records were found to be normal when compared with similar data obtained in other observational studies.

Now since observation in the Del–Rey study was directed primarily towards responses which could occur at any time and did not require the introduction of test conditions, it follows that poverty of environmental stimulation would not be expected to yield much evidence of retardation. The child left to his own devices on his back in his crib can bring his hand to his mouth, grasp his bedclothes, vocalize, observe his own hands, grasp his own hands, grasp his own foot, bring foot to mouth, etc. These are the items which were observed. One of the major findings of the Del–Rey study was that the untutored infant does do these things, and does them within the usual age range of home-reared babies.

In regard to such responses it *may* be that the Creche babies are normal. The relevant facts can be discovered only by observers each spending full time observing a few infants. If all Creche infants were to be observed it would necessitate the presence of many additional observers or caretakers. The reader is reminded that the Del–Rey investigation, involving only two infants, took a major part of the time of the two observers for one year. To devote one year, or even one month to observing each Creche subject cannot be proposed in an institution which has severe limitations of caretaker personnel. In contrast to the requirements of an observational study of development, the testing time in the Creche study was only 10 to 30 min per subject.

If we cannot compare Del and Rey with the Creche babies in terms of observational data, it is likewise not possible to compare them in terms of test data. It is impossible to estimate in retrospect with any degree of confidence how Del and Rey would have scored at various times during the first year on the Cattell infant scale. We arrive, therefore, at the following conclusion: It is likely infants with restricted learning opportunities are normal on 'observational' items but retarded on 'test' items. It is believed that the latter, but not the former, are influenced by environmental limitations. If this is a correct interpretation, the Del–Rey study and the Creche

study are two sides of the same coin. However, to establish that this is the case appears to be a very difficult research assignment.

We consider next the work of Spitz. The observations by Spitz which seem most closely related to the present study concern the institution called Foundling Home. Here, as at the Creche, there was a shortage of personnel. Although the mothers were present in the institution for several months, they seem to have had little contact with their children aside from breast-feeding them. Pinneau [9] points out that Spitz does not explain why this was the case. Despite the presence of the mothers in the institution the adult–child ratio in the nursery is reported to be about 1 to 8. The children spent most of their time for many months on their backs in their cribs, as did the Creche infants. At one point Spitz reports that a hollow worn in their mattresses restrained their activity. This, however, was definitely not true of the Creche infants.

Since Spitz's studies have been extensively reviewed and criticized by Pinneau, only a limited amount of space will be devoted to them here. Spitz used some form of the Hetzer–Wolf baby tests. There is no doubt that their standardization leaves much to be desired. Spitz reports scores for the Foundling Home group and a control group of 17 home-reared infants. In the second month both groups had mean DQs between 130 and 140. The private home group remained at that level but the mean of the Foundling Home group dropped precipitously to 76 by the sixth month and to 72 by the end of the first year. Spitz believes that this decline in DQ was due to the emotional consequences of separation from the mother, but Pinneau has pointed out that most of the decline took place prior to the prevalent age of separation. Pinneau indicates further that at least some of the decline is probably due to inadequate test standardization.

We compare our data with those of Spitz with considerable hesitation because the two sets of data were obtained by tests whose comparability is unknown. In numerical terms the results of the two studies in the second half of the first year seem to agree fairly well, Spitz's mean for this period being about 74 and ours 63. But the findings for the first half-year present some apparent differences. Our subjects drop from a mean of 97 to a mean of 72 between the second and third months, and drop only ten additional points thereafter. Spitz's group starts higher and declines for a longer period.

Spitz's data and ours agree in finding that environmental conditions can depress infant test scores after the second month of life. We disagree with Spitz in regard to the interpretation of the cause of the decline. He believes it to have been due, in the case of his subjects, to a break of the emotional attachment to the mother. This could not have been the cause of the decline of the Creche infants. Since the conditions for the formation of an emotional tie to a specific individual were never present, no breach of attachment could have occurred. We have noted above Pinneau's demonstration that even Spitz's own data do not support his interpretation. We believe that Spitz's data as well as ours are satisfactorily interpreted in terms of restricted learning opportunities. We suggest that an analysis of the relationship between test items and the conditions prevailing in the Foundling Home would reveal that retardation could readily be explained in terms of restriction of learning opportunities. But such restriction is not inherent in institutional care. Klackenberg has recently presented a study [7] of infant development in a Swedish institution, in which the adult–child ratio was 1 to 2 or 3, in which no retardation was found.

Discussion of the Creche 4- and 5-year-olds

We have no doubt that on many tests the Creche 4- and 5-year-olds (and also 2- and 3-year-olds) would be retarded, perhaps to a marked degree. We think this would be particularly true in regard to tests involving more than a very modest amount of language comprehension and language usage. The language handicap of institutional children with limited adult contact has been sufficiently demonstrated [8].

It is likely that on some performance tests the Creche children also would score below available norms. On the Healy Picture form board, for example, most of the incidents represented are outside the experience of Creche children. We assume that the older Creche children are retarded on some tests, but we wish to determine whether retardation is general or whether it is related to specific environmental handicaps.

We chose the draw-a-man test, the Knox cube test and the Porteus maze test because it was thought that the Creche environment might affect these tests less than other tests. So far as the Knox cubes are concerned, it is difficult to imagine how one can deprive a child of the experience of visually remembering just-touched objects, except through loss of sight. So far as the Goodenough is concerned, both human beings and two-dimensional representations of them were familiar to the subjects. They were also familiar with the idea of drawing and with the use of pencils. Knowledge of the use of pencils may also play a part in the Porteus maze test. It is uncertain what other experience may play a role in this test.

The results show clearly that on these tests the Creche children approximated the performance of children in normal environments. In other words, the retardation which was found to exist between 3 and 12 months of age did not produce a general and permanent intellectual deficit. It is possible for infants who have been retarded through limitations of experience at an early age level to perform normally, at least in some respects, at later age periods. The assumption that early retardation produces permanent retardation does not receive support from our data.

Emotional and personality effects

No doubt many readers would like to know the emotional and personality consequences of the Creche regime. So would we. But to the best of our knowledge no objective and standardized procedures with adequate norms are available which would enable us to compare the Creche infants with other groups of children in these respects. This is equally true of studies conducted earlier.

In the absence of objective techniques, we can only report a few impressions. The Creche infants were readily approachable and were interested in the tests. Very few testing sessions were postponed because of crying, from whatever cause. There was very little shyness or fear of strangers, perhaps because each infant saw several different adults. In the cribs there was very little if any crying that did not seem attributable to hunger or discomfort. However, some of the older babies developed automatisms such as arching the back strongly, or hitting some part of the body with the hand, which may have represented a type of 'stimulation hunger'. It was almost always possible to get the infants over 2 months of age to smile by stroking their chins or cheeks or by shaking them slightly. The older children, like the infants, were friendly and approachable. However, such observations are not meant to imply that other personality consequences could not be found if adequate techniques existed.

Summary and conclusions

This study has been concerned with the development of children in an institution in Beirut, Lebanon, called the Creche, in which 'mothering' and all other forms of adult–child interaction are at a minimum because the institution is seriously understaffed. The children come to the institution shortly after birth and remain until 6 years of age. Contact with the mother ceases upon the child's entrance to the institution and contact with mother-substitutes is slight because the adult–child ratio is 1 to 10.

Opportunity for developing infant skills through practice is very slight. In the early months the infants are swaddled. For many months the infant lies on his back, and is even fed in a supine position. He is not propped up, carried about, or provided with the means of practising many activities.

Data on behavioural development were obtained by giving the Cattell infant scale to all infants between 2 and 12 months of age and the Goodenough draw-a-man test, the Knox cube test, and the Porteus maze test to all children between 4½ and 6 years of age. Comparison data were available from American norms and from certain groups of Lebanese subjects.

It was found that in terms of developmental quotients, the mean quotient at 2 months was approximately 100. Between 3 and 12 months the mean was 63. In the tests given at the 4- and 5-year level, the mean scores were roughly 90.

Possible interpretations of these data have been discussed at some length. Our conclusions may be summarized as follows:

(1) It is uncertain whether the normality of behaviour at 2 months shows that maturation plays a major role in early development, or whether experience, limited as it was, provided the essential requirements for learning the responses which were tested.

(2) The retardation prevailing between 3 and 12 months of age seems to be due to lack of learning opportunities in situations comparable to the test situations. It is possible that an observational approach in the day-by-day situation might reveal that some behaviours developed normally.

(3) The infants did not undergo loss of an emotional attachment. There is nothing to suggest that emotional shock, or lack of mothering or other emotion-arousing conditions, were responsible for behavioural retardation.

(4) Retardation in the last 9 months of the first year to the extent of a mean DQ of 65 does not result in a generally poor performance at $4\frac{1}{2}$ to 6 years, even when the child remains in a relatively restricted environment. The study therefore does not support the doctrine of the permanency of early environmental effects.

(5) It is believed that the objective data of other studies, as well as this one, can be interpreted in terms of the effects of specific kinds of restrictions upon infant learning.

References

1. ARTHUR, GRACE. (1947). *A point scale of performance tests* (Rev. Form II). Psychol. Corp., New York.

2. CATTELL, PSYCHE. (1940). *The measurement of intelligence of infants and young children.* Psychol. Corp., New York.

3. DENNIS, W. (1957). Performance of Near Eastern children on the draw-a-man test. *Child Dev.* **28**, 427–30.

4. —— and DENNIS, M. G. (1951). Development under controlled environmental conditions. *In* (Dennis, W. (Ed.)) *Readings in child psychology.* Prentice-Hall, New York, pp. 104–31.

5. GOODENOUGH, FLORENCE. (1926). *The measurement of intelligence by drawings.* World Book Co., New York.

6. KHAMIS, S. H. and POWERS, L. E. (1955). Report on infant mortality survey of rural Lebanon. Mimeographed report, Am. Univ. of Beirut.

7. KLACKENBERG, G. (1956). Studies in maternal deprivation in infants' homes. *Acta pediatr.* **45**, 1–12.

8. McCARTHY, DOROTHEA. (1951). Children's speech. *In* (Carmichael, L. (Ed.)) *Manual of child psychology*, 2nd rev. ed. Wiley, New York.

9. PINNEAU, S. R. (1955). The infantile disorders of hospitalism and anaclitic depression. *Psychol. Bull.* **52**, 429–52.

10. RIBBLE, MARGARET. (1943). *The rights of infants.* Columbia Univ. Press, New York.

11. RIBBLE, MARGARET. (1944). Infantile experience in relation to personality development. *In* (Hunt, J. McV. (Ed.)) *Personality and the behavior disorders.* Vol. 2. Ronald Press, New York, pp. 621–51.

12. SPITZ, R. A. (1945). Hospitalism. An inquiry into the genesis of psychiatric conditions in early childhood. *Psy-*

cho-anal. Study Child **1**. Int. Univ. Press, New York, pp. 53–74.

13. —— (1946). Hospitalism: A follow-up report. *Psycho-anal. Study Child* **2**. Int. Univ. Press, New York, pp. 113–17.

14. —— (1946). Anaclitic depression. *Psycho-anal. Study Child* **2**. Int. Univ. Press, New York, pp. 313–42.

15. SPITZ, R. A. and WOLF, KATHERINE M. (1949). Autoerotism. Some empirical findings and hypotheses on three of its manifestations in the first year of life. *Psycho-anal. Study Child* **3–4**. Int. Univ. Press, New York, pp. 85–120.

16. SPITZ, R. A. (1951). The psychogenic diseases in infancy: An attempt at their etiologic classification. *Psycho-anal. Study Child* **6**. Int. Univ. Press, New York, pp. 255–75.

17. WAKIM, S. (1956). Child care in Mieh-Mieh. M.A. Thesis, Library of the Am. Univ. of Beirut.

24 Stimulation in the neonatal period

ANNELIESE F. KORNER AND
ROSE GROBSTEIN†

OBSERVATIONS incidental to a study of behaviour genetics in neonates [7] suggest that when babies cry and are picked up to the shoulder, they not only stop crying, but they frequently become visually alert, and they scan the environment. We were struck by several implications of this observation. If generally true, this type of soothing would induce a state which is otherwise quite rare in the neonate and which is considered by some to be the optimal state for the infant's earliest learning. According to P. H. Wolff's [13] observations, this state of alertness occurs spontaneously but from 8 to 16 per cent of the time in the first postnatal week, and it only very gradually increases over subsequent weeks. The infant thus spends only a very minor part of his day in alertness. Yet, in terms of his locomotor helplessness, visual prehension is one of the few avenues at his disposal to make contact and to get acquainted with the environment. If regularly soothing of this type induces a state of alertness, it follows that a baby picked up for crying will have earlier and many more opportunities to scan the environment than an infant left crying in his crib.

† From 'Visual alertness as related to soothing in neonates: implications for maternal stimulation and early deprivation'. *Child Dev.* **37**, 867–76 (1966). Reprinted by permission of the Society for Research in Child Development, Inc. Copyright © 1966.

In a recent symposium entitled 'The crucial early influence: Mother love or environmental stimulation' Fantz [6], referring to his findings that infants discriminate from birth among visual stimuli, concluded that perceptual experiences play a crucial role in early development. In fact, he could distinguish babies reared at home from institutional infants through their visual responses by the second month of life. While Fantz stressed the importance of perceptual experiences through environmental stimulation, he also stated that the effects of early stimulation would be better understood 'if one could pin down the specific kinds of sensory stimulation and perceptual experience often provided optimally by a loving mother'. Our observation that babies, when picked up for crying, frequently become visually alert may thus capture one important pathway by which maternal ministrations may inadvertently provide visual experiences.

In this study we set out to investigate how frequently soothing of the type described elicited visual alertness. With the design used to study this problem, it was possible to explore an additional hypothesis. Bell [1] suggested that infants born to primiparous mothers may, for a number of reasons, respond differently to tactile stimulation than infants of multiparous mothers. We explored the relation between parity and visual alertness in response to soothing by including both types of infants.

Sample

The sample consisted of 12 newborn, breast-fed baby girls; 6 were born to primiparous mothers and 6 to multiparae. Boys were excluded because it was quite apparent that the comfort derived from being picked up and put to the shoulder was offset by the discomfort of being held close within hours of a circumcision. The babies ranged from 45 to 79 h in age; the average was 55 h old. All were Caucasian. Their birth weights ranged from 6 lb 8 oz to 8 lb 13 oz. They all had normal vaginal deliveries, received Apgar scores of 8 and above at birth, and they were found to be healthy newborn infants on physical examination.

Method

The infants were tested in a treatment room adjoining the nursery. Temperature and illumination approximated conditions in the nursery. The infants were tested individually after being brought to the treatment room in their own bassinets. They were dressed in shirts and diapers. To facilitate pickups, the infants were placed on the mattress underneath the plastic bassinet usually used for diapering and dressing infants. Since we were interested in soothing crying babies, they were all tested within $1\frac{1}{2}$ h before a feeding. Occasionally, we had to rouse a sleepy baby by moving her or by flicking her foot. The tests described below were initiated only when the baby was crying. Minimum time between experiments was 1 min. Since we were interested in comparing each infant with her own tendencies

in the various experimental positions, it was of little consequence whether some infants cried harder than others at any given trial. Also, enough trials were given to each infant to randomize the degree of agitation over all the trials.

Diapers were changed before the experiments were started irrespective of need. All infants were tested in four positions:

(1) Six trials on the left shoulder.
(2) Six trials on the right shoulder.
(3) Six trials sitting up.
(4) Six control trials in which the baby lay on her back without intervention by the observers.

The 'sit-up' experiments were introduced because it was noted that handling and the upright position alone frequently induced alertness. It was noted, for example, that many babies are alert when they are carried out to their mothers for feeding. In addition to the handling and the upright position, the experience of being put to the shoulder involves warmth, containment, the sense of smell, and the opportunity to establish mouth contact with the shoulder. Differential effects of the two positions could thus be studied.

To ensure comparability of handling, the same person did all the interventions. When picked up, the baby's head was supported, and her hands were kept out of reach of her mouth. The same was done in sitting up a baby. Trials in the various positions were done at random.

For 30 s following an intervention, alert and scanning behaviour was recorded. During the control experiments, the same was done for 30 s without an intervention. When the infant opened her eyes during the 30-s experimental period, the trial was scored as 'yes'. In each instance, the same was done for scanning behaviour. Babies varied a great deal in the degree of alertness. Some drowsily opened their eyes; others actively looked around, lifting the head and

Observer reliabilities

Reliabilities between two observers were calculated on the basis of dividing the number of agreements by the combined number of agreements and disagreements. Percentages of agreement were as follows:

TABLE 24.1. *Frequency of Eyes Opened in Response to Soothing*

Subject	Controls	Situps	Left	Right
'Multips':				
M1	2	0	6	6
M2	2	5	6	6
M3	0	2	3	4
M4	0	1	4	6
M5	3	4	6	3
M6	0	0	5	6
Totals	7	12	30	31
Percentage of trials	19	33	83	86
'Primips':				
P1	1	0	6	6
P2	1	0	6	6
P3	0	0	6	6
P4	5	3	6	6
P5	4	5	6	6
P6	1	0	2	4
Totals	12	8	32	34
Percentage of trials	33	22	89	94

exploring the experimenter. Some had brief, others had sustained, periods of alertness. Since visual pursuit can be elicited even in drowsy babies [15], and since it is difficult to equate several brief periods of alertness with one sustained period, the degree and the duration of alertness were not considered in the ratings. 'Yes' was scored when the infant opened her eyes and when she scanned the environment at any one time during the of 30 s observations. In addition to these observations, the number of spontaneous alert and scanning episodes between experiments was noted for 10 of the 12 subjects.

(1) Opening eyes during 'sit-ups' and during controls: 96 per cent.
(2) Opening eyes between experiments: 98 per cent.
(3) Scanning during 'sit-ups' and during controls: 97 per cent.
(4) Scanning episodes between experiments: 95 per cent.

Reliability ratings for opening of eyes and scanning during 'pick-ups' would have required a third observer. Since there was very little disagreement between what constituted alerting and scanning behaviour during 'sit-ups' and controls and between experiments (the percentages of agreement ranging from 95 to 98), it was felt to be unnecessary to introduce a third observer to rate alert and scanning behaviour during 'pick-ups'.

Results

Incidence of alerting in response to soothing

Our data confirmed the observation that, when crying infants were put to the shoulder, they not only stopped crying, but each of them also opened

result in the infant's opening her eyes significantly more often than when no intervention was made.

Incidence of scanning in response to soothing

Since the degree of alertness varied when an infant opened her eyes, active scanning probably was a better measure for testing the effect of soothing on visual alertness. Table 24.3 demonstrates that, even with this more

TABLE 24.2. *Significance Levels Between Paired Positions*

	Control-Sitting	Control-Left	Control-Right	Sitting-Left	Sitting-Right	Left-Right
'Multips'	N.S.	**	**	**	**	N.S.
'Primips'	N.S.	**	**	**	**	N.S.

** = Significant at the 1 per cent level; N.S. = not significant.

her eyes and alerted in the large majority of trials. Table 24.1 summarizes the raw data for 'primips' and 'multips'.† The figures above the totals represent the number of trials out of six in which each baby opened her eyes in each position. The figures below the totals represent the percentage of trials in which alerting occurred in each position.

An analysis of variance was performed. The difference between 'primips' and 'multips' was not found to be significant. By contrast, the difference of reactions to the various positions was found to be significant at the 1 per cent level. Calculations of significance levels between paired positions resulted in the findings displayed in Table 24.2.

The results suggest that handling and the upright position alone did not

† The terms 'primips' and 'multips' will be used for convenience henceforth to refer to the offspring of primiparous and multiparous mothers, respectively.

stringent criterion for alertness, each baby in this sample alerted and scanned when put to the shoulder, and most did in the majority of the trials.

An analysis of variance was performed. Even though, in absolute terms, the 'primips' scanned more, the difference was not statistically significant. By contrast, the difference of reactions to the various positions was again significant at the 1 per cent level. Calculations of significance levels between paired positions resulted in a table identical to Table 24.2.

Spontaneous alerting and scanning between experiments

Spontaneous alerting and scanning between experiments was recorded only in 10 out of 12 cases. The incidence among babies of these episodes varied greatly. The average number of times the 'primips' opened their eyes between experiments was 7·8; for 'multips', the average was only 3·2. The 'primips' scanned on the average of 6·5 times, the 'multips' only 3 times. These differences between 'primips' and 'multips' did not reach significance, probably because of the small number of observations. It is of interest, however, that there is a consistent trend among the three types of observations: In each instance

positions. By contrast, M3 and P6 had difficulty with both, even when put to the shoulder. There also were marked differences in the capacity to sustain alertness. In some babies these episodes were fleeting; in others they were maintained for long periods of time.

TABLE 24.3. *Frequency of Scanning in Response to Soothing*

Subject	Controls	Situps	Left	Right
'Multips':				
M1	1	0	5	4
M2	0	1	4	5
M3	0	0	2	1
M4	0	0	3	5
M5	2	3	5	3
M6	0	0	5	6
Totals	3	4	24	24
Percentage of trials	8	11	66	66
'Primips':				
P1	0	0	6	6
P2	1	0	4	4
P3	0	0	6	5
P4	4	3	6	6
P5	4	4	6	6
P6	0	0	0	1
Totals	9	7	28	28
Percentage of trials	25	19	77	77

the 'primips' alerted and scanned more frequently than the 'multips'. This suggests that differences may exist in arousal levels between 'primips' and 'multips'. Our data on crying, not reported here, which shows highly significant differences between 'multips' and 'primips', would support this hypothesis.

Individual differences

As Tables 24.1 and 24.3 demonstrate, there were marked differences among babies in their tendency to alert and scan. For example, P4, P5, and M5, tended to alert and scan readily in all

There were particularly marked differences among the infants in their proneness to alert and to scan between experiments. Some babies never did alert and scan, others did very rarely, and a few did quite frequently (range 0–15 instances, with a mean of 5·5). Infants M3 and P6, who had difficulty alerting when put to the shoulder, also showed very few instances of alerting and scanning between experiments (3 and 0 instances, respectively). By contrast, those infants who alerted and scanned most between experiments were not necessarily the same babies who had the highest frequency of these behaviours when picked up. Very probably, the amount of handling during the entire experimental session affected babies differently, arousing some, not affecting others. One may infer from this that there may be individual differences among babies in the ease with which the state of arousal is changed through manipulation.

Discussion

Visual alertness in the neonate has become the concern of many studies (e.g. [5, 6, 9, 10, 13–15]). This concern on the part of some investigators stems from the observation that visual alertness is not as reflex as most neo-natal behaviour and, to a large extent, qualitatively resembles the later capacity of attentiveness. In terms of psychoanalytic theory, visual alertness is probably the clearest example of a primary autonomous ego function observable in the newborn. In view of the neonate's locomotor helplessness, visual prehension is one of the infant's few avenues for learning and for getting acquainted with the environment.

Our experiments show that this state of visual alertness, so important for learning, can readily be induced by picking up a crying newborn and putting him to the shoulder. It was possible to do this without difficulty even at a time when, according to Wolff's [13] findings, the newborn is least likely to be alert, namely, when he is hungry. Wolff's observations demonstrated that during the first week of life his subjects spent, on the average, only 11 per cent of the time in the state of alert inactivity and that 86·4 per cent of this 11 per cent occurred within the first hour after a feeding.

One can only speculate about the causes of the association between this kind of soothing and visual alertness. Neurophysiologically, what may occur is that the soothing action of this intervention lowers the infant's state of arousal, with the result that the infant goes from crying into the next lower state on the continuum of states and arousal.† Waking activity, the next lower state on this continuum, was prevented by the motor restraint imposed by being held to the shoulder. This restraint may have lowered the infant's state of arousal one step further, resulting in the state of alert inactivity. In fact, by preventing the distracting effects of the infant's motor activity, the physical restraint may have enhanced the likelihood of alert behaviour. Wolff and White [15] found this relation to hold: They increased the infant's capacity for attentive behaviour by inhibiting motor activity through the use of a pacifier.

In psychological terms, the association of soothing and visual alertness may involve the prototype of a reaction which may hold true throughout life: By reducing the intensity of internal needs, the organism can turn outward and attend the external world. Descriptively, this corresponds well with the sequence of events as we observed them.

Our data did not suggest that handling or the upright position alone induced a state of alertness. This was true because, in most cases, handling alone did not lower the infant's state of arousal sufficiently to reduce crying to the point of alertness. The observation that many infants are quietly alert when brought to a feeding suggests that handling and the upright position

† For a definition of states of arousal see [12].

are more successful in inducing alertness in non-crying or sleepy infants. In those states of arousal, the stimulation of touch, motion, and positional change are rousing rather than soothing. In an intense form, labour and birth which entail extreme stimulation of this type may have arousing effects with similar results. Brazelton [3] observed that, for a few hours after delivery and before going into a relative state of disorganization, all of his subjects were alert and responsive. They fixed and followed a red ring visually for several minutes at a time. They also attended and often visually followed auditory stimuli. Brazelton's observations of the alertness of the newly delivered baby are easily confirmed by casual observation. All one has to do is to watch babies as they are admitted to the newborn nursery from the delivery room: most of them have their eyes wide open and are highly alert.

Of relevance to the alertness-producing effects of both soothing and handling are the numerous studies dealing with the effects of handling and early stimulation on both animals and infants. For the most part, these studies show the importance of early stimulation for the growth and development of the young organism. The specific factors which account for the more favourable development of the 'handled' group are usually not spelled out. Levine [8], noting profound psychophysiological effects of infantile stimulation in the rat, concluded that the sensory routes and mechanisms underlying these effects are not known. He suspects that proprioceptive and kinesthetic stimulation may indicate the sensory routes of effective stimulation. Casler [4] and Yarrow [16], in reviews of maternal deprivation studies, concluded that early tactile stimulation appears necessary for normal human development. Our own observations suggest that tactile stimulation may activate visual behaviour. Activation of the visual modality through tactile stimulation may thus be one of the pathways through which early stimulation takes effect. We find support of this hypothesis in White and Castle's [11] study which demonstrated that institution-reared infants given small amounts of extra handling during their first weeks of life later showed significantly more visual interest in their environment than non-handled controls.

In the earliest days of life, infant care, for the most part, invites soothing rather than rousing interventions. It is the handling involved in soothing rather than rousing which may make the difference in the neonates' earliest opportunities for visual experiences. Infants in institutions, while usually given adequate physical care, generally are not picked up and soothed when they cry. This may be partly responsible for their earliest deficit.

Mothers of home-reared infants differ, of course, in their readiness to soothe their crying newborn. Our observations suggest that picked-up infants will have many more opportunities to get acquainted with the environment than babies left crying in their cribs. In particular, they will have many more occasions to explore their mothers. Their visual explorations will occur when comforted. This may lower their stimulus barrier under conditions which minimize the danger of being overwhelmed.

Fantz's [6] findings suggest that visual and perceptual experiences during the neonatal period have lasting developmental effects. With

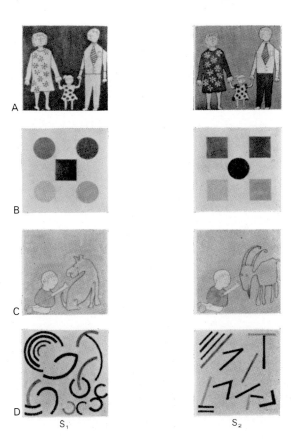

PLATE I. Visual stimuli shown in sets from A (*top*) to D (*bottom*). S_1 is shown on the left, S_2 on the right for each set. All stimuli except S_1 in set A are chromatic. For set A the violation was the change from an achromatic to a chromatic picture; for set B, the violation was a change in form; for set C, content; and for set D curvature.

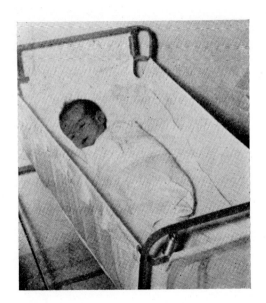

PLATE 2

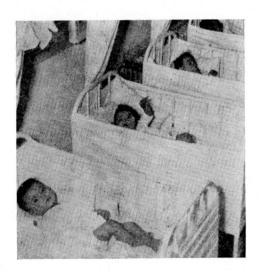

PLATE 3

PLATE 4

PLATE 5

PLATE 6. Infant 'looking chamber' for testing visual responsiveness to targets exposed under controlled-stimulus conditions. The patterned objects are visible in a box on the table, each with a handle for sliding it in the chamber. Observer is looking on one side of the target through the peep-hole, which is hidden by the timer.

PLATE 7. Characteristic investigatory responses.

PLATE 8. Posture and expression characteristic of 'play'.

this in mind, our observations raise a host of developmental questions. For example, do babies who are carried around a great deal learn to rely more heavily on the visual modality in their exploration of the environment than babies who do not have this experience as much? How does the development of the infant of another culture who is constantly carried around by his mother differ in this respect? With the added opportunities of exploring the mother, are there differences in time and depth in the infant–mother bond formation and in the development of differentiating self from non-self? Also are there differences in the onset and strength of stranger and separation anxiety? As Benjamin [2] has shown, babies who rely heavily on the visual modality will experience stranger and separation anxiety earlier and more severely.

Our observations have not only experiential implications. We also found organismic differences among the infants. Babies differed greatly in their capacity for alert behaviour. This finding is confirmed by our larger study [7] involving a bigger sample of neonates and much longer observations. It is reasonable to believe that varying opportunities for visual experiences will affect babies differently depending on their own disposition. Thus an infant with high sensory thresholds may demonstrate the effects of maternal neglect or sensory deprivation more acutely than the infant more capable of providing visual experiences for himself.

References

1. BELL, R. Q. (1963). Some factors to be controlled in studies of the behavior of newborns. *Biol. Neonat.* **5**, 200–14.
2. BENJAMIN, J. D. (1959). Prediction and psychopathological theory. *In* (Jessner, Lucie and Pavenstedt, Eleanor (Eds.)) *Dynamic psychopathology in childhood.* Grune and Stratton, New York, pp. 6–77.
3. BRAZELTON, T. B. (1961). Psychophysiologic reactions in the neonate: II. Effect of maternal medication on the neonate and his behaviour. *J. Pediat.* **58**, No. 4, 513–18.
4. CASLER, L. (1961). Maternal deprivation: a critical review of the literature. *Monogr. Soc. Res. Child. Dev.* **26**, No. 2 (Serial No. 80).
5. FANTZ, R. L. (1958). Pattern vision in young infants. *Psychol. Rec.* **8**, 43–7.
6. —— (1966). The crucial early influence: mother love or environmental stimulation? *Am. J. Orthopsychiat.* **36**, No. 2, 330–1. (Abstract.)
7. KORNER, ANNELIESE F. (1964). Some hypotheses regarding the significance of individual differences at birth for later development. *Psycho-anal. study Child* **19**, 58–72.
8. LEVINE, S. (1962). Psychophysiological effects of infantile stimulation. *In* (Bliss, E. (Ed.)) *Roots of behavior.* Paul Hoeber, New York, pp. 246–53.
9. LING, BING-CHUNG. (1942). A genetic study of sustained visual fixation and associated behavior in the human infant from birth to six months. *J. genet. Psychol.* **61**, 227–77.
10. WHITE, B. L. (1963). The development of perception during the first six months of life. Paper read at Amer. Ass. of Advancement of Science.
11. —— and CASTLE, P. W. (1964). Visual exploratory behavior following postnatal handling of human infants. *Percept. mot. Skills* **18**, 497–502.
12. WOLFF, P. H. (1959). Observations of newborn infants. *Psychosom. Med.* **21**, 110–18.
13. —— (1965). The development of attention in young infants. *Ann. N.Y. Acad. Sci.* **118**, 815–30.

14. —— (1966). The causes, controls and organization of behavior in the newborn. *Psychological issues*. Int. Univ. Press, New York.

15. —— and WHITE, B. L. (1965). Visual pursuit and attention in young infants. *J. Am. Acad. Child Psychiat.* **4**, No. 3, 473–84.

16. YARROW, L. J. (1961). Maternal deprivation: toward an empirical and conceptual re-evaluation. *Psychol. Bull.* **58**, 459–90.

25 Early stimulation and subsequent exploration

JUDITH RUBENSTEIN†

RECENT evidence suggests that stimulation facilitates the infant's development, and his cognitive development in particular [3, 17, 21, 22]. Data on the effects of early experience on exploratory behaviour in the human infant are inconsistent, seemingly varying with the age of the subjects and with the measures of exploratory behaviour. Comparing institutionalized babies with home-reared ones at $3\frac{1}{2}$ months of age, Rheingold [19] found no differences in responsiveness to novel objects, despite the greater amount of stimulation found in the homes and despite the careful quantification of responses. No differences in exploratory interest were clinically apparent on a cube manipulation test at 8 months, following 2 months of experimentally added stimulation of institutionalized babies [18]. Although home-reared babies exhibited a greater variety of responses to a novel object, they did not differ from institutionalized ones at 12 months in the number of responses to this object [3]. On the other hand, clinically assessed 'apathy' characterized institutionalized infants at 6 months of age [5, 6], and a global evaluation of exploratory behaviour in adopted infants found it

† From 'Maternal attentiveness and subsequent exploratory behavior in the infant'. *Child Dev.* **38**, 1089–100 (1967). Reprinted by permission of the Society for Research in Child Development, Inc. Copyright © 1967.

related to maternal stimulation at 6 months [23]. Perhaps the period between $3\frac{1}{2}$ and 6 months is in some way 'critical' for the emergence of this relation between stimulation and exploration.

In studies of institutionalized and adopted infants, emotional trauma attributable to the discontinuity of the mother figure [3] may be confounding the effects of quantity of stimulation. The purpose of the present study was to assess exploratory behaviour at 6 months as a function of different levels of stimulation at 5 months, with the discontinuity factor controlled. Babies reared at home by their biological mothers were chosen for study.

On the assumption that maternal attentiveness is the chief source of varied stimulation for the young home-reared infant, the hypothesis was proposed that 5-month-old infants whose mothers are more attentive exhibit more exploratory behaviour at 6 months of age than do infants whose mothers are less attentive. It was hypothesized that infants of highly attentive mothers, compared with infants of relatively inattentive mothers: (a) exhibit more exploratory interest in a novel stimulus presented alone; (b) exhibit stronger preference for novel over familiar stimuli.

As a corollary interest, the relations between quantity of maternal attentiveness and two indices of variety of stimulation were measured to examine the assumption that maternal attentiveness provides not only more but also more varied stimulation.

Method

Sample

Forty-four white home-reared babies, in their fifth month when first visited, cared for from birth by their biological mothers, were drawn from three Child Health Stations in Brooklyn, New York. Having been at least $5\frac{1}{2}$ lb at birth, and without known birth injury, each baby lived in an intact nuclear family, with no extended relatives, with no siblings over 5 years of age, and with the mother not employed outside the home.

Three groups of infants, receiving high, medium, and low attentiveness, were selected from a larger group of 77 whose mothers were screened for maternal attentiveness. The criteria for the three attentiveness groups were established prior to data collection. The first 44 Ss to meet the criteria (see below, *Operational definitions and measures*) constituted the sample, with the restriction that the groups be balanced for sex. The high- and medium-attentiveness groups (HA and MA, respectively) each had 8 males and 7 females; the low attentiveness group (LA) had 6 males and 8 females.

The three groups were comparable on the following characteristics: mother's age (HA, 22·5; MA, 24·0; LA, 22·1 years), birth weight (HA, 7·0; MA, 6·9; LA, 7·3 lb), and father's occupation. Classified according to Hollingshead's [8] seven-point occupational scale, approximately two-thirds of the fathers in each group were manual workers. There were no fathers in the highest two categories,

professionals or owners of large- or medium-sized businesses.

Maternal attentiveness is related to ordinal position ($X^2 = 4\cdot75$, $p = 0\cdot05$). First-born babies received significantly more attention than did later-born ones.

Overview

The study was conducted in four phases, comprising an initial contact, two home observations of maternal attentiveness and other aspects of stimulation, and the testing of exploratory behaviour in the infant. The purpose of each phase is described briefly; details follow in subsequent sections.

Phase 1. The clinic records were screened for the names of infants meeting the birth-weight, health, and family-composition criteria. As each infant approached his fifth month, the study was described to his mother, and the baby's participation was requested (see below, *Procedures*). If the mother agreed, an appointment was made for the first home visit.

Phase 2. In the baby's fifth month, the first home observation was made. Maternal attentiveness and the auxiliary stimulation variables (see below, *Operational definitions and measures*) were time-sampled. The total maternal attentiveness score derived from this home observation was the basis for the *initial* classification of the S in one of the three attentiveness groups. This initial classification determined whether or not S participated in Phase 3, the second home observation. If S was classified MA, the classification was considered final, and an appointment was made for Phase 4; if S was classified HA or LA, the classification was considered tentative, and an appointment was made for Phase 3.

Phase 3. Still in the baby's fifth month, a second home observation was made. Time-sampling was carried out as in Phase 2. The total maternal attentiveness score based on this visit was averaged with the score from the first visit. Based on this average, a final classification of high, medium, or low attentiveness was made. An appointment was made for Phase 4.

Phase 4. In the second or third week of the infant's sixth month, the observer of Phases 1, 2, and 3 introduced the examiner of Phase 4, who then tested the infant's exploratory behaviour (see below, *Operational definitions and measures*, and *Administration of the exploratory behaviour tests*).

Operational definitions and measures

Maternal attentiveness is defined by the number of times the mother was observed to look at, touch, hold, or talk to her baby. During the baby's fifth month an observer visited the homes of the HA and LA Ss twice on two separate days, and the MA Ss once, and time-sampled 3 h per day while the baby was awake. (The baby was considered 'asleep' when he had been lying quietly for 5 min, eyes closed, breathing regularly.) One observation lasted 10 s, followed by 10 s of recording the behaviours on a checklist. Ten minutes of recording were followed by 5 min of rest, yielding 360 observations per day. A daily attentiveness score is the number of observations during which any form of attentiveness occurred. HA and LA final scores are the averages of the two daily scores. A pilot study revealed the daily attentiveness scores to be stable

(day 1 $\times$ day 2, $r_{tt} = 0.91$, $N = 13$ mothers), an inter-observer reliability to be high ($N = 94$ observations, 97 per cent inter-observer agreement). Spot-checks during the course of the study revealed that inter-observer agreement was maintained ($N = 120$ observations, 98 per cent agreement).

The criteria for classification were: 180 or over, high attentiveness; 108 or under, low attentiveness (50 per cent and 30 per cent, respectively); 109 to 170, medium attentiveness.

Indices of exploratory behaviour were:

(1) Looking at, tactile and oral manipulation of, and vocalization to a single novel stimulus presented within reach for 10 min (bell test). Scores represent total time engaged in each activity.

(2) Looking at and manipulation of ten novel stimuli versus a familiar stimulus (pairs test: the bell, now 'familiar', was paired with ten different novel objects, in alternating position, each paired presentation lasting one minute). Manipulation on the pairs test included both tactile and oral manipulation; tactile manipulation included both moving the object and quiet tactile contact, unlike tactile manipulation on the bell test which excluded quiet tactile contact. Scores on the pairs test represent the algebraic difference between the total time exploring the novel stimuli and the total time exploring the familiar stimulus. A plus score indicates relative preference for the novel. The size of the difference score indicates strength of preference.

Responses were recorded on a Rustrak Model 92, four-channel event recorder. Pilot data indicated high inter-observer reliability (agreement on nine Ss was over 90 per cent for all variables; Spearman *r*s were over 0·90 for all variables). Observer agreement was maintained.

Auxiliary variables: variety of stimulation

Presenting play opportunity. Each 10-s observation period was scored as having or not having contained an explicit presentation of a play opportunity by the mother, that is, either the mother presented a toy (see below), or she engaged in personal social play, for example, patticake, bouncing the baby up and down, tickling and laughing, etc. Personal social play was the primary component of this variable.

Availability of toys within reach of the infant. A toy is defined as an object with which the child could play. Arbitrarily excluded were food, food receptacles, bed and personal clothing, furniture, people, and pacifiers. Included were items such as ashtrays, cigarette containers, etc. 'Within reach' (WR) means that the child could touch the object with his hand if he extended his arm forward or to the side. The 'number of toys WR' was obtained by summing over the 360 observations per day (and averaging over the 2 days where applicable). The number of *different* toys per day constitutes 'variety of toys WR'. Inter-observer agreement for 'presenting play opportunity' and for 'variety of toys WR' is 93 per cent and 91 per cent, respectively ($N = 940$ observations).

Procedure

Each mother was approached via phone if the house had one, in person at home if not. The study of the development of what holds the interest and attention of young infants was introduced, and permission was requested to visit the home on a typical day or two to observe the infant in the course of his usual daily activities and to visit on another day to present the infant with certain toys to see what he chose to play with. Emphasis was given to the idea of the normal daily activities continuing as usual during the home visit. The mothers seemed to go about their usual daily activities, including housework, as requested. Anecdotal evidence supports this view: in describing the study to their friends some mothers mentioned that activities should proceed as usual; one actually left for the afternoon, leaving the baby to be 'observed'. A small stipend was given the mothers for their co-operation.

Administration of the exploratory behaviour tests

The exploratory behaviour tests were given in the second or third week of the sixth month of life. Feeding and nap times were avoided. The baby was seated on his mother's lap at the kitchen table which was covered by a standard white plastic cloth. The mother was instructed to support the baby but not to assist or interact with him. The examiner, seated opposite and wearing a black blouse with no jewellery, was not the same person as the observer of maternal attentiveness and was unaware of the purposes and hypotheses of the study. The observer of maternal attentiveness amused the siblings, answered the door, and prevented interruptions of the baby tests.

The test was preceded by a 1-min habituation period. The bell was then rung and placed on the table within reach of the baby for 10 min. Since it was attached to a string tied to a stick in the examiner's hand, it could be pulled quickly into place after a fall. A buffer toy was presented for 5 min, followed by the pairs test. If a baby cried, a test was interrupted until the mother soothed him.

Results

Reliability data

The main study confirmed the pilot study's indications of the reliability of the measures. Of the 32 mothers who

combined. A Jonckheere *k*-sample test against ordered alternatives [10, 20] was applied to the ranks.† This test is designed to test the null hypothesis against the prediction that the *k* averages will occur in a specific order. It assumes only that scores are at least ordinal. The test yields a statistic, S, which is essentially a measure of the extent to which the ranks of each group overlap the ranks of each other

TABLE 25.1. *Mean Scores (in Seconds) for Measures of Exploratory Behaviour*

Measures of exploration	Maternal attentiveness			Significance levels†
	Low	Medium	High	
Bell test:				
Looking	204	252	275	0·02
Tactile manipulation	259	283	339	0·07
Oral manipulation	181	150	180	n.s.
Vocalization	11	13	32	0·03
Pairs test				
Looking	75	113	197	0·001
Manipulation	107	111	267	0·01

† Non-parametric trend analysis: Jonckheere's *k*-sample test against ordered alternatives.

met the criteria for HA or LA classification on the first visit, 29 met them when their scores from two visits were averaged. The pairs test proved internally consistent in the pilot study. Odd–even reliability coefficients for the difference scores were 0·80 for looking and 0·68 for manipulation, $N = 15$. The main study validated these findings: r_{tt} looking $= 0.76$, r_{tt} manipulation $= 0.84$, $N = 44$.

Major findings

Table 25.1 presents the means for the bell and pairs tests. The bell test scores are the mean number of seconds, of a possible 600, spent exploring the bell. For the pairs test the table presents the mean difference scores. Because none of the sex differences was significant, the data for both sexes were

group, in the predicted direction. Significance levels are presented in Table 25.1. Table 25.2 presents significance levels of 1-tail subcomparisons among groups based on the Mann-Whitney *U* statistic. Subcomparisons on tactile manipulation of the bell were included despite a significance level of 0·07 on the Jonckheere test because of the prior expectation that the extremes would be more sensitive to differences than the middle group would be.

Two of the four responses on the bell test, looking and vocalizing, and both pairs test measures are significant on the Jonckheere test. The differences between HA and LA groups are

† A non-parametric test was used because the assumptions of parametric tests, particularly the assumption of normal distribution, were not met.

significant for five variables. The differences between HA and MA groups are significant on the pairs test only. Differences between MA and LA groups are not significant at all.

The intercorrelations of the dependent measures are presented in Table

based on Mann–Whitney U reveal that HA mothers offered their babies a significantly larger variety of toys and significantly more play opportunities than did LA mothers or MA mothers (HA versus LA: $p = 0.002$ for both variables; HA versus MA: $p = 0.02$ for both variables). However, LA and

TABLE 25.2. *Significance Levels of Subcomparisons on Measures of Exploratory Behaviour (Mann–Whitney)*

Measures of exploration	Maternal attentiveness groups		
	High versus low	High versus medium	Medium versus low
Bell test			
Looking	0·025	n.s.	n.s.
Tactile manipulation	0·05	n.s.	n.s.
Vocalization	0·03	n.s.	n.s.
Pairs test			
Looking	0·01	0·05	n.s.
Manipulation	0·01	0·01	n.s.

25.3. Looking and manipulating are highly correlated within tests, but are not related to their equivalents across tests. Oral manipulation is negatively related to other variations in the bell test, probably because it is difficult for the infant to explore visually and manually while the object is in the mouth.

Table 25.4 presents the means on the auxiliary variables. While the groups do not differ significantly on the number of toys within reach of the baby (Kruskal-Wallis $H = 0.02$ n.s.), they do differ on the variety of toys within reach ($H = 11.24$, $p < 0.01$) and on the number of play opportunities offered by the mother ($H = 12.60$, $p < 0.01$).† Two-tail subcomparisons

† Data on number of toys are available on 43 Ss, variety of toys on 42 Ss. While an overall relation between play and attentiveness is artificially inflated as are part–whole correlations in general, the subcomparisons among groups are of particular interest.

MA mothers did not differ significantly from each other on either variable. These relations parallel those between maternal attentiveness and the pairs test variables: the HA group exceeded the other two groups, which did not differ significantly from each other.

Discussion

The results indicate a positive relation between a quantified measure of sensory–social stimulation and the infant's exploratory behaviour within the normal range of stimulation. These results are consistent with the positive relation found in home-reared infants between maternal nurturance and preference at 6 months for non-realistic representations of a face [12]. The finding of a relation between maternal stimulation and exploratory behaviour in adopted infants at 6 months [23] and the apathy noted in institutionalized infants of the same age [5, 16]

TABLE 25.3. *Intercorrelations of Measures of Exploration*

| | Bell test | | | | Pairs test | |
	Looking	Tactile Manipu- lation	Oral Manipu- lation	Vocaliza- tion	Looking	Manipu- lation
Bell test						
Looking	—	0·71**	−0·37	0·10	0·22	0·03
Tactile manipulation	—	—	−0·43	0·20	0·32*	0·25
Oral manipulation	—	—	—	0·00	0·08	0·08
Vocalization	—	—	—	—	0·29*	0·29*
Pairs test						
Looking	—	—	—	—	—	0·80**
Manipulation	—	—	—	—	—	—

* $p = 0.05$.   ** $p = 0.01$.

TABLE 25.4. *Mean Scores on Availability of Toys and Play Opportunities*

| | Maternal attentiveness | | |
	Low	Medium	High
Number of toys within reach	221	191	232
Variety of toys within reach	3·1	3·9	7·5
Number of play opportunities	4·6	9·5	20·1

suggest that the importance of maternal attentiveness for exploration at 6 months is generalizable to a variety of rearing environments. Further, the fact that our home-reared Ss experienced no discontinuity of mother figure suggests that the apathy of institutionalized infants cannot be attributed wholly to emotional trauma associated with maternal separation. The addition of stimulation might do much to offset the ill effects of group care.

To account for the motivational basis of exploratory behaviour, a 'need for stimulation' [11] or for 'variation' [6] has been postulated. The organism is thought to require stimulation in moderate (not minimal) quantities in order to maintain 'arousal' [1], 'activation' [6], or 'complexity' [4], at 'optimal' [11] or 'normal' [6] levels.

By exploring or withdrawing from novel stimuli, the organism attempts to control the amount of stimulus input. The results of this study are interpreted as suggesting that what is experienced as an 'optimal' level differs from individual to individual, depending in part on what level of stimulation characterized his past experience, that is, on his adaptation level [7]. The infants were situated in familiar surroundings and given the choice of attending to novel or to familiar stimuli. They behaved such that discrepancy between present and past input was minimized [9]. The infant whose past contained little varied stimulation was less responsive to novelty than was the infant accustomed to a high degree of varied experience.

These results contrast with those

predicted by the conceptualization of 'need' or 'drive' as increasing with deprivation. While short-term deprivation has been found to increase the need for stimulation [2], our findings imply that long-term deprivation may dull it. It is suggested that deprivation may increase the need for stimulation only when superimposed upon a background of non-deprivation, for example, in organisms whose customary level of stimulation is suddenly reduced. Viewed in these terms, both the Ss in this study and those suddenly deprived of stimulation behave alike: they act to minimize the discrepancy between present input and past levels of stimulation.

Relations between maternal stimulation and the infant's exploration have been found at 6 months, but less consistently at earlier [19] or later ages [3]. Since Rheingold's measures of exploration at $3\frac{1}{2}$ months were similar to the bell test, either the period between $3\frac{1}{2}$ and 6 months is more sensitive to stimulation than is the earlier period, or a cumulative effect of 6 months is required.

Particularly puzzling is the unanticipated finding that the same individuals were not high on both measures of exploratory behaviour. Medinnus and Love [13] found a similar lack of intercorrelations among various measures of curiosity in older children. The pairs test is more sensitive than the bell test, both in that range of scores is wider and in that the MA group is differentiated by it. Perhaps exploratory behaviour is less confounded with activity level in a choice situation such as the pairs test, which offers the active but non-curious infant the option of playing with the 'familiar' object, in addition to the option of inactivity which is the only alternative to exploration on the bell test.

The results suggest that the relation between stimulation and exploration may not be linear. On the more sensitive test, the pairs test, the LA and MA groups are homogeneous in exploration, though both fall well below the HA group. The maternal-attentiveness groups were defined in terms of the percentage of the time-sampling units during which the mother was attentive, with the HA group comprising those attentive in 50 per cent of the units or more. Contrary to the expectation that a threshold, if any were found, would be low (suggested by White's [21] studies of changes in visual attentiveness as a function of small changes in relatively unstimulating environments), a high threshold emerged. Before any differences in exploratory behaviour appear as a function of maternal attentiveness, attentiveness in at least 50 per cent of the time-sampling units seems to be required. Approximately 63 per cent of the babies sampled received less than 50 per cent attentiveness. Thus, within the range of our sample, a high threshold implies that the concern is not with a small group of 'deprived' babies, those whose mothers are extremely inattentive. Rather, the relatively small group receiving a high degree of attentiveness is apparently advantaged over the remaining majority.

Conceivably, it is the variety inherent in large quantities of attentiveness that is critical. Repetitive, unvarying stimulation is not expected to facilitate exploration. Piaget [15] in particular stresses the importance of variety for the differentiation of schemata through the processes of assimilation and accommodation. Increasingly differentiated schemata enable the infant to interact with novel objects in increasingly varied ways, thereby producing more varied changes in stimulation, which in turn reinforce exploration. Moreover, the notion of adaptation level suggests that the greater the variety of stimuli in the infant's past the more responsive to variety he is likely to be. The MA and LA groups both offered less variety than did the HA group, but did not differ from each other in this regard. The pattern of relations between maternal attentiveness and exploration on the pairs test may be attributable in part to the pattern of relations between maternal attentiveness and variety.

The results confirm previous findings of the greater early susceptibility to environmental influence of language as compared with other developing functions [16, 19, 22]. HA babies vocalized nearly three times as much as did LA babies, a difference greater than any on the other measures of reaction to novel stimuli.

While the relation between maternal attentiveness and the infant's exploration is interpreted as suggesting that attentiveness may facilitate exploration by the infant, this relation may be the result of an association between high-exploratory behaviour and other infant characteristics which elicit more maternal attentiveness. Studies of maternal attentiveness as a function of maternal attitude prior to the birth of the infant [14] suggest that maternal behaviour is controlled, at least in part, by other than infant characteristics. But the role of the infant may be more potent than is now suspected.

Future studies might well concentrate on the effects of variety as compared with quantity of stimulation at various ages, consider the possibility of a non-linear relation with differences in exploration emerging as a function of stimulation exceeding a high threshold, and emphasize tests of exploration which control for activity level.

References

1. BERLYNE, D. E. (1960). *Conflict, arousal and curiosity*. McGraw-Hill, New York.
2. BEXTON, W. H., HERON, W., and SCOTT, T. H. (1954). Effects of decreased variation in the sensory environment. *Can. J. Psychol.* **8**, 70–76.
3. COLLARD, ROBERTA. (1962). A study of curiosity in infants. Unpublished doctoral dissertation, University of Chicago.
4. DEMBER, W. (1961). Alternation behavior. *In* (Fiske, D. and Maddi, S. (Eds.)) *Functions of varied experience*. Dorsey, Homewood, Ill., pp. 227–52
5. FISCHER, LISELOTE. (1952). Hospitalism in 6-month-old infants. *Am. J. Orthopsychiat.* **22**, 522–33.
6. FISKE, D. and MADDI, S. (1961). A conceptual framework. *In* (Fiske, D. and Maddi, S. (Eds.)) *Functions of varied experience*. Dorsey, Homewood, Ill., pp. 11–56.
7. HELSON, HARRY. (1964). *Adaptation-level theory*. Harper and Row, New York.
8. HOLLINGSHEAD, A. B. (1956). Two-factor index of social position. Yale Univ. Press, New Haven.
9. HUNT, J. McV. (1960). Experience and the development of motivation: some reinterpretations. *Child. Dev.* **31**, 489–504.
10. JONCKHEERE, A. R. (1954). A distribution-free *k*-sample test against ordered alternatives. *Biometrika* **41**, 133–45.
11. LEUBA, C. (1955). Toward some integration of learning theories: the

concept of optimal stimulation. *Psychol. Rep.* **1**, 27–33.

12. LEWIS, M. (1965). Exploratory studies in the development of a face schema. Paper presented at the American Psychological Association Symposium on the Origins of Social Behavior, Chicago.

13. MEDINNUS, G. and LOVE, J. (1965). The relation between curiosity and security in pre-school children. *J. gen. Psychol.* **107**, 91–8.

14. MOSS, H. (1966). Sex, age, and state as determinants of mother–infant interaction. Paper presented at the Merrill-Palmer Conference, Detroit.

15. PIAGET, J. (1952). *The origins of intelligence in children.* Int. Univ. Press, New York.

16. PROVENCE, SALLY and LIPTON, ROSE. (1961). *Infants in institutions.* Int. Univ. Press, New York.

17. REBELSKY, FREDA, NICHOLS, IRENE, and LENNEBERG, E. (1963). A study of infant vocalization. Paper presented at the meeting of the Society for Research in Child Development, Berkeley, California.

18. RHEINGOLD, HARRIET. (1956). The modification of social responsiveness in institutional babies. *Monogr. Soc. Res. Child Dev.* **21**, No. 2 (Whole No. 63).

19. —— (1961). The effect of environmental stimulation upon social and exploratory behavior in the human infant. *In* (Foss, B. M. (Ed.)) *Determinants of infant behaviour.* Wiley, New York, pp. 143–77.

20. SIEGEL, S. (1956). *Nonparametric statistics for the behavioral sciences.* McGraw-Hill, New York.

21. WHITE, B. (1963). The development of perception during the first six months of life. Paper presented to the American Association for the Advancement of Science, Cleveland.

22. YARROW, L. (1961). Maternal deprivation: Toward an empirical and conceptual re-evaluation. *Psychol. Bull.* **58**, 459–90.

23. —— (1963). Research in dimensions of early maternal care. *Merrill-Palmer Quart.* **9**, 101–14.

VII | **Fear and exploration**

CONVENTIONALLY, fear and exploration have been used to designate the two polar points of an approach–avoidance dimension. Thus, stimuli low in intensity [6] or low in impact [3] are considered to elicit approach, inspection and investigation, whereas those stimuli of high intensity or impact elicit fear, withdrawal, or flight. Unfortunately this type of formulation is essentially *a posteriori* and does not enable one to predict the response of an individual in any particular stimulus situation. This is chiefly due to the lack of operational definitions for the stimulus attributes themselves.

Rubinstein's paper (Chap. 25) forms a natural link between this and Part VI, in illustrating how one form of early experience, increased attention from mother, has particular effects on subsequent exploration.

In reviewing the available mammalian evidence, Bronson (Chap. 26) implies that 'fear of novelty' is an instinctive and adaptive reaction of many species, which is manifested in late infancy. Hutt (Chap. 28) observes, however, that there is no evidence of fear of novelty *per se* in primates and certainly none in humans, and argues that the effects of novelty may differ according to its source, i.e. whether it is object-novelty, environment-novelty, or person-novelty. In general, the empirical evidence seems to support such a distinction. The novelty of an object, a toy for instance, or even a picture (Chap. 27) is seen against a familiar background and readily attracts attention. A strange environment on the other hand, means that the whole frame of reference, the whole background, is new and tends to inhibit exploration (Chap. 29 of this book and [2]). Such anxiety, moreover, can have a proactive effect in that the distress of the children is often only partly alleviated by the mother's subsequent presence.

The response to a strange person is much more ambiguous: if the stranger talks to the child or approaches it, flight or distress responses may be elicited [5]. This reaction was considered by Spitz [7, 8] and Benjamin [1] to be intimately linked with that of separation anxiety, both stemming from a fear of 'object-loss'. Tennes and Lampl [9] demonstrated the distinctness of fear-of-stranger and separation-anxiety responses; although generally the latter is found to precede the former, the contrary relationship found by Tennes and Lampl is due to their method of testing these responses. Moreover, while separation anxiety might legitimately be used as an index of attachment, fear of strangers certainly can not.

As the infant becomes increasingly independent visual novelty accordingly becomes more important in directing its attention whereas stimulus complexity appears to be more effective in maintaining that attention. The final emancipation of the human infant may be seen in the emergence of play—when, able to leave the mother to explore, he attains mastery over parts of his environment which he then uses to serve his own objectives [4].

References

1. BENJAMIN, J. D. (1961). Some developmental observations relating to the theory of anxiety. *J. Am. Psychoanal. Ass.* **9**, 652–68.

2. COX, F. N. and CAMPBELL, D. (1968). Young children in a new situation with and without their mothers. *Child Dev.* **39**, 123–31.

3. FISKE, D. W. and MADDI, S. R. (Eds.) (1961). *Functions of varied experience.* Dorsey, Ill.

4. HUTT, C. (1966). Exploration and play in children. *Symp. Zoo. Soc. London* **18**, 61–81.

5. MORGAN, G. A. and RICCUITI, H. N. (1969). Infants' responses to strangers, during the first year. *In* (Foss, B. (Ed.)) *Determinants of infant behaviour.* Vol. 4. Methuen, London.

6. SCHNEIRLA, T. C. (1965). Aspects of stimulation and organization in approach/withdrawal processes underlying vertebrate behavioural development. *In* (Lehrman, D. S., Hinde, R. A., and Shaw, E. (Eds.)) *Advances in the study of behavior.* Academic Press, New York.

7. SPITZ, R. A. (1950). Anxiety in infancy: a study of its manifestations in the first year of life. *Int. J. Psycho-anal.* **31**, 138–43.

8. —— (1965). *The first year of life.* Int. Univ. Press, New York.

9. TENNES, K. H. and LAMPL, E. E. (1964). Stranger and separation anxiety. *J. nerv. ment. Dis.* **139**, 247–54.

Development of fear

GORDON W. BRONSON†

A POTENTIAL to fear the strange must be regarded as inherent in many animal species—it is no longer tenable to maintain that all instances of fear have roots in a painful experience. This article examines the nature of the fear potential: it traces the development of the fear of novelty in young animals and identifies factors which can affect the course of such development. The relevant evidence is reviewed for those mammalian species on which sufficient developmental data are available: humans, other primates, and dogs.

Whether one finds similarities or differences in the fear reactions of animals across this range of species depends on the level of detail at which behavioural comparisons are made. The present analysis focuses on the general form of aversive reactions, thereby stressing similarities in the developmental patterns of these animals. The rather limited material documenting fear behaviour in humans appears in sharper focus when viewed in the context of developmental patterns observed in other species.

Fear is identified here as an aversive reaction to novel visual patterns. Aversive reactions to nonvisual stimuli, such as pain and sharp sounds, which appear before the fear of novelty has

† From 'Development of fear in man and other animals'. *Child Dev.* **39**, 409–32 (1968). Reprinted by permission of the Society for Research in Child Development, Inc. Copyright © 1968.

developed, are called 'distress reactions'. From the evidence reviewed, such distress reactions appear to be precursors to the fear of novelty. Learned fears, in the traditional sense of the term, are not examined in this survey.

The development of fear under normal rearing conditions

Studies of the different species are reviewed separately to minimize confusion arising from differences in maturity at birth and variations in the rate of development. Ages at which significant sensory and motor developments occur in the various species provide rough guides for making cross-species comparisons.

Humans

While the evidence is not conclusive, it seems probable that an encoding of the familiar is prerequisite to the fear of novelty [11]. If so, infants must be capable of visual memory before a fear of visual novelty can develop. The first clear evidence of visual memory appears in human infants at about 2 months of age: visually induced smiling begins at around this age [1], showing that visual patterns can now be recognized. Similarly, in a study by Fantz [18], infants less than 2 months old showed no difference in their reactions to new versus previously presented visual patterns, while after this age they spent less time gazing at 'familiar' than at novel patterns. (Note that studies which indicate that infants can distinguish visual patterns in the first weeks of life (e.g. [17, 63]) are not evidence of an ability to encode such patterns; furthermore, it is quite possible that these early visual reactions are mediated by subcortical systems and do not imply true pattern perception [10].)

Strange persons produce the earliest fear reactions reported for human subjects; however, it is apparent that infants can distinguish a stranger from mother some time before the age when strangers provoke fear. Ambrose [1] reported an increasing reticence to smile at strangers beginning shortly after age 3 months in home-reared infants and after age 4 months in institution-reared infants. Polak, Emde, and Spitz [54] also found that smiling at strangers decreased after age 4 months in their institution-reared infants. Although visual discrimination is clearly implied by the waning of the smiling responses to strange faces, Ambrose [1] was reluctant to infer the existence of fear at these early ages, since the infants showed no reaction other than the reticence to smile. Bridges [8] has made the same reservation, noting that her institution-reared infants could distinguish a strange face by 6 months but did not show signs of fear (i.e. crying, body rigid) until around 7 months.

Other studies confirm that clearly defined fear reactions first appear some months after the age when smiling at strangers begins to wane. Polak *et al.* [54] and Spitz [62] reported fear reactions to strange persons beginning at about 7 months in institution-reared infants, and perhaps somewhat earlier in home-reared infants [62]. Schaffer and Emerson [58] found that about 15 per cent of their sample of home-reared infants showed a fear of strangers (crying, turning head away) as early as 6 months; the majority, however, did not give this reaction until around 8 months of age. The authors added that the initial fear of strangers occurred about 1 month after the age when infants could no longer be comforted by a strange person in mother's absence, offering further evidence that a fear of strangers follows some time after the age when the infant has distinguished mother as a specific person. Freedman [20] reports a range of 7–10 months for the first appearance of crying and stiffening of the body at the approach of a stranger. Morgan and Ricciuti [52] observed infants at $4\frac{1}{2}$, $6\frac{1}{2}$, $8\frac{1}{2}$, $10\frac{1}{2}$, and $12\frac{1}{2}$ months as a stranger approached: the two youngest age groups gave positive responses; fearfulness first appeared at $8\frac{1}{2}$ months and increased in intensity through age $12\frac{1}{2}$ months. Fear reactions were more intense when infants were alone in the crib than when seated on their mother's laps. Bayley [12] identified those instances of crying, during monthly tests of physical and mental development, which were provoked by the strangeness of the examiners and their procedures. In spite of efforts to allay such fears, the incidence of crying increased from around 10 per cent at 5- and 6-month testings to over 20 per cent at 9, 10, 11, and 12 months.

These studies are in rather close agreement in indicating that for most infants a fear of strange persons appears at around 7–9 months of age. Experimental studies of fear reactions to novel situations or strange objects during this age-range have not been found, but anecdotal evidence suggests that such reactions develop along with the fear of strange persons.

Although fear reactions to visual stimuli seem to emerge gradually during the second 6 months of life, aversive reactions to non-visual stimuli are present much earlier. Since it will be argued that these early 'distress reactions' are precursors to the fear of novelty, studies of infant distress must be examined. Bridges [8], observing infants in a foundling home, described a pattern consisting of crying, muscle tensing, and diffuse movements which could be provoked by discomfort, pain, or sharp sounds; she concluded that such distress behaviour was clearly present by 3 weeks of age, and perhaps occurred even earlier. Rocking, patting, wrapping in warm blankets, and the opportunity to suck seemed to quiet distressed infants. Subsequent experiments give additional support to Bridges' observations: Ambrose (personal communication, 1967) and Gordon and Foss [25] have demonstrated the quieting effect of mechanically rocking newborn infants; Cohen [13] and Kessen and Leutzendorff [33] reported a decrease in activity when a rubber nipple was inserted in the mouth of the neonate; Bridger and Birns [7], causing distress by immersion of a foot in ice water, could quiet the infant either by inserting a nipple in the mouth or by rocking the head from side to side; McKee and Honizik [42], in a review of sucking behaviour in humans and other mammals, concluded that sucking quiets infants (human and otherwise) suffering from diverse types of discomfort. These procedures, which are effective in quieting infants without necessarily removing the cause of the distress, are components of the normal maternal activity in response to an upset infant.

The mothering activities which quiet distressed infants involve direct physical contact. At later ages—that is, from roughly the end of the first year onward—common observation indicates that the mere presence of the mother within the child's visual field can often allay tensions provoked by novel situations. This development evidently depends upon the formation of a visual attachment to the mother; hence the age at which such attachment develops is an important parameter affecting fear behaviour. Schaffer and Emerson [58], in a study of home-reared infants, concluded that most infants show an attachment to the specific mothering person by about the third quarter of the first year. Since this is also the age at which visual fears develop, it is evident that as the infant begins to be disturbed by visual novelty he also begins to find comfort in a visual awareness of the mother's presence.

Monkeys

Monkeys are born relatively mature and develop rapidly. Harlow [29] and Hinde, Rowell, and Spencer-Booth [33] observed visual exploration at 3 days; and Mowbray and Cadell [53] reported good visual orientation towards small objects by about 1 week after birth. At 10 days, the monkey walks about easily [33].

The only available reports of early fear reactions in monkeys concern animals which were reared apart from their mothers. While at later ages the quality of the fear reactions of such animals differs from normal patterns, in the absence of other data it is assumed that the age at which fear reactions first appear is not greatly affected by an early separation from the mother.

Bernstein and Mason [6] observed

a fear grimace and screech when small objects were introduced into the home cages of 1-month-old monkeys (the earliest age tested); the response was greater to objects of a more complex shape. Harlow and Harlow [30] reported fear of a mechanical bear beginning at about 20 days: crouching if alone in the cage, and 'fleeing' to the cloth mother-surrogate if it was present. (Since this early fleeing did not occur in the absence of the mother-surrogate, the behaviour was evidently aimed at gaining maternal security rather than at retreat from the frightening object.) The authors noted that fear reactions became stronger throughout the third and fourth months and that fear was less intense in the presence of the mother-surrogate. On the basis of these two studies, it can be tentatively concluded that the fear of novelty in monkeys appears at about 3–4 weeks of age, that is, some 3 weeks after the capacity for the perception of visual patterns.

Distress reactions in infant monkeys have not been specifically studied; however, Hansen [28] noted that monkeys raised with cloth mother-surrogates showed convulsive jerking, frequent distress calls, and mouthing of their own bodies, particularly during the first month. Such reactions are not characteristic of mother-reared animals. Maternal activities which might comfort infant monkeys are implied in Harlow's [29] observation that monkeys prefer mother-surrogates which are cloth covered and which rock.

Harlow and Harlow [30] concluded that attachments begin to develop during the first weeks of life; by 3 weeks the frightened monkey flees to the mother. Sackett, Porter, and Holmes [57] have shown that mother-separated monkeys, who had had contact with humans for only the first 3 weeks of life and had then remained relatively isolated until tested when $2\frac{1}{2}$ years old, turned towards a human rather than another monkey when placed in an apparatus offering these choices. A second group, raised in pairs following the initial 3 weeks of human contact, oriented towards the monkey in the above test. These results indicate that attachments do begin in the initial weeks, but they also indicate that later experience can shift the object of allegiance.

.   .   .   .   .

Summary of normal development

On the evidence available, the development of fear behaviour follows similar patterns in humans, monkeys, and dogs.

A fear of visual novelty develops some time after the ability to perceive visual patterns. The interval varies with the complexity of the animal: roughly 6 months in humans, 3 weeks in monkeys, and 2 weeks in dogs. Since the conditions under which fear was demonstrated varied considerably for the different species, these intervals can be regarded as only approximations; however, the ordering of the species is probably correct. (Such ordering has been interpreted by Hebb [31] as support for his theory that more complex nervous systems require more extensive visual experience to develop codifications of the familiar and that the fear of visual novelty can only appear after a sense of the familiar has developed; Hebb's hypothesis is examined in detail elsewhere [11].)

Distress reactions appear at or shortly after birth in response to diverse types of disturbing stimuli. The range of stimuli producing distress cannot be adequately compared across species, since data are incomplete, but extreme temperatures and pain are probably universal; visual novelty is not effective. Sucking activity, or being rocked, will quiet distressed mammals, and contact with a soft object also appears to be effective for primates.

The process of attachment formation normally begins before the fear of novelty has developed. Experiments on dogs and monkeys show that attachments can also be formed for at least a limited period after the age when fear reactions begin to appear, and common observation of the behaviour of adopted infants indicates that this is also true for humans. The fear of a novel stimulus is reduced in the presence of objects to which attachments have been formed.

Effects of maternal deprivation and early sensory restriction on the development of fear

Fortunately, the experimental deprivation of human infants is not possible; but, as a consequence, reports of the behaviour of humans reared in unusual circumstances are often difficult to interpret. Since studies of chimpanzees reared apart from their mothers provide a useful perspective for understanding abnormal patterns of human development, experiments conducted on chimpanzees are presented before consideration of the data on humans.

Chimpanzees
Too little is known about the normal development of fear reactions in chimpanzees to justify their inclusion in the preceding section; however, studies of the effects of early maternal deprivation can be interpreted with-

out detailed knowledge of normal developmental patterns.

A number of chimpanzees at the Yerkes Laboratories were separated from their mothers at birth and raised in restricted environments to about 2 years of age. The degrees of restriction varied: some were raised with a companion chimpanzee, some in bare cages, some with abstract patterns projected on to cage walls, and some could receive a visual reward by pushing levers. Later tests showed that the behavioural differences among animals in these different groups were minimal. The variables that emerged as significant were common to members of all experimental groups: separation from mothers at birth, the limitation of experience by confinement in the rearing cages, and no contact with human handlers.

In a series of papers [49–51], the behaviour of these 2-year-old animals was compared with that of wild-born chimpanzees of about the same age. Presented with novel objects either in the home cage or in new surroundings, or introduced into a strange empty room, the experimental animals reacted by crouching, rocking, and swaying, with no attempt to retreat from the novel objects; several hours of exposure produced little change in behaviour. Wild-born animals of the control group showed less fear: they began by actively moving about, followed by approach and exploration of the new objects; no stereotyped rhythmic behaviour occurred. The authors concluded that the early separation from the mothers, rather than the general restriction of the early environment, was the essential factor responsible for the development of stereotyped behaviour patterns (i.e. rocking and swaying). Although these chimpanzee experiments confounded maternal separation and sensory restriction, there is evidence giving support to the author's interpretation. Berkson, Mason, and Saxon [5] observed these same experimental animals after they had lived for 3 years in large outdoor cages in the company of other animals: stereotyped behaviour remained the dominant response when the chimpanzees were frightened by a novel situation. Davenport, Menzel, and Rogers [15] found that stereotyped behaviour did not develop when normally reared 1½-year-old chimpanzees were kept in isolation for a 6-month period. These latter two studies seem to eliminate confinement in a monotonous environment *per se* as the primary cause of stereotyped behaviour, but they do not rule out *early* sensory restriction, imposed through an initial post-natal period, as the significant factor causing stereotypy. However, since Davenport and Menzel [14] have reported that a review of the laboratory records showed that stereotyped behaviour never occurred in those animals which had been reared in cages with their mothers, but was always observed in chimpanzees which had been separated from their mothers at birth, it seems reasonable to conclude that early maternal deprivation was the primary cause of the stereotyped behaviour.

In addition to the abnormal form of their fear reactions, the above experimental animals also seemed to be more intensely afraid: the wild-born chimpanzees soon mastered their fear and began to explore the novel objects, whereas the experimental animals remained frightened for several hours. It must be recognized that, although the abnormal form of the fear reaction can be reasonably attributed to maternal deprivation, it is not clear from the available evidence whether the intensity of the fear was a consequence of maternal separation or of the early environmental restriction.

Daily observations of these same mother-separated animals, made while they remained undisturbed in their home cages, show the evolution of patterns of stereotyped behaviour from infancy until the animals were released from isolation at about 2 years of age [14]. These behaviours fell into two main categories: rhythmic rocking, swaying or turning movements, and other repetitive activities (primarily thumb or toe sucking and exaggerated chewing movements). Thumb or toe sucking was the first to develop, appearing some time during the first or second month. By 3 or 4 months, rhythmic activities of the entire body began to appear, first in the form of 'pivoting' while in a horizontal position, then, in the second 6 months, as rocking or swaying. By the second year, mouthing activities had largely disappeared, apparently having been superseded by the rhythmic rocking or swaying. Developmental charts of individual chimpanzees show that each animal produced a diversity of stereotyped behaviours during the first year, with particular patterns of rocking or swaying emerging as characteristic of individual animals during the second year.

It is evident that rhythmic behaviour occurred in mother-separated animals even when alone in a familiar environment. However, Berkson and Mason [4] have shown that the intensity of such activity increased when deprived chimpanzees were presented with visual novelty or a loud noise, or when they were hungry, or after an amphetamine injection. These authors concluded that intensity of stereotyped behaviour is a function of the general level of arousal.

To summarize: the early appearance and the pervasiveness of stereotyped behaviour in chimpanzees raised without mothers imply that such animals are disturbed from an early stage of development, that even in the familiar home environment they suffer chronic mild tension, and that the effects of early deprivation carry over into adulthood. That fear provokes stereotyped behaviour in deprived animals is shown by the increased intensity of these reactions in novel situations.

Humans

The studies of humans reared in institutions where mothering was minimal have not specifically focused on fear behaviour. However, in view of the reactions noted in chimpanzees, the high incidence of rocking behaviour found in institution-reared infants assumes a particular significance.

An early study by Bridges [8] described the development of rocking in institution-reared infants: 2- to 3-month-old infants moved their heads from side to side; by age 5 months they would sway while lying down; and 9-month-old infants would rock from a sitting position, sometimes humming rhythmically. Later studies support these observations and emphasize the pathognomic significance of such behaviour. Provence and Lipton [55] compared the development of infants in an institution with that of normal infants; among the distinguishing characteristics was the high incidence of rocking, which appeared in some institution infants at 4 or 5 months of age (while lying down) and was observed in all infants by age 8 months

(in a sitting position). Thumb-sucking declined as rocking developed, a phenomenon also observed in the maternally deprived chimpanzees. Brody [9] proposed a continuum ranging from normal infant reactions of rocking or bouncing when excited, through disturbed repetitive rocking which seemed to 'lull' the infant, to agitated energetic rocking, sometimes with head banging, where the infant seemed temporarily beyond external influence. She considered the latter two forms to be products of unusual patterns of mothering, and she noted that they may be accompanied by a dominance of tactual over visual modes of establishing contact with the environment.

Hutt and Hutt [34] noted that stereotyped behaviour, including repetitive movements of various parts of the body as well as rocking, is a frequent characteristic of autistic children. In an experimental study of 3- to 5-year-old autistic children, they found that stereotypy increased as the environment was made more complex by adding first a box of blocks and then a (passive) person to an originally empty room. It seems that novelty heightens stereotyped behaviour in autistic children and that even moderate degrees of visual novelty increase tensions in such individuals. Bender [3] noted that 'whirling', as well as rhythmic body activity, is a frequent characteristic of schizophrenic children.

The observation by Brody [9] that disturbed infants avoided visual exploration of the environment is of particular significance, since such self-imposed restriction will effectively decrease the perception of novelty. Others have made similar observations. Schopler [59], reviewing the accepted diagnostic signs of autism, noted as characteristic the obsessive desire for maintaining a familiar visual environment and also the marked preference for touch, taste, and smell as modalities for relating to the environment. In an experimental study of 7- to 9-year-old children diagnosed schizophrenic, Schopler [60] demonstrated a marked avoidance of visual modes in the exploration of novel objects, but normal use of tactile exploration. Hutt and Ounsted [35] concluded that the characteristic eye avoidance of autistic infants and children is also an expression of excessive fearfulness.

In light of the material presented earlier showing that rocking is highly effective in soothing distressed infants and the evidence that maternal deprivation produces rhythmic rocking in chimpanzees, it seems reasonable to conclude that chronic rocking or swaying in young disturbed humans is an attempt to reduce tensions associated with some form of maternal deprivation. Furthermore, since such activities increase in disturbed children (and chimpanzees) when they are confronted with even moderately novel situations, and since it has been shown that the perception of visual novelty is avoided if possible, it can be inferred that such disturbed children are also characterized by an excessive fear of visual novelty.

Monkeys

A review of experiments conducted on monkeys supports the view that rearing apart from mothers produces animals prone to stereotyped rhythmic behaviour and that such animals are also unusually afraid of visual novelty. Mason and Green [45] reported that mother-separated monkeys, raised alone in cages that allowed an open view of the laboratory, remained largely immobile, clutching themselves, and rocking and swaying, when placed in an empty room at 1–2 years of age. A control group of wild-born monkeys of about the same age moved actively about the room. Similarly, Mason [44] found that 9-month-old monkeys, raised apart from their mothers but in cages that allowed sight of the laboratory, responded to a strange environment by crouching and clasping themselves, rocking and swaying, and sucking parts of their bodies. In contrast to these effects, Jensen and Tolman [37] found that monkeys raised with their mothers in small cages showed no crouching, rocking, or swaying when placed in strange cages at 5 or 7 months of age, although they emitted piercing screams when separated from their mothers. Green [26] reported crouching and trembling to be the primary reaction of 2½-year-old mother-deprived monkeys presented with novel objects in a strange cage, whereas 1½-year-old animals raised in visually restricted environments, but with mothers present to age 4½ months, showed no crouching and seemed less disturbed by the novel situation. Griffin and Harlow [27] observed stereotyped behaviours, including oral activities, in mother-separated monkeys beginning in the first month; the intensity of stereotyped behaviour increased when animals were transferred to more open cages at age 3 months, while general exploratory activities dropped dramatically; one animal died following transfer, probably from a refusal to eat in the strange surroundings. Harlow and Harlow [30] reported crouching and rocking in response to novel situations by monkeys raised with wire mother-surrogates; animals reared by cloth 'mothers' also showed these reactions, but apparently with less intensity.

It is clear that early maternal deprivation produces enduring effects on fear behaviour. The possible contribution of early environmental restriction in the promotion of enduring fearfulness, however, is more difficult to assess. Only one experiment conducted on monkeys provides clear evidence that such restriction can, in some circumstances, produce enduring effects on fear behaviour. Mason and Sponholz [46] compared the behaviour of two groups of monkeys raised without mothers; members of one group were raised in cages within sight of other monkeys, while monkeys of the second group were raised in total isolation. When tested by pairing with another isolation-reared monkey at 16 months of age, all of the monkeys showed the crouching and rocking characteristic of mother-deprived animals; however, the less restricted animals were able partially to overcome their fear and engage in some social activity. Even after many hours together, the previously isolated animals did not develop social responses. Of particular interest is the observation that after a subsequent 2 years of living in a cage that permitted sight of other animals, each originally isolated subject was still 'traumatized' when tested with another monkey. For subjects raised without mothers, it appears that rearing in visually limited environments produces a heightened fearfulness which is not easily reversed by subsequent experience. It remains to be shown, however, that such early environmental restriction would have enduring consequences for animals raised with their mothers.

Observations of the development of monkeys illustrate another phenomenon: the changing pattern of fear reactions with increased age. Bernstein and Mason [6] described the development of fear reactions in mother-deprived monkeys which were reared in separate cages but with no attempt to greatly restrict sensory experience. Behaviour was observed when small objects were introduced into the home cages. Monkeys 1 month old gave a fear grimace and screech, sometimes accompanied by a convulsive jerking of the entire body; there was no attempt to move away from the object at 3 months, the response was again a fear grimace and screech, plus crouching and rocking behaviour; as at 1 month, there was no attempt to retreat from the source of fear. Animals first tested at age 7 months showed retreat reactions plus components of aggressive behaviour: ears went back and 'barks' replaced the screech, although the fear grimace remained present; crouching and rocking were less frequent. Active avoidance, with components of threat behaviour, became the dominant pattern of later ages, although rhythmic rocking again appeared strongly at 16 months. While these animals showed the stereotyped rocking behaviour characteristic of primates reared apart from their mothers, they also demonstrated the emergence of active patterns of retreat and of aggressive behaviour when faced with a frightening object. The change from immobilization to retreat as well as the development of aggressive reactions, can apparently occur in the absence of the mother, although the evidence above [26, 45] indicates that immobilization remains a dominant tendency in mother-deprived monkeys. Green [26] also noted another change towards increased aggression in older animals: observing the behaviour of $1\frac{1}{2}$- and 5-year-old wild-born monkeys when confronted with novelty, Green found that increasing the complexity of the novel objects produced a decrease in 'threat barking' in the younger animals, but led to intensified aggression in the older monkeys. Coping with novelty by a show of aggression appears to develop more slowly than retreat reactions to frightening objects.

.   .   .   .   .

Summary of the effects of abnormal rearing

Stereotyped rhythmic behaviour is characteristic of mother-deprived primates. Such behaviour appears before the age at which novelty provokes fear, remains a frequent activity when the animal is in a familiar environment, and, after the fear of novelty develops, appears with increased intensity in unfamiliar situations. It can be inferred that such activity reduces tensions arising from various sources, including the fear of novelty. Chimpanzees raised with a sibling in place of the mother and monkeys raised with inanimate 'mother-surrogates' also develop such abnormal behaviours, indicating that mother animals possess important attributes not offered by these substitutes. (These conclusions can also be applied to dogs if it is assumed (1) that 'whirling' is analogous to rhythmic rocking and (2) that early separation from mother was the significant variable in dog experiments.)

While the evidence is somewhat tentative, it seems probable that maternally deprived primates have an unusually intense fear of visual novelty and that such heightened fearfulness remains characteristic well beyond infancy. (Such enduring fearfulness was found also in mother-separated

dogs; however, because of the design of the canine experiments, the effects cannot be unequivocally attributed to maternal deprivation.)

When primates are raised without the mother, rearing in restricted environments intensifies the fear of novelty; such heightened fearfulness is not easily attenuated by later experience with diversified environments. This is seen most clearly in an experiment with mother-separated monkeys; experiments on dogs, while giving some support to this position, are less conclusive because of the undetermined contribution of early separation from the mother. It has not been shown that early environmental restriction would have enduring effects on animals which were raised with their mothers.

Observations of monkeys and dogs show that the response to novel objects develops from an initial tendency towards immobilization (with vocalization), to active retreat, and later to aggressive reactions. Since motor abilities develop in advance of this sequence, the maturation of motor capacities cannot account for this changing pattern of fear responses. This developmental pattern is retarded in animals raised in conditions producing excessive fearfulness.

Discussion

Where the evidence is available, patterns of aversive reactions as well as the variables which affect their development are found to be generally similar for humans, other primates, and dogs. The various theoretical interpretations which have been proposed to account for such general patterns are examined in detail elsewhere [11]. The present discussion treats the data on a more descriptive level, organizing the material in terms of three hypothetical developmental stages. This approach, which is of particular relevance to issues in human development, must sacrifice claims to cross-species generality: only for primates are the data sufficient to identify such stages. Although observations on dogs support the argument at various points, it is uncertain whether the proposed pattern of primate development is appropriate to non-primate species in all details.

Developmental stages are defined by the types of stimuli found to be capable of producing aversive reactions and by the changing role of the mother in relieving tensions. It will be argued that a normal development of aversive reactions at later ages depends on successful transitions through earlier developmental stages, and that the mother plays an essential, but changing, role in promoting such developments.

The first developmental stage coincides with the period when distress reactions are dominant—visual novelty is not yet a basis for fear. Relief from distress is dependent on direct maternal contact; in some instances mothering behaviour is closely integrated with infant reflexes (i.e. rooting and sucking; in furry primates, clinging), while at other times, the mother's activity (i.e., holding, rocking) seems not to depend on infant responses for its effectiveness. Attachment to the mother begins within this stage.

Some time after development of the capacity for encoding visual patterns, the emerging fear of visual novelty introduces the second stage. At the beginning of this second stage, aversive reactions remain similar in form to the distress response observed in the

previous stage: in humans, crying and muscle tensing dominate the reaction; monkeys, possessing more developed motor abilities, flee to the mother. Retreat from the threatening object, followed by aggressive responses, appear later in the second stage. Attachment to the mother has encompassed her visual characteristics by about the time the infant enters this stage: the mere visual presence of the mother is often effective in reducing tensions provoked by novelty. However, common observation shows that the severely frightened toddler may also seek comfort from maternal activities which had alleviated distress in the previous stage—that is, in maternal contact and being rocked.

A third and final stage can be identified, although comment will be brief since it is not well documented by the material under review. Increasingly throughout the juvenile period, the fear of novel situations is mastered without direct reference to the mother. This growing independence has been reported in various primate species: humans [24], chimpanzees [56], and monkeys [36]. How much this increasing ability to cope with novelty in the absence of the mother is a function of a general decrease in fear as the environment becomes more familiar, and how much it is due to the development of new techniques for mastery of threatening objects—for example, through the gradual emergence of aggressive reactions—is not clear. It is evident that for humans this final stage emerges gradually through the mid-childhood years and that during this transitional period cognitive references to the mother may often serve as substitutes for her immediate presence—for example, the child's awareness that mother awaits at home remains a source of security to the child throughout the latency period.

The abnormal behaviours observed in primates raised without adequate mothers indicate that the development of normal fear reactions at later stages depends on successful transitions through the earlier periods. As infants, mother-deprived primates develop behaviours which appear to be substitutes for maternal care—for example, stereotyped sucking and rocking activities. Stereotyped rhythmic activities remain characteristic of maternally deprived primates at later stages of development, implying that a primitive condition akin to distress remains chronic at ages when normally reared individuals less frequently experience tensions which, for their relief, are dependent on infantile modes of mothering.

The earliest reactions to visual novelty are similar to distress reactions, suggesting that the transition to the second stage occurs when a new stimulus dimension—vision—becomes capable of provoking previously existing aversive mechanisms. Later within this stage, more complex aversive reactions develop: first, retreat; later, aggression. In normally reared animals, the more primitive forms of aversive response gradually disappear; maternally deprived primates, however, continue to give the abnormal forms of response which they developed in the initial developmental stage (i.e. stereotyped behaviours) and are slow to evolve the more mature aggressive type of reactions to novelty.

Maternally deprived primates seem to remain chronically afraid of visual novelty. In light of evidence that the maternal presence normally provides security to the young as they explore and master their visual environment, it is reasonable to suggest that such deprived animals remain unusually fearful because mothers were absent throughout the second developmental stage, a time when exploratory behaviour is usually a major activity. Unfortunately, no primate studies directly test this hypothesis; in all experiments, the separations from mothers commenced at birth, so it cannot be clearly demonstrated that the resulting heightened fear of novelty was primarily due to maternal deprivation through this second developmental period. (Two of the canine studies [47, 48] lend some tentative support to the hypothesis. Separated from their mothers at age 4 weeks— the beginning of the second developmental stage—the dogs remained chronically afraid of visual novelty. It must be recognized, however, that, because these animals were raised in limited environments, the results might also be explained in other terms.)

If the hypothesis is correct—if, in normal development, the mastery of the fear of visually complex environments is based on the security provided by the presence of the mother during the second stage of development—the unusual behaviours observed in primates deprived of adequate mothers from birth onward must be viewed as the cumulative effects of deprivations suffered through two developmental stages: stereotyped activities are a consequence of deprivation of maternal contact beginning in the first developmental stage, while the enduring fear of visual novelty stems from the absence of a security-giving mother as novelty is encountered during the second stage. The failure of such animals, as adults, to achieve an independent mastery of environmental complexity—the final developmental stage—indicates that such mastery depends on successful transitions through earlier stages.

It seems reasonably certain that the development of normal patterns of fear behaviour is dependent on the maternal presence and that the salient qualities of 'mother' differ in the different developmental stages. Less clear is the contribution of general sensory stimulation to developments within the different stages. Studies conducted on rodents and dogs indicate that animals subjected to diverse types of excitatory stimulation during the first developmental stage are often less fearful when confronted by novel situations at later ages [41] see also, [19, 31]. The types of stimulation which have produced such effects are those which might be expected to provoke distress reactions, that is, cooling, pain, and rough handling. While not demonstrated in primates, it remains possible that in these species also an easy mastery of frightening situations in later periods presupposes some minimal degree of excitatory stimulation during the initial stage of development.†

Evidence that development of normal patterns of fear behaviour depends on exposure to a diversified environment during the second de-

velopmental stage is suggestive, but far from conclusive. It was noted earlier that the studies on dogs which have been cited as evidence for the enduring effects of rearing in monotonous environments could alternately be interpreted as studies of maternal deprivation. One primate study [46] showed that mother-separated monkeys were, as adults, less fearful if raised in relatively diversified environments, but it remains to be shown that environmental diversity is an important parameter for animals which are raised with their mothers. On theoretical grounds, one might expect that the opportunity to explore visually complex environments while still of an age when the mother provides security for such enterprises would produce a more confident animal, but there is no experimental evidence that will directly test this prediction.

A final comment concerns the role of fear in childhood pathology. From the evidence reviewed earlier, fear in normal human infants seems similar to that observed in other animals: it is a reaction to novelty found in the immediate perceptual environment, and it wanes quickly when the perceptual world returns to the familiar. In cases of infant pathology, however, clinical theory proposes another phenomenon: since changes in the immediate perceptual environment do not alleviate

---

† The thesis that the distress reaction of infancy is a precursor to the fear of novelty gains further support from evidence that the excitatory stimulation of animals during the initial stage of development can affect the intensity of fear reactions at later ages. A neurological explanation of such developmental continuity was suggested in a previous paper [10]: in mammals which are born relatively immature, behaviour during the first weeks of life is mediated by primitive networks located at the level of the brainstem; as the more

sophisticated neural systems of the forebrain mature to levels where they become functionally significant, more complex behaviours, including the fear of novelty, emerge. Since the activity of these more complex neural systems is modulated by the primitive networks which mediate behaviour during the neonatal period, experiences which affect neural development during this earliest stage will influence the intensity of complex fear reactions at later ages.

tensions, chronic emotional disturbance is frequently attributed to the existence of frightening fantasies. This explanation, based mainly on an extension into infancy of phenomena observed in older subjects, at times attributes remarkable intellectual powers to the immature neocortex (e.g. [40]). Studies of the behaviour of chimpanzees and monkeys reared apart from their mothers raise possibilities of another explanation of chronic infant tension. These animals showed symptoms analogous to those frequently found in infant pathology—stereotyped rhythmic behaviour, an excessive fear of visual novelty, and a general failure to develop normal social responses—yet it seems unlikely that these animals are capable of developing such fantasies as are often assumed to be the basis of infant pathology. The behavioural characteristics of such maternally deprived animals imply a heightened fear of visual novelty. Since even the degree of visual complexity inherent in a normally diversified environment seems to be a source of tension, the chronic nature of the disturbance need not be attributed to frightening fantasies. Such excessive fearfulness is bound to affect developing cognitive structures; therefore, some cognitive distortions are bound to occur. However, if the studies of other species are

granted relevance to humans, the frightening fantasies of disturbed children must be recognized as a consequence, not the initial cause, of the pathology. The mechanisms by which the presence of the mother normally aids the young towards a comfortable familiarity with environmental diversity remain an area of great uncertainty. If we better understood the details of such processes, it might appear that some human infants, although raised by the mother, are nevertheless partially deprived, either because of the particular pattern of mothering or because of the special constitutional characteristics of the infant (see [39] for consideration of the nature of maternal stimuli which might act to alleviate infant tensions, and [59] for possible constitutional variations which might make normal patterns of mothering inappropriate for some infants). Whether the basis of the deprivation lies primarily in unusual characteristics of the infant or the mother, it is suggested that some forms of early human pathology have roots in disturbances beginning in the initial post-natal period and that such disturbances lead to a pervasive fear of visual complexity; this is an alternative to the assumption that infant pathology is initiated by frightening fantasies.

References

1. AMBROSE, J. A. (1961). The development of the smiling response in early infancy. *In* (Foss, B. M. (Ed.)) *Determinants of infant behaviour*. Vol. 1. Wiley, New York.

2. BAYLEY, N. (1932). A study of the crying of infants during mental and physical tests. *J. genet. Psychol.* **40**, 306–29.

3. BENDER, L. (1947). Childhood schizophrenia. *Am. J. Orthopsychiat.* **17**, 40–56.

4. BERKSON, G. and MASON, W. A. (1964). Stereotyped behavior of chimpanzees: relation to general arousal and alternative activities. *Percept. mot. Skills* **19**, 635–52.

5. —— and SAXON, S. V. (1963). Situa-

tion and stimulus effects on stereo-typed behaviors of chimpanzees. *J. comp. physiol. Psychol.* **56**, 786–92.

6. BERNSTEIN, S. and MASON, W. A. (1962). The effects of age and stimulus conditions on the emotional responses of rhesus monkeys: responses to complex stimuli. *J. genet. Psychol.* **101**, 279–98.

7. BRIDGER, W. H. and BIRNS, B. (1963). Neonates' behavioral and autonomic responses to stress during soothing. *In* (Wortis, J. (Ed.)) *Recent advances in biological psychiatry.* Vol. 5. Plenum, New York.

8. BRIDGES, K. M. B. (1932). Emotional development in early infancy. *Child Dev.* **3**, 324–41.

9. BRODY, S. (1960). Self rocking in infancy. *J. Am. Psycho-anal. Ass.* **8**, 464–91.

10. BRONSON, G. W. (1965). The hierarchical organization of the central nervous system: implications for learning processes and critical periods in early development. *Behav. Sci.* **10**, 7–25.

11. —— (1968). The fear of novelty. *Psychol. Bull.* **69**, 350–58.

12. CLARKE, R. S., HERON, W., FETHER-STONHAUGH, M. L., FORGAYS, D. G., and HEBB, D. O. (1951). Individual differences in dogs: preliminary report on the effects of early experience. *Can. J. Psychol.* **5**, 150–6.

13. COHEN, D. J. (1967). The crying newborn's accommodation to the nipple. *Child Dev.* **38**, 89–100.

14. DAVENPORT, R. K., JR. and MENZEL, E. W., JR. (1963). Stereotyped behavior of the infant chimpanzee. *Arch. gen. Psychiat.* **8**, 99–104.

15. —— —— and ROGERS, C. M. (1966). Effects of severe isolation on 'normal' juvenile chimpanzees: health, weight gain, and stereotyped behaviors. *Arch. gen. Psychiat.* **14**, 134–8.

16. ELLIOT, O. and SCOTT, J. P. (1961). The development of emotional distress reactions to separation in puppies. *J. genet. Psychol.* **99**, 3–22.

17. FANTZ, R. L. (1958). Pattern vision in young infants. *Psychol. Rec.* **8**, 43–7.

18. —— (1964). Visual experience in infants: decreased attention to familiar patterns relative to novel ones. *Science* **146**, 668–70.

19. FOX, M. W. and STELZNER, D. (1966). Behavioural effects of differential early experience in the dog. *Anim. Behav.* **14**, 273–81.

20. FREEDMAN, D. G. (1961). The infant's fear of strangers and the flight response. *J. Child Psychol. Psychiat.* **2**, 242–8.

21. —— KING, J. A., and ELLIOT, O. (1961). Critical period in the social development of dogs. *Science* **133**, 1016–17.

22. FULLER, J. L. and CLARK, L. D. (1966). Genetic and treatment factors modifying the post-isolation syndrome in dogs. *J. comp. physiol. Psychol.* **61**, 251–7.

23. —— and —— (1966). Effects of rearing with specific stimuli upon post-isolation behavior in dogs. *J. comp. physiol. Psychol.* **61**, 258–63.

24. GESELL, A. and ILG, F. L. (1946). *The child from five to ten.* Harper, New York.

25. GORDON, T. and FOSS, B. M. (1966). The role of stimulation in the delay of onset of crying in the newborn infant. *Quart. J. exp. Psychol.* **18**, 79–81.

26. GREEN, P. C. (1965). Influence of early experience and age on expression of affect in monkeys. *J. genet. Psychol.* **106**, 157–71.

27. GRIFFIN, G. A. and HARLOW, H. F. (1966). Effects of three months of total social deprivation on social adjustment and learning in the rhesus monkey. *Child Dev.* **37**, 533–47.

28. HANSEN, E. W. (1966). The development of maternal and infant behavior in the rhesus monkey. *Behaviour* **27**, 107–49.

29. HARLOW, H. F. (1962). Development of affection in primates. *In* (Bliss,

E. L. (Ed.)) *Roots of behavior.* Harper, New York.

30. —— and HARLOW, M. K. (1965). The affectional systems. *In* (Schrier, A. M., Harlow, H. F., and Stollnitz, F. (Eds.)) *Behavior of nonhuman primates.* Vol. 2. Academic Press, New York.

31. HEBB, D. O. (1949). *The organization of behavior.* Wiley, New York.

32. HINDE, R. A. (1966). *Animal behaviour.* McGraw-Hill, New York.

33. —— ROWELL, T. E., and SPENCER-BOOTH, Y. (1964). Behaviour of socially living rhesus monkeys in their first six months. *Proc. zoo. Soc.* (Lond.) **143**, 609–49.

34. HUTT, C. and HUTT, S. J. (1965). Effects of environmental complexity on stereotyped behaviours of children. *Anim. Behav.* **13**, 1–4.

35. —— and OUNSTED, C. (1966). The biological significance of gaze aversion with particular reference to the syndrome of infantile autism. *Behav. Sci.* **11**, 346–56.

36. JAY, PHYLLIS. (1965). The common Langur of northern India. *In* (De-Vore, I. (Ed.)) *Primate behavior.* Holt, Rinehart, and Winston, New York.

37. JENSEN, G. D. and TOLMAN, C. W. (1962). Mother–infant relationship in the monkey, macaca nemestrina: the effect of brief separation and mother–infant specificity. *J. comp. physiol. Psychol.* **55**, 131–6.

38. KESSEN, W. and LEUTZENDORFF, A. (1963). The effect of nonnutritive sucking on movement in the human newborn. *J. comp. physiol. Psychol.* **56**, 69–72.

39. —— and MANDLER, G. (1961). Anxiety, pain, and the inhibition of distress. *Psychol. Rev.* **68**, 396–404.

40. KLEIN, MELANIE. (1955). On identification. *In* (Klein, M., Heinmann, P., and Money-Kryle, R. E. (Eds.)) *New directions in psycho-analysis.* Tavistock, London.

41. LEVINE. S. (1962). The effects of infantile experience on adult behavior. *In* (Bachrach, A. J. (Ed.)) *Experimental foundations of clinical psychology.* Basic Books, New York.

42. McKEE, J. P. and HONZIK, M. P. (1962). The sucking behavior of mammals: an illustration of the nature–nurture question. *In* (Postman, L. (Ed.)) *Psychology in the making.* Knopf, New York.

43. MARR, J. N. (1964). Varying stimulation and imprinting in dogs. *J. genet. Psychol.* **104**, 351–64.

44. MASON, W. A. (1960). Socially mediated reduction in emotional responses of young rhesus monkeys. *J. soc. abnorm. Psychol.* **60**, 100–4.

45. —— and GREEN, P. C. (1962). The effects of social restriction on the behavior of rhesus monkeys, IV: Responses to a novel environment and to an alien species. *J. comp. physiol. Psychol.* **55**, 363–8.

46. —— and SPONHOLZ, R. R. (1963). Behavior of rhesus monkeys raised in isolation. *J. psychiat. Res.* **1**, 299–306.

47. MELZACK, R. (1954). The genesis of emotional behavior: an experimental study of the dog. *J. comp. physiol. Psychol.* **47**, 166–8.

48. —— and SCOTT, T. H. (1957). The effects of early experience on the response to pain. *J. comp. physiol. Psychol.* **50**, 155–61.

49. MENZEL, E. W., JR. (1963). The effects of cumulative experience on responses to novel objects in young isolation-reared chimpanzees. *Behaviour* **21**, 1–12.

50. —— DAVENPORT, R. K., JR., and ROGERS, C. M. (1963). The effects of environmental restriction upon the chimpanzee's responsiveness to objects. *J. comp. physiol. Psychol.* **56**, 78–85.

51. —— —— and ——. (1963). Effects of environmental restriction upon the chimpanzee's responsiveness in novel situations. *J. comp. physiol. Psychol.* **56**, 329–34.

52. MORGAN, G. A. and RICCIUTI, H. (1969). Infants' responses to strangers during the first year. *In* (Foss, B. M. (Ed.)) *Determinants of infant behaviour.* Vol. 4. Wiley, New York.

53. MOWBRAY, J. B. and CADELL, T. E. (1962). Early behavior patterns in rhesus monkeys. *J. comp. physiol. Psychol.* **55**, 350–7.

54. POLAK, P. R., EMDE, R. A., and SPITZ, R. A. (1964). The smiling response to the human face, I: Methodology, quantification and natural history. *J. nerv. ment. Dis.* **139**, 103–9.

55. PROVENCE, S. and LIPTON, R. C. (1962). *Infants in institutions.* Int. Univ. Press, New York.

56. REYNOLDS, V. and REYNOLDS, FRANCES. (1965). Chimpanzees of the Budongo Forest. *In* (DeVore, I. (Ed.)) *Primate behavior.* Holt, Rinehart, and Winston, New York.

57. SACKETT, G. P., PORTER, M., and HOLMES, H. (1965). Choice behavior in rhesus monkeys: effect of stimulation during the first month of life. *Science* **147**, 304–6.

58. SCHAFFER, H. R. and EMERSON, P. E. (1964). The developments of social attachments in infancy. *Monogr. Soc. Res. child Dev.* **29** (3, Serial No. 94).

59. SCHOPLER, E. (1965). Early infantile autism and receptor processes. *Arch. gen. Psychiat.* **13**, 327–35.

60. —— (1966). Visual versus tactual receptor preference in normal and schizophrenic children. *J. abnorm. Psychol.* **71**, 108–14.

61. SCOTT, J. P. and FULLER, J. L. (1965). *Genetics and the social behavior of the dog.* Univ. of Chicago Press, Chicago.

62. SPITZ, R. A. (1946). The smiling response: a contribution to the ontogenesis of social relations. *Genet. Psychol. Monogr.* **34**, 57–125.

63. STECHLER, G. and LATZ, E. (1966). Some observations on attention and arousal in the human infant. *J. Am. Acad. Child Psychiat.* **5**, 517–25.

64. THOMPSON, W. R., MELZACK, R., and SCOTT, T. H. (1956). 'Whirling behavior' in dogs as related to early experience. *Science* **123**, 939.

65. WELKER, W. I. (1959). Factors influencing aggregation of neonatal puppies. *J. comp. physiol. Psychol.* **52**, 376–80.

27 | Attention to novelty

MICHAEL LEWIS, SUSAN GOLDBERG, AND
MARILYN RAUSCH†

THE dimension of novelty and familiarity is an important stimulus property influencing attentional behaviour [1–3]. One definition of novelty and familiarity is based on the assumed frequency with which certain stimuli have occurred in the organism's experiential history [4]. Experimentally, novelty and familiarity can be defined by controlling the frequencies with which stimuli occur. A stimulus S_1 is defined as familiar when it has been presented repeatedly for n trials. The occurrence of a second stimulus S_2 on trial $n+1$ defines S_2 as a novel event. S_2 can be any event discriminable from S_1. The present experiment, using visual stimuli, seeks to investigate this problem with pre-school children.

Method

Twenty Ss, 10 experimental and 10 controls, $3\frac{1}{2}$ years of age, were each seated at a table enclosed in a uniform grey room approximately 5×5 ft. The visual stimuli were presented, by rear-screen projection, approximately $2\frac{1}{2}$ ft from S's head. Total fixation time (TF) or the total time S oriented his head and eyes towards the screen was recorded by two independent observers (inter-observer reliability, $r = 0.94$).

Four different sets of stimuli were

† From 'Attention distribution as a function of novelty and familiarity', *Psychon. Sci.* **7**, 227–8 (1967). Reprinted by permission of the authors and Psychonomic Soc., Inc.

presented (see Plate 1) and the order of presentation was the same for both experimental and control groups. Set A was presented first, followed by sets B, C, and D. The control group received seven trials of A_1, each trial 30 s in duration with a 30-s inter-trial interval. The experimental group received six trials of A_1, followed by one trial of A_2. This procedure was the same for each set.

Results

Response decrement

Fig. 27 presents the mean TF for each trial for each set. The response to familiarity for each set (see trials 1–6) is response decrement. A linear function, $y = ax + b$, with a relatively steep negative slope fits the data; r^2 varies in the range 0.61–0.81 and 0.61–0.69 for the experimental and control groups, respectively. Between-set differences were determined by obtaining trial 1–6 differences for each S for each set and comparing this distribution by a Friedman two-way analysis of variance [5]. No significant set differences in response decrement for either the control or experimental groups was found. Moreover, no experimental-control group differences in response decrement were found for any of the sets.

Response recovery

The response to a novel stimulus can be determined by observing the difference between the predicted TF on the regression line and the observed TF. The criteria of response recovery was an increase of more than two S.D. from the predicted point. The control group showed no significant increases whereas the experimental group's data was: A_2 (4·7 S.D., $p < 0·5 \times 10^{-6}$); B_2 (2·8 S.D., $p < 0·5 \times 10^{-3}$); C_2 (4·0 S.D., $p < 0·5 \times 10^{-5}$); and D_2 (8·6 S.D., $p < 0·5 \times 10^{-10}$). For both

repeated stimulation (S_1) and recovery occurs when S_1 is varied (S_2). Sokolov [2] argues that response decrement and recovery are mediated by some central process such as memory or neuronal model formation. Novelty is defined as the lack of match between the external event and the model and results in attentive behaviour. Within this theoretical system, rate of response decrement can be viewed as a function

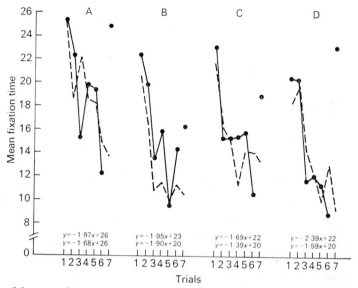

FIG. 27.1. Mean total fixation time for each trial, stimulus sets A–D for experimental group (solid line) and control group (dotted line). The seventh trial is indicated by an isolated point for the experimental group. For each set, the lower equation represents linear function for the control group, the upper equation, the experimental group.

experimental and control groups response recovery also occurred whenever sets changed. This is seen most clearly for the control group for trial 1 of each new set which shows a significant increase for each change (by sign test, $p < 0·01$).

Discussion

TF for the $3\frac{1}{2}$-year-old can be considered part of the orienting reflex in that response decrement occurs to

of the speed of model acquisition whereas response recovery is a function of discrimination ability, model formation and the nature and degree of the violation (S_2—distortion, change in complexity, form, shape, colour, etc.). The present study shows that distribution of attention can be a function of novelty and familiarity. Further, attention can be sustained over relatively long periods (in this case, for 30 min) by varying the visual input.

References

1. BERLYNE, D. E. (1960). *Conflict, arousal, and curiosity*. McGraw-Hill, New York.
2. SOKOLOV, Ye. N. (1963). *Perception and the conditioned reflex*. (Trans. by S. W. Waydenfeld). Macmillan Co., New York.
3. CANTOR, G. N. (1963). Responses of infants and children to complex and novel stimulation. *In* (Lipsitt, Lewis P. and Spiker, Charles C. (Eds.)) *Advances in child development and behavior*. Vol. 1. Academic Press, New York.
4. LEWIS, M. (1965). Exploratory studies in the development of a face schema. Paper presented at the Symposium on the Origins of Social Behavior, American Psychological Association Meeting, Chicago.
5. SIEGEL, S. (1956). *Non-parametric statistics for the behavioural sciences*. McGraw-Hill, New York.

28 | Exploration of novelty

CORINNE HUTT†

Novelty as a determinant of exploration

Exploratory behaviour is essentially stimulus selection behaviour, and as such is a characteristically pervasive behaviour of many young mammals. It thus has an immediate attraction for those interested in the activities of such organisms when they are not constrained, restricted, nor limited by the demands of the experimental situation. As Berlyne [17] commented:

Most of the standard experimental situations used by psychologists are designed to study the effects of one stimulus factor at a time; the stimulus of interest is made to predominate in determining behaviour, and the influence of other background stimuli is reduced to a minimum. . . . As soon as the experimental situation is made more complex by introducing several conspicuous stimuli at once or as soon as animals are studied in surroundings resembling their natural environments in which their receptors are inundated with an endless variety of stimuli coming from all directions, a new question arises: 'To which stimulus will this animal respond?'

To which must be added an equally important question, 'And why?'

   .   .   .   .   .

Some definitions of novelty

Berlyne [17] has distinguished three categories of novelty along a temporal

† From 'Specific and diversive exploration'. In *Adv. Child Dev. Behav.* 5, 120–80 (1970). Copyright © 1970. Reprinted by permission of Academic Press, Inc.

dimension: *complete novelty, long-term novelty,* and *short-term novelty.* Two additional categories are those of *absolute novelty* (when an aspect of a stimulus has not been encountered before) and *relative novelty* (when otherwise familiar aspects of elements are combined in an unexpected manner). Whether these latter types of stimulus-change can properly be regarded as novel and thus different in kind from other, hardly distinguishable stimulus-changes involving incongruity, surprise, etc., is doubtful. These reservations increase with attempts to vary the degree of novelty of a stimulus. The most valid definition of novelty seems to be one in terms of a temporal dimension, within which complete novelty appears to have different behavioural consequences from long- and short-term novelty [93, 94]. But even on this dimension a constraint upon its applicability seems desirable, namely that it should not be applied to relatively contemporaneous events, particularly if all these are ordinarily familiar and the novelty arises simply from its difference from a set—as in a sequence of tones. Such effects seem more appropriately attributable to stimulus-change, unless we accept that stimulus-change by definition is novel. In human studies, for instance, the case might be made for differentiating between short- and long-term novelty in terms of days and months. Although an attempt at such terminological precision may appear contrived, the application of colloquial terms in situations where a certain degree of specificity is implied, does lead to unnecessary confusion.

The trichotomy of novelty to be proposed here is an attempt to reconcile at least some of the discrepant results in the literature in a manner that makes them biologically meaningful. It is proposed that novelty differs according to its source, and can be of three kinds: (a) object-novelty; (b) environment-novelty; and (c) conspecific-novelty, or in the human more simply stated as person-novelty. Much of the literature hitherto has confused novelty emanating from these three sources and it would be instructive to examine the more relevant animal and human results while attempting to partial out the effects due to the individual sources.

This categorization of novelty is justified on several grounds: (a) there are species-specific and differential reactions to each type of novelty; (b) within a species, and particularly in the human, these reactions appear at different but nevertheless specific periods in ontogeny; (c) a good deal of empirical data already demonstrates the distinctive effects of each; and (d) the evolutionary significance of each is likely to differ according to the species.

Novelty in a biological context

Most theoretical formulations in psychology have erred in prematurely assuming a generality for their models that subsequent work has failed to substantiate. Those relating to exploratory behaviour are no exception. Just as *Rattus norvegicus* upheld or demolished a considerable body of learning theory for decades [10], so too was he the progenitor of explora-

tory theory. One of the features of this parochialism is that there is a tacit assumption that concepts like reward, novelty, complexity, have an equivalent valency for all species. Novelty is assumed to have similar effects upon all animals, in that moderate degrees elicit exploration and extreme degrees avoidance. And yet it would seem biologically nonsensical for a number of disparate species to react in the same way to certain situations, irrespective of their social organization, their ecology, their physical structure, and their neuromuscular organization. Laboratory rats, for example, react differently to novelty than do voles and wild rats [77, 8, 158]. In an extensive study of 187 mammals and 20 reptiles, Glickman and Sroges [71] found very great variation in reactions to novel objects even within an order. These authors also demonstrated the differences in exploratory activities as a function of the habitat: the *Colobus* monkeys, for example, are tree-dwelling and leaf-eating and their exploration is predominantly visual; a *Cecopethicus* monkey like the baboon, in contrast, which is ground-dwelling and has to manipulate a number of obstacles like rocks and plants in searching for food, shows immediate approach towards, and very active manipulation of, novel objects. From their analyses of exploratory patterns these authors concluded that 'at least within an order, habitat will be a more potent predictor of quantity of response than some crude index of brain development' ([71], p. 182).

Among the mammalian species, rats, macaques, baboons, chimpanzees, and humans seem generally exposed to the most varied habitats. Macaques live in geographically very distinct areas; baboons, under persistent predation from humans, have had to find new territory and food sources [119], chimpanzees need to obtain food from diverse sources and are able to improvise tools for some of their requirements [109], and humans are the most widely distributed species of all. A measure of the success of these species is their ability to survive in such a variety of habitats. They are also notably exploratory animals. Hence it seems reasonable to suppose that their respective exploratory tendencies have conferred a distinct advantage. Man's particular success in diversity can be ascribed to a 'hypertrophy of curiosity'. It is suggested that selection pressures have acted upon man in a manner so as to favour those individuals with the greatest exploratory tendencies. Consequently we now find in man an 'innate' attraction to novelty (object). To posit this, one requires only an elaborated form of the orienting reaction. In other words, it is postulated that novel objects elicit an orienting reaction which is immediately followed by approach and active exploration. Thus, fear of object-novelty *per se*, of whatever degree, would not be manifest. This will not necessarily be true of the other classes of novelty, but detailed discussion of these aspects may be suspended until experimental data have been reviewed. It would also follow that stimuli which did not elicit the orienting reaction would not elicit exploration.

.   .   .   .   .

Sources of novelty

Considering the significance of novelty in determining orienting, attention, and exploration, it is regrettable that studies of curiosity and exploration in young children are so few. Most young

mammals, and primates in particular, acquire information about their environment through their exploratory activities. Curiosity in the human infant and child are only too characteristically manifest, as any caretaker will vouch, and yet we know relatively little about what stimulus attributes make a child direct his attention to one object from a host of possible alternatives, how he explores it, how effectively he processes the information [64], and when he becomes satiated with it. Although much is known about the properties of random polygons that determine visual attention and preference, a similar knowledge of the effective parameters of commonplace and manipulatable objects is sadly lacking. The revolution in pedagogic theory in recent years, which has resulted in the substitution of 'exploratory learning' for 'teaching', appears to have had little impact on the study of the basic motivational and cognitive processes of their subjects.

Object-novelty. (a) *Infrahuman primate studies*. Harlow and his colleagues showed that monkeys would readily manipulate puzzle-devices introduced into their cages and incidentally solve problems [79, 81, 82] or learn a discriminant response [83]. Carr and Brown [45–47] similarly found approach and manipulation of objects of different materials by Rhesus monkeys which waned after a period of exposure to these objects. Mason, Harlow, and Rueping [121] found that manipulation of a number of objects by infant monkeys increased steadily over the first few weeks of life, and they attributed this to maturational or reinforcement effects. Welker [179, 180] demonstrated increased responsiveness to novel objects in chimpanzees, this responsiveness also decreasing with time. The chimpanzees showed 'preferences' for those stimulus objects upon which their manipulations could effect changes and for those objects left inside as opposed to outside their cages; these animals also manipulated a heterogeneous set of objects more than an equivalent but homogeneous set. Of these workers, only Welker [178] described a fear reaction to novelty: 1- to 2-year-old chimpanzees showed initial withdrawal or caution whereas 3- to 4-year-olds approached and manipulated readily. It is not clear whether this fear is specific to this age in most infrahuman primates. Certainly Glickman and Sroges found evidence of fear in only 19 out of 100 adult primates and in many of these cases the fear was due to idiosyncratic features of the object (e.g. to rope but not to block) or of the animal. No evidence of age-specific fear reactions was observed in the subadult animals.

(b) *Human studies.* A human infant of 7 months was shown to grasp and manipulate novel objects with alacrity [94]. In this case the object was presented to the child by a familiar adult; no signs of fear or caution were observed. The stimulus objects in this study were those which were completely novel, i.e. the child had not encountered them previously in his life. Attention spans were found to decrease with repeated presentation of an object, and reciprocally the frequency with which the child dropped the object increased. During any particular session the frequency of toy-dropping (of equally familiar toys) generally increased from beginning to end, but this trend was dramatically inhibited by the presentation of a new toy (Fig. 28.1).

In a comparison of the social and exploratory responses of first-born children with later-born ones, Collard [49] used 9- to 13-month-old infants; she found manipulatory latencies to be

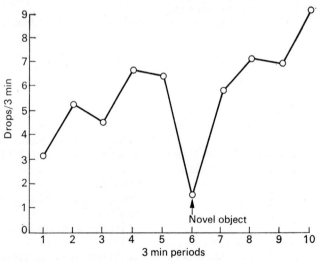

FIG. 28.1. Mean number of drops per 3-min period in 3 continuous 30-min sessions when a *different*, but relatively familiar object was presented every 3 min. A completely novel object was presented as the sixth object (from Hutt, 1967).

far greater in the first-born than in the later-born. The first borns also appeared to be generally more inhibited in their exploration of the toy. But, as Collard has very nicely demonstrated, these children were also more wary of the stranger and manifested more negative reactions towards her, although they engaged in as much play and interaction with their *mothers* as the later-borns did. Hence, the first-born's inhibition of exploration was

would subsequently show a preference for a novel toy even if it was damaged and for a novel toy over two familiar ones.

In an investigation of developmental patterns in the exploration of a novel object, Schaffer and Parry [153] compared 6- and 12-month-old infants. The subjects were presented with a 'nonsense' object which was made out of plastic and which therefore had complete novelty for them. This object

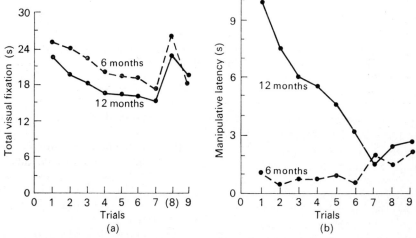

FIG. 28.2. Total length of visual fixation (a) and manipulative latency (b) per trial for 6- to 12-month-old infants (from Schaffer and Parry, 1969).

more likely to have arisen from fear-of-the-stranger (from whom he was required to take the toy) than fear-of-the-object.

Mendel [126] familiarized kindergarten children on certain toys and then offered them a selection from sets containing different proportions of novel toys, on the assumption that an individual would prefer optimally an intermediate degree of novelty. The children showed a clear preference for the set offering 100 per cent novelty. Harris [84] found that young children when familiarized on one or two toys

was presented on 7 successive 30-s trials, with intertrial intervals of 30 s. On the eighth trial a similar-shaped object, but of different colours, was presented, and on the ninth trial the original object was presented again. The objects were moved towards the subject on a mobile tray from behind a screen which occluded any view of the experimenters or observers. A familiar adult sat behind the subject. The results for the two chief measures— total fixation and manipulative latency—are shown in Fig. 28.2. The 6- and 12-month-old infants showed a very similar visual pattern, decrease in fixation with repeated exposure and increased fixation on appearance of the novel object. The two age-groups diverged, however, on the manipulation measure, the older group showing a considerable delay in grasping and handling the new object at first but doing so more readily thereafter. The younger group showed no such hesitation. The authors interpreted the behaviour of the younger children in terms of a failure of perceptual recognition to exert control over overt action: 'these infants registered the information received in terms of familiarity-unfamiliarity but did not act accordingly' (p. 96). But such an interpretation follows only on the assumption that there must be an *avoidance* of novelty. The 'indiscriminate approach behaviour' becomes simply approach-of-novelty if the hypothesis proposed earlier (of an innate attraction-to-novel-objects) is accepted. How then can the latency of the older group upon initial presentation of the object be explained? It was very likely to have been due to the experimental procedure, whereby the object moved forward towards the subject without the aid of a detectable agent. This would be a disconcerting procedure for a 12-month infant whose body of experience, and hence expectations, considerably exceeds that of the 6-month old. Moreover, other primates like monkeys have been shown to manifest persistent fear reactions to stimuli which apparently loomed at them [154]. The latency of the older children is thus more likely to be a function of the manner of stimulus presentation than of the novelty of the object *per se*. The fact that after adaptation to the first object, the appearance of another novel object did not cause an increase in approach latency supports this interpretation, although Schaffer himself (personal communication) does not regard his method of presentation as comparable with 'looming'.

Exploration of a completely novel object by 3- to 5-year-old children was studied utilizing a procedure which permitted access to familiar alternative toys [93]. The subjects were familiarized with the playroom, which contained five commercially available toys. The novel object (see Fig. 28.3) was designed to allow one of several different kinds of feedback to be contingent upon manipulations of the lever:

  (i) none—other than tactile
 (ii) simple visual—counters, which registered manipulations, exposed
(iii) sound—bell + buzzer contingent upon two of the four manipulations
 (iv) sound + simple visual—bell and buzzer, and counters exposed
  (v) complex visual—orange and green lights contingent upon 2 of the 4 manipulations
 (vi) sound + complex visual—(iii) and (v) combined.

The terms 'simple visual' and 'complex visual' refer largely to the relative heterogeneity involved.

Each child was individually familiarized with the playroom and other toys in two pre-exposure sessions. Then followed six experimental sessions of 10 min each at 48-h intervals, on the first of which the novel toy had been introduced into the playroom. Cine recordings of the children's behaviour enabled a detailed analysis to be made of their approach and investigatory responses, their process of habituation to novelty, and any response classes that might be manifested.

The different kinds of incentive had marked effects upon the level of manipulatory response (Fig. 28.3). Condition (vi) did not differ at all from Condition (iv) and hence is not illustrated in the graph. Despite the fact that the counters changed upon each manipulation, the incentive value was inadequate to maintain responsiveness. Lights and sounds were both effective in maintaining response but

the sounds together with the counters were most effective. Nevertheless, all these curves reflected a response decrement in the sixth session.

In this study, where practical considerations necessitated the presence of the observer in the same room as the child, it was found that the latency of approach towards the novel object was considerably less than if the child was alone in the room [93]. The results were interpreted in terms of the 'fear of novelty' being reduced in the presence of the adult. This, however, might not have been the most ap-

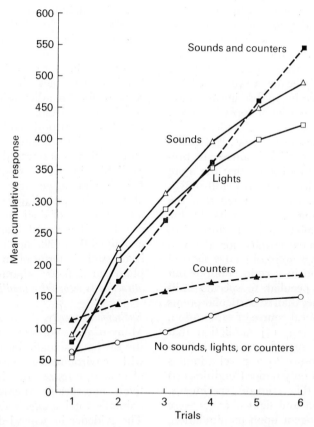

FIG. 28.3. Cumulative response curves obtained during exploration of a novel toy provide different incentives.

propriate interpretation since there had been a difference in the degree of familiarity of the environment for the two groups, the room producing the shorter latency being more familiar to that group since it was often encountered outside the experimental situation as well. A subsequent experiment (unpublished) was thus carried out to test the relative validity of these interpretations. If response latency was due to fear-of-novelty, then the greater the novelty the greater the latency to be expected. Three groups of children were allowed to play in the same situation as already described (a) twice in the presence of the novel toy, (b) once in the presence of the novel toy, the preceding session being only with the other toys, or (c) twice with all the other toys except the novel one. Two weeks later they were tested with the same experimental design as before. The mean latencies of approach were: (a) 45·6 s (S.D. 16·2), (b) 28·1 s (S.D. 12·4), (c) 12·8 s (S.D. 9·5). In fact the results were entirely contrary to prediction, thus indicating that the more novel the object the more readily it was investigated. This suggested that the earlier finding was in fact partly due to the confounding of differences in environment-novelty for the two groups. There were of course signs of apprehension in certain children but these were peculiar to specific individuals rather than to particular points in the temporal course of exploration.

Berlyne's [12, 17] prediction that exploration should wane with continued exposure to a novel stimulus was fulfilled only under Conditions (i) and (ii) in this series of experiments. When sound and light changes were made contingent upon manipulation, responsiveness continued to increase until the fifth session. That this un-

predicted result was largely a matter of response definition and could still be encompassed within the terms of Berlyne's theory will be demonstrated in a subsequent section.

In an area where there seems to be a consensus of evidence that infants and children attend to and prefer novel stimuli more than familiar equivalents, a discordant result strikes a cautionary note. This result stems from an experiment carried out by Hunt and Uzgiris and described by Hunt [92] in which infants were found to prefer mobiles with which they had previously been familiarized to novel ones. The infants were 4 weeks old at the start of the familiarization period and at the time of testing they were 8 to 9 weeks old. Preference was evaluated in terms of differential fixation. The fact that preferential response for three-dimensional novelty could not be demonstrated at an age when that for two-dimensional novelty is manifest [60], is disconcerting since more salient cues would have been available in the former situation. Whether infants younger than the age of 3 months can reliably discriminate novel features of their environment is clearly still a vexed question. Hunt explained the preference for familiarity in his study in terms of an ontogenetic phase in infancy characterized by *attraction to recognitive familiarity*.

Environment-novelty. (a) *Rat studies.* Many of the studies of exploration in the rat have actually been concerned with environment-novelty. Changes of mazes or maze arms involve relatively non-specific alterations in the animal's total *available* environment. The evidence in general does seem to support the notion that there is some initial fear of a completely new environment, particularly if it happens to be an elevated maze. That it is imperative to clarify concepts and terminology in this area is no more clearly illustrated than in the interpretations of results obtained by A. B. Sheldon [156]. In these experiments, rats were put in a strange, and elevated Y-maze and offered the choice of an object with which they were already familiar or of a novel object. The rats predominantly chose the familiar as opposed to the novel object and this preference increased with the degree of familiarity. In other words, where both visual and olfactory cues were familiar, preference was greater than when only one set of familiar cues was available.

These results were interpreted in terms of a positive motivation towards familiarity, which was independent of a fear of novelty, and were seen (mistakenly) as support for Hunt's [92] postulation that, under certain conditions, familiarity elicits approach. Sheldon's explanation, however, was no more than a redescription of her empirical evidence since she failed to specify the precise conditions under which the behaviour was likely to recur or to indicate the mechanism whereby such a preference would be mediated and for which independent evidence might be obtained. An interpretation more consonant with a greater body of evidence would be that the experimental situation was one generative of fear (strange environment plus raised maze), and thus of increased arousal, which is precisely that state in which an animal is known to prefer familiar to novel objects.

In a more recent paper [156] very similar results were attributed to the effects of 'degrees-of-novelty', since it was found that with adaptation to the

unfamiliar environment the novel objects themselves became increasingly preferred. But this still leaves the additive nature of novelty (irrespective of source) to be demonstrated; a more parsimonious interpretation of all Sheldon's results is simply that environment-novelty inhibits exploration in the laboratory rat.

(b) *Primate studies.* The literature is less explicit with respect to primates—human and infrahuman. Perhaps the earliest systematic account of children's reactions to an unfamiliar environment is that given by Arsenian [3], although it is a commonplace observation that children are extraordinarily distressed by a new environment unless reassured by an adult. Arsenian's subjects were 24 children between 1 and $2\frac{1}{2}$ years of age. Sixteen of these children were introduced to a novel situation (room with toys) by themselves, and 8 were accompanied by their mothers or substitutes. The children who were exposed to the strange situation alone exhibited intense distress reactions—crying, screaming, attempts to escape, autistic gestures—which showed some abatement only after 4 or 5 trials. Their approaches to the toys at this time were characterized by conflict. The children accompanied by their mothers also manifested some emotional behaviour initially but this disappeared almost completely after the fourth trial. In general this group's behaviour consisted mainly of 'adaptive' reactions such as play, locomotion, and talk. The departure of the mother on the sixth trial caused distress reactions in some, but not all subjects.

Cox and Campbell [50] investigated the effect of the mother's temporary departure from an unfamiliar situation upon the behaviour of 1 year and 2- to 3-year-old children. During a 12-min exposure to a strange situation, the mother remained with the child during the first 4 min, left the room for 4 min, and returned to it for the final 4 min. Mothers of the control group remained with their children throughout the 12-min period. There was a pronounced decrease in play activity, general movement, and talking in both older and younger children of the experimental group; the majority of the younger children also cried throughout the period the mother was away, whereas none of those in the control group uttered distress vocalizations. In the 1-year-old children return of the mother resulted in only a partial recovery of their earlier activities. Unfortunately, much information that might have been of greater significance than rigorous statistical comparisons between control and experimental groups does not appear to have been obtained in this study. For example, what were the reactions of the children on initial exposure to the new situation? Did the reactions of the older children differ from the younger? How did they react to the return of the mother since they showed less interest in their former activities? In this experimental design, the effects of environment-novelty may well have been confounded with those of 'separation-anxiety'; while, in such a situation, the distinction may be largely a semantic one, this remains to be demonstrated.

Rosenthal [146] investigated the frequency of two forms of dependency behaviour—attention-seeking and proximity-seeking—when 3- to 5-year-old children were exposed to a novel situation with their mothers or mother-substitutes. She found that in a situation which was deliberately designed to be anxiety-provoking, proximity-seeking increased over a 30-min period. More significant still was the finding that even in a pleasant playroom, not designed to evoke any anxiety, proximity-seeking did not decrease over the 30-min period, thus indicating that despite the presence of mother or substitute the new situation was evocative of anxiety.

In an investigation of the 'fear of visual novelty', Bronson [31] concerned himself with children's reactions to strange situations and strange adults. Various response categories relating to 'sensitivity', 'shyness', and 'fear' were sampled from 1 month to $8\frac{1}{2}$ years of age in 30 boys and 30 girls. The sampling was more frequent at the earlier ages. It was found that in boys, precocity in fear of strangeness (i.e. first manifest at 4 to 6 months) was highly predictive of increased fearfulness and shyness up to early school years. The possibility that this early onset and increased intensity of fear were due to a general hypersensitivity was eliminated. The girls, however, were not found to show this continuity in fear and shyness with age: in their case an early expression of fear of novelty was indeed due to a general hyperexcitability, i.e. they tended to cry when confronted with novelty, but also cried in many other situations. Unfortunately, Bronson did not specify the kind of novelty he was considering and has tended to regard visual novelty as a uniform category [28, 29]. This seems unwarranted, particularly in view of his earlier statements, that 'Strange persons produce the earliest fear reactions reported for human subjects', and again '. . . for most infants a fear of strange persons appears at around 7–9 months of age.

Experimental studies of fear reactions to novel situations or strange objects during this age range have not been found, but anecdotal evidence suggests that such reactions develop along with fear of strange persons' ([28], pp. 410 and 411, respectively). Regrettably, anecdotal evidence can be adduced in support of any position.

The most systematic and detailed account of infant reaction to environment-novelty has recently been given by Rheingold [143]. She seems to have been the only worker to have isolated the effects of environment-novelty from other kinds of novelty and related effects. In an elegant study she systematically investigated the effects of a simple but novel environment on the child alone and with its mother, and the modification of these effects by the introduction of toys and of a stranger. The subjects of her study were 10 infants approximately 10 months of age. Her results showed quite unequivocally that exposure to a novel environment caused great distress to the child and almost wholly inhibited any exploratory activity. The presence of attractive toys and of a stranger in that environment did little to ameliorate the child's distress or encourage exploration. In contrast, those infants first exposed to this strange situation in the presence of their mothers showed no distress and explored fairly freely. A most interesting fact that emerged concerned the persistent effects of this fear-of-novelty: those infants who had initially been exposed to the situation alone continued to show some distress reactions and inhibition of exploratory activity even when their mothers were subsequently present and despite the fact that they had spent some time in the room, in contrast to those infants who were initially exposed to the strange situation with their mothers. In other words, the fear of environment-novelty appears to have been so intense that it had a proactive effect on a potentially unalarming situation. This fear was minimized by the presence of the mother or substitute. Rheingold is to be congratulated on her timely clarification of a confused issue by her diligent separation of effects attributable to different agents.

Conspecific-novelty. Conspecific-novelty will not be considered here in any detail since, due to its peripheral relevance to exploratory behaviour as such, it does not fall properly within the terms of reference of this paper. Nevertheless it must be emphasized that in humans it is the most dramatic form of fear-of-novelty. Recognition of pattern or object novelty has been demonstrated in the first few weeks of life. It thus antecedes by a considerable interval the recognition of strangers at approximately 4 months [1, 142]. Nevertheless, while there seems to be no fear of novel patterns or objects, fear of strangers, as Bronson remarked, is one of the earliest manifest fear reactions, appearing between 7 and 9 months of age [65, 132, 152, 161, 166]. Conspecific-novelty, certainly for the human, clearly has a very special significance, being dependent as it is on the formation of adequate affectional bonds.

In summary, several points may be made: (a) there is no evidence of *fear* or object-novelty *per se* in humans, despite a very early *recognition* of it in ontogeny. Rather, object-novelty appears to be maximally effective in releasing exploratory responses, but this potency also wanes relatively quickly upon repeated exposure; (b)

There is no clear evidence of when environment-novelty can first be recognized, but certainly fear of it is manifest at the age of 10 months, and it also effectively inhibits exploration. These effects can be minimized by the presence of a 'security base' though the negative reactions show some resistance to habituation. (c) Conspecific novelty is recognized relatively late in ontogeny but evokes fear early; its effects are primarily of an emotional nature and its influence on exploration is indirect but nevertheless inhibitory.

What is fear of novelty?

A number of theories of exploratory behaviour assume that novelty evokes both approach and investigation as well as fear (e.g. [17, 20, 63, 125]). To avoid difficulties arising from this obvious contradiction, the qualification is generally made that only extreme or intense degrees of novelty evoke avoidance, moderate degrees evoking ambivalence and eventually approach. The lack of independent measures of degree-of-novelty, apart from the behaviour under investigation, makes this a particularly unprofitable tautology.

More recently the intimate relation between fear and exploration has been emphasized to the extent of providing a fear-motivated basis for exploration [77, 110, 111]. This theoretical formulation states that mild increases in fear enhance exploratory activities while high levels of fear result in avoidance. Tests of this theory, however, are largely based on the extent of locomotor activity in elevated mazes, which appear to present the rat with a very special problem since on any raised platform the animal looks for an opportunity to step down. Therefore the results might simply mean that the animals are searching more actively for a way out. Moreover, as M. H. Sheldon [157] has pointed out, to demonstrate that some experimental manipulation has affected locomotor activity is not to show that it has affected exploration directed towards specific environmental features. Where Halliday succeeded in demonstrating greater exploration of the complex arm of a maze by shocked than non-shocked rats, this arm also happened to be the more familiar of the alternatives since the experimental animals had been shocked in a similarly patterned box. Thus, a formidable array of evidence demonstrates that only in those cases where arousal level has been *experimentally* altered (by administration of stimulant drugs, electric shock, or noise) do the animals choose to explore the less novel alternatives presented [23, 87, 155, 156, 171]. Haywood and Wachs, furthermore, emphasized that their results showed a *reduction* in novelty-preference rather than novelty-*avoidance*. Thus, the already slender evidence adduced in support of fear-motivated exploration becomes very tenuous indeed when appropriate measures of exploration are considered.

This raises a further thorny problem, that of adequate measures of exploratory activity. In general, locomotor activity is used as the principal measure of exploration, though studies which have used multiple measures have not found locomotion to correlate highly with others like sniffing [26, 73]. Very few of the studies on rats have maintained their experimental situation in such a manner as to allow the separation of object-novelty and environment-novelty effects. That it is important to do so is suggested by the fact that the domesticated rat, for instance, shows no fear or avoidance of novel objects, while under other conditions it may well show an increased latency to explore a new situation. Apart from elevated mazes, to what degree novelty evokes fear in rats is still an open question.

In the case of monkeys and chimpanzees the inevitable examples offered, of fear evoked by intense novelty, are the almost hysterical reactions released by the sight of an anaesthetized chimpanzee, a snake, or a model of a monkey head [88]. It is indeed debatable whether these stimuli *a priori* are novel, but more pertinent perhaps is the fact that these reactions are very specific to these particular stimuli. In other words, it is their biological significance rather than their novelty that results in the negative reaction. More important, Butler [37], using stimuli similar to those discussed by Hebb (snake, rubber coil, anaesthetized monkey, etc.) found that they did not in any way suppress an instrumental response upon which they were contingent. The monkeys' exploratory behaviour was no more diminished by these supposedly fear-provoking stimuli than by others. Similar results were reported by Wolin, Ordy, and Dillman [182]. A comparable and often cited example in humans is the finding by Buhler and her colleagues and described by Berlyne (p. 176 of [17]) that children showed more fear and distress to partially 'novel' stimuli —like a distorted voice emanating from a familiar face or a mask covering the face of a person who was talking in his familiar voice—than to completely novel stimuli—like the distorted voice, or the mask alone. This finding suggests that it was the violation of a strong and emotive expectancy which resulted in fear. Often, extraneous

parameters of the experimental situation, e.g. sudden movement or gross distortion of the familiar (as just described), may evoke avoidance, but these effects must be distinguished from the effects of novelty *per se*, since they introduce a qualitative rather than a quantitative change. In other words, we should be clear whether we are attributing novelty effects to the stimulus presented, to the mode of presentation, or to an interaction of the two.

When unconfounded with the effects of environment- and/or stranger-novelty, the effect of object-novelty appears to be to elicit approach and investigation. Although the evidence from rats and, to a certain extent, from monkeys and chimpanzees, seems less supportive than the data for humans, it is likely that selection pressures acting differentially on species will militate against uniform reactions to particular attributes of stimuli. Certainly in humans there is no reliable empirical evidence which supports the notion of fear of novelty in any substantial sense. Where a deliberate attempt has been made to create novel but fear- or anxiety-provoking pictures, children manifested not aversion but greater visual exploration [61]. *Degree* of novelty has not been defined adequately nor has it been shown to have systematic effects. A reduction in preference-for-novelty has been demonstrated in cases where the internal parameters (the state) of the animal were experimentally increased by stimulant drugs (e.g. [23, 163]) and in autistic children [97, 102] in whom, it is suggested, the level of arousal is abnormally and chronically high. Moreover, the precise extent of this internal change may be important in view of Gilmore's [68] demonstration that while 'anxious' children approached novel toys as readily as non-anxious children, 'very anxious' children did not.

Summary and conclusions

In attempting to stress the complexity of the concepts and variables in the area of exploratory behaviour it may appear that an integration of the available evidence into a coherent theoretical formulation has been sacrificed. If so, two arguments in defence of this error of omission may be offered: (a) more competent integrative accounts of the field are already available [18, 21]; and (b) the main purpose of this paper has been to clarify, or at least attempt to clarify, some of the issues relating to behavioural definition and analysis, stimulus variables, and theoretical constructs common in this area.

Although most of the collative stimulus properties can conveniently be subsumed under *novelty* and *complexity*, the precise classification of any particular variable seems open to conjecture. This is most manifest in the attempts to elucidate the parameters of stimulus–complexity effective in eliciting exploration. Complexity, and to a certain extent some of its constituents, were seen to vary along a multiplicity of dimensions. The difficulty in ascertaining the critical features on occasion seems insurmountable. The response measures (fixation, number of exposures, statement of preference or interestingness) moreover do not necessarily show a high degree of correlation (e.g. [24, 51, 52, 106]). Although the evidence regarding the effective attributes of complexity in infants and adults is still equivocal, there seems some measure of agreement that immature organisms (young children and retar-

dates) in general show greater fixation of and preference for the more simple and symmetrical figures of a series.

With respect to stimulus novelty the picture is much less confused, but even greater clarity may be achieved by distinguishing not only the temporal dimension but also the source from which the novelty emanates, viz. object-novelty, environment-novelty, and conspecific-novelty. Man has no fear of object-novelty as such and this seems to be a feature of his evolutionary emancipation. There is clearly an association between an animal's adaptability to a diversity of physical conditions and the intensity of its exploratory activities.

Environment- and conspecific-novelty, in contrast to object-novelty, do elicit fear and distress. Although the impact of environment-novelty is maximal in that there is no familiar frame of reference, an explanation of the reaction in terms of 'degree-of-novelty' is a misleading over-simplification, since it certainly does not account for what is very often a more intense reaction to strangers. The evidence suggests that fear of strangers precedes fear of environment-novelty in time of onset. It may be argued that such a classification unnecessarily proliferates conceptual categories which could more parsimoniously be subsumed under some such dimension as 'degree-of-novelty' or 'stimulus-intensity'. But parsimony may often be misleading; it would moreover need to await a definition of such dimensions independent of the behaviour in question.

In this area, not only stimulus variables but response variables too need more precise definition. Discrepancies in the literature relating to the eliciting properties or temporal course of exploration may be resolved with appropriate definition of stimulus conditions and response classes, thus also enabling a more formal distinction between *specific* and *diversive* exploratory activities (Plates 7 and 8). Thus, apparently incongruent formulations accounting for the energizing and directional aspects of exploratory activity may be equally applicable, with the proviso that they apply to different sets of response classes with different antecedent conditions.

The formulations regarding complexity, novelty, and exploration which have been put forward in this paper resulted primarily from an attempt to find consistency in the very large volume of empirical data, but were also influenced by considerations of biological and psychological relevance. They owe little to any entrenched theoretical position. If they succeed in provoking good experiments to invalidate them, the attempt will have been vindicated.

References

1. AMBROSE, J. A. (1961). The development of the smiling response in early infancy. *In* (Foss, B. M. (Ed.)) *Determinants of infant behaviour.* Vol. 1. Methuen, London.
2. ARASTEH, J. D. (1968). Creativity and related processes in the young child: A review of the literature. *J. genet. Psychol.* **112**, 77–108.
3. ARSENIAN, J. M. (1943). Young children in an insecure situation. *J. abnorm. soc. Psychol.* **38**, 225–49.
4. ATTNEAVE, F. (1954). Some informational aspects of visual perception. *Psychol. Rev.* **61**, 183–93.
5. —— and ARNOULT, M. D. (1956). The quantitative study of shape and pattern perception. *Psychol. Bull.* **53**, 452–71.
6. BARNES, G. W. and KISH, G. B. (1961). Reinforcing properties of the onset of auditory stimulation. *J. exp. Psychol.* **62**, 164–70.
7. BARNETT, S. A. (1958). Experiments on 'neophobia' in wild and laboratory rats. *Brit. J. Psychol.* **49**, Part 3, 195–201.
8. —— (1963). *A study in behaviour.* Methuen, London.
9. BARTOSHUK, A. K. (1962). Response decrement with repeated elicitation of human neonatal cardiac acceleration to sound. *J. comp. physiol. Psychol.* **55**, 9–13.
10. BEACH, F. A. (1950). The Snark was a boojum. *Am. Psychol.* **5**, 115–24.
11. BERLYNE, D. E. (1950). Novelty and curiosity as determinants of exploratory behaviour. *Brit. J. Psychol.* **41**, 68–80.
12. —— (1955). The arousal and satiation of perceptual curiosity in the rat. *J. comp. physiol. Psychol.* **48**, 238–46.
13. —— (1957). Conflict and information-theory variables as determinants of human perceptual curiosity. *J. exp. Psychol.* **53**, 399–404.
14. —— (1958). The influence of the albedo and complexity of stimuli on visual fixation in the human infant. *Brit. J. Psychol.* **49**, 315–18.
15. —— (1958). The influence of complexity and novelty in visual figures on orienting responses. *J. exp. Psychol.* **55**, 289–96.
16. —— (1958). Supplementary report: complexity and novelty responses with longer exposures. *J. exp. Psychol.* **56**, 183.
17. —— (1960). *Conflict, arousal and curiosity.* McGraw-Hill, New York.
18. —— (1963). Motivational problems raised by exploratory and epistemic behavior. *In* (Koch, S. (Ed.)) *Psychology: A study of a science.* Vol. 5. McGraw-Hill, New York.
19. —— (1963). Supplementary report: complexity and novelty responses

with longer exposures. *Can. J. Psychol.* **17**, 274–90.

20. —— (1964). Novelty. *New Soc.* No. 87, 23–4.

21. —— (1966). Curiosity and exploration. *Science* **153**, 25–33.

22. —— CRAW, M. A., SALAPATEK, P. H., and LEWIS, J. L. (1963). Novelty, complexity, incongruity, extrinsic motivation, and the G.S.R. *J. exp. Psychol.* **66**, 560–67.

23. —— KOENIG, I. D., and HIROTA, T. (1966). Novelty, arousal and the reinforcement of diversive exploration in the rat. *J. comp. physiol. Psychol.* **62**, 222–6.

24. —— OGILVIE, J. C., and PARHAM, L. C. C. (1968). The dimensionality of visual complexity, interestingness, and pleasingness. *Can. J. Psychol.* **22**, 376–87.

25. —— and PARHAM, L. C. C. (1968). Determinants of subjective novelty. *Percep. and Psychophys.* **3**, 415–23.

26. BINDRA, D. and SPINNER, N. (1958). Response to different degrees of novelty: the incidence of various activities. *J. exp. Anal. Behav.* **1**, 341–50.

27. BRENNAN, W. M., AMES, E. W., and MOORE, R. W. (1966). Age differences in infants' attention to patterns of different complexities. *Science* **151**, 354–6.

28. BRIDGER, W. H. (1961). Sensory habituation and discrimination in the human neonate. *Am. J. Psychiat.* **117**, 991–6.

29. BRONSON, G. W. (1968). The development of fear in man and other animals. *Child Dev.* **39**, 409–31.

30. —— (1968). The fear of novelty. *Psychol. Bull.* **69**, 350–58.

31. —— (1970). Fear of visual novelty: developmental patterns in males and females. *Dev. Psychol.* **2**, 33–40.

32. BROVERMAN, D. M., KLAIBER, E. L., KOBAYASHI, Y., and VOGEL, W. (1968). Roles of activation and inhibition in sex differences in cognitive abilities. *Psychol. Rev.* **75**, 23–50.

33. BURGERS, J. M. (1966). Curiosity and play: basic factors in the development of life. *Science* **154**, 1680–81.

34. BUTLER, R. A. (1953). Discrimination learning by rhesus monkeys to visual-exploration motivation. *J. comp. physiol. Psychol.* **46**, 95–8.

35. —— (1954). Incentive conditions which influence visual exploration. *J. exp. Psychol.* **48**, 19–23.

36. —— (1957). Discrimination learning by Rhesus monkeys to auditory incentives. *J. comp. physiol. Psychol.* **50**, 239–41.

37. —— (1964). The reactions of Rhesus monkeys to fear-provoking stimuli. *J. genet. Psychol.* **104**, 321–30.

38. —— (1965). Investigative behavior. *In* (Schrier, A. M., Harlow, H. F., and Stollnitz, H. (Eds.)) *Behavior of nonhuman primates.* Vol. 2. Academic Press, New York.

39. —— and ALEXANDER, H. M. (1955). Daily patterns of visual exploratory behavior in the monkey. *J. comp. physiol. Psychol.* **48**, 247–9.

40. —— and HARLOW, H. F. (1954). Persistence of visual exploration in monkeys. *J. comp. physiol. Psychol.* **47**, 258–63.

41. CANTOR, G. N. (1963). Responses of infants and children to complex and novel stimulation. *Adv. child Dev. Behav.* **1**, 1–29.

42. —— and CANTOR, G. N. (1964). Children's observing behavior as related to amount and recency of stimulus familiarization. *J. exp. Child Psychol.* **1**, 241–7.

43. —— and —— (1964). (1964). Observing behavior in children as a function of stimulus novelty. *Child Dev.* **35**, 119–28.

44. —— and —— (1966). Functions relating children's observing behavior to amount and recency of stimulus familiarization. *J. exp. Psychol.* **72**, 859–63.

45. CARR, R. M. and BROWN, W. L.

(1959). The effect of the introduction of novel stimuli upon manipulation in Rhesus monkeys. *J. genet. Psychol.* **94**, 107–11.

46. —— and —— (1959). The effect of sustained novelty upon manipulation in Rhesus monkeys. *J. gen. Psychol.* **61**, 121–5.

47. —— and —— (1959). Manipulation of visually homogeneous stimulus objects. *J. genet. Psychol.* **95**, 245–9.

48. CLAPP, W. F. and EICHORN, D. H. (1965). Some determinants of perceptual investigatory response in children. *J. exp. Child Psychol.* **2**, 371–88.

49. COLLARD, R. R. (1968). Social and play responses of first-born and later-born infants in an unfamiliar situation. *Child. Dev.* **39**, 325–34.

50. COX, F. N. and CAMPBELL, D. (1968). Young children in a new situation with and without their mothers. *Child Dev.* **39**, 123–31.

51. DAY, H. (1966). Looking time as a function of stimulus variables and individual differences. *Percep. mot. Skills* **22**, 423–8.

52. —— (1967). Evaluations of subjective complexity, pleasingness and interestingness for a series of random polygons varying in complexity. *Percep. Psychophys.* **2**, 281–6.

53. DEMBER, W. N. and EARL, R. W. (1957). Analysis of exploratory, manipulatory and curiosity behaviors. *Psychol. Rev.* **64**, 91–6.

54. —— —— and PARADISE, N. (1957). Response by rats to differential stimulus complexity. *J. comp. physiol. Psychol.* **50**, 514–18.

55. EISENMAN, R. (1967). Complexity-simplicity: I. Preference for symmetry and rejection of complexity. *Psychonom. Sci.* **8**, 169–70.

56. —— (1968). Novelty ratings of simple and complex shapes. *J. gen. Psychol.* **78**, 275–8.

57. —— and RAPPAPORT, J. (1967). Complexity preference and semantic differential ratings of complex-ity-simplicity and symmetry-asymmetry. *Psychonom. Sci.* **7**, 147–8.

58. ENGEN, T., LIPSITT, L. P., and KAYE, H. (1963). Olfactory responses and adaptation in the human neonate. *J. comp. physiol. Psychol.* **56**, 73–7.

59. FANTZ, R. L. (1961). The origin of form perception. *Scient. Amer.* **204**, 66–72.

60. —— (1964). Visual experience in infants: decreased attention to familiar patterns relative to novel ones. *Science* **146**, 668–70.

61. FAW, T. T. and NUNNALLY, J. (1968). The influence of stimulus complexity, novelty and affective value on children's visual fixations. *J. exp. Child Psychol.* **6**, 141–53.

62. FISKE, D. W. and MADDI, S. R. (Eds.). (1961). *Functions of varied experience.* Dorsey, Homewood, Ill.

63. FOWLER, H. (1965). *Curiosity and exploratory behavior.* Macmillan, New York.

64. FRASER, D. C. (1966). Satiation and exploratory activity. *Nature* **212**, 1613–14.

65. FREEDMAN, D. G. (1961). The infant's fear of strangers and the flight response. *J. Child Psychol. Psychiat.* **4**, 242–8.

66. FRIEDLANDER, B. Z. (1965). Performance differentiation in a child's incidental play for perceptual reinforcement. Paper presented at the meeting of the American Psychological Association, Chicago.

67. —— McCARTHY, J. J., and SOFORENKO, A. Z. (1967). Automated psychological evaluation with severely retarded institutionalized infants. *Am. J. ment. Defic.* **71**, 909–19.

68. GILMORE, J. B. (1966). Play: a special behavior. *In* (Haber, R. N. (Ed.)) *Current research in motivation.* Holt, Rinehart, and Winston, New York.

69. GLANZER, M. (1953). Stimulus satiation: an explanation of spontaneous alternation and related phenomena *Psychol. Rev.* **60**, 257–68.

70. —— (1958). Curiosity, exploratory

drive, and stimulus satiation. *Psychol. Bull.* **55**, 302–15.

71. GLICKMAN, S. E. and SROGES, R. W. (1966). Curiosity in zoo animals. *Behav.* **26**, 151–88.

72. GOLDBERG, S. and LEWIS, M. (1969). Play behavior in the year-old infant: early sex differences. *Child Dev.* **40**, 21–31.

73. GOODRICK, C. L. (1966). Activity and exploration as a function of age and deprivation. *J. genet. Psychol.* **108**, 239–52.

74. —— (1967). Exploration of non-deprived male. Sprague-Dawley rats as a function of age. *Psychol. Rep.* **20**, 159–63.

75. GOY, R. W. (1968). Organising effects of androgen on the behaviour of rhesus monkeys. *In* (Michael, R. P. (Ed.)) *Endocrinology and human behaviour.* Oxford University Press, London and New York.

76. GUILFORD, J. P. (1962). Factors that aid and hinder creativity. *Teach. Coll. Rec.* **63**, 380–92.

77. HALLIDAY, M. S. (1966). Exploration and fear in the rat. *Symp. zoo. Soc. Lond.* **18**, 45–69.

78. HAMBURG, D. A. and LUNDE, D. T. (1966). Sex hormones in the development of sex differences in human behaviour. *In* (Maccoby, E. (Ed.)) *The development of sex differences.* Tavistock Publications, London.

79. HARLOW, H. F. (1950). Learning and satiation of response in intrinsically motivated complex puzzle performance by monkeys. *J. comp. phsyiol. Psychol.* **43**, 289–94.

80. —— (1953). Mice, men, monkeys, and motives. *Psychol. Rev.* **60**, 23–32.

81. —— BLAZEK, N. C., and McCLEARN, G. E. (1956). Manipulatory motivation in infant rhesus monkeys. *J. comp. physiol. Psychol.* **49**, 444–8.

82. —— HARLOW, M. K., and MEYER, D. R. (1950). Learning motivated by a manipulatory drive. *J. exp. Psychol.* **40**, 228–34.

83. —— and McCLEARN, G. E. (1954). Object discrimination learned by monkeys on the basis of manipulation motives. *J. comp. physiol. Psychol.* **47**, 73–6.

84. HARRIS, L. (1965). The effects of relative novelty on children's choice behavior. *J. exp. Child Psychol.* **2**, 297–305.

85. HAYES, J. R. (1958). The maintenance of play in young children. *J. comp. physiol. Psychol.* **51**, 788–90.

86. HAYNES, H., WHITE, B. L., and HELD, R. (1965). Visual accommodation in human infants. *Science* **148**, 528–30.

87. HAYWOOD, H. C. and WACHS, T. D. (1967). Effects of arousing stimulation upon novelty preference in rats. *Brit. J. Psychol.* **58**, 77–84.

88. HEBB, D. O. (1946). On the nature of fear. *Psychol. Rev.* **53**, 259–302.

89. HERSHENSON, M. (1964). Visual discrimination in the human newborn. *J. comp. physiol. Psychol.* **58**, 270–76.

90. —— MUNSINGER, H., and KESSEN, W. (1965). Preference for shapes of intermediate variability in the newborn human. *Science* **147**, 630–31.

91. HOATS, D. L., MILLER, M. B., and SPITZ, H. H. (1963). Experiments on perceptual curiosity in mental retardates and normals. *Am. J. ment. Defic.* **68**, 386–95.

92. HUNT, J. McV. (1965). Intrinsic motivation and its role in psychological development. *In* (Levine, D. (Ed.)) *Nebraska symposium on motivation.* Univ. of Nebraska Press, Lincoln, Neb.

93. HUTT, C. (1966). Exploration and play in children. *Symp. zoo. Soc. London* **18**, 61–81.

94. —— (1967). Effects of stimulus novelty on manipulatory exploration in an infant. *J. Child Psychol. Psychiat.* **8**, 241–7.

95. —— (1967). Temporal effects on

response decrement and stimulus satiation in exploration. *Brit. J. Psychol.* **58**, 365–73.

96. —— (1969). Complexity, curiosity and development. Proceedings of the XIXth International Congress of Psychology, London.

97. —— (1969). Exploration, arousal and autism. *Psycholog. Forschung*, **33**, 1–8.

98. —— (1970). How children explore. *Sci. J.* **6**, 68–71.

99. —— Bernuth, H. v., Lenard, H. G., Hutt, S. J., and Prechtl, H. F. R. (1968). Habituation in relation to state in the human neonate. *Nature* **220**, 618–20.

100. —— and McGrew, P. L. (1969). Do children really prefer complexity? *Psychonom. Sci.* **17**, 113–14.

101. —— and —— (1969). The multi-dimensionality of visual complexity: effects on children's preferences and fixations. Paper presented at the London Conference of the British Psychological Society.

102. Hutt, S. J. and Hutt, C. (1968). Stereotypy, arousal, and autism. *Human Dev.* **11**, 277–86.

103. —— and —— (1970). *Direct observation and measurement of behavior.* Charles C. Thomas, Springfield, Ill.

104. —— —— Lenard, H. G., Bernuth, H. v., and Muntjewerff, W. J. (1968). Auditory responsivity in the human neonate. *Nature* **218**, 888–90.

105. —— Lenard, H. G., and Prechtl, H. F. R. (1969). Psychophysiology of the newborn. *Adv. child Dev. Behav.* **4**, 128–72.

106. Kagan, J. and Lewis, M. (1965). Studies of attention in the human infant. *Merrill-Palmer Quart.* **11**, 95–127.

107. Kimura, D. (1963). Speech lateralization in young children as determined by an auditory test. *J. comp. physiol. Psychol.* **56**, 899–902.

108. Kish, G. B. and Antonitis, J. J.

(1956). Unconditioned operant behaviour in two homozygous strains of mice. *J. genet. Psychol.* **88**, 121–9.

109. Lawick-Goodall, J. V. (1968). The behaviour of free-living chimpanzees in the Gombe Stream Reserve. *Anim. Behav. Monogr.* **1**, 161–311.

110. Lester, D. (1967). Sex differences in exploration: towards a theory of exploration. *Psychol. Rec.* **17**, 55–62.

111. —— (1968). Two tests of a fear-motivated theory of exploration. *Psychonom. Sci.* **10**, 385–6.

112. Leuba, C. (1955). Toward some integration of learning theories: the concept of optimal stimulation. *Psychol. Rep.* **1**, 27–33.

113. —— and Friedlander, B. Z. (1968). Effects of controlled audio-visual reinforcement on infants manipulative play in the home. *J. exp. Child Psychol.* **6**, 87–99.

114. Lewis, M. and Goldberg, S. (1969). The acquisition and violation of expectancy: an experimental paradigm. *J. exp. Child Psychol.* **7**, 70–80.

115. —— —— and Rausch, M. (1967). Attention distribution as a function of novelty and familiarity. *Psychonom. Sci.* **7**, 327–8.

116. —— Kagan, J., and Kalafat, J. (1966). Patterns of fixation in infants. *Child Dev.* **37**, 331–41.

117. Lieberman, J. N. (1965). Playfulness and divergent thinking: an investigation of their relationship at the kindergarten level. *J. genet. Psychol.* **107**, 219–24.

118. Maccoby, E. E. (1966). Sex differences in intellectual functioning. *In* (Maccoby, E. E. (Ed.)) *The development of sex differences.* Tavistock, London.

119. Marais, F. N. (1939). *My friends the Baboons.* Methuen, London.

120. Marler, P. J. and Hamilton, W. J. (1966). *Mechanisms of animal behavior.* Wiley, New York.

121. Mason, W. A., Harlow, H. F., and Rueping, R. R. (1959). The

development of manipulatory responsiveness in the infant Rhesus monkey. *J. comp. physiol. Psychol.* **52**, 555–8.

122. MAY, R. B. (1963). Stimulus selection in preschool children under conditions of free choice. *Percept. mot. Skills* **16**, 203–6.

123. McCALL, R. B. and KAGAN, J. (1967). Attention in the infant: effects of complexity, contour, perimeter and familiarity. *Child Dev.* **38**, 939–52.

124. McDONALD, D. G., JOHNSON, L. C., and HORD, D. J. (1964). Habituation of the orienting response in alert and drowsy subjects. *Psychophys.* **1**, 163–73.

125. McREYNOLDS, P. (1962). Exploratory behaviour: a theoretical interpretation. *Psychol. Rep.* **11**, 311–18.

126. MENDEL, G. (1965). Children's preferences for differing degrees of novelty. *Child. Dev.* **36**, 453–65.

127. MEYERS, W. J. and CANTOR, G. N. (1966). Infants' observing and heart period responses as related to novelty of visual stimuli. *Psychonom. Sci.* **5**, 239–40.

128. —— and —— (1967). Observing and cardiac responses of human infants to visual stimuli. *J. exp. Child Psychol.* **5**, 16–25.

129. MONTGOMERY, K. C. (1951). The relationship between exploratory behavior and spontaneous alternation in the white rat. *J. comp. physiol. Psychol.* **44**, 582–9.

130. —— (1953). Exploratory behaviours as a function of 'similarity' of stimulus situations. *J. comp. physiol. Psychol.* **46**, 129–33.

131. MOON, L. E. and LODAHL, T. M. (1956). The reinforcing effect of changes in illumination on lever-pressing in the monkey. *Am. J. Psychol.* **69**, 288–90.

132. MORGAN, G. A. and RICCIUTI, H. N. (1969). Infants' responses to strangers during the first year. *In* (Foss, B. M. (Ed.)) *Determinants of infant*

behaviour. Vol. IV. Methuen, London.

133. MOSS, H. (1967). Sex, age and state as determinants of mother–infant interaction. *Merrill-Palmer Quart.* **13**, 19–36.

134. MULLER-SCHWARZE, D. (1968). Play deprivation in deer. *Behaviour* **31**, 1–2.

135. MUNSINGER, H. and KESSEN, W. (1964). Uncertainty, structure and preference. *Psychol. Monogr.* **78**, (Whole No. 596), 1–24.

136. —— and —— (1966). Stimulus variability and cognitive change. *Psychol. Rev.* **73**, 164–78.

137. —— and —— (1966). Structure, variability and development. *J. exp. Child Psychol.* **4**, 20–49.

138. —— —— and KESSEN, M. L. (1964). Age and uncertainty: developmental variation in preference for variability. *J. exp. Child Psychol.* **1**, 1–15.

139. —— and WEIR, M. W. (1967). Infants' and young children's preference for complexity. *J. exp. Child Psychol.* **5**, 69–73.

140. MYERS, A. K. and MILLER, N. E. (1954). Failure to find a learned drive based on hunger: evidence for learning motivated by 'exploration'. *J. comp. physiol. Psychol.* **47**, 428–36.

141. PAYNE, B. (1966). The relationship between a measure of organization for visual patterns and their judged complexity. *J. verb. Learn. verb. Behav.* **5**, 338–43.

142. POLAK, P. R., EMDE, R. N., and SPITZ, R. A. (1964). The smiling response. II. Visual discrimination and the onset of depth perception. *J. nerv. ment. Dis.* **139**, 407–15.

143. RHEINGOLD, H. L. (1969). The effect of a strange environment on the behaviour of infants. *In* (Foss, B. M. (Ed.)) *Determinants of infant behaviour.* Vol. IV. Methuen, London.

144. —— STANLEY, W. C., and DOYLE, G. A. (1964). Visual and auditory

reinforcement of a manipulatory response in the young child. *J. exp. Child Psychol.* **1**, 316–26.

145. ROBINSON, R. (1968). Visual performance in the newborn. Paper read to the Spastics International Study Group, Oxford, England.

146. ROSENTHAL, M. K. (1967). Effects of a novel situation and of anxiety on two groups of dependency behaviours. *Brit. J. Psychol.* **58**, 357–64.

147. RUMP, E. E. (1968). Is there a general factor of preference for complexity? *Percep. Psychophys.* **3**, 346–8.

148. SAAYMAN, G., AMES, E. W., and MOFFETT, A. (1964). Response to novelty as an indicator of visual discrimination in the human infant. *J. exp. Child Psychol.* **1**, 189–98.

149. SACKETT, G. P. (1963). A neural mechanism underlying unlearned, critical period, and developmental aspects of visually controlled behavior. *Psychol. Rev.* **70**, 40–50.

150. SALAPATEK, P. (1968). Visual scanning of geometric figures by the human newborn. *J. comp. physiol. Psychol.* **66**, 247–58.

151. —— and KESSEN, W. (1966). Visual scanning of triangles by the human newborn. *J. exp. Child Psychol.* **3**, 155–67.

152. SCHAFFER, H. R. and EMERSON, P. E. (1964). The development of social attachments in infancy. *Monogr. Soc. Res. Child Dev.* **29**, Serial No. 94, 1–77.

153. —— and PARRY, M. P. (1969). Perceptual-motor behaviour in infancy as a function of age and stimulus familiarity. *Brit. J. Psychol.* **60**, 1–10.

154. SCHIFF, W., CAVINESS, J. A., and GIBSON, J. J. (1962). Persistent fear responses in Rhesus monkeys to the optical stimulus of 'looming'. *Science* **136**, 982–3.

155. SHELDON, A. B. (1968). Preference for familiar situation independent of fear of novelty. *Psychonom. Sci.* **13**, 173–4.

156. —— (1969). Preference for familiar versus novel stimuli as a function of the familiarity of the environment. *J. comp. physiol. Psychol.* **67**, 516–21.

157. SHELDON, M. H. (1968). The effect of electric shock on rats choice between familiar and nonfamiliar maze arms: a replication. *Quart. J. exp. Psychol.* **20**, 400–404.

158. SHILLITOE, E. E. (1963). Exploratory behaviour in the short-tailed vole *Microtus agrestis. Behaviour* **21**, 145–54.

159. SMOCK, C. D. and HOLT, B. G. (1962). Children's reactions to novelty: an experimental study of 'curiosity motivation'. *Child Dev.* **33**, 631–42.

160. SOKOLOV, E. N. (1963). Higher nervous functions: the orienting reflex. *A. Rev. Physiol.* **25**, 545–80.

161. SPITZ, R. A. (1950). Anxiety in infancy: a study of its manifestations in the first year of life. *Int. J. Psycho-anal.* **31**, 138–43.

162. STENSON, H. H. (1966). The physical factor structure of random forms and their judged complexity. *Percep. Psychophys.* **1**, 303–10.

163. STRETCH, R. (1963). Effects of amphetamine and pentobarbitone on exploratory behaviour in rats. *Nature* **199**, 787–9.

164. SYMMES, D. (1959). Anxiety reduction and novelty as goals of visual exploration by monkeys. *J. genet. Psychol.* **94**, 181–98.

165. TAYLOR, D. C. (1969). Differential rates of cerebral maturation between sexes and between hemispheres: evidence from epilepsy. *Lancet*, 140–42.

166. TENNES, K. H. and LAMPL, E. E. (1964). Stranger and separation anxiety. *J. nerv. ment. Dis.* **139**, 247–54.

167. TERWILLIGER, R. F. (1963). Pattern complexity and affective arousal. *Percep. mot. Skills* **17**, 387–95.

168. THOMAS, H. (1965). Visual-fixation

responses of infants to stimuli of varying complexity. *Child Dev.* **36**, 629–38.

169. —— (1966). Preferences for random shapes: ages six through nineteen years. *Child Dev.* **37**, 843–59.

170. THOMPSON, R. F. and SPENCER, W. A. (1966). Habituation: a model phenomenon for the study of neuronal substrates of behaviour. *Psychol. Rev.* **73**, 16–43.

171. THOMPSON, W. R. and HIGGINS, W. H. (1958). Emotion and organisation behaviour: experimental data bearing on the Leeper-Young controversy. *Can. J. Psychol.* **12**, 61–8.

172. THORPE, W. H. (1963). *Learning and instinct in animals.* (2nd ed.) Methuen, London.

173. TORRANCE, E. P. (1962). *Guiding creative talent.* Prentice-Hall, Englewood Cliffs, N.J.

174. —— (1963). *Education and the creative potential.* University of Minn. Press, Minneapolis.

175. VITZ, P. C. (1966). Preference for different amounts of visual complexity. *Behav. Sci.* **11**, 105–14.

176. WALKER, E. L. and WALKER, B. E. (1964). Response to stimulus complexity in the rat. *Psychol. Rec.* **14**, 489–97.

177. WALLACH, M. A. and KOGAN, H. (1965). *Modes of thinking in young children: A study of the creativity-intelligence distinction.* Holt, Rinehart, and Winston, New York.

178. WELKER, W. I. (1956). Effects of age and experience on play and exploration of young chimpanzees. *J. comp. physiol. Psychol.* **49**, 223–6.

179. —— (1956). Some determinants of play and exploration in chimpanzees. *J. comp. physiol. Psychol.* **49**, 84–9.

180. —— (1956). Variability of play and exploratory behaviour in chimpanzees. *J. comp. physiol. Psychol.* **49**, 181–5.

181. WICKELGREN, L. W. (1967). Convergence in the human newborn. *J. exp. Child Psychol.* **5**, 74–85.

182. WOLIN, L. R., ORDY, J. M., and DILLMAN, A. (1963). Monkeys' fear of snakes: a study of its basis and generality. *J. genet. Psychol.* **103**, 207–26.

29 Exploration in a strange environment

HARRIET L. RHEINGOLD†

THE strangeness of a stimulus affects behaviour. In a strange environment, for example, many animals explore little and show 'emotional' responses (see [3, 5], for reviews). Although the effect of a strange *person* upon the behaviour of *human* infants has often been studied—most recently by Morgan and Ricciuti [4], and Cald-well—the effect of a strange *environment* has less often been investigated. Of special relevance for the present studies are two reports; Bayley's [2] that the strangeness of place and persons during psychological tests was one cause of crying in infants and Arsenian's [1] that crying and 'autistic' gestures appeared in children, 11 to 21 months of age, when they were placed alone in a strange room.

In the animal studies, most of the subjects had been raised in laboratories and hence it may be assumed that they had experienced a restricted environment. Similarly, Arsenian's subjects were reared in an institution and thus, according to her, might have had less experience in strange environments than home children. When the studies to be reported here were begun, it was expected that human infants

reared in normal environments—assumed to provide varied stimulation —would not be as distressed as organisms from narrower environments.

In a series of four experiments, the effects of a strange environment upon the behaviour of different groups of infants approximately 10 months of age were investigated. This age was chosen as the earliest at which reasonably proficient creeping could be expected. In the first experiment, the strange environment was empty; in the second experiment, it contained toys; and in the third, it contained a person. For a different group of subjects in each experiment, the strange environment contained the subject's own mother. In the fourth experiment, the effects of the four conditions—empty, toys, person, and mother—were simultaneously examined in still other groups of infants.

The mother's presence was used to provide a contrasting condition; it was known from preliminary work in the laboratory that subjects at this age would creep around the room and not cry in an environment that contained their mothers. Arsenian's [1] data, although the subjects in her study were somewhat older than those here reported, supported these observations.

The main purpose of the studies was to discover the effect of a strange environment upon the infant's behaviour. A second purpose was to

† From 'The effect of a strange environment on the behavior of infants'. In *Determinants of infant behaviour* (Foss, B. (Ed.)), Vol. 4. Methuen, London (1969). Reprinted by permission of the Tavistock Institute of Human Relations.

measure the effect of prior exposure to the environment *with* the mother upon subsequent exposure without her (the effect of familiarization). A third purpose was to measure the effect of prior exposure *without* the mother upon subsequent exposure to an environment now containing her (the persisting effect of a strange environment).

Two classes of responses to the environment were selected for study in each experiment: vocal behaviour, which was considered to be a measure of emotional responses; and locomotor activity, which was considered to be a measure of exploratory behaviour.

Experiment 1

Method

Subjects. The Ss were 10 normal white infants, 4 male and 6 female. They ranged in age from 9·1 to 10·1 months; mean age was 9·6 months. Mean DIQ on the Bayley Infant Scale of Mental Development was 112, with a range from 104 to 126. The mean DMQ on the Bayley Infant Scale of Motor Development was 114, with a range from 94 to 127. Their fathers had an average of 16·6 years of education; range was 11 to 20 years. Their mothers had an average of 14·9 years of education; range was 12 to 16. As a group, therefore, the Ss were somewhat above average in developmental status, and they came from homes of above average educational level.

The Ss were obtained by telephoning mothers of infants born at the University of North Carolina Memorial Hospital. Rate of refusal was negligible. Age was the primary criterion for selection. The records of subjects were discarded only if they could not creep (three Ss in this experiment), or if before the test was begun they did not easily allow the

experimenter (E) to take them from their mothers (none in this experiment).

The strange environment. The strange environment was a room not seen by Ss before the experiment (Fig. 29·1). It was approximately 9 ft wide, 18 ft long, and 9 ft high. The walls were painted off-white and the floor was covered with an embossed white vinyl material. An electric baseboard heater of grey metal on the right wall was 4 ft wide and 7 in high. In general, the room presented a relatively homogeneous environment; there was little to attract Ss' attention and nothing in it of an obviously fear-provoking nature.

The floor was marked by means of $\frac{1}{4}$-in-wide buff-coloured masking tape into a matrix of 18 cells, each approximately 3 ft square. Lighting was provided by four 150-watt cove lights on the right wall; incident light at floor level was approximately 7 ft-candles. On the left wall there were two one-way vision mirrors, each approximately 3 ft above the floor; from these windows, observers (Os) outside the experimental room followed and recorded Ss' behaviour.

Procedure

On the day before the test, Ss and their mothers spent an hour in the laboratory to adapt Ss to the general environment and to E. Immediately upon first entry to the laboratory, each S was given a pretest: he was placed in a crib with three toys in a small examining room for 3 min, while E and the mother, in an adjoining room, observed his behaviour through a one-way vision window. If an S cried before the end of 3 min the pretest was ended and the mother and E returned at once. The pretest was designed to ensure that all the *S*s who could not stay alone in *that* environment would not by chance be assigned to one or the other groups. The *S*s who lasted three minutes were called 'tolerators'; the others, 'non-tolerators'. On the adaptation day, the Bayley scales of mental and motor development were also administered.

On the test day, *S*s were carried into the strange environment by *E* who talked softly to them and placed them

cushion on the floor in cell 52 (column 2, row 5), facing the infant. Each mother was told that she could look at and smile to *S* and could put an arm around him if he required support, but she was directed not to talk to *S*, play with him, or entice him to come to her; she was not, on the other hand, to push him away.

The measures
Vocal responses. From tape recordings of the infants' vocal responses two

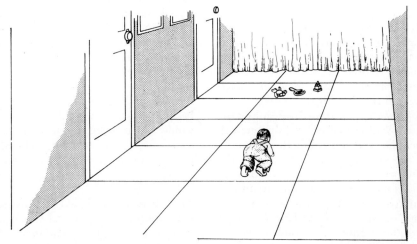

Fig. 29.1. The strange environment. Infant is in the start cell; the toys identify cell 52.

in cell 22 (column 2, row 2 in Fig. 29.1) in a creeping position, facing the long axis of the room. As a signal to time the trials, *E* said 'Start' when *S* was placed, then left the room, closing the door.

The duration of a trial was 3 min. At the end of 3 min *E* entered the room, picked *S* up, and carried him to an adjoining room. The inter-trial interval was 1 min. During the interval *S* did not see his mother, but *E* talked to him, showed him a toy, and patted him if he was emotionally upset.

The mother, when present, sat on a

measures were calculated: *latency of crying* and frequency of non-distress *vocalizations*.

Latency of crying was the number of seconds from *E*'s placing of *S* in cell 22 until onset of *S*'s crying. Crying was defined as continuous, rhythmical, wailing sounds. Typically the onset was sudden, following a holding of the breath. The crying was often loud. It had the characteristics of a cry of pain and appeared to be as distressing for the infant to experience as it was for the observers to hear. As a response measure, it was used only for these acute sounds, and was sharply differentiated from such milder distress vocalizations as protests and fusses.

Frequency of *vocalizations* was the number of 30-s periods in which there occurred discrete voiced sounds of a non-protest, often cheerful, nature.

All the measures reported are the average of measures made independently by the 2 *O*s. Observer agreement for each vocal measure yielded product-moment correlations of 0·99.

Locomotor activity. On a plan of the floor drawn on paper, two *O*s traced *S*'s path through the room and recorded the second at which he crossed successive lines. From these timed tracings, three measures were calculated: *number of lines crossed, time to cell 52, and time in cell 52.*

Number of lines crossed was simply the number of lines *S* crossed or touched, including lines bounding the perimeter of the room. *Time to cell 52* was the number of seconds from *E*'s placing of *S* in the test environment until *S* entered cell 52; it measured time to contact with mother. *Time in cell 52* was the number of seconds *S* was in cell 52. When the mother was present, it measured time in proximity to, or in contact with, her.

Again, all reported measures are the average of the two *O*s' measures. The product-moment correlations of agreement between the measures of two *O*s were 0·99 for lines crossed; 0·99 for time to cell 52; and 0·94 for time in cell 52.

A few words are necessary to explain that *S*s were removed from the room when they gave the distress cry and to point out the effect of their removal upon the other measures. Once an infant gave the distress cry, it was observed that he continued to cry without abatement. The longer he was allowed to cry, the less the possibility of calming him in the intertrial interval and therefore of carrying him through subsequent trials. Furthermore, it was observed that *S*s who cried did not creep around the room. They stayed in the start cell, lying on the floor, face down, or at most they crawled to the entrance door and *stayed* there. It follows then that when a *S* was removed, measures of locomotor activity were based on the assumption that, had he been allowed to stay, he would not have crossed any more lines. The data on locomotor activity are therefore less firmly based in reality than the data on latency of crying.

Duration of trial was longer by some seconds than latency of crying, because *E* waited to make sure that *S* would not recover spontaneously. As a measure, it was of course related to latency of crying.

Plan of experiment 1

The ten *S*s were assigned at random to two groups, Group A and Group M, subject only to the requirement that each group contain an equal number of tolerators.

For both groups there were 5 trials, each planned to be 3 min in duration, with an inter-trial interval of 1 min. For Group A, *S*s were placed in the strange environment for the first four trials without their mothers and for the next trial with their mothers. For Group M, *S*s were placed in the same environment but with their mothers present for the first two trials, with their mothers absent for the next two trials, and with their mothers present again in the last trial (Table 29.1).

The effect of the strange environment was measured by comparing the performance of the two groups in trials 1 and 2. The effect of familiarization was measured by comparing the performance of the two groups in trials 3 and 4. The persisting effect of the strange environment on responses to the environment now containing the mother was measured by comparing the performance of Group A in trial 5 with the performance of Group M in trials 1 and 2. In passing, attention will be drawn on occasion to the effects of experimental conditions *within* a group. Within-group effects

haviour. The results, however, showed a marked difference between the two trials in all experimental conditions except those in which the mother was present from the beginning. Where differences between trials occurred, the results of each trial will be considered separately.

Effect of the Strange Environment

The differences in performance between Groups A and M on trials 1 and 2 provide a measure of the effect of the strange environment.

TABLE 29.1. *Design of Experiment 1 and Means of Measures*

Groups and measures	Trials				
	1	2	3	4	5
Group A	Alone	Alone	Alone	Alone	Mother
Latency of crying	46·0 s	5·6 s	3·3 s	0·3 s	73·5 s
Lines crossed	4·0	0·6	0·7	0·2	7·6
Duration of trial	86·5 s	21·0 s	7·0 s	2·5 s	157·8 s
Group M	Mother	Mother	Alone	Alone	Mother
Latency of crying	180·0 s†	180·0 s†	65·5 s	45·0 s	99·8 s
Lines crossed	15·9	13·7	6·5	1·9	6·8
Duration of trial	180·0 s	180·0 s	87·9 s	55·3 s	180·0 s

† Indicates that no *S* cried.

were not tested but they offer additional confirmation of the findings.

Two measures, latency of crying and number of lines crossed, were subjected to statistical test. The Mann-Whitney test was used, and all p values are two-tailed. Other measures (e.g. frequency of vocalizations, duration of trial) are reported in the text or the tables but differences between them were not tested.

Results

Two trials of each experimental condition were planned in order to obtain a more representative sample of be-

In trial 1, four of the five *S*s in Group A cried when placed alone in the environment. Mean latency of those who cried was 12·5 s; mean latency for the group was 46·0 s (Table 29.1). In trial 2, all 5 *S*s cried with a mean latency of 5·6 s. In contrast, no *S* in Group M cried at any time during trials 1 and 2. If, for statistical purposes, 180 s is taken as a measure of latency for *S*s who did not cry, the difference between the groups in latency of crying was significant ($p < 0.01$).

Measures of vocalizations support the findings on measures of crying.

No *S* in Group A uttered a vocalization of a non-protest nature, but all *S*s in Group M vocalized one or more times in both trials. Specifically, Group M *S*s vocalized during 3 or more of the six 30-s periods in trial 1, and during 2 or more periods in trial 2.

The findings on vocal behaviour therefore indicate that a strange environment without the mother produced crying; with her, it did not. Her presence, instead, supported vocal vocalizations of a non-protest nature.

Locomotor activity was minimal in Group A (Table 29.1). In trial 1 they crossed a mean of 4·0 lines, and in trial 2, a mean of 0·6 lines. Group M, in contrast, crossed 15·9 lines in trial 1 and 13·7 lines in trial 2. The difference between the groups on trial 1, although large, were not statistically significant; on trial 2 it was reliable ($p < 0.01$); and on both trials combined, it was also reliable ($p < 0.01$). The strange environment entered alone therefore inhibited locomotor activity; the presence of the mother in the strange environment supported it.

The responses of Group A on the whole differed markedly from trial 1 to trial 2; in trial 2 they cried sooner and crossed fewer lines. The responses of Group M, on the other hand, were similar from trial 2.

No *S* in Group A went to cell 52 in trials 1 and 2. In the absence of the mother, then, *S*s did not enter cell 52. All of Group M, however, went to cell 52. In trial 1 they took 30·5 s to reach it and spent 97·7 s there; in trial 2 they took 33·9 s to reach it and spent 93·6 s there. Once again, the behaviour of Group M showed considerable similarity from trial 1 to trial 2, thus providing a standard with which to compare Group A's behaviour.

Effect of prior exposure with the mother

In trials 3 and 4, *S*s in Group A were placed alone in the strange environment for the 3rd and 4th consecutive times. Group M *S*s, in contrast, were placed in it alone for the first time, following two trials in which the mother had been present and during which they had an opportunity to become familiar with the strange environment. All *S*s in Group A cried, as they had in trials 1 and 2, and they cried earlier on each successive trial (Table 29.1). But now, 4 of the 5 *S*s in Group M cried in both trials 3 and 4. Latency of crying, however, was greater on each trial than Group A's on the same trials ($p < 0.01$ for trial 3, $p < 0.05$ for trial 4).

In passing, it can be seen that Group M on trials 3 and 4 responded much the same as Group A on trials 1 and 2.

Prior exposure *with* the mother therefore postponed crying, when compared with prior exposure *without* the mother; but at the same time the data also show that the strange environment when encountered for the first time by the infant alone produced a measure of distress.

Locomotor activity was also reduced for both groups in trials 3 and 4 (Table 29.1). Group A crossed less than one line in each trial. In contrast, Group M crossed 6·5 lines in trial 3, a performance that was reliably different from Group A's ($p < 0.05$); they also crossed more lines in trial 4, but here the difference was not statistically significant. These findings show that prior exposure with the mother supported more activity on the first trial when alone than prior exposure without the mother. By the second trial, the effect of familiarization had disappeared.

Locomotion to cell 52 is also of interest here. As in trials 1 and 2, no *S* in Group A went to cell 52 in trials 3 and 4. Now that it is clear that *S*s did not go to cell 52 if the mother did not occupy it, the next question asks whether *S*s, who had gone to cell 52 when the mother was there, would go there in her absence. The data show that only one *S* went to cell 52 in trial 3, and that he stayed there for only 2 s; none went in trial 4.

In summary, prior exposure with the mother had an effect—it postponed crying and supported locomotor activity. At the same time, the effect of being alone in the strange environment was marked: *S*s of Group M cried now, although they had not in trials 1 and 2, and they crossed fewer lines.

Persisting effect of the strange environment

How did the responses of *S*s to an environment now containing the mother, after four trials alone, compare with the responses of *S*s to an environment that contained the mother from the beginning? The differences in latency of crying and in number of lines crossed between trial 5 for Group A and trials 1 and 2 for Group M are large (73·5 s versus 180·0 s for latency of crying; 7·6 versus 15·9 and 13·7 for number of lines crossed) but are not statistically significant. Nevertheless, three *S*s in Group A cried at a mean latency of 2·5 s. Of these three *S*s, two did not go to the mother.

The findings, then, are not straightforward. It is clear, however, that the performance of three of the five *S*s was markedly affected; for them, there was a persisting effect. The mother's presence therefore did not dissipate distress and support activity in all *S*s.

It may also be seen that Group M's performance in trial 5 was markedly different from its own performance in trials 1 and 2. Some *S*s cried (latency of crying for the group in trial 5 was 99·8 s) and they were less active (6·8 lines crossed in trial 5 versus 15·9 in trial 1 and 13·7 in trial 2). All *S*s, however, went to cell 52 and reached it in less time than in trials 1 and 2 (16·9 s versus 32·2 s) and stayed with the mother longer (131·2 s versus 95·1 s). As a group they too showed the effects of being alone in the environment for the preceding two trials.

Some subject variables of interest, such as sex of *S*s, and whether tolerator or not, will be evaluated later for the four experiments combined.

Summary

The results of this experiment show that a strange environment, of the kind studied here, inhibited exploratory behaviour and evoked emotional distress. For a control group of *S*s, the same environment containing the mother supported exploratory behaviour and, instead of crying, evoked many non-protest vocalizations. When the mother was removed, this second group explored less and eventually cried, but they nevertheless explored more and took longer to cry than the *S*s who had been placed in the strange environment without their mothers. Familiarity with the environment had an effect. Also, the mother in the environment did not uniformly inhibit distress and support exploratory behaviour in all *S*s, if they had first been exposed to the strange environment by themselves. The effect of the strange environment persisted. Lastly, successive entries into the environment were anticipated by many *S*s who cried earlier and earlier.

Experiment 2

Because the strange environment by itself produced so much apparent distress and supported so little exploratory activity, toys were added to the room in this experiment. It was anticipated that the presence of toys might support behaviour better than an empty environment and that their attractiveness might diminish the emotional response.

The number of trials in the strange environment without the mother was reduced from 4 to 2, because trials 3 and 4 for Group A in Experiment 1 added no new information on the effect of the strange environment. The design then was as follows: Group T (Toys) entered the room alone for trials 1 and 2 (Table 29.2). For trials 3 and 4, the toys were removed and the mothers were present in their place. Group M, on the other hand, entered the room with only the mothers present for trials 1 and 2 and then with toys instead of their mothers for trials 3 and 4. As a result, the effect of a strange environment which contained toys could be contrasted with the effect of one which contained the mother (trials 1 and 2 for Groups T and M). The effect of prior exposure with the mother could also be measured by comparing trials 3 and 4 for Group M with trials 1 and 2 for Group A. In addition, the effect of prior exposure without the mother upon responses to the environment when the mother was present could also be compared (trials 3 and 4 for Group T in contrast to trials 1 and 2 for Group M).

Method

Subjects. The *S*s were 8 normal white infants, 4 male and 4 female. They ranged in age from 9·6 to 10·0 months;

mean age was 9·8 months. Mean DIQ on the Bayley mental developmental scale was 104; scores ranged from 96 to 114. Mean DMQ on the Bayley motor developmental scale was 106; scores ranged from 99 to 116. Their fathers had an average of 18 years of education, ranging from 12 to 23 years. Their mothers' education ranged from 12 to 17 years, with an average of 15 years. Subjects were obtained in the same way as in Experiment 1. The records of three other *S*s were not used; two could not crawl and one could not be removed from the mother before the beginning of the test.

The Strange Environment. The room was the same as in Experiment 1. In the toy condition, 4 colourful toys were placed on the floor close to the start cell; they were a pull toy containing marbles, a large plastic bolt with nuts, a large ball, and a string of wooden beads.

Procedure

Duration of trials was reduced from 3 to 2 min. Since the early onset of distress had markedly reduced the duration of trials for *S*s without their mothers, a shorter length of trial might serve to equalize duration of trials between the two groups. As before, two groups of *S*s were formed by random assignment.

In all other respects the experiment was carried out in the same way as Experiment 1. The same measures were used, and again all scores were the averages of the measures recorded independently by 2 *O*s. Product-moment correlations of agreement were 0·99 for latency of crying; 0·98 for periods in which vocalizations were heard; 0·97 for number of lines crossed; 0·96 for time to cell 52; and 0·91 for time in cell 52.

Results

Effect of the strange environment

The responses of the two groups in trials 1 and 2 show the effect of the different environments.

All *S*s in Group T cried in trials 1 and 2; latency of crying was 36·2 s in trial 1, and 2·0 s in trial 2 (Table 29·2). Group M behaved differently—none cried in either trial. Furthermore, no *S* in Group T vocalized, but all *S*s in Group M did; as a group they gave

between the groups was statistically significant ($p < 0·05$).

The toys in the environment might have been expected to evoke some manipulation from Group T. Actually, the response was minimal. In trial 1, only one *S* manipulated a toy briefly before crying. Of the three other *S*s, one looked at the toys and two just touched one of the toys. In trial 2, none made contact with a toy.

No *S* in Group T went to cell 52 in either trials 1 or 2. All *S*s in Group M, in contrast, did go in both trials. They

TABLE 29.2. *Design of Experiment 2 and Means of Measures*

Groups and measures	Trials			
	1	2	3	4
Group T	Toys	Toys	Mother	Mother
Latency of crying	36·2 s	2·0 s	63·2 s	62·8 s
Lines crossed	4·2	0·0	7·6	10·8
Duration of trial	55·6 s	2·2 s	101·1 s	90·0 s
Group M	Mother	Mother	Toys	Toys
Latency of crying	120·0 s†	120·0 s†	120·0 s†	66·0 s
Lines crossed	16·2	10·6	4·8	5·4
Duration of trial	120·0 s	120·0 s	120·0 s	115·0 s

† Indicates that no *S* cried.

one or more vocalizations in three of the four 30-s periods in each trial. These findings indicate that, even with toys in it, the strange environment produced an emotional response. With the mother present, the same environment produced no distress but instead evoked vocalizations of a non-protest nature.

With so shortened a trial and with so much emotional distress, Group T crossed only 4·2 lines in trial 1 and none at all in trial 2 (Table 29.2). Group M *S*s were much more active; they crossed 16·2 lines in trial 1 and 10·6 lines in trial 2. The difference

took a mean of 17·1 s to reach the mother in trial 1 and of 36·8 s, in trial 2. In trial 1 they spent 47·1 s in proximity to the mother, and 71·9 s in trial 2.

Effect of prior exposure with mother

The performance of Group M in trials 3 and 4, when contrasted with that of Group T in trials 1 and 2, supplies a measure of the effect of prior exposure with the mother. Whereas all *S*s in Group T cried in trial 1, no *S* in Group M cried in trial 3 (Table 29.2). Moreover, three of the 4 *S*s vocalized, but not as freely as during the two preceding trials with the mother (for the group, vocalizations occurred in only one of the four 30-s periods). All *S*s in Group M, furthermore, manipulated the toys throughout the entire trial.

The conclusion, then, is that familiarity with the environment eliminated crying, fostered vocalizations, and encouraged manipulation of the toys; in every respect, they behaved differently from *S*s who entered the same environment without prior familiarization.

In trial 4, however, latency of crying was 66·0 s (Table 29.2). Now, only one *S* vocalized and only 2 *S*s manipulated toys—and then for only part of the trial. The effect of familiarity had been dissipated.

Persisting effect of the strange environment

In trials 3 and 4, Group T faced an environment that previously had occasioned distress but that now contained the mother. The group means show that Group T *S*s cried earlier in both trials than Group M in trials 1 and 2 (who in fact did not cry at all). They also crossed fewer lines in trial 3 than Group M in trials 1 and 2 (Table 29.2). These differences, however, although large, were not statistically significant.

Examination reveals the reason for the lack of significance. Two *S*s in Group T cried almost at once in both

trials upon seeing their mothers and one of these stayed unmoving in the start cell. The other two *S*s did not cry, vocalized, went to cell 52, and moved about the room in a fashion similar to all *S*s of Group M in trials 1 and 2.

For the group, then, the effect of exposure to the strange environment did not persist. For two of the four *S*s, however, the effect was marked—they were emotionally distressed by the mother's appearance.

Summary

The strange environment, even when furnished with toys, proved to be distressing; *S*s cried early and tended not to move around the room. But, as in Experiment 1, the same environment with the mother in it, supported exploratory behaviour and occasioned no distress. Prior exposure with the mother had an effect: *S*s did not cry, moved about, and played with the toys—for one trial; on the next trial they behaved as did *S*s without prior exposure. The appearance of the mother, after experience with the toys, produced distress in some *S*s but not in others. Toys in the strange environment, therefore, were no substitute for the mother, unless the mother had first been part of that environment. Even then, toys supported behaviour for only one trial.

References

1. ARSENIAN, J. M. (1943). Young children in an insecure situation. *J. abnorm. Soc. Psychol.* **38**, 225–49.
2. BAYLEY, N. (1932). A study of the crying of infants during mental and physical tests. *J. genet. Psychol.* **40**, 306–29.
3. BERLYNE, D. E. (1960). *Conflict, arousal, and curiosity.* McGraw-Hill, New York.
4. MORGAN, G. A. and RICCIUTI, H. N. (1969). Infants' responses to strangers during the first year. *In* (Foss, B. M. (Ed.)) *Determinants of infant behaviour.* Vol. 4. Wiley, New York.
5. WELKER, W. I. (1961). An analysis of exploratory and play behavior in animals. *In* (Fiske, D. W. and Maddi, S. R. (Eds.)) *Functions of varied experience.* Dorsey, Homewood, Ill.

Subject Index